SMOOTH WORDS

SMOOTH WORDS

Women, Proverbs and Performance in Biblical Wisdom

CAROLE FONTAINE

T & T CLARK INTERNATIONAL
A Continuum imprint
LONDON • NEW YORK

For my Implied Reader

Published by T&T Clark International
A Continuum imprint
The Tower Building, 11 York Road, London SE1 7NX
15 East 26th Street, Suite 1703, New York, NY 10010

www.tandtclark.com

Copyright © 2002 Sheffield Academic Press
First published as JSOTS 356 in 2002
This edition published 2004

British Library Cataloguing-in-Publication Data
A catalogue record for this book is available from the British Library

ISBN 0567042707 (paperback)

Typeset by Sheffield Academic Press
Printed on acid-free paper in Great Britain by Cromwell Press Ltd, Trowbridge,
Wilts

CONTENTS

LIST OF ILLUSTRATIONS AND TABLES

Illustrations

Tables

ACKNOWLEDGMENTS

No project of this size and length comes to fruition without considerable support and assistance from others, and this is especially true when the regular challenges of life and health continually raise barriers to its completion. First of all, I must thank my long-suffering publisher, Professor David Clines, who allowed me the time and space needed to do my work at my own pace, despite innumerable setbacks and delays in the process. This book was begun during the death of both parents, and took me through several bouts of illness, as well as other family and institutional stresses. Through it all, David was a gentle, supportive presence who kept on waiting for results without a hint of chagrin or impatience—though he was entitled to both!

The research presented here was also supported in substantive ways by two institutions and a granting agency. Andover Newton Theological School not only assisted me through the vehicle of two sabbatical semesters, but also made travel funds available so I might present the Queen of Sheba materials from Chapter 3 at the International Meeting of the Society of Biblical Literature in Dublin, Ireland, in 1996. Major portions of Chapters 3 and 4 were done while on leave as a Research Fellow at the University of Amsterdam, in the Department of Humanities/Theology, arranged through the gracious auspices of Professor Athalya Brenner. Travel funds for this and an ongoing project were made available through funding provided by the Luce Foundation to the Theology and the Arts Program at Andover Newton Theological School. I extend my special thanks to the Andover Newton professors in Theology and the Arts who made the travel possible for me, as part of my projects as Artist-in-Residence at Andover Newton. President Benjamin Griffin and Dean Elizabeth Nordbeck both provided me with ongoing encouragement, understanding and often, direct substantive support of my work, and I would like to express my gratitude to them both. Our small, 'free-standing' seminary is not always an easy place in which to nurture 'pure' scholarship, yet they have managed to do just that.

Portions of Chapter 2 appeared earlier in 'The Social Roles of Women in the World of Wisdom', in Athalya Brenner (ed.), *A Feminist Companion to Wisdom Literature* (FCB, 9; Sheffield: Sheffield Academic Press,

1995), pp. 24-49, and are reprinted here with the publisher's permission. Section Three of Chapter 2, 'Cosmic Domain', began its life as 'The Personification of Wisdom', in J.L. Mays (ed.), *Harper's Bible Commentary* (San Francisco: Harper & Row, 1988), pp. 501-503, which was later omitted in the second edition, and appears here with permission of the publisher, changed out of all recognition. In fact, both earlier pieces have been so substantially revised and enlarged that it is more appropriate to say that they give theme and direction to what appears here, rather than simply repeating what has already been said in another place.

There are several persons whose influence on my work and life deserve special acknowledgment here. Professor Claus Westermann was a primary conversation partner in the formation of this work, and had planned to write the Preface to it; my own snail's pace did not allow for completion of the manuscript before his death in June 2000, at the age of 90. However, he read the work as it progressed, both urging me to greater authorial voice as a woman and rejoicing in my strength when I found it. His impact on my scholarly life is felt throughout this work, but most particularly in the proverbial critique of the 'fool' in Chapter 2, which he felt to be a 'feminist' voice in the text whose potential female authorship ought not to be discounted. For his care as a reader, his helpful responses to my work on the Queen of Sheba, his delight in 'The Wisdom of Newtons', as well as so much else, I can only remain astonished by his generosity and grateful for his role in my development as a scholar.

There are other professors, of course, whose work in the field of wisdom literature was a constant companion as I thought and wrote: Father Roland Murphy, my former dissertation director, has never deserted his slowest student, and his continuing work on Proverbs and the Song of Song set a high standard for his 'daughter' to emulate. The recent commentaries of Michael Fox and Richard Clifford have likewise been critical for some portions of this study, as have the works of many other wisdom scholars.

And then there are the Women—a sort of scholarly Matriarchate without whose work, as well as encouragement, chiding, joshing and material support for mine has made all the difference. Professor Athalya Brenner of the University of Amsterdam, a wise woman extraordinaire and human dynamo, has had a role in my emergence as a feminist writer that cannot be underestimated. It was she who prodded me to work in the midrash on the Queen of Sheba, even though I considered it outside my field; she several times arranged opportunities to give papers on that topic, and provided an ongoing life-support during the times my family struggled with deaths, unemployment or changes in my health. Her presence 'in' my computer in the middle of the night via e-mails sent when we were both on-line, half a world away, reminded me over that years that I am not alone, and that the passion for feminist analysis is best experienced in the company of friends. For all this, I offer my deep thanks.

The work and friendship of Professor Claudia Camp of Texas Christian University has been an ever-present companion to me for well over 20 years, since we first met in graduate school in the 1970s at Duke University. In many respects, this work might be thought of as a companion volume to her study, *Wise, Strange and Holy: The Foreign Woman and the Making of the Hebrew Bible* (Sheffield Academic Press, 2000). Her work on the missing and estranged sisters of the Hebrew Bible admirably fills the gap I found in Proverbs on the topic of real, rather than metaphorical, sisters. I advise the reader to become friends with this whimsical yet explosive look at how gender ideology shaped the whole program of 'scripture-making'. The work of other women, less well known to me personally perhaps but no less important to me as a scholar, needs to be mentioned here: Gerlinde Baumann, Barbara Geller, Judith Hadley, Christl Maier, Carol Meyers, Carol Newsom, Susan Niditch, Sylvia Schroer and Gale Yee all added their voices to the synthesis found here, and my work would be weaker had I not had theirs upon which to build.

Outside of my scholarly world, there were many others whose presence in my life and on this project have made a critical difference. Producers Tracey Benger and Mila Marvizon, both of whom I met when they were working for the production company Film Roos, have impacted my feminist research by asking me crazy questions no student would dream of putting to the esteemed professor. (Thank you!) Working with them on episodes on Solomon, I fell in love with Sheba, and they are largely responsible, along with Professor Brenner, for dragging me across the time-line, kicking and screaming, into variant after variant. The angels of the Trask Library at Andover Newton, Cynthia Bolshaw, Head of Circulation, and S. Diana Yount, Associate Director and ILL manager, both assisted me in the acquisition of resources with speed, accuracy and humor. Gail Griffin, Beth Clark and Dawn Sorensen keep my office computer and Internet access up and running. My squad of health care professionals, pain management counselors Kathy Gill and Donna O'Connell-Gilmore, and physical therapist Jenny Marshall, kept me going physically during the times when there was only tunnel and no light.

Next, over the years I have been blessed with extraordinary students who have served as Research and Teaching Assistants, proof-readers, library grunts, computer management consultants, travel companions and trusted allies. There is a story to tell about each and every one of them, but only their names can be listed here: Rev. Cara Davis, Rev. Rick Fowler, Rev. Gen Heywood, Mary-Jane Jenson, Rev. Gary McCaslin, Rev. Lee Milligan, Cathy O'Connell, Rev. Simeon Olapade, Rev. Lynne Phipps, Rev. Carol Ramsey-Lucas, Rev. John Tamillio III, and Rev. Carole York-Robinson all contributed their labor to the production of this manuscript. Special notice needs to be given to former students Rev. Carolyn Lambert, Lee Parsons, Margaret Tabor, Deborah Vickers, Jackie Clement and KyooWan Yi, all of whose help went well beyond the call of duty. The students of GLANTS (Gays and Lesbians at Andover Newton Theological School) and those of the student fellowship of the Unitarian Universalist Association (UUCANS) at my institution have always served as special friends and allies, and I thank them for their not inconsiderable support. In those days before feminist biblical hermeneutics could be considered typical or desirable among seminary professors, the folks of GLANTS and UUCANS always let me know that there was a human (and not just a scholarly) reason for pursuing the kind of research that I did.

My husband, Dr Craig W. Fontaine, has been an unfailing supporter of my work and career, making computer and financial resources available to me on a scale that finds little comparison in other professional marriages that I have observed. From the time of graduate school, when he first taught me about 'cognitive maps', to his time as a corporate leader in the development of web-based education, his expertise and willingness to share it with me has been a genuine blessing. He is the one who has managed the burdens of household chores, income taxes and the perennial fights with health insurance companies, while this research took shape. Whether it has been lifting a box of proofs or uplifting my flagging spirits, I cannot imagine having completed this task without his immeasurable support, and gourmet cooking. The poem in 'The Wisdom of Newtons' on the Good Man is about Craig, and I am glad to be able to add it as a fitting conclusion to my own collection of student proverbs and instructions.

So, I conclude by saying that this book is for all those mentioned here: the ones who cooked and cleaned, xeroxed and searched, proof-read and met planes, conversed and laughed, comforted and cared, supported and sustained, installed hardware and de-bugged software, graded and groused, meowed and cheered. Thank you! I don't need to tell you that I could not have done this without you; you already know that. Thank you all!

Carole R. Fontaine
June 2001

ABBREVIATIONS

AB	Anchor Bible
ABRL	Anchor Bible Reference Library
ANET	James B. Pritchard (ed.), *Ancient Near Eastern Texts Relating to the Old Testament* (Princeton: Princeton University Press, 1950)
AOAT	Alter Orient und Altes Testament
AOR Diss	American Schools of Oriental Research
AJSL	*American Journal of Semitic Languages and Literature*
BA	*Biblical Archaeologist*
BARev	*Biblical Archaeology Review*
Bib	*Biblica*
BIS	Biblical Interpretation Series (Leiden)
BJS	Brown Judaic Studies
BL	Bible and Literature (Sheffield)
BM	Bibliotheca Mesopotamia
BTB	*Biblical Theology Bulletin*
BZAW	Beihefte zur *ZAW*
CANE	Jack M. Sasson (ed.), *Civilizations of the Ancient Near East* (New York: Charles Scribner's Sons, 1995)
CBQ	*Catholic Biblical Quarterly*
CBQMS	*Catholic Biblical Quarterly*, Monograph Series
GCT	Gender, Culture, Theory
CIS	*Corpus inscriptionum semiticarum*
EA	*El Amarna* (refers to the numbering of the letters in VAB 2/1 and Rainey, AOAT, 8th edn)
FAT	Forschungen zum Alten Testament
FCB	Feminist Companion to the Bible
FFC	Folklore Fellow Communications
FOTL	The Forms of the Old Testament Literature
GFC	Garland Folklore Casestudies
HR	*History of Religions*
HSM	Harvard Semitic Monographs
HTR	*Harvard Theological Review*
IBT	Interpreting Biblical Texts
JAF	*Journal of American Folklore*
JCS	*Journal of Cuneiform Studies*

JNES	*Journal of Near Eastern Studies*
JSOT	*Journal for the Study of the Old Testament*
JSOTSup	*Journal for the Study of the Old Testament*, Supplement Series
JTS	*Journal of Theological Studies*
KUB	Keilschrifturkunden aus Boghazköi
LAI	Library of Ancient Israel
OBO	Orbis biblicus et orientalis
OTL	Old Testament Library
RA	*Revue d'assyriologie et d'archéologie orientale*
RB	*Revue biblique*
SBLDS	SBL Dissertation Series
SBLMS	SBL Monograph Series
SHR	Studies in the History of Religions (Supplements to *Numen*)
SO	Sources Orientales
STAR	Studies in Theology and Religion (Leiden)
THeth	*Texte der Hethiter* (Heidelberg)
VAB	Vorderasiatische Bibliotek, II (J.A. Knudtzon, *Die El-Amarna-Tafeln*, Anmerkungen und Register bearbeitet von O. Weber and E. Ebeling, 1-2 (Leipzig, 1907-15; rpt., Aalen, 1964)
VT	*Vetus Testamentum*
VTSup	*Vetus Testamentum*, Supplements
WAW	Writings from the Ancient World (SBL; Atlanta, GA: Scholars Press)
WMANT	Wissenschaftliche Monographien zum Alten und Neuen Testament

TO THE READER

Thank you for picking up this book; I hope it feels good in your hands, a good weight, and a pleasure to hold. As I sit here writing this work on women and wisdom, I think of you, Gentle Reader,[1] and I try to imagine your questions and responses.[2] In my mind's eye, we are not encountering each other through this page, but we are strolling through my favorite museum collections. It is not the best of days for me: I am using my cane and leaning on your arm, glad that you offered to carry my bag.

But on this day, we do not mind moving slowly, because we are looking at all the artifacts that women's culture leaves behind from the ancient Near East. These are not the names of great victories in battle carved upon massive stones, nor are there many grand scenes of women storming the gates of patriarchal power, leading company upon company of amazons. Rather, we are stopping to look at the thread in a hunter's kit from Egypt and wondering who spun it, and who tied up the savory herbs that are part of that bundle for bringing home food. We are sighing as we look at a small handmade paddle-doll found buried with a girl-child's little mummy. We are studying the inscriptions on the ceilings of an Egyptian woman's coffin and wondering about Isis's wings and how much they remind us of the wings of the Israelite god, stretched out to protect the one who prays. We are musing over clay tablets and papyrus scrolls, laughing and marveling at Hathor's ears or the *Dea Nutrix*, as she stands, generously carved with big hips and two hands beneath her breasts, in a sort of ancient Near Eastern 'wonder bra' pose, offering herself to the worshiper. We read the legacy of women's names, and ponder the probable weight of splendid necklaces so

---

1.   I know this form of address makes you think of Miss Manners and her way of sweetly coercing you to a standard of polite interaction that privileges form over substance. In fact, I am thinking more of that earnest female authorial voice that we find when a Brontë addresses the breathless yearning of her audience: 'Reader, I married him!'

2.   As you can tell already, I am carrying on a conversation for us that asks you to interact with these footnote asides.

heavy that counterweights must be slung over the shoulder to hold them properly in place. We look closer, seeing that those weights are each in the shape of the word *neferet*, 'beautiful'. Long before modern culture held women to a standard that ordains them to forever strive to hold the eye of the men around them, the ancient world was putting a mirror and a spindle in the hands of baby girls to express *the* elemental works of the female: beauty and handiwork. We begin to get a sense of how long has been the road to our self-conscious appropriation of the blessings and curses of our culture's construction of the gender and the female sex. We feel very close to the dead queens, shy girls and hard-working slave women so long gone.

This book, like all my work as a feminist, is a response to my students and their ministries as they try to make their way in a patriarchal church that only vaguely knows what to do with them. It seeks to honor their questions—and yours, Gentle Reader, as I imagine them—and affirm their gifts as woman-persons. In one sense, I do not work very differently from the 'pastoral theologians' of the early church and Jewish communities of the Exile. Exegesis of a text held sacred is a profoundly practical matter. People for whom this text is sacred cannot simply pass by on the other side when matters of justice are at issue. Since the church is one of the last remnants of a feudal, androcentric worldview that sustains the second-class status of women in the Western world and developing countries, we must confront its treatment of women in direct ways. As long as the text has the power to inform behavior, then feminists must be passionate readers and exegetes.[3]

Let me note for you now that although what I present here is the fruit of long study and work that I am prepared to defend, I must tell you that I am often in pain as I write, and like Job, I must reserve to myself the right to recant and 'take it all back' if necessary. The Talmud tells us that a doctor is required to restore lost health to a patient because, among other reasons, a person in pain cannot properly perceive the Divine Presence. Yet I wonder if there might not also be a place for the Jobs of this world among the ranks of theologians, those who write out of a place of uncertainty and pain, rather than doctrine and ideals. The 'normals' set the bar for every-thing else, and many of us are shut out of any standard 'fulfillment' by the specific circumstances of our bodies. This is as much the case with gender, race, class, age, sexual orientation or state of health or mind. People who

---

3.   Even if only out of self-defense! But there are better reasons to read the Bible than that—read on.

move with ease must pardon us when we linger over the past; we are resting and reviving as we pause.

Why do I write, then? There is much to be said for the medical benefits of distraction through intense involvement in a fascinating project. But, in fact, a student's dream answers the questions better. A survivor of sexual abuse had dreamt, after a first class session in Wisdom Literature, that she was dressed in a grey suit with a clerical collar, waiting amidst a crowd of other applicants for a Field Education job interview. In her dream, I walked straight up to her as the priest's collar was beginning to choke, causing her unbearable panic, and held out my hand. 'Come with me if you want to live,'[4] this wisdom teacher told her. 'I'm with the Resistance.' And she realized, as she walked away with me, that although she was frightened by the possibilities, she had a sense of being safe. And free.

Viva la Resistance!

---

4. Actually, I think the *Vorlage* of this scene may have come from the movie *The Terminator*.

Chapter 1

W/WISDOM THE SIGNIFIER

Why Another Book on Wisdom?[1]

What is it that 'Wisdom', the third traditional division of the *Tanak* or Hebrew Bible, signifies? The answer given to that question will depend entirely on whom one queries and what text they may be reading when they make their answers. To the elite reader—one trained in the biblical languages, professionally employed in the literary or theological criticism of those texts, with or without specific commitments to religious ideologies of whatever sort—'Wisdom' probably signifies a specific body of biblical literature. This 'body' can be narrowly defined (Proverbs, Job, Qoheleth) or more broadly situated in later Hellenistic philosophical speculation, apocryphal works, Gnostic systems of Christology, or even the Jewish mystical tradition of the Qabbalah. For such readers, Wisdom may represent a strictly defined subject area, springing out of a matrix of changing social conditions that roughly coincide with the history of the kingdoms of Israel and Judah, down through the formation of the Diaspora and the first Christian communities.

---

1. New entries in the field include the following: Dianne Bergant, *Israel's Wisdom Literature: A Liberation-Critical Reading* (Philadelphia: Fortress Press, 1997); Anthony R. Ceresko, *Introduction to Old Testament Wisdom: A Spirituality for Liberation* (Quezon City, Philippines: Claretian Publications, 1999); Richard J. Clifford, *The Wisdom Literature* (IBT; Nashville: Abingdon Press, 1998) and *Proverbs: A Commentary* (OTL; Louisville, KY: Westminster/John Knox Press, 1999); Michael V. Fox, *Proverbs 1–9* (AB, 18a; New York: Doubleday, 2000); Claudia V. Camp, *Wise, Strange and Holy: The Strange Woman and the Making of the Hebrew Bible* (JSOTSup, 320; CGT, 9; Sheffield: Sheffield Academic Press, 2000); Roland Murphy and E. Huwiler, *New International Biblical Commentary: Proverbs, Ecclesiastes, Song of Songs* (Peabody, MA: Hendrickson, 1999). New entries in one-volume commentaries include R.C. van Leeuwen, 'Proverbs', in Carol Newsom *et al.* (eds.), *New Interpreter's Bible*, V (Nashville: Abingdon Press, 1997), and Carole R. Fontaine, 'Proverbs', in James L. Mays (ed.), *Harper Collins Bible Commentary* (San Francisco: Harper, rev. edn, 2000), pp. 447-65.

Even for such well-trained scholars, however, there is a decided ambiguity[2] about the subject 'Wisdom': does it represent a 'way of thinking', some sort of intellectual tradition perhaps, or a 'movement' championed by a specific social class (urban scribes, for instance), or simply an index of literary forms used in didactic settings? In fact, Wisdom may be understood as all of these things and more, as introductory textbooks on 'Old Testament' Wisdom make clear.[3] In the present work, 'wisdom' (little 'w') will refer in linguistic terms to those texts and textual signifiers used by bearers of the tradition, elite or traditional. These texts and signifiers, roughly contiguous with the 'wisdom books',[4] are themselves indeterminant and contextual in nature, constructed through the interplay of interwoven discourses of a variety of communities (ancient, modern, Jewish, Christian, feminist and literary). At the level of 'character', Wisdom (capitalized, as befits a named character) designates that mediating female personification/hypostasy found in Proverbs and elsewhere, who may or may not be the vestigial remains of a scribal goddess retained within the Bible's patriarchal system of monotheism. The 'good news' in the adoption of these definitions, despite their untidy insistence on certain historical and literary points of order, is that an empowered,[5] resisting reader may not only speak about what W/wisdom *was* but about what W/wisdom *is* and might become.

The undecidability of the meaning of W/wisdom[6]—*Ḥokmâ*, in the Hebrew Bible—is present in the texts themselves, where wisdom flows

2.   Or a delightful elasticity, depending on one's readerly temperament.

3.   Roland E. Murphy, *The Tree of Life: An Exploration of Biblical Wisdom Literature* (Grand Rapids, MI: Eerdmans, 2nd rev. edn, 1996); James L. Crenshaw, *Old Testament Wisdom* (Atlanta: John Knox Press; London: SCM Press, 1981); Gerhard von Rad, *Wisdom in Israel* (trans. James D. Martin; Nashville: Abingdon Press, 1972); Claus Westermann, *Roots of Wisdom: The Oldest Proverbs of Israel and Other Peoples* (Louisville, KY: Westminster/John Knox Press, 1995).

4.   It is with some hesitation that I engage in the standard circular reasoning so dear to biblical studies: if we had not named the books 'wisdom', would we still be calling its genres 'wisdom'?

5.   An empowered reader is an engaged one who looks beyond the literal meaning of the surface text, a reader who can read upside down, backwards and in between the lines, one capable of reading, evaluating and using the work of specialized, elite scholarly readers while not actually having to become one.

6.   I am indebted to Professor Athalya Brenner for the terminology that names this effect so admirably (A. Brenner, 'Introduction', in A. Brenner and C.R. Fontaine [eds.], *A Feminist Companion to Wisdom and Psalms, 2nd Series* [FCB, 2; Sheffield: Sheffield Academic Press, 1998).

from one overlapping meaning to another and back again, meandering over a territory marked by the diverse lexical meanings assigned to the very same word when it appears in different contexts. When Jonadab, a '*ḥākām*', helps Prince Amnon concoct a plot to seduce his half-sister Tamar in 2 Samuel 13, clearly the meaning of 'wise' in that story differs from its use in Exod. 35.25-26, where all the women 'wise of heart' bring 'whatever was in their hands' to offer in the building of the Tabernacle. In one place, the adjective 'wise' cannot mean simply 'skilled', and certainly carries no distinctive moral value, whereas in the other the term is almost 'technological' in its use. When we compare the story of the crafty 'court-wise' counselor plotting with the king's son to the episode of recently freed slave women in the wilderness with proficiency in a specific craft or crafts, an expertise that they readily devote to their redeemer god in a public religious context, we see again the several 'wisdoms'. For neither story is it possible to establish a reliable, historical facticity, so we must continually remind ourselves that we only see these wisdoms through the medium of a text, and at the will of its author—how this compares to 'reality' is to be discovered. So, although elite readers often do so, one actually may *not* speak of a monolithic 'Wisdom', be it movement, world view or literary style, that is always and everywhere the same, open to systematic and final classifications, without violating the indeterminacy with which the Hebrew Bible itself uses the term. Perhaps this is a clue to the meaning of the use of 'W/wisdoms' (*ḥokmôt*) in Prov. 9.1: we must always ask, Which W/wisdom? Which text? When and where? Read by whom? Without a consideration of these factors, the 'how' and 'what' questions, however clever or fascinating, remain of academic interest only.

For feminist critics, W/wisdom may mean something altogether different than the meanings proposed by their (self-declared) 'disinterested, ideology-free' academic forbears or current colleagues. For reformer Christian feminists, Wisdom, now hailed as 'Sophia'[7] has increasingly been explored as a 'Way Out'. That is, Wisdom might be understood as a cognitive and imaginative road map into women's experience perhaps, or a reworked, woman-friendly Christology that has the virtue of being textually located within the New Testament's own understanding of its incarnate Hero. In eagerness to

---

7. Observe the nice Greek name change—yet another way well-meaning scholarship colludes in the inscription of the methodological and semantic preeminence of the New Testament over its earlier Hebrew ancestor. Yes, such texts *are* in Greek, but this erasure of early Jewish traditions of Wisdom in favor of Hellenistic philosophical or Gnostic ones follows a pattern in Christian scholarship that is all too familiar.

embrace the female figure of personified Wisdom as a theological forerunner and/or literary Sender/Parent of Jesus as the Christ, these readers have built 'W/wisdom liturgies' and set up a paradigm of resistance to androlatrous portraits of their Redeemer. 'Creation' has been dragged out of its metaphysical closet, where its main function was to provide the costume and scenery changes for Salvation History, and steered toward center stage as a focus, a value and a biblically coded call to ecological repentance. These teachers, critics, priests, pastors, laywomen/men have even become so vocal as to spawn a conservative outcry of 'Jesus is Lord!' in response to the challenges raised by feminist reappropriation of biblical imagery.[8]

That 'Wisdom' in the hands of women theologians can be viewed as a theology so threatening that true believers are urged to name it 'Heresy' is decidedly something to be said in its favor,[9] but for other feminist readers the picture is not quite so rosy. With further analysis, W/wisdom's 'way out' all too often proves to be a 'way back in' to the dualistic, hierarchical, phallogocentric, male-exclusive theologies that feminists are committed to resisting. For every good wife praised for her strength and effectiveness, there is an loud, adulterous, vain, nagging woman to be found in the shadow she casts, the two together reinforcing the 'good girl/bad girl' codifications of patriarchal musings on the nature of the female Other. Even when only one of these 'character archetypes' appears, her very presence invokes her absent sister, and the interpretive cycle that socializes women based on the roles assigned to them *by* men for the benefit *of* men begins anew.

Wisdom scholars have been pointing out since the close of the Second World War that the 'wisdom way' is to categorize, observe and learn in

8.   Although everywhere else conservative theologies prefer to insist that meaning and theological priority resides in the 'plain sense' of Scripture (that is, its 'literal meaning', assuming one can be agreed upon), when a female Mediator is found, the text is suddenly discovered to be 'metaphorical' in nature.

9.   As one feminist German artist writes, 'Patriarchal values are of meaning only in their sublation'; i.e., only the juxtaposition of an opposite value that destabilizes the 'true' meaning assigned to a text or act by patriarchal system can give a transformational, wholesome energy to patriarchal structures that still dominate the lives of the great majority of the world's women (Gisela Ecker [ed.], *Feminist Aesthetics* [trans. Harriet Anderson; Boston: Beacon Press, 1986]); unfortunately, I am unable to locate the precise page after much searching; my compliments to Professor Daniel Boyarin (whose *Carnal Israel: Reading Sex in Talmudic Culture* [Berkeley: University of California Press, 1993]) contains a similar 'demi-reference', thus providing a format for this reference).

response to those observations. Such perceptual activities always seek to assign, discover or impose some sort of 'order' on a world of chaotic—but not unrepeatable—experiences. If the 'order' discovered/imposed through the speeches of Lady Wisdom still places females on the negative side of the binary equations of wise/foolish, own/foreign, male/female—is this an order for which modern women should yearn or seek to accommodate themselves? A literalist of any sort, Christian or Jew, male or female, might well give similar answers to this question, grounded in the inviolable, almost mythical 'authority' of the biblical text that is interpreted as life teachings by their religious communities. Feminists committed to a hermeneutic of resistance will read the question differently, and craft a variety of responses.

Testing the Limits of Method and the Method of Limits

The goal of this work is to use the book of Proverbs to explore the textual nexus of some of the questions outlined above and their practical 'political' ramifications in the lives of real (and not just 'textual') women. We will take our examples from the 'then's' and 'now's', especially where they come together in the wisdom books of the Hebrew Bible. To do this, we must press our questions back into the dawn of the formation of ancient Near Eastern bureaucracies and scribal traditions (though we cannot say for certain if pre-Exilic kingdoms of Judah and Israel had any such institutions). We must turn over the rocks of ancient Israel's 'uniqueness' to examine the common metaphorical ground beneath an allegedly monotheistic Bible's texts and those of the goddess-worshiping, yet relentlessly patriarchal, societies all around them.[10] We must venture into the world of the village as well as that of the city elite, in each place visiting the mother's 'inner chamber' (bedroom)[11] along with the public square where the fathers do business. The resisting readers of the Hebrew Bible's W/wisdom texts will find that the journey on W/wisdom's Way takes them from threshing floor to sacrificial altar, from fertility to philosophy, from

---

10. Gerda Lerner, *The Creation of Patriarchy* (New York: Oxford University Press, 1986); Tikva Frymer-Kensky, *In the Wake of the Goddesses: Women, Culture and the Biblical Transformation of Pagan Myth* (New York: Fawcett Columbine, 1992).

11. Carol Meyers, 'Returning Home: Ruth 1.8 and the Gendering of the Book of Ruth', in Athalya Brenner (ed.), *A Feminist Companion to Ruth* (FCB, 3; Sheffield: Sheffield Academic Press, 1993), pp. 85-114, esp. pp. 94-114.

the riverbed of the Nile all the way to the top of the temple-towers of
Mesopotamia. Adventurous readers may choose to leap the boundaries of
the Common Era and move from Jewish sacred literature to 'mystical
experience' of later Judaism or to its theological offspring, Christianity.
Such a traveler might start with the metaphors of the Tree of Life and the
rivers of Eden, only to recognize that others traveling the same thought-
line may wind up traversing the Jordan in the shadow of the Cross. The
study of W/wisdom leads in many directions.

Many of our explorations will be about wisdom as a form of expert,
almost ritualized, 'performance' practiced by women as well as male
sages, and despite our difficulties with date or life-setting, we will assume
some level of verisimilitude between representations of wisdom use in the
text and the way 'it actually happened'. This is possible because some
genres where users presume a common cultural code (proverbs used in
letters, for example) *do* exist elsewhere in the ancient Near East, although
they are *not* represented in Israel. Hence, we will be searching for wisdom
as a display of proficiency in a craft or facility in the mastery of linguistic
tropes (whether generic or semantic). To do so, we must consider the wisdom of women's hands outside Proverbs and the wisdom of 'Lady
Tongue', in whose 'hand' is the power of life or death. We must ask questions not just about how Lady Wisdom 'works' in the texts that feature
her, but also about the way that women worked in society—even where
evidence of their labor is scant or inferential at best, largely erased or considered self-evident. Often their only textual residue is in their customary
citation as so-and-so's mother, wife, daughter or sister. We must assess the
literary roles assigned to women in biblical wisdom literature, whether as
trollops or teachers of Torah, and be vigilant in searching out the gaps,
inconsistencies, contradictions and silences of those textual representations and our appropriations of them.[12]

Following the way of wisdom, the study here on women as 'performers'
and carriers (tradents) of the wisdom tradition seeks to impose some order
on a welter of reported and/or constructed experiences towards which our
texts gesture. It should be clear, though, that the order imposed or
discovered can only be one that acknowledges basic *dis-order*: *dis-order*
in the tradition, its interpreted teachings and our own souls. In such an
endeavor, it may be that Woman Stranger is as useful a guide as her lofty

---

12. Just how effective would that well-off, perfect wife and SuperMom of Prov. 31
appear without a squad of unnamed maids or daughters who hasten to do her bidding?

twin, Woman Wisdom;[13] that a goddess may be as serviceable a character as a god; and that a Redeemer is in the eye of the beholder. But that W/wisdom existed in women, and that women exemplified W/wisdom we cannot doubt: even our thoroughly male-biased texts make no secret of it. As a playful reworking of a couplet from the Middle Kingdom Egyptian 'Instruction of Ptah hotep', a valued counselor to Pharaoh, declares:

> More so than the best malachite,[14]
> Good Speech[15] is quite hidden from sight—
> and yet, it is found
> with the slavegirl profound
> At her grindstone displaying Insight![16]

As many feminist critics who have gone ahead have pointed out, the matter of choosing the 'legitimate' subject matter of scholarly and/or theological discourse has worked to the profound disadvantage of those who search for 'women's history'. Never mind that a golden Matriarchal Age as envisioned early on by Neo-Pagan thealogians is notoriously hard to locate textually[17]—even in the accepted 'canonical' texts that one is obliged to cover, finding the proverbial 'woman behind the man'[18] is no easy task, given the predilections and biases of male authorship in antiquity.[19] What is to be done then? In order to give a fuller picture of women's participation in the wisdom traditions of the ancient Near East,

13. The alert reader has by now recognized that I am using the terms Woman Wisdom and Lady Wisdom interchangeably to refer to the female character Wisdom. Both terms are found in scholarly literature, with feminists usually giving some preference to the term 'Woman Wisdom' coined by Claudia Camp.

14. Literally, 'a green stone'.

15. I.e. W/wisdom.

16. Carole R. Fontaine, 'Modern Look at Ancient Wisdom: The Instruction of Ptahhotep, Revisited', *Biblical Archaeologist* 44 (1981), pp. 155-60.

17. One may argue here about the validity and scholarly value of data provided by 'archeomythology', a method that assumes a general correspondence and meaning of artistic symbols as they move through time and space.

18. 'Behind every great man is a woman.'

19. Elizabeth Schüssler Fiorenza, *In Memory of Her: A Feminist Theological Reconstruction of Christian Origins* (London: SCM Press, 1983); Berenice Carroll (ed.), *Liberating Women's History: Theoretical and Critical Essays* (Chicago: University of Chicago Press, 1976); Carole R. Fontaine '"A Heifer From Thy Stable": On Goddesses and the Status of Women in the Ancient Near East', in Alice Bach (ed.), *The Pleasure of Her Text: Feminist Readings of Biblical and Historical Studies* (Valley Forge, PA: Trinity Press International, 1990), pp. 69-95.

we must consciously read outside the lines of Hole-y Writ, seeking wise women and their ways in the cultures contemporaneous and contiguous with those that produced the Bible. We will freely rummage through the archives of Israel's neighbors, holding up their literary and archaeological patterns, looking for a proper 'fit' in hopes of filling in the gaps we find in our own text traditions. If we find ourselves reading with head turned sideways and eyes a-squint, such is the hazard of feminist readings, but the returns outweigh the difficulties.[20]

Additionally, there is a reason why visual art has fluttered onto these pages, even though our subject is largely literary. The literary history of ancient women must be traced through material culture—which includes art and inscriptions, as well as similar finds from parallel cultures—because as members of the non-elite (usually), women were seldom represented in the 'official' written histories of their time. When we find a mother who writes, a slave woman who quotes proverbs, or a queen who drafts marriage contracts, we should take note, for here are examples of women who were wise going about their business. If a funerary stele helps us settle a question about women's authorship, then we must place it alongside biblical verses for consideration. As an artist, my interpretive responses to the text are often in the form of some visual rendering. Cartoon or vignette from a medieval manuscript that illustrates our point, I offer the visible evidence of iconography for your eyes' consideration.

Further, where reliable data are scarce, we would be foolish to limit ourselves to only one time period. Just as Hebrew wisdom texts had precursors in their world, these images and characters have retained a vigorous afterlife in Jewish, Christian and Islamic retelling, mainstream and sectarian. For that reason, readers here will find themselves—from time to time—visiting medieval Europe or Yemen, pagan Iceland, or post-modern ghettos, wherever our texts or characters have found a foothold in women's practice. Whether in the exotic Queen of Sheba of folklore or the entrenched practices of African American resistance[21] to a modern white supremacist society, the dynamics of women carriers of wisdom will be considered fair game.

Since we mean to resist the restrictions imposed by supposedly neutral methodologies that keep us straightjacketed in 'proper questions' (that is, the questions of interest to mainstream/malestream scholarship), we must

---

20. Still, it *is* a strain. I recommend ice-packs at the end of a day of suspicion and resistance.

21. 'My mama didn' raise no fool!'

also read with an eye to 'differences': perspectives of race, class, gender, ethnicity, age, ability, and so on, that can so shape the formation and reception of our textual images. When Job complains about his awful plight,[22] he and commentators usually miss the fact that he is only living the daily life of an average woman slave: no honor, no hope, no sense of meaning in a world that has so characterized one in terms of function.[23] W/wisdom, when in the possession of a 'foreigner' like Sheba, Queen of the South in the New Testament, can play a powerful role in shaming the 'insiders' who miss the great miracles in front of them. Clearly, then, social and psychic location informs the making of meaning in any text.

Standard Feminist Statement of Disclosure

If the methodological position adopted here—that reading and making meaning is a multifaceted act—holds true, then the subject position of the author (understood as the one who reads) deserves the attention of the careful reader. While it may be tedious to be regaled constantly with the feminist theologian's statement of radical, passionate reading as shaped by personal experience and commitments, it is nevertheless necessary. Feminist criticism requires

> a politically explicit hermeneutics which resists ideological closure and the imposition of orthodoxy; which embraces polysemy and conceives of meaning as a process rather than as an ahistorical entity; which accords integrity to subjectivity and imagination in interpretation, maintaining an awareness of the limitations of rational logic and 'scientific' reading.[24]

That being said, I will also comment that, in the opinion of this reader/ writer, the present emphasis on 'autobiographical' criticism and disclosure of social location favors those who are either temperamentally suited to a confessional style or who have serene lives they do not mind sharing. In the current feminist climate, a will-to-privacy is apt to be mistaken for ideological obstinacy or a failure to meet feminist standards. For all these good and sufficient reasons, and because I do not aspire to a disinterested stance, I confess—but only grudgingly. As a visual artist, anyone can

22. See especially Job 29–31.

23. Further, one might argue that Job's distressed state is *still* better than that of a female slave, since sexual exploitation, routine in their settings, forms no part of Job's abuse.

24. David Rutledge, *Reading Marginally: Feminism, Deconstruction and the Bible* (BIS, 21; Leiden: E.J. Brill, 1996), p. 162.

know whatever it is important to know about me simply by viewing my work; words seem both inadequate and clumsy.[25]

As a classically trained 'bible geek(-ette)', I studied with wonderful men at fine universities and was dispatched to do as I had been done by: those who study the Torah to teach it to others are authorized with special blessings as they undertake this work of the soul. I was fortunate in finding academic employment, and have remained with the first institution that hired me, a mainstream Protestant seminary not attached to a university. I progressed through the ranks of privilege to attain full professorhood before the age of 40. I am, at present, a 'post-denominational sacramentalist of Northern European decent', a 'California Anglican' when in the west[26] but a Unitarian Universalist when in New England where I teach and make art.

While this gives the bare bones of a personal history, in many ways it omits exactly what such a statement is designed to elicit. To know that I am white, a professor, a woman, and a modest success at what I do must surely present a lopsided picture of the passions that formed me. Though I do not seek to deny the ease of advantages and entitlements of my current social location, knowledge of a childhood spent in an African American ghetto precariously poised on the edge of the rich[27] multicultural setting of Miami, Florida, during the years of the Civil Rights movement is rather more to the point in understanding my hermeneutic position and political commitments. Raised in the midst of the great-grandchildren of slaves, a white Southern upper-class, a retired Jewish population on Miami Beach,[28] and a patchwork of Caribbean groups, multicultural hermeneutics are not simply theoretical for me. Rather, diversity of interpretation is a way of keeping faith with the street people, the gangs, the Holocaust survivors, the Haitian prostitutes, the Cubanos, and all the others who formed me. From snake-handling cults to fundamentalist Southern Baptist churches, the religious scene I grew up in has very little representation in the worlds in which I now travel, except in this way: I have been taught by experience to look for the underside of traditions, to see power in unofficial places, and the dogged resilience of the working women[29] who were my models has helped me in my own survival as a person and an academic.

---

25. See my 'Journey through the Pit: A Pictorial Account of One Woman's Descent into Shadow and Beyond', *Anima* 15 (1988), pp. 53-66.

26. Sort of 'Roman Catholic-Lite': all of the ritual, only half the fat!

27. 'Rich' in the sense of diverse, extravagant, spicy and dangerous.

28. The sixth borough of New York City.

29. In the southern urban ghetto, the racist dominant society mandates that women

Beyond the impact of these early years, there are a few other salient disclosures to be made. I have been married for 29 years (at present writing) to the same feminist man, but I am not a mother; I am handicapped by a medical condition which causes chronic pain and progressive disability; I have always had a paintbrush, a drill, a soldering iron, a needle or some other instrument of art or craft in my hands. I know 'beauty' to be a primary mechanism of my survival to adulthood, despite the effects of malnutrition and the lingering sense of a violent, unjust and unpredictable world. Perhaps more biblical scholars should have direct personal experience of the Ku Klux Klan, Haitian priestesses, Baptist revivals and unrelenting pain: because of these things the world of the biblical text was sometimes a comfort, a refuge, or a call to envision something different. It was with no easy conscience that I came to realize that women had been largely excluded from real and meaningful membership in the household of God as the biblical authors and later interpreters conceived of it. It is with some hope that serious, radical rereading can bring back a sense of what might happen were Wisdom allowed to build Her house. To that end, we will turn our attention to women in the many dimensions of the World of Wisdom: the private domain of the home, the public domain of the marketplace, the cosmic domain of the wisdom goddesses of the ancient world, all places where women use wisdom texts or are used by them. We will end with 'The Wisdom of Newtons', a foray into women's midrash by modern mothers seeking the way of wisdom, provided in the instructions and proverbs created by my students and me. We may never be able to fill in the gaps of women's past history, but we can dedicate ourselves to reclaiming W/wisdom's heritage in the present and the future.

are more likely to have jobs than men, even though those jobs are usually menial and do not pay a living wage. Until I went to college, I had never met girls or women who had not worked, or expected that they would have the luxury of 'staying home' with their children.

Chapter 2

TEXTUAL WOMEN: THE SOCIAL ROLES OF WOMEN
IN THE PRIVATE, PUBLIC AND COSMIC DOMAINS

Preliminary Considerations

The women of the wisdom books of the Hebrew Bible are well known to us through their stereotypic representations: we have them as good wives, devoted mothers, wicked prostitutes, slick adulteresses, hard-working slaves and lusty daughters to be controlled.[1] As such, these textual ladies are frequent topics of discussion for the Sages who are thought to have composed much of the book of Proverbs, or at the very least compiled and edited oral materials and their written derivatives into a collection of wisdom teachings for the young men they taught.

But did the lived experience of real women of the past find its way into the wisdom traditions—the literary forms, pragmatic content and theological speculations—of the book of Proverbs, or are we given only a male view of women's wisdom? To explore these questions, we will consider first the attitudes concerning textual women found in Proverbs, then the social roles played by women in the formation of the wisdom traditions— as much as can be reasonably deduced,[2] and finally, the reflection of both as they impact the creation of the character of Woman Wisdom. Following

---

1. This chapter represents a substantially revised and enlarged version of my 'The Social Roles of Women in the World of Wisdom', in Athalya Brenner (ed.), *A Feminist Companion to Wisdom Literature* (FCB, 9; Sheffield: Sheffield Academic Press, 1995), pp. 24-49. For other studies, see Claudia Camp, *Wisdom and the Feminine in the Book of Proverbs* (BL, 11; Sheffield: Almond Press, 1985); Athalya Brenner, 'Some Observations on the Figurations of Woman in Wisdom Literature', *FemCompWisLit*, pp. 50-66; Silvia Schroer, 'Wise and Counseling Women in Ancient Israel: Literary and Historical Ideals of the Personified Ḥokmâ', in Brenner (ed.), *Wisdom Literature*, pp. 67-84, and *Die Weisheit hat ihr Haus gebaut: Studien zur Gestalt der Sophia in den biblischen Schriften* (Mainz: Matthias Grünewald Verlag, 1996).

2. By 'wisdom traditions' I mean the social realities that produced the texts known as 'wisdom literature'.

chapters will examine stories in which women are shown using proverbs —a bit of pragmatic revenge, perhaps, for all the texts that used *them*; but here we begin with our focus on how the sayings in Proverbs use women —as topics, tropes, referents and symbols.

If we wonder whether the sages are in fact telling the truth about women's lives, we must also raise a query here concerning the main form they use in making their points: the brief literary proverb composed of one line (a 'traditional saying') or two (an 'artistic proverb', more likely to have originated as a written, literary creation), many of which probably originated in an oral context.

These little units of folklore, so beloved to students of oral art precisely for their brevity, carry their own limitations imposed by their pithy quality. Often proverbs and sayings make their point by proposing oppositions; they are teaching tools that aim to force a 'correct' choice by presenting hearers with obvious choices, one of which is usually better than another. Another strategy is to make an artful 'comment' on a particular 'topic', again with an eye to structuring the hearer's choices along a particular path. While the form may masquerade as 'neutral' in its observations on life, in reality, it is anything but impersonal or disinterested! The saying form that predominates in Proverbs, so often depicting life from the male vantage point of genuine choice and full moral agency, displaces the everyday real, lived experience of women, who neither have such choices available to them, nor are they viewed by the male culture, for the most part, as full moral agents. Their displaced voice must echo from 'below' the text, forced to chant along docilely with the majority view. If the proverb is an oppositional one, ancient women hearers/users must decide between two options, neither of which may concern itself with the real alternatives allowed women. If the saying works, on the other hand, by an extended comment on a topic, there is not much likelihood that either the topic *or* the comment is reflective of a female 'point of view'—even where women themselves are used as the topic or comment!

The biblical proverb form, with its inherent dependence on dualities, is thus a *gendered* one, whether it contains explicit male/female content or not. 'Choose between these two!' demand the scribal teachers of their male students, invoking parental authority to undergird the role of the teacher.[3] Thus is the patriarchal economy of thought preserved, inscribed,

3.   Similar observations on the discourse strategies of the Instruction form may be found in Carol A. Newsom's 'Woman and Discourse of Patriarchal Wisdom: A Study of Proverbs 1–9', in Peggy L. Day (ed.), *Gender and Difference in Ancient Israel*

and assimilated by a new generation. In such indoctrination it is neither the ability to choose nor the injunction to do so that constitutes the problem for those interested in a liberating hermeneutic; rather it is the foreclosure on diverse possibilities and outcomes caused by the focus on dichotomous thinking. There are more fluid ways to apprehend and represent the world; and, eventually, the plaintive question, Where is Wisdom? found in Job and Qoheleth will give expression to the way the *either/or* construction of reality also betrays men when they find themselves in changed or unpredictable circumstances.[4]

The Social Location of the Sages, Male and Female: Who Are They? Why Do They 'Write'?

It might be useful to pause here to give our own definition of 'sage', the general term that describes the social role of one participating in the wisdom tradition. John G. Gammie and Leo G. Perdue consider the definition of 'sage' to be 'one who has composed a book or piece belonging to the wisdom literature of the ancient Near East'.[5] Other scholars, like R. Harris, working out of cuneiform and hieroglyphic sources, consider 'sage' under the traditional rubrics proposed by A. Leo Oppenheim, that is, 'scribe as bureaucrat, poet and scholar', and then try to adduce evidence of Mesopotamian women who might have fit into such roles.[6] We will adopt a fuller definition here, reckoning as a 'sage' any practitioners or tradents (carriers) of the wisdom tradition, in addition to those who composed or copied wisdom books. Sages, then, are any persons who routinely perform one or more of the following tasks associated with the wisdom tradition: authorship, scribal duties (copying, collecting, editing), counseling, skilled production and/or management of economic resources (especially where confirmed by the text itself), conflict resolution, teaching, mourning and healing. By using this broader definition, we are able to number women

(Philadelphia: Fortress Press, 1989), pp. 142-60.

4. For a perspective on social crisis during the postexilic period, see Gerlinde Baumann, 'A Figure with Many Facets: The Literary and Theological Functions of Personified Wisdom in Proverbs 1–9', in A. Brenner and C. Fontaine (eds.), *A Feminist Companion to Wisdom and Psalms* (FCB, 2nd series, 2; Sheffield: Sheffield Academic Press, 1998), pp. 44-91.

5. John G. Gammie and Leo G. Perdue (eds.), *The Sage in Israel and the Ancient Near East* (Winona Lake, IN: Eisenbrauns, 1990), p. x.

6. R. Harris, 'The Female "Sage" in Mesopotamian Literature (with an Appendix on Egypt)', in Gammie and Perdue, *Sage*, pp. 5-6.

among the sages because of their practice, even where we cannot attribute authorship of specific texts to them.

In general, the wisdom tradition reflected in Proverbs presents us with paradigmatic illustration of the great paradox observed elsewhere in patriarchal literature with respect to women: that the elevated female figures, such as Lady Wisdom (Prov. 1–9) or the Strong Woman (Prov. 31.10-31), may be inversely proportional to the 'truth'[7] of real women's lives. That is, such fine figures may just as easily be an index of women's lack of power and status, a drugged sop thrown to a beaten dog. Such figures and their negative counterparts must always be examined on a case by case basis in conjunction with whatever ethnographic and economic data that can be adduced.[8]

It is possible to explain the presence of characters like Woman Wisdom in such androcentric contexts as an example of male 'bad conscience': 'Wisdom: can't live with Her, can't live without Her.' As we shall see, these celebrated representations serve to bind up a variety of ideas about women and goddesses and give expression to their role in the great scheme of things—but from the male point of view.[9] One of the most remarkable things about these characters in Israel's traditions is their mobility and strength of presence. They move easily between the public domain of the gates, walls and marketplaces and the private domain of women's worlds, and they do so, for the most part, without the typical female humility formulae. Lady Wisdom stretches out her hand without asking permission to do so. While that act may not have been reflective of

---

7.   Whatever that may be! A woman's own view of her life may not qualify as truth where she is continually forced to internalize and act out of gendered roles and choices made *for* her by patriarchal culture—but I remain reluctant to deny full subjectivity (subject-hood) to women who find themselves in such circumstances— since that would be most women, then and now.

8.   For example, adoration of the Virgin Mary in historical Catholicism does not correlate positively with a high value placed on women or their freedom to fill a variety of high-status roles. Likewise, the 'Cult of True Womanhood' in Victorian England coincided with attempts to restrict the social roles of women to the private domain of the household.

9.   Claudia Camp, 'Woman Wisdom as Root Metaphor: A Theological Consideration', in K.G. Hoglund, E.F. Huwiler, J.T. Glass and R.W. Lee (eds.), *The Listening Heart: Essays in Wisdom and the Psalms in honor of Roland E. Murphy, O. Carm.* (JSOTSup, 58; Sheffield: JSOT Press, 1987), pp. 45-76, now *Wise, Strange and Holy: The Strange Woman and the Making of the Hebrew Bible* (JSOTSup, 320; GCT, 9; Sheffield: Sheffield Academic Press, 2000), pp. 72-93.

her ancient sisters' condition, it is a goal toward which her modern daughters may press.[10]

It should be remembered, however, that these cosmic literary figures, textual ladies, as well as the social roles of real women that influenced them, come to us from the male sages' perspective; the 'facts' about women's lives recorded here express only a partial truth, or at least the only parts the authors felt to be worthy of comment. Even so, wisdom literature is usually considered by scholars to present a portrait that is more closely related to actual social reality (as known by males) because of its pragmatic concerns.[11]

One of the peculiarities of dealing with Israel's wisdom tradition is the special need to consider the effects of 'foreign influence' on these texts and their world-view because the subject materials so patently demand this methodological awareness. One cannot speak of wisdom without speaking of Egypt or Mesopotamia, though speaking of wisdom in those 'primary'[12] societies is a rather different enterprise, requiring differing areas of expertise of their interpreters. The sages were comparative thinkers: because of their association 'vertically' through time with 'tradition' and 'horizontally' (across cultures during the same time period) with wisdom contacts in other cultures, they did not perform their intellectual activities in a theological, ethical, literary or practical vacuum. In the midst of Israel's culture, which self-consciously emphasized its theological 'uniqueness', the sages worked with the connections and similarities of their teachings to those of their neighbors, creating a kind of intellectual ecumenism, as it were. They were 'wise' precisely because they honed their thought on the

10. There is a modern 'proverb' to be sought here: if Wisdom's waiting hand is ignored, should human women be surprised when their testimony goes unheard? Is the daughter greater than the mother? 'Like mother, like daughter...our mother was a Hittite...'

11. Put another way, didactic literature is largely pointless if its teachings are not viewed as relevant to the audience's reality. For a discussion of how texts embody 'social verisimilitude', see Carole R. Fontaine, 'Heifer', p. 72.

12. 'Primary' societies are those that influence the civilizations around them, for whatever reason. In the ancient Near East, Egypt and Mesopotamia represent the primary societies based on the economic and cultural advantages brought by settling next to major rivers, the Nile, the Euphrates and the Tigris. Israel and those other cultures occupying the 'land bridge' between the two great river valley civilizations are 'secondary': their cultures were first incubated in the primary areas, and then transmitted by trade, emigration and war. Naturally, 'secondary' cultures routinely modify the received traditions of their more fortunate neighbors, introducing changes that better harmonize with their unique experience.

wisdom of the ages and the experience of the cultures that preceded and surrounded them.

Similarly, our 'ancient ecumenicists' in Israel demand of interpreters a sensitivity to literary issues, since we are so clearly dealing in most cases with artistic products of verbal artisans, and not merely with a tradition of scribal copies or unedited collection of oral materials. Literary artistry was a matter of great concern to our authors, and so a literary method is in order to study the language acts that they produced.

One more introductory note is necessary when we think of the social locations and social roles of women sages in Israel and their refraction in the text of Proverbs. The origin of the wisdom traditions in the scribal bureaucracy and schools of the surrounding primary river valley cultures is well documented, but the situation is not nearly so clear in Israel.[13] The diversity of the origins of Israel's wisdom traditions may be blurred if we make normative the experience of Mesopotamia and Egypt, where sages were elite servants of the royal bureaucracy. It is easy to 'under-observe' the role of the 'folk', elusive creatures that they are—certainly the group among whom most of our women sages must be sought—in the origins of Israel's wisdom. In this respect, questing after the 'folk sage' is a task beset by the same methodological problems as the task of searching out the 'female sage'. While it is true that we should probably associate the formation of some of our texts with the needs of the royal establishment, the vigorous stream of folk wisdom that fed into the great river of Israel's wisdom often receives less attention than it ought, thus concealing the importance of Israel's tribal and oral heritage in shaping the later products of the monarchies.[14]

With respect to the educational enterprise of training sages to carry on the wisdom tradition, many scholars have underestimated what must have been the amazing impact of the movement from cuneiform and/or hiero-glyphic syllabaries to the more-or-less straightforward phonetic alphabet

13. See, for example, James L. Crenshaw's conclusions in *Education in Ancient Israel: Across the Deadening Silence* (ABRL; New York: Doubleday, 1998): analogies based on Egypt and Mesopotamia are essentially faulty in that they underestimate the difference between learning and using cuneiform and alphabetic scripts, but such epigraphic evidence as we have from Judah and Israel supports a conclusion that schools—of what sort we cannot specify entirely—did exist from the eighth century onwards (pp. 85-113).

14. Westermann, *Roots of Wisdom*, a less than careful translation of *Wurzeln der Weisheit: Die ältesten Sprüche Israels und anderer Völker* (Göttingen: Vandenhoeck & Ruprecht, 1990).

of Hebrew and Aramaic used by our Israelite tradents of later times. The scribal education demanded for the mastery of hieroglyphics in Egypt and the diplomatic languages of Mesopotamia was still necessary in Israel to some extent for the purposes of diplomacy during the early period of the monarchy, but was not so vital once the switch to Aramaic as the language of diplomacy had been made (from the eighth century BCE onward).[15] However, even in the early era, the fact that some required specialized training to become professional scribes scarcely rendered the rest of the non-elite and under- or differently educated population functionally incapable of oral composition in their own language! Modern concepts of 'literacy' are less than helpful as we attempt to reconstruct the situation in ancient Israel: it is quite possible that many could read, but not write. Writing/reading of certain sorts (economic and political list keeping, seals of ownership, law codes, etc.) may well have been fairly common— certainly true for the later Iron Age and following periods—while artistic 'compositions' still continued to be governed by a world in which orality and its 'registers' dominated the majority of linguistic productions.[16] Certainly, wisdom literature's repeated emphasis on the 're-oralization', to use Susan Niditch's helpful term,[17] of wisdom teaching—these pithy teachings were to be remembered, used, repeated, applied, learned—suggests that women should be given an equal place as wisdom tradents, since they were no less proficient at oral composition and strategic use of wisdom genres in their day-to-day life. There is no reason to assume that the folk—women included—were without insights into human experience or lacked the linguistic capacities to give verbal expression to such gleanings in the form of traditional sayings, parables, riddles, laments and so on. Nor were the folk—women included—without the daily conflicts that make proverbial forms so useful for settling disputes in traditional societies; a survey of proverb use among the various peoples of Africa indicates how vital such a folk tradition can be—even in the absence of professionally trained and supported scribes![18]

15. Crenshaw, *Education*, p. 107.

16. Susan Niditch, *Oral World and Written Word: Ancient Israelite Literature* (LAI; Louisville, KY: Westminster/John Knox Press, 1996), pp. 39-77, 108-30 et passim.

17. Niditch, *Oral World*, pp. 95-98. Cf. Prov. 31.26, where the wife 'opens her mouth' with wisdom and has Torah 'on her tongue'.

18. See Carole R. Fontaine, *Traditional Sayings in the Old Testament: A Contextual Study* (BL, 5; Sheffield: Almond Press, 1982), for further discussion.

Sage Women in the Private Domain

Positive Roles: Wife/Mother as Sage

If women were not normally included among those who might receive a scribal education and the training needed to become an official court scribe, author or counselor, then where *should* the search for their connections to the wisdom movement begin? As is often the case in the study of women's lives in the past, we look for women's participation first in the arena to which patriarchal culture routinely assigns them, the 'private domain' of the home. Initially, we will seek the association of women with 'wisdom' by surveying the traditional roles of wife and mother.[19]

Wife (Proverbs 5.18; 12.4; 18.22; 19.13-14; 21.9, 19; 25.24; 27.15-16; 30.23; 31.10-31). The position of wife is the one most approved by the sages, along with that of 'Mother'.[20] Despite regular delineation of women as potential troublemakers, the Sages see an able, active, fruitful wife as an undisputed prerequisite for male advancement in the public world (cf. 12.4; 31.10ff.), a theme repeated in Egyptian materials as well. For them, finding a discerning, industrious woman to oversee one's household is no less than a divine blessing (18.22; 19.14). Women were the managers of the private world of the home with its extremely time-consuming tasks of daily survival. The primary duties of wives fell within the realm of childcare, production and processing of food, and manufacture of textiles and clothing for home use and sale (see discussions below). As it happens, these were excellent tasks to be performed by those whose primary focus was on the safety and well-being of young children. 'Women's work' had to be amenable to frequent interruption and 'multi-tasking'. It was a source of immediate pride and gratification because of its immediacy and tangible nature. Obviously, women's sexual services were important to the men of patriarchal societies for providing legitimate male heirs to inherit the father's name and estate, as well as recreational benefits. Even beyond that, however, women were critical to the successful continued functioning of any extended family.

Ancient Near Eastern materials, textual and material, show both the

---

19. Carole R. Fontaine, 'The Sage in Family and Tribe', in J.G. Gammie and L.G. Perdue (eds.), *The Sage in Israel and the Ancient Near East* (Winona Lake, IN: Eisenbrauns, 1990), pp. 155-64, and Claudia Camp, 'The Female Sage in Ancient Israel and in the Biblical Wisdom Literature', in Gammie and Perdue (eds.), *Sage*, pp. 185-204.

20. Unfortunately for them, not all wives successfully became mothers.

knowledge of a woman's importance in the management of the domestic sphere, and a certain fear of it, too. Assyrian proverbs start from the public domain and proceed to the private, proclaiming as they ponder the given 'order' in society:

> People without a king are [like] sheep without a shepherd.
> People without a foreman are [like] a canal without a regulator.
> Workers without a supervisor are [like] a field without a cultivator.
> A household without a master is [like] a woman without a husband.[21]

This being acknowledged, however, the sages among Israel's neighbors are not too happy about the implications of the woman's role as her husband's Grand Vizier of the household. From Ugarit, we read in *The Instructions of Shube-Awilim* a profound ambivalence on the topic:

> Do not open your heart (too much) to the woman you love,
> Seal it up, however much she importune.
> You should k[eep?] your wealth in your strong room,
> Do not let your wife learn what is in your purse... (Section ii, lines 16-19)

> Do not buy [an ox? In the springtime],
> Do not choose a girl to marry on a h[oliday].
> "(Even) a bad ox will look good in (that) season,
> A ba[d] girl [just wears] g[oo]d [clothe]s for the occasion..." (Section iii, 10'-13')[22]

In a more generous vein, all these domestic, managerial tasks and their relationship to a woman householder's wisdom find an apt summation in an Iron Age Neo-Hittite funeral stele from Marash showing Aramaic influence (eighth–seventh century BCE; Figure 1).[23] Our dead mother is shown dressed in high-status clothing (her outer robe bears a fringe), seated before an incense stand, with a spindle in her hand with which she is industriously plying her womanly craft. Before her stands a scribe, clearly of lower status (since he is shown in a smaller size), with his tablet and stylus at the ready to record his mistress's words or accounts. The tableau formed here is quite telling: the mother of the house outranks the male who serves her, and each is pictured with the 'tools' of their trade.

21. Benjamin Foster, *Before the Muses: An Anthology of Akkadian Literature*. I. *Archaic, Classical, Mature* (Bethesda, MD: CDL Press, 1993), p. 339.

22. Foster, *Before the Muses*, I, pp. 334-35.

23. Ilse Seibert, *Women in the Ancient Near East* (New York: Abner Schram, 1974), plate 56; also in E. Akurgal, *The Art of the Hittites* (trans. C. McNab; New York: Harry Abrams, 1962), plate 138.

Figure 1.   The Sage Wife. (Neo-Hittite funeral stele from Marash [Iron Age: c. 8–7 BCE]. Digital painting by Carol Fontaine.

As has been suggested by other feminist historians, what 'text' is to men, 'textiles' are to women.[24] It may be that some of her elite status was based on her sale of the textiles she is shown processing, since we know that many women did do a brisk business in the export of their woven work (see discussion of the Strong Woman of Prov. 31 below).[25] Whether the scribe is recording her last words (an instruction to her daughters, perhaps? See Chapter 4, below) or calculating the tally on her shipments of

---

24. Rozsicka Parker, *The Subversive Sticth: Embroidery and the Making of the Feminine* (London: Woman's Press, 1986); Tova Rosen, 'Circumcised Cinderella: The Fantasies of a 14th Century Jewish Author', *Prooftexts* 20 (2000), pp. 87-110; Miriam B. Peskowitz, *Spinning Fantasies: Rabbis, Gender, and History* (Berkeley: University of California Press, 1997).

25. Elizabeth Wayland Barber, *Women's Work: the First 20,000 Years* (New York: W.W. Norton, 1994), pp. 164-84.

flax and woolens is impossible to decide, but in either case, this woman of worth has something of substance about her, either in speech or products, that is worth recording by a man. Even in death, she is rest-less, depicted as engaged in work for the support of her household! Here is indeed an ancient witness, 'carved in stone', to the 'truth' of the English proverb-ditty: 'A man may work from sun to sun, but woman's work is never done.'

Missing Mothers-to-Be: Daughters and Sisters. Oddly enough, daughters and sisters are almost wholly missing from the book of Proverbs. While young male students are advised to 'Say to Wisdom, "You are my sister"...' (7.4), real, living sisters—so key in epic traditions of the ancient Near East and other cultures as harbingers of doom to fathers or rescuers of brothers (see 'Ugarit' below)—have entirely disappeared from the sages' collection of wisdom teachings on women, as have daughters (mentioned only meta-phorically as the twin suckers of a leech in 30.15). To what should these lacunae be attributed? We speculate here that it is the liminal nature of these two groups of females that is responsible for their absence: under male control (the sages only hope!), they do not yet seem to have achieved the status of wife/mother, the only reason for their existence. If they have been successfully married off, they are naturally considered under the rubric of that penultimate domestic role. Otherwise, without a mate and a child, they exist as non-persons in the sages' collection.

The custom obtaining broadly throughout the ancient Near East is that the man acquiring a wife pays 'bride-price' to her male guardian; the bride's family in turn supplies the girl with a 'dowry'. We see a cycle of economic exchange instituted here: what comes into a family as dowry goes out to another family to pay bride-price. Law codes are filled with regulations stipulating the wife's entitlement to her dowry, and its disposi-tion in cases of divorce, death, and so on, as well as covering disputes where bride-price is involved. Clearly, the disposition of daughters repre-sented a strong economic commitment required by her family of origin, and the excellence of her personal reputation and that of her family helped set a high 'bride-price', so necessary to her brothers' acquisition of fitting wives.

Documents on the strange institution of 'sistership' from the city-state of Nuzi in Mesopotamia provided added information about the status and economic problems associated with unmarried daughters. We find there that a father has three options with respect to the 'disposal' of his unmarried daughters: he might negotiate bride-price and give her in marriage; he might give her in adoptive 'daughtership' or 'daughter-in-lawship' to another man, again with the goal of arranging a marriage of full status for her at a later date, or he might choose to sell her as a slave. Upon the father's death, it was not automatically the case in Nuzi that the right to negotiate a sister's marriage fell to the interested brother. Unless the deceased gave explicit permission for the brother to arrange the sister's marriage, authority over her in this matter seems to have gone to the mother as a matter of course— though the ranking male of the bereaved household was still understood to have some authority over the girl in other matters. A brother who *was* given the right to dispose of his sister by his parent's will had the same options as his father with regard to negotiating an immediate marriage or a 'daughter-ship/daughter-in-lawship' arrangement. But two features are unique to the brother's duties in regard to a sister left under his authority legally: there are no attested examples of a brother selling his sister into slavery (which doesn't mean it never happened), and he might choose to dispose of his sister in the institution of 'sistership'.

'Sistership' could be negotiated by the brother or by the sister herself, and involved her being transferred as the adopted 'sister' to another man, who would then have the right to negotiate her bride-price to be retained by himself outright, or to share in the future bride-price along with the natural brother. From these texts, scholars also presume that, as adopted sister, the woman lived in the household of her adopted brother, hence giving him a considerable economic advantage in her ongoing domestic work in exchange for room and board. Since the evidence from these texts does not always allow us to paint a full portrait of the legal and social ramifications of this custom, we may only draw limited conclusions. First, it is notable that the sister *must* have given her consent to her entry into 'sistership', suggesting a world of domestic discord, machinations and uneven strategies existing in sibling relations. A woman who had been badly treated in her family of origin might readily cede herself and her financial prospects in marriage to another guardian with considerable glee, knowing she had deprived her natural brother of a substantial resource. Secondly, while it is not always clear why a brother would choose to exercise his option of 'sistership' when negotiating (and keeping!) the bride-price himself would seem more immediately advantageous, it is apparent from these proceedings that the disposition of sisters might represent a valuable financial option in times of fiscal disaster for the family.[26]

---

26. B.L. Eichler, 'Another Look at the Nuzi Sistership Contracts', in M. Ellis (ed.), *Essays on the Ancient Near East in Memory of Jacob Joel Finkelstein* (Memoirs of the

In the postexilic period to which the editing of Proverbs is usually assigned, matters of inheritance were of key importance. Perhaps the troubling absence of any genuine human sisters in the Book of Proverbs should be related to the financial impact of the sister on the family: she is blessing or burden, a useful unpaid drudge until such time that she can be 'converted' into a bride-price that outweighs the outlay of her dowry.

Patriarchal culture socializes a woman to regard becoming a wife/ mother as the most important occurrences of her life (Exod. 1.21; Song 8.8-14). Her circumstances are precarious without such status (consider the lot of poor Tamar, either one). Without her own household, such a daughter/sister is likely to be seen as a social burden by her family and an object of shame and humiliation within her culture (Ruth; Gen. 30; 1 Sam. 1.1–2.10). When she successfully marries or becomes a mother, emotions of great exaltation and social exoneration are attributed to her (Gen. 21.6-7; 1 Sam. 2.1-10; Prov. 30.23). No longer a suspect vehicle of bad luck, curse or perversity, she is finally whole and productive as she was taught to be.

We may note here that the socially constructed goal of marriage for a woman is not some sort of 'romantic' fulfillment, but rather finding a context in which her fertility and economic assets are channeled 'honorably'—at least to the thinking of the Sages! What might they have thought if they had recognized that man, the measure of all things in their eyes, was of less interest to a female's story of her own life than the child he might father, or the household he would cede to a woman's control? Having helped to create women who pursue their allotted roles, did the teachers feel a bit of chagrin, perhaps, that man ceased to be the center of a woman's life, even though his love is better to her than seven sons by his own way of thinking (Hannah and Elkanah)? Did our Sages ever recognize their own role—and that of their fellows—in creating the very stereotyped predatory female behaviors that they later decry?

That a daughter or sister might choose to remain unmarried, or once widowed, to remain so, is beyond our sages' comprehension. Ben Sira, the sage of the later period (c. 180 BCE) whose proverbial compositions build on the imagery found in Proverbs, best sums up male wisdom's view of woman's purpose—and her propensity for straying from it!—in his sentiments on daughters:

Connecticut Academy of Arts and Sciences, 19; Hamden, CT: Archon Books, 1977), pp. 45-59.

A daughter is a secret anxiety to her father,
and worry over her robs him of sleep;
when she is young, for fear she may not marry,
or if married, for fear she may be disliked;
while a virgin, for fear she may be seduced
and become pregnant in her father's house;
or having a husband, for fear she may go astray,
or, though married, for fear she may be barren.

Keep a strict watch over a headstrong daughter,
or she may make you a laughingstock to your enemies,
a byword in the city and assemble of the people,
and put you to shame in public gatherings.
See that there is no lattice in her room,
no spot that overlooks the approaches to the house.
Do not let her parade her beauty before any man,
or spend her time among married women;
for from garments comes the moth,
and from a woman comes woman's wickedness.
Better is the wickedness of a man than a woman who does good;
it is woman who brings shame and disgrace (Sir. 42.9-14, NRSV).

We have here a potent explication of the *true* focus of this sage's view of womanhood, as exemplified in daughters: it is the trouble they might cause to men that sets the agenda for the social control of their behavior. Nowhere does Ben Sira indict any male in the potential misbehavior he suspects to be lurking in any daughter's conduct,[27] nor does his worry for the success of her marriage have anything whatsoever to do with the daughter's happiness and/or fulfillment. As Claudia Camp notes, the fate of a straying, married daughter has direct economic and status impact on the father—she returns to his house to live with her shame and rejection.[28] The daughter in this passage seems to have no concern about dowry or bride-price, but no doubt these economic realities undergird part of her father's worry: can he arrange a good bride-price and supply a suitable dowry? What if she is found 'impure' and returned to him after

---

27. Warren C. Trenchard, *Ben Sira's View of Woman: A Literary Analysis* (BJS, 38; Chico, CA: Scholars Press, 1982), pp. 129-65, where the author argues that Ben Sira's condemnation is extended to *all* daughters, and not just 'bad' ones.

28. Claudia Camp, 'Understanding a Patriarchy: Women in Second Century Jerusalem through the Eyes of Ben Sira', in A.-J. Levine (ed.), *Women Like This: New Perspectives on Jewish Women in the Greco-Roman World* (Atlanta: Scholars Press, 1991), pp. 1-40.

he has already spent the bride-price he must now return! Will her dowry be safe in her new household? What if *he* dies before the whole complex business is negotiated: will the family that survives him be capable of seeing to the settlement of this unowned female, or will she find some way to ruin them all in the breach?

Violence or abuse, scarcity or family misfortune, ill-health or infant mortality—none of these occurrences, very real possibilities for a woman in any society, seems to cast a shadow on the horizon of this sage's concerns for the wretched daughter God uses to curse men. He finishes off his argument in the most convincing way a sage knows, by citing a proverb to lay the blessing of 'traditional wisdom' over his personal musings (v. 14). Nowhere is there a better text to demonstrate that proverbial teachings about women are *actually* about men! His prurient fantasies of adolescent sex are indeed the stuff of nightmares; his ideal remedy is as poisonous as his lurid dreams of his daughter's nakedness in the arms of another man. He suggests a cruel and extreme punishment for a teenager who has yet to commit any crimes: wholesale isolation. Only such radical action can guard a man against the misfortune of having fathered girls.

Turning the tables on this laughingstock of a sage, we must treat him like the bad dream he is, tossing his androcentric concerns onto their head in the same way the morning shakes out the skirts of the earth to empty the world of evil-doers who have proliferated by night (Job 38.12-13). Beneath his diatribe, we may glimpse another reality in the life and the laughter of Ben Sira's girl. Though destined for an 'honorable' marriage that will please her father, she is a desiring subject capable of seeking her own mate. She and her lover set the parameters of their sexual encounters before and after courtship with no hint of the economic legalities intruding on their desire—*not* the father who thinks he owns her sexuality! Within marriage, she is capable enough to cause her husband's dislike, implying not just poor execution of her wifely obligations, but also a hearty capacity for critique of her husband's performance of *his* duties. We hear nothing of her mothering and nurturing abilities, but we see her as intent upon finding a partner, choosing between options, looking eagerly for a suitable choice, and engaging married women in conversation about the real nature of married life and its possibilities.[29] She knows her own beauty, and seeks a better venue for its appreciation than she ever found in her father's eyes.

---

29. The married women may in fact be her most important source of information on pregnancy and child-rearing, and hence keeping her from them imperils the very outcome of success as mother/wife that her father wishes for her.

Headstrong? By Ben Sira's evaluation, perhaps so; in another context, we might see her as having many of the same traits that make the Strong Woman of Proverbs 31 such an excellent and efficient mate.

Mother (Proverbs 1.8; 4.3; 6.20; 10.1; 15.20; 19.26; 20.20; 23.22, 25; 28.24; 30.11, 17 paired with 'father'; Proverbs 29.15; 31.1, mother alone). 'Mother' appears as the second half of the standard antithetical word-pair (father/mother), an instructional tool much favored by the Sages in their discourse on parental prudence, responsibilities and control. The mother is the epitome of power and influence expressly because she *is* a mother, and, at some point in her life, probably the mistress of her own domestic unit. As such, she is a powerful presence in the home, exemplifying domestic organization, propriety and the child's first contact with religious and ethical instruction (so, emphasis on the 'mother's torah' in 1.8; 6.20). In fact, one reason 'Lady Wisdom' (cf. Prov. 1.20-33; 3.13-20; 4.5-9; 8; 9.1-6) is imaged as female may be the all-encompassing roles played by the mother in the typical family. When added to the literary memories of bygone goddess figures who served as m/patrons of the scribal bureaucracies that produced wisdom materials, we encounter a female entity of almost mythic dimensions, present at creation and mother to human endeavors of all kinds (Prov. 8; Job 28).

Because of her role as initial instructor to her children and domestic staff, the mother pays special attention to proper behavior in order to secure the success of her offspring (Prov. 10.1; 15.20; 23.25; 29.15). The outcome of child-rearing reflects directly upon her performance (and that of the father). Due to her supervision of the home, she anticipates compliance, deference and appreciation from her household, including her grown male children (Prov. 30.17; 31.28). Close reading shows that many of the references to 'father/mother' in Proverbs relate to the solicitude owed to parents during their later years of frailty. As they cared for the child, now the child ought to care for them (Prov. 19.26; 20.20; 23.22; 28.24; 30.11, 17), a theme also found in Egyptian wisdom literature. These strongly motivational proverbs are in agreement with the religious and social duties of covenant duties (Exod. 20.12; 21.15, 17; Deut. 5.16; 21.18-21; 27.16; Sir. 3.1-16), forming a sort of 'social welfare' system for the care of the aged. The imposing body of proverbs and admonitions advising *against* abuse of the mother and father suggests that all might not be so peaceful in the patriarchal home, however. Just as parents use verbal warnings and physical intimidation to control their children and preserve the family's honor (Prov. 19.18; 22.15; 29.15, 17; cf. Deut. 21.18-21), 'elder abuse' may have been a control mechanism favored by grown children to deal with parental complaints and demands.[30]

Proverbs 31.10-31 presents the best all-around depiction of the idealized mother of wisdom literature. A fully operational biological 'woman' in the context of a family, she is a source of both sexual services and childbearing/nurturing functions. She is an able manager and economic planner, an indefatigable worker, a woman of business, a wisdom teacher and a doer of charitable deeds. For all of her considerable contributions to the life of the family and the broader society, patriarchy treasured her and she merits its highest praise. The poem in praise of the 'The Strong Woman' (a more literal translation than 'virtuous' or 'capable wife') summarizes well:

> A strong woman who can find? She is far more precious than jewels.
> The heart of her husband trusts in her, and he will have no lack of gain.
> She does him good, and not harm, all the days of her life.
> She seeks wool and flax, and works with willing hands.
> She is like the ships of the merchant, she brings her food from far away.
> She rises while it is still night and provides food for her household and tasks for her servant-girls.
> She considers a field and buys it; with the fruit of her hands she plants a vineyard.
> She girds herself with strength, and makes her arms strong.
> She perceives that her merchandise is profitable. Her lamp does not go out at night.
> She puts her hands to the distaff, and her hands hold the spindle.
> She opens her hand to the poor, and reaches out her hands to the needy.
> She is not afraid for her household when it snows, for all her household are clothed in crimson.
> She makes herself coverings; her clothing is fine linen and purple.
> Her husband is known in the city gates, taking his seat among the elders of the land.
> She makes linen garments and sells them; she supplies the merchant with sashes.
> Strength and dignity are her clothing, and she laughs at the time to come.
> She opens her mouth with wisdom, and the teaching of kindness is on her tongue.
> She looks well to the ways of her household, and does not eat the bread of idleness.
> Her children rise up and call her happy; her husband too, and he praises her:

---

30. John Pilch, '"Beat his Ribs While He Is Young" (Sirach 30:12): A Window on the Mediterranean World', *BTB* 23 (1993), pp. 101-13.

'Many women have done excellently, but you surpass them all'.
Charm is deceitful, and beauty is vain, but a woman who fears the LORD is
   to be praised.
Give her a share in the fruit of her hands, and let her works praise her in the
   city gates (NRSV).

This text nicely illustrates the manifold tasks that were allotted to the
good wife or 'Woman of Worth'[31]—she says little, but does much. Not
only did this tireless woman work with her own hands at the day-to-day
tasks of spinning, weaving and sewing, she is also shown managing her
household so well that she has surplus to sell. None of her servants are idle
and no one fears 'shortfalls' as fruitful seasons draw to a close. Along with
these managerial tasks of economic allocation, she implicitly serves as
teacher to her household and even finds time to do good works for the
poor. She exemplifies male expectations about female honor and shame: a
woman's honor comes from protecting her 'shame', that is, by concealing
herself in the inside of the house and turning all her attention inward,
toward the goal of servicing the men in her life.[32] Most interestingly, in
her role of wife, our Strong Woman goes beyond the boundaries of her
own front door: she sells goods she has produced, makes important pur-
chases of real estate, and puts in crops according to her plans (vv. 16, 24).
She has crossed thresholds to the public domain, a possible dishonor for
her menfolk, but because she does so in service of them, bearing the produce of her inward works, her potential violation of cultural norms instead
brings honor to her men at the public gate.

When we hear the continued intonation of the much-loved androcentric
proverb, 'A woman's place is in the home,' a thoughtful reader might call
attention to the differences between the modern family setting and the
biblical one which was a pre-industrial, agrarian economic unit, possibly
in a village setting, but always essential to the survival goal of the family
unit. Such a household, living in close proximity to one or two other
related families, sharing a common hearth and courtyard, aimed at being

31. See Camp, *Wisdom*, pp. 79-96.
32. For discussions of the 'honor and shame' mentality that dominates the cultures
that produced the Bible, see L.N. Bechtel, 'Shame as a Sanction of Social Control in
Biblical Israel: Judicial, Political, and Social Shaming', *JSOT* 40 (1991), pp. 47-76;
D.D. Gilmore (ed.), *Honor and Shame and the Unity of the Mediterranean* (American
Anthropological Special Publication, 22; Washington, DC: American Anthropological
Association, 1987); Lilian R. Klein, 'Honor and Shame in Esther', in Athalya Brenner
(ed.), *A Feminist Companion to Esther, Judith and Susanna* (FCB, 7; Sheffield: Shef-
field Academic Press, 1995), pp. 149-75.

self-sufficient economically.[33] The wife in biblical times was the uncontested ruler of this private domain; interference in her realm was held to be as unwise as troubling one's servants over trivial matters. So reads Prov. 11.29: 'Those who trouble their households will inherit wind, and the fool will be servant to the wise' (compare Ben Sira 4.30; 7.20). Possessor of intimate knowledge of her household, such a woman was *expected* and *required* to make decisions, to perform meaningful and productive acts on behalf of her kin. The home was her arena, and archaeologists of Iron Age Israel's village life, such as Carol Meyers, have demonstrated how multi-faceted and crucial was the managerial and technological work performed by these 'homemakers' of the past (Fig. 2).[34]

Other Home-Based Roles: Household Manager, Teacher, Counselor, Maid. Within the description of the Strong Woman is substantial evidence of one of the roles we have posited above as belonging to the Household Sage, that of economic manager of the domestic unit. While we would expect the Lady of the House to know how much food she had available on site, to supervise her maids and children, and even to engage in the traditional tasks of spinning and weaving, we are a bit more surprised to learn that her wifely duties might also extend to extra-domestic responsibilities like ordering food from the outside world, buying and selling property to increase her family's holdings, marketing surplus produce from her domestic unit, and so on. While these rather broadly flung initiatives take her to the marketplace, both to gather information relevant to her

33. For a masterly portrait of the Iron Age Israelite village family, see Carol Meyers, 'The Family in Early Israel', in Leo G. Perdue, Joseph Blenkinsopp, John J. Collins and Carol Meyers, *Families in Ancient Israel* (Louisville, KY: Westminster/ John Knox Press, 1997), pp. 1-47. In fact, the reason why this proverb no longer applies is because the modern Western household is neither economically self-sufficient nor able to do without the woman's paycheck from work outside the home. With the rise of industrialization, when textiles, women's traditional form of earning a living while at home, was moved into factories and paid 'slave wages' in comparison to men's higher wage standards, poor working women were forced to move out from the home in order to provide for their children. This situation remains largely in force at present time, despite 'flex time', 'personal time' and possibilities for 'tele-commuting'—none of which will affect women at the lower ends of the social and occupational scale, but all of which may compromise women's orderly climb up the male career ladder of success.

34. Not to mention tedious and time-consuming! See Carol Meyers, *Discovering Eve: Ancient Israelite Women in Context* (Oxford: Oxford University Press, 1988), and discussions below.

Figure 2. Spinning Woman (Italy, fifteenth century. After T. Metzger and M. Metzger, *Jewish Life in the Middle Ages: Illuminated Hebrew Manuscripts of the Thirteenth to the Sixteenth Centuries* [New York: Alpine Fine Arts Collection, 1982], p. 200, illus. 282.)

long-range planning and to engage in the actual work of the transactions needed to realize her goals, we must note that it is her role *inside* the private world that makes these activities acceptable and laudable by her men. The portrait presented here then is necessarily that of a 'landed', upper-class woman whose household is 'well off'; clearly, her entrepreneurial skills would not be so stellar or successful if she had less to work with, or was scrabbling out a living from resources that were continuously being squandered by a foolish male head of household. Often the possibilities for women in the royal or upper classes as economic managers move them out of the kitchen and into the palace audience chambers.

The economic records and personal correspondence of queens available to us from the various archives of ancient Near Eastern city-states and empires fully attest that our 'Strong Woman' of Proverbs 31 is no fanciful invention of Hebrew wisdom poetry. Everywhere—Mesopotamia, Egypt, Anatolia—we find women moving out of their assigned powers in the household world to accrue reputation and success in a more public arena, using the very same skills they honed in women's world of the home. Queens of smaller city-states might find themselves in charge of palace, archive, workshop and temple responsibilities whenever their kings or other salient menfolk were away at war, as they often were. Queen Shibtu of eighteenth-century Mari, a Mesopotamian city-state, left an enormous amount of correspondence that witnesses to her able stewardship of her husband Zimri-Lim's holdings. In his absence she not only administered all facets of the palace-temple economic endeavors, she also conducted diplomatic correspondence, oversaw all 'public works' in Mari itself, and even found time to sustain a presence of power in her father's royal court in Aleppo. Modern persons might well marvel at how the reconstructed portrait of life at Mari overturns our expectations of 'backward' ancients: they not only had ice-cubes at Mari, they had Shibtu as well![35] The *naditu* women of Middle Bronze Age Sippar, cloistered unmarried women from elite families who were dedicated to the service of a god, were a major force in real estate and loan assistance, judging from the economic records they left behind. They regularly used scribes to record their dealings, and even though their 'occupation' required them to produce no children, they often managed to leave their inheritance to younger women *naditu* whom they had adopted as surrogate sisters.[36] Like the alewives of Mesopotamia, who made loans to farmers, ran a 'tab' for regular customers, and conducted their business dealings without any male oversight, all these 'professional' women managed to employ their talents in commerce in a world that sought to understand them primarily in terms of their ability to breed. To the record of the queens and princesses of Mari, we might also add the women (often *sisters* of the ruling males in matrilineal Anatolia) who ran the Hurrian city-states of upper Mesopotamia during their male leaders' absence, the indefatigable queens of the New Kingdom Hittite empire (see next chapter), the militant pre-Islamic queens of Arabia, and the able royal women—Ahmose-Nefertari, Hatshepsut, Tiye, Nefertiti, Ankhesenaton, and Nefertari, to name the most notable—of the royal households of New Kingdom Egypt.[37] When the Bible speaks of 'public' women—Deborah, Bath-Sheba, Queen Sheba, Jezebel, Athalya, Huldah—taking assertive roles in political dealings (and political contexts always suggest some socio-economic power base at work), such characters and

35. Fontaine, 'Heifer', pp. 167-72.

36. Daniel C. Snell, *Life in the Ancient Near East, 3100–332 B.C.E.* (New Haven: Yale University Press, 1997), p. 53.

37. S.R. Bin-Nun, *The Tawannana in the Hittite Kingdom* (THeth, 5; Heidelberg: Carl Winter, 1975); Nabia Abbott, 'Pre-Islamic Arab Queens', *AJSLL* 58 (1941), pp. 1-22; Barbara S. Lesko, *The Remarkable Women of Ancient Egypt* (Providence, RI: B.C. Scribe Publications, 1987), pp. 1-11.

their doings cannot be regarded as mere fictions[38] when read against the background context of the opportunities given upper-class women in the rest of the Fertile Crescent.

Figure 3. The Teaching Mother. (Ink-and-wash illustration from 'Mashal ha-qadmoni of Isaac ibn Sahula', Germany [c. 1450]. After Metzger and Metzger, *Jewish Life*, p. 294, illus. 292).

Although not fully exegeted in Prov. 31, the mother's roles in teaching, counseling and conflict resolution within the home are also tasks that qualified her as a practitioner of wisdom. First, a mother finds authority in her nurturing relationship to her offspring, as we see in a charming ink-and-wash illustration from the illuminated manuscript 'Mashal ha-qadmoni of Isaac ibn Sahula', an Ashkenazi text from Germany of the early modern period (c. 1450). In it, we see a mother and a grandfather holding a toddler by each hand, encouraging first steps by a baby who is looking somewhat bemused. The mother stands on the right and coaxes the child toward her; the older man stands to the left, the direction from which the child has come. There is a tenderness of expression on the mother's face as she bends down toward the boy and urges him on, all the while providing safety in the process and the desirable end of her embrace for the adventurous youngster (see Fig. 3).[39]

38. This is not to imply that the Bible's history of these women is in fact accurate, only that the notion of women acting in public contexts is perfectly credible.

39. Codex Hebr. 107, folio 79v (Munich: Bayerische Staatsbibliothek), after Thérèse

The 'mother's teaching' is mentioned in Prov. 1.8 and 6.20. It is interesting to note the variant term used in 31.26: *torat-hesed*, 'torah of kind-
ness',[40] suggesting that her teachings may differ from those of the fathers.
Further references acknowledge a mother's sorrow when her child does
not heed her instruction (10.1 and, by implication, 15.20). While no examples of the mother's 'Torah' survive in Proverbs, with the exception of the
passage by the Queen-mother cited below, the fact that this pedagogy is
always mentioned as parallel to the 'father's instruction/commandment'
(1.8; 6.20) shows that it was held in high esteem in this traditional society.
The mother's role as the instructor of very young children of both sexes,
girls of all ages and the female domestic work force, is one of the great
sources of her power, marking her as an 'authority' within the household.
Well into a male child's adulthood, his mother was still a source of
authority and wisdom (see Bath-Sheba, below). In fact, this tendency to
defer to the mother's counsel was one of the reasons that Protestant
Reformers felt the need, even beyond their general position of iconoclasm,
to diminish the role of Mary of Nazareth in Christian theology and piety—
for what man, even a messiah, does not listen to his mother?[41]

Part of the mother's teaching tasks no doubt found further expression in
counseling and conflict resolution, as she modeled effective ways of
settling disputes and managing the men of the extended family. While
modern persons may look askance at some of the 'crafty' and manipu-
lative behavior displayed by the wives and mothers portrayed in the
biblical tradition, it should be remembered that the use of 'indirect means'
(e.g. such as gossip, shaming behavior, untruths, promotion of 'harem'
rivalries, etc.) are typical strategies employed by those who do not have
direct access to power.[42] When wives and mothers are not allowed to give

Metzger and Mendel Metzger, *Jewish Life in the Middle Ages: Illuminated Hebrew
Manuscripts of the Thirteenth to the Sixteenth Centuries* (New York: Alpine Fine Arts
Collection, 1982), p. 204, fig. 292.

40. 'Hesed' is notoriously difficult to translate: it means 'steadfast love' as guaran-
teed through covenantal relationship; it carries aspects of fidelity, ultimacy and
intimacy, and evokes a religious connotation, since it is this love that God shows for
Israel.

41. Allison P. Coudert, 'The Myth of the Improved Status of Protestant Women:
The Case of the Witchcraze', in Brian P. Levack (ed.), *Witchcraft, Women and Society:
Articles on Witchcraft, Magic and Demonology: A Twelve Volume Anthology of Schol-
arly Articles*, X (New York: Garland, 1992), pp. 85-113.

42. Esther Fuchs, 'Who Is Hiding the Truth? Deceptive Women and Biblical
Androcentrism', in Adela Yarbro Collins (ed.), *Feminist Perspectives on Biblical*

peremptory orders, they readily turn to other methods to make their influence felt. In fact, the counsel of women was valued in Israel, if we are to attribute any credence at all to the stories handed down to us. Husbands who do not heed the subtle advice of their wives—like Job and Nabal—are doomed to endless repetition of narrative episodes (Job),[43] or disappear from the story altogether (Nabal). That such women could also be perceived as irritating 'nags' is also the case: Job silences his wife, telling her she is speaking like a fool, and David is so enraged with Queen Michal's comments on his public behavior that the story does away with her altogether, first causing her to disappear from the plot (just as Saul's whole royal dynasty has disappeared from the plot of Israel's struggle for a king), and later telling the reader that she was denied her opportunity to achieve her full status through child-bearing (2 Sam. 6.23).[44]

Mantic Mothers and Wives. Elsewhere in the ancient Near East we meet another form of the wise wife-mother's counsel when she interprets dreams. While this 'mantic' understanding of wisdom has more to do with wisdom's relationship to oracular traditions, it is nevertheless worth mentioning that in Mesopotamia, Egypt and Anatolia, much of the interpretation of the symbolic language of dreams fell to trusted women, usually within the family, and enhanced their status as practitioners of wisdom. (We need only remember the role that dream interpretation plays in the establishment of wise or godly young men in the royal courts of Egypt and Babylon.) Dreams in the ancient world were considered 'real' messages with clear impact on one's 'path', if only one could understand their meanings. Within the Hebrew Bible, only Jer. 29.8 suggests that dreams and their interpreters are 'bad' in and of themselves; elsewhere they appear as genuine, if ambiguous, messages from the Hebrew God. In particular, this ability to 'translate' the register of dream phantasms into intelligible guidance in the real world strikes us as an extension of the dimension of women's verbal performance of wisdom.

Scholarship (Chico, CA: Scholars Press, 1985), pp. 137-44, and ' "For I Have the Way of Women": Deception, Gender, and Ideology in Biblical Narrative', *Semeia* 42 (1988), pp. 68-83; see also Camp, *Wisdom*, pp. 124-39.

43. Carole R. Fontaine, 'Folktale Structure in the Book of Job: A Formalist Reading', in Elaine Follis (ed.), *Directions in Biblical Hebrew Poetry* (JSOTSup, 40; Sheffield: JSOT Press, 1987), pp. 215-16.

44. J. Cheryl Exum, *Fragmented Women: Feminist (Sub)versions of Biblical Narrative* (Valley Forge, PA: Trinity Press International, 1993).

In the Epic of Gilgamesh, we meet one such wise mother. This obstreperous king, part god, part man (and apparently the least desirable part of each), was such a trouble to the people of his city-state Uruk that they sought help from the gods to control his sexual appetites. In response, the gods created a 'double', a champion so well matched to Gilgamesh, that this new companion would divert the king's focus from regular mortals. However, before the double, Enkidu, ever arrives in Uruk to challenge Gilgamesh, his coming is heralded in a dream:

> For Gilgamesh arose to reveal his dreams,
>   Saying to his mother:
>   · 'My mother, I saw a dream last night:
> There appeared the stars in the heavens...
> Like the essence of Anu[45] it descends upon me.
> I sought to lift it; it was too stout for me...
> I loved it and was drawn to it as though to a woman...
>
> [The wise mother of Gilgamesh who] is versed in all knowledge,
> Says to her lord;
> [Beloved and wise Ninsun], who is versed in all knowledge,
> Says to Gilgamesh:
> 'Thy [*rival*],—the star of heaven,
> which descended upon thee...
> [A stout com]rade who rescues [a friend is come to thee].
> [He is the mightiest in the land]; strength he has.
> [Like the essence of Anu], so mighty his strength
> [That thou didst love him and] wert [drawn] to him [as though to a
>   woman],
> [Means that he will never] forsake [th]ee.
> [This is the mean]ing of thy dream.

This is not the only dream the king brings to his mother for interpretation. He has a second dream, also concerning Enkidu. Now the double-champion is symbolized by an axe to which Gilgamesh is immediately drawn (as though to a woman) and which he places at his mother's feet. Again, the wise mother Ninsun has the key to the interpretation of her son's dream: 'The axe which thou sawest is a man...'[46]

---

45. The lord of the sky.

46. 'The Epic of Gilgamesh', trans. E.A. Speiser, in James B. Pritchard (ed.), *Ancient Near Eastern Texts Relating to the Old Testament, 3rd Ed. with Supplement* (Princeton: Princeton University Press, 1969), pp.75-76 (hereafter cited as *ANET*). Gilgamesh's dreams appear in column v of Tablet I of the Akkadian version and Tablet II, cols i and ii of the Old Babylonian version.

Within the Hittite Empire of the thirteenth century BCE, we see dreams come to a special prominence, as the new Queen, Pudukhepa, from the southern province of Kizzuwatna brought the traditions of dreams, vows and oracles into a new place of esteem in the religion of the great empire (for more on this queen, see Chapter 3). Warnings about health and welfare of the royal family might be transmitted in dreams, and vows made to avert the predicted disaster—vows often forgotten when the dreamer awoke, thus angering the gods and calling for another round of oracular consultation with the Wise Woman/Old Women of the region. Evil dreams might be both interpreted and removed by the Wise Woman, and pregnant women could not be led to the birthing stool until they had experienced the requisite purification dream.[47] In Egypt, dreams were similarly understood to have cosmic meaning. The goddess Hathor might give a dream (the so-called 'incubation' dream) to a seeker who slept in her temple; both she and the mother goddess Isis might be invoked to remove an illness whose meaning had been revealed in such a way.[48] In Mt. 27.19 we find an interesting notice that the wife of Pilate sent counsel to her husband about his treatment of Jesus, based on the fact that she had 'suffered much over him today in a dream'. Here is another example of a woman displaying wisdom in the interpretation of dreams, but wisdom that could be safely ignored by the man to whom it was directed because it came from a woman.

We may also add to the roles performed by wife and mother those of 'healer' and 'mourner', both of which are particularly associated with wisdom (see discussion below). It is the mother, wife and sister to whom the care of sick family members is assigned (see the unfortunate case of Tamar in 2 Sam. 13), so that the activity of nursing was probably taught to daughters and female slaves as part of the Mother's Torah. Likewise, the women of the household are mourners par excellence: the Wise Woman of 2 Sam. 14.2 pretends to be mourning in order to carry out her plan to prick the conscience of the king; the harlots of 1 Kgs 3.18-19 implicitly bring their cause for mourning over a dead child to the wise king for a settlement.[49]

---

47. Gabriella Frantz-Szabó, 'Hittite Witchcraft, Magic and Divination', in Jack M. Sasson (ed.), *Civilizations of the Ancient Near East*, III (New York: Charles Scribner's Sons, 1995), pp. 2013-15 (hereafter *CANE*).

48. J.F. Borghouts, 'Witchcraft, Magic, and Divination in Ancient Egypt', *CANE*, III, pp. 1775-85; Kent R. Weeks, 'Medicine, Surgery and Public Health in Ancient Egypt', *CANE*, III, pp. 1787-98.

49. Michael Coogan (ed. and trans.), 'Aqhat', in *Stories from Ancient Canaan* (Louisville, KY: Westminster Press, 1978), p. 41; cf. also 'Kirta', p. 69.

Maid: Cult Functionaries, Servants or Daughters? (Proverbs 9.3; 27.27; 31.15 [Heb., נערות*, nᵉʿārôt; NRSV: 'servant girls ']; 30.23, [Heb.,* שפחה*, šiphâ; NRSV: 'maid ']).* In the gynocentric households portrayed in the book of Proverbs, female servants are a necessity for the upper-class mistress, even if a largely ignored one in terms of literary characterization in Proverbs. Such servants belonged to the well-off household, and might be of any age, marital status, nationality, and hold varying statuses within the household based on these factors or a special competence in some area of household duties. Sometimes, such servants were given as a wedding or other sort of gift, but could even be the results of the spoils of war (cf. Gen. 12.16; 29.24, 29). In most 'normal' circumstances, such a female servant was under the direct control of the female head of the household, who might also assign her to provide sexual services to the master of the house (Gen. 16; 30).

In fact, we find three kinds of 'maids' in Proverbs: those who belong to Woman Wisdom (9.3); those who work in the household (27.27; 31.15); and the maid (*šiphâ*) in 30.23 who supplants her mistress, no doubt based on sexual services to the man of the house. The serving women of Woman Wisdom might well be viewed as cultic functionaries, serving Wisdom in her (as yet to be demonstrated) 'cult' as personal goddess to scribes, bureaucrats and their households. This would be in keeping with other cults in the ancient Near East, where women, high-born or otherwise, might be dedicated to the service of a particular deity. Further, in some mythologies from the region, such 'servants' are themselves divine: Ninitta and Kulitta, a pair serving the Hittite mother-goddess, are such minor deities, as is Ninshubur, 'Lady of the East Wind', who serves as Grand Vizier (*sukkal*) to the martial fertility goddess of Sumer, Inanna. These maids would have high status indeed, and so we should not automatically assume that Wisdom's serving women are mere slaves in Wisdom's sight, slogging along behind her, cleaning up after the messianic banquet Wisdom ordered them to serve to men. We must also object to translators' continued characterization of such women as 'girls', since modern readers are more apt to think of this terminology in terms of 'age', when in fact, it refers to lesser status vis-à-vis the mistress who commands them. A better term might be 'serving-woman' or 'slave-woman', since the age of the female in question often cannot be decided from the sparse information given in context.

In reflecting on the lot of serving women and their relation to the exercise of wisdom, a few scattered historical notices shed some light on their lives. In Mesopotamia, most affluent households only had from one to five slaves (in some periods, only two to four), and close reading of the

Bible's traditions on this subject seem to suggest about the same rate of ownership. They might bear special slave names, be forced to wear a metal arm-band, special hairstyle or tattoo (the *abbuttu*) that marked their status as property. Slaves, and certainly serving women, were used to provide household labor, since supervision of agricultural work (where they might be able to escape more easily) was more difficult to arrange in terms of 'man-power'. Sexual exploitation by the men of the household seemed to be the order of the day, and in the best cases might bring about manumission if the woman bore sons to her master. Slaves employed in textile work in the royal or temple 'factories' might also produce goods on their own time that they might sell independently or retain for their own personal use, suggesting some possibility for a form of non-sexual 'advancement'.[50] In Anatolia, we find that slave women served as 'wise women' and are recorded as 'informants' who recite ritual texts so they may be recorded for the archives, thus giving a direct connection to some of the remarks made here.[51] Slaves in Israel were also possessors of knowledge: the story of the healing of the Syrian general Naaman in 2 Kings 5 is facilitated by the captive Israelite maidservant who serves his wife. She advises her mistress, 'Would that my lord were with the prophet who is in Samaria! He would cure him of his leprosy' (5.3), who must repeat that information to her husband, though the biblical text leaves out this stage of female transmission of knowledge of possible medical remedies for a sick member of the household.[52] Further, even so great a sage as the Egyptian vizier Ptahhotep might comment that even slave women could be noted for their abilities in 'good speech' (= wisdom). That we will later find an 'uppity' Egyptian slave addressing an effective proverb to Pharoah and his sage in order to gain her own objectives should occasion no surprise then, given this expanded portrait of the lowest status woman of the household (see Chapter 3 for discussion).

Carol Meyers has suggested that the $n^e\,'\bar{a}r\hat{o}t$ in Prov. 27.27 and 31.15 should be understood not as servants, but unmarried daughters of the household, since this word elsewhere often refers of girls of marriageable age.[53] If this is so, then it highlights again the low status of the daughters

50. Snell, *Life*, pp. 54-55, 123.

51. See Fontaine, 'Heifer', p. 173.

52. I am indebted to Professor Marcia White for bringing this slave and her text to my attention.

53. C. Meyers, T. Craven and R.S. Kraemer (eds.), *Women in Scripture: A Dictionary of Named and Unnamed Women in the Hebrew Bible, the Apocrypha/ Deuterocanonical Books, and the New Testament* (Boston: Houghton Mifflin, 2000), p. 307.

of the house whom we previously described as 'missing'. While the terminology for 'son' is readily and repeatedly emphasized in Proverbs (the
singular appears 45 times in 41 verses; plural occurs 8 times in 8 verses),
the daughters go unmentioned as such—except for those of the leech in
30.15. This is a fitting situation, given how daughters were viewed under
patriarchy: dangerous liabilities to be worked, traded and bred. Indeed,
what could be more telling to both the ancient daughters or modern
readers than to find themselves lumped among the unspecified drudges
who empower the household?

*Negative Roles: the Scolding Wife/Mother, Widow, the Adulteress, the
Prostitute and the Uppity Slave*

The Scolding Wife/Mother (12.4; 19.13; 21.9, 19; 25.24; 27.15-16). At the
opposite end of the continuum from the wife/mother who soothes with
words of encouragement is the scold or nag. A woman whose linguistic
skills included the ability to make negative assessments of the men in her
household was likely to be viewed unfavorably for such a 'talent'. Wrath-
ful, verbally disparaging, peevish women were considered curses upon
men that destroyed their daily peace (12.4; 19.13; 21.9, 19; 25.24; 27.15-
16). The role of language use is key here, as it is in the more familiar,
sexually adventurous negative counterparts of wife/mother discussed
below. As much as a scolding wife might be viewed negatively, it is worth
noting that this general role of the female scold has been transferred to the
behaviors attributed to Woman Wisdom in Prov. 1–9 (see below).[54]

The Widow (15.25; cf. 22.28; 23.10-11). Appearing only here in the book
of Proverbs, the widow is a slightly different type of 'negative' variant of
the wife/mother, since the negatives attaching to her come from her loss
(rather than betrayal) of her husband and the legal and economic protection he and his family provided for her and her offspring. Given the economic arrangements of patriarchal social systems, the plight of the widow
and her children might be extreme—recall Naomi and Ruth forced to
subsist on the 'left-overs' Ruth gleaned after the reapers of Boaz's field. A
woman who had been left with land or other goods meant to ensure her
survival often became a target for the unscrupulous who hoped to take
advantage of her lack of official male protection. Our proverb notes that

---

54. Athalya Brenner and Fokkelien van Dijk-Hemmes, *On Gendering Texts:
Female and Male Voices in the Hebrew Bible* (Leiden: E.J. Brill, 1993), pp. 113-30.

when the proud attempt to meddle with a widow's land, God himself serves as her protection, in lieu of the human husband, and 'makes firm' her boundary marker, while simultaneously bringing down the houses of her oppressors. (Similar statements on behalf of the orphan are made in 23.10-11.)[55]

Of course, the system whereby women are not considered full persons economically capable and legally empowered to look after their own welfare and holdings goes unquestioned by our sages, as it does by the rest of their society. Nevertheless, we may see here a persistent irritant within the social structures of patriarchy: women *do* own land, run households and rear children without male assistance. It was not considered either an easy or good thing that such women should exist in those circumstances—most widows would probably have agreed with this estimation!—and so the prophetic and legal traditions try to limit the amount of ill that can be done to such 'loners'. Legal activity on the widow's behalf is also a testimony to the fact that women and children alone must have been considered easy prey by some. In the postexilic period, fears of alienation of patrimony through land passing to 'foreign' wives and their offspring becomes a pointed subtext for all of the exhortations for Judean men to put away such inconvenient and inappropriate relatives, and most certainly added to the fund of troubles brought about by the presence of 'strange' foreign women within the community.[56] Further, many early Christian women, virgins and widows, eagerly seized upon the new religion's offer of freedom from male control by the embrace of a chaste life, thereby scandalizing the cultures whose insistence upon compulsory heterosexuality forced women into a marital straightjacket, will-they or nil-they.[57] The abiding fear of the anomalous female, whether without husband by choice or ill fate, suggests that our sources are less than candid about the actual successes of women in retaining and managing their own property.

---

55. R.E. Murphy, *Proverbs* (WBC; Dallas, TX: Word Books, 1998), pp. 114, 171, 175.

56. J. Blenkinsopp, 'The Social Context of the "Outsider Woman" in Proverbs 1–9', *Biblica* 72 (1991), pp. 457-73; T. Eskenazi, 'Out from the Shadows: Biblical Women in the Post-Exilic Era', in Athalya Brenner (ed.), *A Feminist Companion to Samuel-Kings* (FCB, 5; Sheffield: Sheffield Academic Press, 1994), pp. 252-71.

57. Stevan Davies, *The Revolt of the Widows: The Social World of the Apocryphal Acts* (Carbondale, IL: Southern Illinois University Press, 1980).

The Adulteress (Proverbs 2.16-19; 5.3-8, 20; 6.24-26, 29, 32; 7.5-27; 22.14; 23.27-28; 30.20; 31.3) Prostitute (RSV, 'harlot'; Proverbs 6.26; 7.10; 23.27; 29.3).[58] Like their counterparts, the prostitute and the foolish woman, the 'loose woman' and 'adulteress' are major preoccupations of the sages. The figurative and effective antithesis of the dependable wife and supportive mother, the loose woman embraces all that male society pronounces unacceptable in women. The phrases referring to her, *'iššâ zārâ*, 'foreign, strange woman', 'foreigner', betray an innate xenophobic distrust. Such women tend to be seen as ripe for sexual misconduct, and their actions jeopardize group standards concerning ethnicity, inheritance customs and sexual conventions.[59]

Males in Israel and Judah were urged not to compel their own daughters to engage in prostitution (as, for example, in repayment of a family's debt) and this furnishes another connection for 'Woman Stranger's' deportment. Sexual activity outside of wedlock was supplied primarily through encounters with out-group, alien and unrelated women whose irreclaimable 'honor' presented no particular problem ('shame') for the in-group men who patronized them. Biblical pejorative, especially in the prophetic corpus, castigates foreigners as participants in 'loose' sexual practices, perhaps cultic in nature. Her supposed affinities for such 'degeneracies' made the foreign 'Woman Stranger' into a likely partner for prohibited or adulterous proceedings.

The barely disguised, almost mythic depiction of the adulteress (*mᵉnā'āpet*) underscores her association with Woman Wisdom, the ideal who is the 'patron' of the sages and the true, divinely authorized female exemplar. Like Wisdom, the adulteress's mastery of language is paramount: her utterances are sweet, but they engender death rather than life (5.3-6; 7.5, 21; 22.14). A man who falls into her trap harms himself and runs foul of the statutes of the covenant (6.24-35), but the one who turns to Wisdom receives abundance and long life. The rhetorical mechanism at work reflects, first, a transfer of motifs from goddess mythology of surrounding cultures and then a consequent distribution of those

58. See the section below, 'Wisdom in the Cosmic Domain', for discussion of the mythic overtones to this negative figure.

59. For discussion, see Harold C. Washington, 'The Strange Woman (אשה זרה נכריה) of Prov. 1–9 and Post-Exilic Judaean Society', pp. 157-85, and Gale Yee, 'The Socio-Literary Production of the "Foreign Woman" in Proverbs', pp. 110-26; and pp. 127-30, both in A. Brenner (ed.), *A Feminist Companion to Wisdom Literature* (FCB, 9; Sheffield: Sheffield Academic Press, 1995).

elements into 'good' and 'evil' groupings.[60] The fertility goddesses of Israel's neighbors undeniably had significant connections with death and the underworld, but these associations have life-giving benefits for their societies. These links are split in half: Woman Wisdom represents all the positive qualities of the goddesses, whereas Woman Stranger (loose woman/adulteress) has assimilated all of the detrimental aspects of that mythology. Among her traits, the sages refer to disloyalty to one's mate, death-dealing language and conduct, sexual licentiousness (especially when allied to foreign cultic practice; cf. 7.14), explorations into the public domain rightfully monopolized by males, failure to parent and extravagant sensual cravings. While a 'contentious' wife's verbal henpecking was a kind of water torture for her spouse ('a continual dripping of rain'), the adulterous wives of one's neighbors represented language-based dangers of another sort. Such women were a source of slick enticements and forbidden gratifications. To fall prey to their blandishments was disaster (5.3; 6.29-35; 7.19-23; 12.4)—far better were constancy and awareness of the 'wife of one's youth', who provided all a man and his household could ever need (5.18; 31.10-31).

This portrayal opens a window into the circumstances of women in societies where negotiated marriages and gender asymmetry predominate. Oddly enough, compared to other sections of Scripture, Proverbs gives the adulteress her own voice—perhaps to generate male horror, or to let her condemn herself out of her own mouth. The adulteress articulates the reality of her circumstances, as she sees them, when she says, 'I have done no wrong' (30.20) or, 'Stolen water is sweet, and bread eaten in secret is pleasant' (9.17). Married into a situation not of her own choosing, with perhaps even less attention to her own fulfillment in performance of 'conjugal duties', she assertively pursues her own satisfaction. In her defiance of conventional standards, she becomes a full, desiring subject who selects her own partner and has no regrets concerning her actions. What is viewed by others as her *dis-grace* is in fact grace when viewed from within the confines of her life. She has no 'shame', for she has turned away from the inward room of her marriage to find satisfaction outwardly, beginning her search in public arenas in which no honorable woman would place herself.

---

60. Claudia Camp, 'Wise and Strange: An Interpretation of the Female Imagery in Proverbs in Light of Trickster Mythology', in Brenner (ed.), *Wisdom Literature*, pp. 131-56, highlights this rhetorical strategy, although she does not necessarily link it to goddess mythology; see her revision now also in *Holy*, pp. 72-93.

Consider the warning against her in Prov. 7.4-27 (NRSV):

> Say to wisdom, 'You are my sister', and call insight your intimate friend,
> that they may keep you from the loose woman, from the adulteress with her
> smooth words.
> For at the window of my house I looked out through my lattice, and I saw
> among the simple ones, I observed among the youths, a young man without
> sense,
> passing along the street near her corner, taking the road to her house in the
> twilight, in the evening, at the time of night and darkness.
> Then a woman comes toward him, decked out like a prostitute, wily of heart.
> She is loud and wayward; her feet do not stay at home;
> now in the street, now in the squares, and at every corner she lies in wait.
> She seizes him and kisses him, and with impudent face she says to him:
> 'I had to offer sacrifices, and today I have paid my vows;
> so now I have come out to meet you, to seek you eagerly, and I have found
> you!
> I have decked my couch with coverings, colored spreads of Egyptian linen;
> I have perfumed my bed with myrrh, aloes, and cinnamon.
> Come, let us take our fill of love until morning; let us delight ourselves with
> love.
> For my husband is not at home; he has gone on a long journey.
> He took a bag of money with him; he will not come home until full moon'.
> With much seductive speech she persuades him; with her smooth talk she
> compels him.
> Right away he follows her, and goes like an ox to the slaughter, or bounds
> like a stag toward the trap until an arrow pierces its entrails.
> He is like a bird rushing into a snare, not knowing that it will cost him his
> life.
> And now, my children, listen to me, and be attentive to the words of my
> mouth.
> Do not let your hearts turn aside to her ways; do not stray into her paths,
> for many are those she has laid low, and numerous are her victims.
> Her house is the way to Sheol, going down to the chambers of death.

We can see here that for the sage, this female figure is an embodiment
of all the wifely virtues turned upside down. Instead of re-oralizing the
approved tradition by 'opening her mouth with wisdom' (Prov. 31.26), *this*
female uses her smooth words to snare her innocent (but not very resisting!) prey, acting as a sort of tutor in folly. In so far as she uses language
so seductively, she is a kind of perverse, if unofficial, 'author'; certainly
her oral performances are full of allure! She comprehends well the ways
of her household, and uses that knowledge to aid her in her wicked pursuits. She understands her religious obligations (7.14), as well as the
delights of seduction (vv. 15-16), so she represents a formidable figure of

'anti-wife', one who brings death and not life to the men she seeks. Like the strong woman of Prov. 31, the adulteress also leaves the realm of the household, but this time to do it evil rather than good! *Her* textiles are all for entrapment and adornment; *her* surplus is a primal sexual energy that her husband, in his absence, can neither absorb nor control. No children sing her praises at the gate, though if the sages had their way, she would be dragged there like pregnant Tamar, ripe for a judgment of death. Instead, the sage must content himself with telling her ways to young men with all the salacious delight of a storyteller controlling young children through fear with stories of the boogie-man.

Given the subjectivity that the sages so relentlessly attribute to *all* women, that is, the overwhelming desire to become successful mothers, it is only fair to factor that motivation into our reading of the adulteress and loose woman, if not the prostitute. No mention is made anywhere of this type of female's children or abilities in parenting, which is a bit odd, given the text's unceasingly negative portrayal of her. *Had* she been a mother, her wayward activities would surely have reflected adversely on her children, making her boys into children of shame and her girls into potential followers in their mother's wicked ways—like mother, like daughter! claims Ezekiel after all.[61] Fox calls attention to the sages' choices in depiction of the adulteress in 7.6-27: rather than a 'languorous, sultry femme fatale...friendly neighbor...or desperate nymphomaniac', Strange Woman in this passage is a 'turbulent', 'defiant' character motivated by a 'deep disquiet'.[62] Her proposition of the young fool on his way home is studded with elements that imply that this is neither the first time nor the last that she has engaged in such activity as she searches for gratification. This in turn implies that her promiscuous behavior has not really brought her the fulfillment that is, by implication, clearly not available at home with her husband. What could propel such an unhappy woman into the streets to find a naive, hapless bedmate for her extramarital activities? Does she *really* think that the inexperienced adolescent she chooses out of many other choices can bring her pleasure, or should we look for another reading, one with the advantage of taking the sages' own view of women and their desires seriously?

In the reading proposed here, we take the position that our strange woman is no mother, but seeks to become one. In v. 10, she is only

---

61. Judg. 11.1-2, 7; Ezek. 16.44; see Chapter 3 below for discussion of Ezekiel's use of this mashal.

62. Fox, *Proverbs 1–9*, p. 253.

'*dressed* as a prostitute', not in fact actually one of that trade. Further, as the verse continues its initial description of her, it is said that she is 'guarded of heart' (*n^eṣurat leb*), that is, her thoughts and motivations are hidden. The time is the dark of the moon (vv. 9, 20)—the midpoint of her menstrual cycle, meaning that she is fertile—and her mention of sacrifices in v. 14 may imply again, less subtly, that she is not menstruating, and hence is a suitable sexual partner. Her husband is gone and will continue to be absent during the time she might possibly conceive—even if she had any lingering hope that she might be able to gain a child by him. She chooses a young—fertile—partner of little experience because he is easily manipulated in his eager, untried state; his implicit lustiness can be channeled by her for her own satisfaction. Further, if her plan is successful, the boy would never breathe a word of his forbidden encounter, nor seek to claim her child as his own. Denied the one thing—a child—that will make her a woman of value to her culture, she takes matters into her own hand to remedy this situation. She is not deterred by danger; in fact, her risks add 'zest' to the hunger for personhood via maternity previously denied satisfaction. In her audacity, she undercuts the male-dominant world-view that suggests that her husband be the center of her world, better even than seven sons if he happens to love her. Neither prayer for fertility nor an accessible husband can meet her need, so she manages the situation herself. Thus, she functions as a temptation to women who might imitate her actions, the men who supply her lack, and the husband whose own behavior has proved so inadequate. Given the world of the sages, this *is* strange, indeed!

The positive roles, mostly drawn from the world of the household, that qualify average women as practitioners of wisdom are balanced by negative ones in the dichotomous thinking of the sages, as we have just seen. While a good wife (and by implication, mother) might be seen as a gift 'from the Lord' (Prov. 18.22; 19.14), a wife who nags, brings shame, or acts foolishly is just as much of a possibility, and a dreadful one at that (Prov. 11.16, 22; 12.4; 14.1; 19.13; 21.9, 19; 25.24). The good wife and mother whose sexuality when properly contained—that is, kept under the control of men—brings life, is inverted in the negative character of the 'adulteress' or 'loose' or 'foolish woman', who appears as the composite figure of 'Woman Stranger', the evil twin of Woman Wisdom, in Proverbs 1–9.[63] While women in their proper roles (wife, mother, daughter, sister)

63. See Claudia Camp's excellent study of this multivalent symbol, 'What's So Strange about the Strange Woman?', in David Jobling, Peggy L. Day and Gerald T.

within the home might well be viewed as 'flowing water'—almost always a symbol of life in the arid Near East, but still dangerous because of its fluid movement—by the sages (Prov. 5.15-20), their negative counterparts are seen as similarly threatening. Those who follow Woman Stranger's ways 'go down to death' (Prov. 2.18-19; 5.5-6; 22.14), never to be seen again. Like the efficacious wisdom on the tongue of the good woman, crafty language use is a hallmark of this negative incarnation of the wise wife: the words of the adulteress or loose woman are 'smooth', dripping honey (Prov. 2.16; 5.3; 7.5). For men who believe that 'Death and life are in the power of the tongue, and those who love it will eat its fruits' (Prov. 18.21, RSV), Woman Stranger's command of language, her perverse re-oralization of tradition with herself cast in the role of desiring subject (i.e. the male role) signifies the power of the tongue. To the sages this is damning indeed, and a clear indication that she embodies the reversal of true, life-giving wisdom.

Looking at the imagery used by the male sages to describe the figures of wife/mother and loose woman/seductress, we may observe a basic similarity in the sage's depiction of each. The good woman is a 'well', 'cistern', 'flowing water', and a 'fountain' whose love 'intoxicates' her husband (Prov. 5.15-20, NRSV). Wells and cisterns were dug out through intensive male labor; fountains and springs represent water that comes to surface usefulness without such human interventions, but even there the water must then be channeled or managed by the communities who make use of it. In contrast, the adulteress/seductress is consistently associated with Sheol, the marshy Pit of the underworld inhabited by the dead. The difference is one of degree for the sages: female reality is associated with murky, underground places of hidden power. Men who dig down only a little bit—as difficult as the digging may be—may find a well that gives flowing water, and hence life, even though that life comes with the risks associated with loss of control (i.e. 'intoxication'). Even such life-giving waters must be rigorously controlled by men. Those unfortunate males who penetrate too deeply into the secret places of female sexuality dig themselves into a cosmic pit from which there is no emergence. In both cases, the images evoke the powerful male fear of being swallowed up and washed away by watery caverns of female potency. Only intensive labor or complete avoidance will serve men when they venture into female domains.

Sheppard (eds.), *The Bible and the Politics of Exegesis* (Cleveland, OH: Pilgrim Press, 1991), pp. 17-31, now revised in her *Holy*, pp. 40-71.

Though a prostitute's services may be acquired for little expense ('a loaf of bread'), the hidden cost can actually deprive an unsuspecting man of his life and his livelihood (6.26; 7.22-23, 27; 23.27; 29.3). Like the goddesses Inanna, Ishtar and Anat, who bear their lovers down to the underworld, the harlot is described as a 'deep pit' (23.27), whose house is 'the way to Sheol [= the underworld from which none but deities return]' (7.10-27). Her clothing is distinguishing (with or without a veil, depending on the time period; compare Gen. 38.14 with Song 5.7) in order to signal her availability, a feature preserved in other ancient Near Eastern societies (where a veil is usually the symbol of married or noble status). Her deportment is another indication of her deviance, for she is brash and domineering, openly haunting public places where she scavenges for quarry (7.11-12). Since there is no secure evidence for cultic prostitution in the Hebrew Bible, the prostitutes featured in Proverbs are probably 'secular' ones, whose action is generated by practical necessity (Lev. 19.29) or unruly disposition. Prostitutes often surface as dangerous characters in the wisdom instructions and proverbs of surrounding nations: such women are thought to be intrinsically 'disloyal' because of their many associations with men and their supposed economic autonomy, and as such make unsatisfactory wives (7.19-20; Lev. 21.7-9, 14). The Counsels of Wisdom, an Akkadian text from about 1500–1000 BCE is explicit in its advice:

> Don't marry a prostitute, whose husbands are legion,
> Nor a temple harlot, who is dedicated to a goddess,
> Nor a courtesan, whose intimates are numerous.
> She will not sustain you in your time of trouble,
> She will snigger at you when you are embroiled in controversy.
> She has neither respect nor obedience in her nature.
> Even if she has the run of your house, get rid of her,
> She has her ears attuned for another's footfall (lines 72-80).[64]

The Uppity Slave Woman (30.23). The serving maid (*šipḥâ*) who has found an elevated place in the household in 30.23 is used as the second half of an antithetical word-pair, juxtaposed with 'mistress' (גברה; *geḇîrâ*). Locked in perpetual struggle for the favored attention of the powerful male, when the mistress and maid exchange places, it is an emblematic sign that 'all hell has broken loose'. According to the orderly world-view

---

64. Foster, *Before the Muses I*, pp. 329-30. A variant of line 80 reads, 'As to the household she enters, she will break [it] up./The man who married her will not have a stable home life' (p. 330).

of ancient wisdom, which, in modern liberationist view, finds itself entirely too comfortable with the status quo, such reversals are hardly viewed as positive. Men might also find themselves the topic in such topsy-turvy tinkerings with social order; we hear this in Egyptian laments and admonitions from the Middle Kingdom:

> Now see for yourself:
> The arbitrator is a robber,
> The peacemaker makes grief,
> He who should soothe makes sore (*The Eloquent Peasant*).[65]

> See, he who had nothing is a man of wealth,
> The nobleman sings his praise.
> See, the poor of the land have become rich,
> The man of property is a pauper.
> See, cooks have become masters of butlers,
> He who was a messenger sends someone else.
> See, he who had no loaf owns a barn,
> His storeroom is filled with another's goods.
> See the baldhead who lacked oil
> Has become the owner of jars of sweet myrrh... (*The Admonitions of Ipuwer*).[66]

If one wanted to speak of troubling shifts in the public order, then high and low status male characters were juxtaposed in their encounters in the public domain. To discuss these concerns in the private world of the family, then women, children and slaves are featured in the comparisons.

When ancient wisdom authors truly sought to convey the scandal of the lowliest of the low stealing the prerogatives of the highest of the high, only the citation of the long-standing jealousies of the slave woman and her glee at the comeuppance of her mistress would do. Turning again to the Middle Kingdom composition *The Admonitions of Ipuwer*, we find the 'uppity' behavior of slave women cited:

> Lo, gold, lapis lazuli, silver and turquoise,
> Carnelian, amethyst, *ibht*-stone and...
> Are strung on the necks of female slaves.
> Noblewomen roam the land,
> Ladies say, 'We want to eat!'...

---

65. Miriam Lichtheim, *Ancient Egyptian Literature: A Book of Readings*. I. *The Old and Middle Kingdoms* (Berkeley: University of California Press, 1975), p. 179. Similar 'problems' of status reversal also form a trope in Mesopotamian wisdom literature and laments (William Lambert, *Babylonian Wisdom Literature* [Oxford: Clarendon Press, 1960]).

66. Lichtheim, *Literature*, I, p. 157.

> There is no remedy for it,
> Ladies suffer like maidservants,
> Singers are at the looms in the weaving-rooms,
> What they sing to the goddess are dirges,
> Those who told...are at the grindstones.
> Lo, all maidservants are rude in their speech,
> When the mistress speaks, it irks the servants...[67]

The 'uppity' behavior of female slaves consists in their ready appropriation of the ornaments of womanhood normally denied to them, the acquisition of status through the snaring of a husband (especially their mistresses'!), their fertility (in comparison to their higher-status mistresses'), and their use of indecorous speech toward their mistresses. This is a standard motif in narrative texts, which will be explored later in terms of wisdom 'performance' (cf. Egyptian Westcar Papyrus 'Three Tales of Wonder'), and could also serve as a reason for mild or severe punishment (cf. Code of Hammurabi §§146-47; Gen. 16.3-5).[68]

It is not only the Egyptian wisdom corpus that warns against the uppity slave woman and the trouble she can bring to a man's house and a mistress's peace of mind. *The Counsels of Wisdom* from Mesopotamia sing the same song:

> You must not make a slave girl important in your house,
> She must not rule your bedroom like a wife
> ...
> Let your people have this to tell you:
> 'The household that a slave girl rules, she will break up' (lines 66-71).[69]

What interests us here as we survey the world of wisdom's women is the clear attribution of a consciousness on the part of slave women that their status is inferior, and their willingness to take action to reverse that situation. Resourceful and able to seize the moment when the scales of status are tipping, these women are obviously possessed of innate intelligence and the drive to improve their lot—sure signs of a pragmatic wisdom, even if one which operates at the end of the social continuum of status! That their *speech* is what so often gives offence is another mark of their wisdom, however negatively perceived in their own cultures: speech

---

67. Lichtheim, *Literature*, I, pp. 152-53.

68. G.R. Driver and John C. Miles, *The Babylonian Laws* (2 vols.; Oxford: Clarendon Press, 1955).

69. Foster, *Before the Muses*, I, p. 329.

functions as a marker for internal thought, planning and self-knowledge. No wonder the Old Kingdom Egyptian sage Ptahhotep warns his young successor about ignoring such facts:

> Don't be proud of your knowledge,
> Consult the ignorant and the wise;
> The limits of art are not reached,
> No artist's skills are perfect;
> Good speech is more hidden than greenstone,
> Yet may be found among maids at the grindstones (*The Instruction of Ptahhotep*).[70]

Women Sages in the Public Domain

Positive Roles: Women as Authors and 'Official' Sages

As noted previously, cuneiform specialist Rivkah Harris considers it is highly unlikely that many Mesopotamian or Egyptian women ever received full scribal educations (or would have wanted to, had it been possible).[71] Since knowledge is power, and training is the key to success, this acted as an effective limit on 'professional' roles females could fill in their societies. Since women were not allowed or expected to fill most public roles, educating them for such positions would have seemed bizarre within this ancient context of stratified societies, with hereditary roles passed down from fathers to sons.

Why were women excluded from the 'professions', we might ask? It may well have been initially a value-free response to the demands a woman experiences when tending a child (and mothers in traditional societies normally nursed their children for two or three years). Those who think about the nature of 'women's work' have outlined *not* what *might* be desirable for the care giver, but what is *possible* for a woman caring for a baby or toddler. The work that women can do well under such circumstances has to conform to the 'baby first' mentality needed for successful nurturing; that is, the mother's or care giver's work cannot put the child at risk.[72] Further, it should not be too demanding in the amount of concentration required, since the care giver will experience frequent interruptions. It

---

70. Lichtheim, *Literature*, I, p. 63.

71. Harris, 'Female Sage', pp. 3-10, where she comments that 'female' and 'sage' were contradictions in terms in the ancient Near Eastern world.

72. War-making, plowing with large animals, horse-breaking, metal-working and even ceramics present potential threats to a curious child's well-being.

must be work that is easily resumed and easily stopped, the kind of work where a woman could 'mind her place'. If such work takes place within the territory routinely inhabited by the child (e.g. at home or in a home-based workshop where children are not endangered) and produces something that mother and child actually need (such a food or clothing), so much the better. Women who found themselves engaged in the cycle of pregnancy, nursing and care giving could not spare the time and dedicated energies needed to pursue a 'career'—but this should not be construed to mean that they had forgotten how to think or use language effectively! Outside of women's work in the home and garden, it is likely that women were a sporadic and unreliable part of the more general workforce, ones who probably only performed menial jobs on a part-time basis (child-rearing cycles permitting), and so seldom attained the level of skill needed for 'professional' success.[73] An exception to this generalization would be the occasional training available to daughters of royal houses or members of professional families. Christian and Jewish traditions of women scribes in Middle Ages show that such women might indeed make a contribution to such a specialized craft requiring intensive training, but they are always ideally placed for such ventures: daughters of scribal houses, princesses or women religious, all women for whom a household staff might be imagined as taking up the care of the children or home/convent while the woman in question practiced her skill.[74]

As always, upper-class and lower-class women might experience more freedom of choice and movement.[75] Women as a group tend to do better in

73. Judith Brown, 'Note on the Division of Labor by Sex', cited in E.W. Barber (ed.), *Women's Work: First 20,000 Years* (New York: Norton, 1994), pp. 29-30.

74. Binyamin Richler, *Hebrew Manuscripts: A Treasured Legacy* (Cleveland: Ofeq Institute, 1990), pp. 41-42; Jonathan G. Alexander, *Medieval Illuminators and their Methods of Work* (New Haven: Yale University Press, 1992), pp. 18-23; Alice Taylor, 'Armenian Illumination under Georgian, Turkish, and Mongol Rule in the Thirteenth, Fourteenth, and Fifteenth Centuries', in T.F. Matthews and Roger S. Wieck (eds.), *Treasures in Heaven: Armenian Illuminated Manuscripts* (New York: Pierpont Morgan Library, 1994), pp. 88-89.

75. Upper-class women have more social possibilities open to them because they are related to males of high status who may make exceptions for them, die and leave them in power, or bequeath significant economic resources into their control. Women of low status usually have more freedom of movement than middle-class women, precisely because their low status frees them from the social codes governing 'respect-ability'. Gender restrictions are often far more loosely applied to poor women (so with Tal Ilan on the postbiblical period in her *Jewish Women in Greco-Roman Palestine* (Peabody, MA: Hendrickson, 1995), p. 228.

societies that are more egalitarian, less ranked and stratified so that distinctions between the public 'assigned' power of men and the private,
informal power of women blur. Because of this, ancient Israel with its two
'pioneer' periods of the Settlement and postexilic times actually offered
more scope for women's inclusion in the world of wisdom. That is, we are
able to look for 'women sages'—composers and users of wisdom genres
—in the same kinds of situations, often informal, where one might look
for traditional 'folk' sages of the villages.

With respect to authorship of wisdom texts, scholars have not yet
decided whether dictating one's text rather than writing it down oneself
(for which a full-blown scribal education would have been a prerequisite)
compromises the quality of the authorship—in modern minds, if not in the
minds of the ancients.[76] There is a variety of folk genres usually composed
by women—lullabies, working songs, love songs, etc.—and so we must be
prepared to see some argument for women as both oral composers and
literary authors even where their work may not have survived. Most of us
working on these topics have found, in the absence of data on the invisible
members of society—women, children, slaves—that we must work by, as
Harris puts it, 'controlled inference'.[77] We also must evaluate better the
meaning of slavery and low status and how this intersects with our understanding of wisdom tradents, whom we implicitly perceive as having high
status roles. If women trained as scribes to serve royal princesses or priestesses—at Mari or in the cloisters of Sippar—were slaves, albeit ones of
high status, how shall we number them among the wise? Are they only
'semi-sage', because they are slaves, or are they perhaps 'super-sage',
because they practice their craft without the full authorizing qualities of
entitlement that come when a free man engages in his profession? How
does the fact that such women scribes, according to Harris, usually served
only other women affect our ascription of status to them?[78] At any rate, as
we will see below in the next chapter, the low status of a slave woman did
not stop her from using proverbial wisdom to gain her ends.

Mesopotamia and Egypt: Remains and Reminders

These questions aside, it is still true that some few women did find their
way into the scribal elite and may even be reckoned as successful practi-

---

76. Again, Niditch's work is most helpful in mapping out the different kinds of
relations between oral composition, performance, dictation and literary composition in
the production of biblical texts (*Oral World*, pp 109-29).

77. Harris, 'Female Sage', p. 3.

78. Harris, 'Female Sage', p. 7.

tioners of that high literary art. Enheduanna of Ur, high priestess of the
Nanna, the moon god, and devotee of Inanna, goddess of love and war,
composed a series of hymns to temples, and a great poem of praise to her
goddess.[79] Her work became a definitive part of the scribal corpus and
represents the first non-anonymous poetry in historical record. One female
scribe of Mesopotamia, Ninshapatada of Old Babylonian Uruk, produced a
composition that was so excellent an example of the scribal tradition that
her work found its way into the official 'canon' at Larsa and was used to
train subsequent scribes in literary technique. In contemporaneous times,
too, the historical information that she so carefully incorporated into her
flattering appeal to King Rim-Sin to spare her conquered city of Durum is
considered invaluable for the reconstruction of historical dates and scribal
conventions.[80] Her crafty rhetoric, used on behalf of her folk group to
achieve the very desirable end of continued existence, shows that she was
well educated by scribal school and female experience. At least two
Assyrian proverbs are considered to be of possible female authorship,
based on their content:

> My mouth can make me the rival of men.
> My mouth has made me renowned among men.[81]

Do we have here perhaps a female scribe's reflection on the success her
training has brought her? It is tempting to think so, but the reader should
be aware that either sex may take on the 'voice' and subjectivity of the
other during the mysterious event of composition.

Other Mesopotamian women may also have composed extant texts and
some served as scribes.[82] In particular, judging from the Maqlû incantations, sorceresses were thought to be powerful users of word and action to
harm unsuspecting victims, and this may perhaps be related to traditional
compositions passed from one generation of women to another. In the
cosmic domain as well, goddesses were portrayed as having knowledge of
writing and the production of texts, as we shall see below.

---

79. Fontaine, ' Heifer', pp. 77-80.

80. Harris, 'Female Sage', p. 8, and W.W. Hallo, 'Sumerian Historiography', in H.
Tadmor and M. Weinfeld (eds.), *History, Historiography, and Interpretation: Studies
in Biblical and Cuneiform Literatures* (Jerusalem: Magnes Press, 1983), pp. 9-20 (17-
18).

81. Foster, *Muses, I*, p. 340.

82. Harris, 'Female Sage', pp 9-10, 14-17, and W.W. Hallo, 'The Women of
Sumer', in D. Schmandt-Besserat (ed.), *The Legacy of Sumer* (Bibliotheca Mesopotamia, 4; Los Angeles: Undena Publications, 1976), pp. 23-34 (30-33).

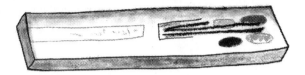

Figure 4. Girl's Scribal Palette. (New Kingdom Egypt, Amarna Period. Ivory 6 ins. × 1 in., with inscription, 'For Princess Meritaton' [Metropolitan Museum of Art, New York City, NY].)

In the Metropolitan Museum of Art in New York City, a tiny toy 'scribal palette', fully functional and supplied with inks, water pot and pen, is inscribed with the name of a royal princess from the New Kingdom period, who, at least for a time, must have shown some interest in 'playing scribe' (Figure 4). *Her* scribal palette is made of ivory, not wood, with ivory-handled brushes. She is only given a toy, however: the more rare or difficult to make pigments are not supplied to her (blue-green, yellow, red, blue). But it is clear someone loved her and honored her desire for this symbol of male power, since the incription reads 'For Princess Meritaton', making her one of the charming little princesses born to Akhenaton and Nefertiti, and so often pictured in tableau of the royal family. As always, a princess might be humored in her wishes due to her special access to power, whereas a 'regular' female would not.

However, the normal status pattern of women being excluded from education for positions they could not hold prevailed, with daughters of the elite having more options than their lower-class sisters, although again, no texts by women or for women can be directly identified. From the Middle Kingdom (but not the Old or New Kingdom), we find passing mention of the *seshet*, the feminine form of the masculine word for 'scribe', *sesh*. However, scholars suggest that this is to be understood as 'painter of her mouth' (i.e. 'cosmetician'), since the term is usually embedded in a list of other titles relating to the low-status 'beauty industry'. Even so, one woman *seshet*, Idwy from the Middle Kingdom, had her own scarab, a mark of high status, suggesting that she may really have been a scribe. In New Kingdom family portraits, women sometimes have scribal kits located beneath their chairs in these scenes, but these may actually belong to her menfolk and have been placed with the women for the sake of artistic balance.[83] At any

83. Gay Robbins, *Women in Ancient Egypt* (Cambridge, MA: Harvard University Press, 1993), p. 111.

rate, the handful of mentions of the *seshet* throughout the long history of the Egyptian civilization reminds us that, while not all women were excluded from literacy and its professions, in fact very few indeed are documented. Specialized knowledge remained a closed guarded item of male status.

Authorial Evidence from Canaan

Moving out of the civilizations where cuneiform and hieroglyphic syllabaries contained thousands of entries that a scribe must memorize in order to do his job and into the southern Levant,[84] changes in the 'technology' of literacy may have worked to the benefit of all non-elite members of society. In this region, although scribes of the Bronze and Iron Age Transitions might make use of cuneiform for their diplomatic correspondence with the large river valley civilizations, their own literature and texts in indigenous languages were eventually written down by means of an alphabet that consisted of a very limited number of signs, rather than the encyclopedic syllabaries of the pictorial languages. This switch from the picture/syllable mode of recording language to the phonetic meant that literacy was well within the intellectual grasp of anyone with time and opportunity to learn. In a strange little episode in Judg. 8.14, we find the hero Gideon coming upon a young lad during his skirmishes against invaders who is able to 'write' for him the names of the elders of Succoth, who had earlier refused aid to Gideon and his men, apparently helping Gideon devise a 'hit list' for the ingrates of the town.[85] Whether Gideon writes down the names, or the young man, clearly the story would have us believe that names were written down by someone who was not a professional scribe. If shepherds or lesser sons of lesser tribes can be viewed as literate during this period without straining the audience's credulity, then we must make room for the possibility that women, especially ones keeping household records of stores, may have been familiar with writing as well, at least by the time of this episode's composition. Epigraphic evidence consisting of short texts—abecedaries, inscriptions, graffiti, bless-

---

84. The area abutting the Mediterranean comprising modern Syria, Lebanon, Israel and Palestine.

85. We encounter a customary problem in the Hebrew of this verse, since the male pronominal suffixes do not let us know for certain which male is doing the writing for whom. One presumes that Gideon did not know the names of the elders and so the lad supplied them. Whether he or Gideon is the subject of the verb 'to write' here is not clear, but regardless of identity, this story suggests that literacy was not unknown in tribal Israel, which is at least possible, if not 'provable'.

ings, curses, oracles, letters and sealings—from sites like Gezer, 'Izbet Ṣarṭah, Kuntillet 'Ajrud, Ketef Hinnom, En Gedi, Khirbet Beit Lei, Ḥorvat 'Uza, Samaria, Dan, Arad, and Tel 'Ira confirms that the populations of the Iron Age increasingly made use of the written word for a variety of purposes.[86]

Within the Hebrew Bible, we must not rule out the possibility that women sages may have contributed to the stock of folk proverbs that found their way into the book of Proverbs and nestled among the artistically crafted two-lined proverbs created (most probably) by the court sages. Since mothers were teachers to their household, and traditional society relies heavily on proverbs to pass along inherited knowledge, we may certainly assume that women used proverbs, whether they composed and/or wrote them or not (see Chapter 3 below). It is hard to believe that the Female Scold, so noxious to her kinsmen, did not take some proverbial insights as part of the text for her sermons against the idiocies of her menfolk.

Figure 5. The Fool (Fifteenth-century Italy/Germany [Ms. Parm 2998]. After Metzger and Metzger, *Jewish Life*, p. 209, illus. 304).

An 'F' Voice? On a Fool and his Folly
It may be necessary then to re-evaluate our view of the 'voice' of authority that speaks in the book of Proverbs. Why must it be viewed monolithically

86. Niditch, *Oral World*, pp. 45-59.

as an 'M' (male) voice in the text, and not potentially as an 'F' (female) one? Do not mothers, as well as fathers, warn their sons to be on their guard against unacceptable females?[87] It is not possible at present, however, to point to any one proverb and say with certainty that it was authored by a woman, since the content of a proverb is not an invariable guide to its origin. Proverbs about the family, or herbcraft, for example, need not be composed by women, although they reflect the (supposed) interests and specialities of women. Certainly, one may well question whether women wrote the standard sage's lament against the unpleasant 'nagging wife' as the sole scapegoat for domestic discord (cf. Prov. 21.9, 19; 25.24; 27.15), though it is not unheard of in folk literature to find gender-critical proverbs in use by older women to guide the behavior of adolescents, male and female.[88] It may be that women's critique of male behavior should be sought in the book of Proverbs' litany of faults to be found in 'the fool', as Claus Westermann has suggested.[89]

Consider the teachings of Proverbs on this group of men:

12.23: One who is clever conceals knowledge, but the mind of a fool broadcasts folly.

14.7:   Leave the presence of a fool, for there you do not find words of knowledge.

15.5:   A fool despises a parent's instruction, but the one who heeds admonition is prudent.

17.12: Better to meet a she-bear robbed of its cubs than to confront a fool immersed in folly.

17.21: The one who begets a fool gets trouble; the parent of a fool has no joy.

17.25: Foolish children are a grief to their father and bitterness to her who bore them.

18.6:   A fool's lips bring strife, and a fool's mouth invites a flogging.

---

87. See, for example, Rebekah's disgust at the possibility of yet another Hittite daughter-in-law in Gen. 27.43, as well as her clever use of this gambit as a way to remove Jacob from danger at Esau's hand. On identifying the 'F' voice in the text, see Brenner and van Dijk-Hemmes, *Gendering Texts*.

88. One African-American pastor tells me that she was raised with the adage, 'Keep your dress down, and your drawers up.' One might add other common proverbs on sexual behavior: 'Why should a man keep a cow, if he can get milk for free?'; 'It's as easy to fall in love with a rich man as a poor one'; 'Soon ripe, soon rotten'; and of course, 'Marry in haste, repent at leisure.'

89. Personal communication to author. See also proverbs on the 'lazy man' for another potential area of female critique of male behavior (Prov. 10.26; 12.24, 27; 13.4; 15.19; 19.24; 20.4; 21.25; 22.13; 24.30; 26.13-16).

18.7:   The mouths of fools are their ruin, and their lips a snare to
         themselves.
23.9:   Do not speak in the hearing of a fool, who will only despise the
         wisdom of your words.
26.6:   It is like cutting off one's foot and drinking down violence, to send
         a message by a fool.
26.11:   Like a dog that returns to its vomit is a fool who reverts to his folly.
29.11:   A fool gives full vent to anger, but the wise quietly holds it back.
         (NRSV)

Heard in a different voice—a female one—these proverbs seem striking in their evocation of the ruin that a fool causes to his family, whether as head of the household or unruly son. The emphasis on parenting is also noticeable here—along with the proverbial mothering of Mama Bear—which may suggest a mother's typical interest in the well-being of her offspring as well as a father's. A final trope in these proverbs worthy of note is the fool's relationship to language: it affords him neither protection or precision in his interactions with others; it is rather an index of his hot-headedness and quarrelsome nature. An Assyrian proverb, possibly authored by a woman, makes the point well: 'The wife of the tongue-tied talker is a slave girl.'[90]

Whereas women's 'foolishness' in Proverbs is spoken of primarily in terms of their sexuality or unwillingness to conform to the patriarchal standards set for their behavior as female, the male fool is another matter entirely. He cannot be trusted in any arena of life: unable to learn from his mistakes, he continually blames others, and his speech brings only discord (unlike the torah-of-hesed of the mother of the house). There is no task with which he can safely be entrusted, no words that can dissuade him from his folly, and no hope of peace in his company. If we note the emphases in these proverbs on the one who remains concealed quietly in the background, speaking softly and wisely at the proper time, we are in fact painting a picture of the Lady of the House, who must publicly defer to her menfolk, but who in private is the lynchpin of her household's successful functioning. Claudia Camp's discussion of the story of Abigail and Nabal in 1 Sam. 25 shows the wife-sage taking matters into her own hands to avert disaster with all the dispatch and power of Woman Wisdom. Her husband Nabal, literally named 'Fool', has insulted David and his men, who had protected Nabal's household during their pasturing of flocks. Fortunately, Abigail is told of the insult and speeds out—without

90. Foster, *Before the Muses*, I, p. 340.

benefit of Nabal's permission or knowledge—with gifts and smooth words to soothe David's aggrieved ego. Falling down before him, she says:

> Upon me alone, my lord, be the guilt; please let your servant speak in your ears, and hear the words of your servant. My lord, do not take seriously this ill-natured fellow, Nabal; for as his name is, so is he; Nabal is his name, and folly is with him; but I, your servant, did not see the young men of my lord, whom you sent... (vv. 24-25).

David is pacified, and accepts Abigail's generous provisions and flattering words, commenting:

> Blessed be the LORD, the God of Israel, who sent you to meet me today! Blessed be your good sense,[91] blessed be you, who have kept me today from bloodguilt and from avenging myself by my own hand! For as surely as the LORD the God of Israel lives, who has restrained me from hurting you, unless you had hurried and come to meet me, truly by morning there would not have been left to Nabal so much as one male (vv. 32-34, NRSV).

Upon learning of the disaster so nearly befalling him, Nabal dies of fright. Abigail whose behavior has truly proved her 'fit for a king' becomes one of David's wives as this look at the inner workings of the affluent household concludes. Clearly, here we have a woman who knows what it is like to carry a fool on her back, and has becomes adept at the art of the graceful 'save'. She may not have authored any proverbs on fools, but she has certainly had experience of their content and proved herself as an embodiment of female wisdom. We may think of Prov. 14.1 as a summation of Abigail's story (though there the hands of the fool are female): 'Wisdom builds her house, but Folly with her own hands tears it down.'

A Composition of her Own? Good Queen/Bad Queen 'Authors'. There is, however, one instance within Israel's wisdom tradition where we might reasonably posit female authorship, or at least composition if not the actually writing down of the text. This is the rather remarkable example of an 'Instruction' attributed to the queen mother of King Lemuel in Prov. 31.1-9. The instruction form is a unified composition known from Egypt, and it may consist of proverbs, admonitions and prohibitions, as well as pertinent examples. A king or aging bureaucrat undertook to place his life-

---

91. טַעְמֵךְ; lit., 'your taste', 'discernment'; compare to the praise of the strong wife in 31.18, טָעֲמָה כִּי־טוֹב סַחְרָהּ; 'she tastes that her merchandise is good'. As usual in Hebrew thinking, perception is clearly a body-based activity, and female bodies are no less able than males' to engage in effective discernment.

wisdom into a persuasive literary piece that he then passed on to his successors, one presumes through the method of dictating his reflections to a scribe. That this form found its way to Israel is apparent in the number of fatherly instructions by the sages that add structure to Prov. 1–9 and 22–24 (1.1-19; 2.1-22; 3.1-12, 21-35; 4.1-9, 10-19, 20-27; 5.1-23; 6.20-35; 7.1-27; 22.17-24). There the instructions cited deal primarily with the topics necessary for a young man to make his way in the world of court intrigue and professional circles. Table manners, 'professionalism' and warnings against the wiles of women are among typical themes found in the form.

Let us listen to the words of the royal mother:

> The words of King Lemuel. An oracle that his mother taught him:
> No, my son! No, son of my womb! No, son of my vows!
> Do not give your strength to women, your ways to those who destroy kings.
> It is not for kings, O Lemuel, it is not for kings to drink wine, or for rulers to desire strong drink;
> or else they will drink and forget what has been decreed, and will pervert the rights of all the afflicted.
> Give strong drink to one who is perishing, and wine to those in bitter distress;
> let them drink and forget their poverty, and remember their misery no more.
> Speak out for those who cannot speak, for the rights of all the destitute.
> Speak out, judge righteously, defend the rights of the poor and needy (NRSV).

The queen mother who speaks in Proverbs 31 gives ample evidence of 'the Mother's Torah' ('teaching') spoken of elsewhere in Proverbs (1.8b; 6.20) when she addressed her princely son. Like the male sages, she makes use of direct address, using familial terms ('No, my son! No, son of my womb! No, son of my vows!', 31.2) and feels free to make direct admonitions and prohibitions, making vigorous use of imperatives (vv. 3, 6, 8, 9), showing that she has authority to speak and expects her words to be heard and obeyed. Again, like the male authors of instructions, she takes up usual themes seen in the genre: warnings against drunkenness and women (vv. 3-5), and advice about performing the traditional protective tasks assigned to rulers (vv. 8-9). Her instruction is particularly interesting for its ability to differentiate between appropriate and inappropriate contexts for a single act: the powerful ought not to drink because it will impair their execution of their duties; the powerless, however, might well profit from a drink in which to drown their woes (vv. 4-7). Proverbs 26.4-5 shows a similar attention to the variable nature of experience in its counsel for handling fools, but the queen mother of Proverbs 31 introduces a compassionate and thoughtful note not apparent in the other citation. The counseling queen mothers of the Hebrew Bible are not always viewed so positively as the mother in Proverbs 31 (cf. 1 Kgs 15.9-14; 2 Chron. 22.2-4), so it is clear that they must have exerted enough power over their sons to make them a target for negative comment by authors and editors. Unfortunately, we do not know the content of their counsel, nor the forms it may have used, but that they did counsel and were considered effective in that role must be granted.[92]

Looking outside of Israel, Lemuel's mother is not the only queen known to us who uses the language of wisdom to achieve her goals: Queen Puduḫepa of the Late Bronze Age Hittite empire (see below) also used proverbs to achieve her goals in dealing with the gods.[93] Tiye, the widow of Pharoah Amenophis III and mother of Amenophis IV (Akhenaton), is frequently addressed in the Amarna Letters of the Late Bronze Age as 'a woman/one who knows'. Her knowledge of the political intricacies of treaties and treasure is invoked repeatedly by the Mitannian king Tušratta, who feels that he has been slighted by her son in the matter of 'embassies of joy'. Solid gold statues promised to the Asian monarch by her husband were sent by her son, but upon examination they were found to be fashioned of gold-plated wood! He is thoroughly nonplussed by this breach of brotherly love, since 'gold is as dirt' in Pharaoh's land. This clearly constituted a shaming treaty violation in the northern king's eyes, so he makes his petition to one who 'knows the score'! A frenzied appeal to the queen mother ensues:

> You are the one that knows that I [myself] always showed love [to] Mimmureya, your husband, and that Mimmureya, [your] husband], on the other hand, always showed love to me. A[nd *the things*] that I wou[ld write and] say [t]o Mimmureya, your husband, and that Mimmureya, your husband, [on the ot]ther hand, [would always write and say to me, you, [Keli]ya, and Mane know. But you are the on[e, *on the other hand*, who knows much better than all others the things [that] we said [to one another. No one [el]se knows them (as well)... Wh[y] have you [no]t exposed before Napḫ[urreya] the words t[hat you your]self, and with your own mouth, said to [me]? If [you] do not expose them before him, and *y[ou keep silent*,] *can*

92. Schroer, 'Wise', pp. 74-77.

93. Carole Fontaine, 'Queenly Proverb Performance: The Prayer of Puduḫepa (KUB XXI, 27)', in K.G. Hoglund *et al.* (eds.), *The Listening Heart: Essays in Wisdom and the Psalms in honor of Roland E. Murphy, O. Carm.* (JSOTSup, 58; Sheffield: JSOT Press, 1987), pp. 95-126.

anyone [el]se know? Let [Nap]ḫurreya give me statues of sol[id] gold! He
must cause me no [dis]tress whatsoever, nor [...]. Let him treat m[e] 10
times better [th]an his father did, [wi]th love and evidence of es[teem]...
(EA 26:7-18, 49-57).[94]

In a subsequent letter directed to Akhenaton, still in hot pursuit of those
solid gold statues, Tušratta instructs the Pharaoh to consult Tiye: 'It is
Teye, your mother, whom you must ask about all of them: [*what*] your
father [*would write over and over*], the words that he would speak with me
over and over.'[95] It is clear that Tušratta is counting upon the presence and
diplomatic memory of Queen Tiye to help him resolve his difficulties with
the current Pharaoh; he may even be drawing conclusions about her role
based on his own knowledge of the power of queens in his own land. Her
wisdom (she *knows* the facts of the matter) comes from her *presence* in the
world of royal power; her influence rests upon her ability to bear witness
to what she has heard and to sway her son. While this may not necessarily
make her a specialized 'wise woman' counselor, as some translators would
have it based on Tušratta's terminology,[96] she is clearly an important player
in the give-and-take of royal politics.

The Hebrew Bible is not always so positively disposed to view the
counseling, linguistic activity of its queens, however, especially when they
show themselves crafty enough to manipulate the legal traditions to their
own ends. Just as we have the positive queen mother of Proverbs, she is
balanced by the negative portrait of another queen mother, Jezebel of
Israel (1 Kgs 16.31–22.20; 2 Kgs 9.30-37). Jezebel's pursuit of her own
religious 'reforms' are the source of scandal to the writers of Kings, but it
is in the episode of Naboth's vineyard that we see the Israelite conser-
vatives' fears of educated foreign women fully realized. In 1 Kgs 21.5-16,
we see Jezebel taking matters into her own hands to overturn Israelite
customs of land tenure while her husband sulks. She achieves her aims by
writing letters in Ahab's name, appropriating his seal to authorize her
orders, and furthermore, her entire plot hinges on a sophisticated understanding of community laws and customs, which she subtly manipulates
for nefarious ends. While commentators dispute whether Jezebel actually
conceived of the plan on her own, or wrote the letters herself, it cannot be

---

94. *The Amarna Letters* (ed. and trans. William L. Moran; Baltimore: The Johns
Hopkins University Press, 1992), pp. 84-85. See also EA 27 and 29.

95. Moran, *Amarna*, p. 92.

96. D. Arnold, *The Royal Women of Amarna: Images of Beauty from Ancient Egypt*
(New York: Metropolitan Museum of Art; Harry N. Abrams, 1996), pp. 30, 119.

denied that the authors of this text could fully envision her acting with a kind of perverse wisdom and authority. Jezebel, of course, is only one of many foreign queens who are roundly castigated by the historical writers of the Hebrew Bible for their excessive influence as authoritative counselors or goads to their innocent, unsuspecting husbands (cf. 1 Kgs 11.1-8; 2 Kgs 11).

The good queen/bad queen dichotomy is held together in a single character, Bathsheba, by the later treatment meted out to her in Jewish and Christian traditions, since her role in 1 Kings 1–2 differs markedly from her treatment in 2 Samuel. In the genealogy of Jesus in Mt. 1.6, we see Bathsheba, Solomon's mother, mentioned only as 'the wife of Uriah', a gesture toward the decadent history of David's royal house. She is in fitting company in this passage, however, for the only other three women besides Bathsheba and Mary mentioned as progenitors of Jesus (Tamar, Rahab and Ruth) are also notable for the way their atypical sexual histories and outsider status contribute to the unfolding of divine purpose— even though God never acts on their behalf as he does for male heroes. Critics suggest that the reference to these four mothers occurs precisely to foreshadow the unusual birth of Jesus by Mary of Nazareth: just as in ancient times God used remarkable 'women strangers' to achieve divine political purpose, women whose (sexual) behavior deviated markedly from the norm,[97] so God acts again in the same way through Mary. The point is well made: the outsider women of Matthew 1 may have been Strange Women, but they had their role to play too in the drama of religious history, and by the time of Jesus were generally thought of as proselytes of Judaism. They are not presented in the New Testament for their 'sinful' status, but as righteous converts whose extraordinary stories merit repeating and provide a topology for understanding Jesus' status.[98] We will meet Bathsheba again, this time in her role as 'mother' of wisdom, as she is pre-

---

97. The breakdown of the topology of these four characters is not quite so tidy as some commentators seem to suggest: Rahab's sexuality, though perhaps implicit in her profession of innkeeper, is not a specific feature of the text in Joshua; similarly, a woman, even a married one, answering the call to her king's bedchamber could hardly be supposed to be displaying out of the ordinary behavior in complying. As the Middle Egyptian proverb has it, in the world of royal protocol, 'The one who comes is the one who is called.'

98. Elaine Wainwright, 'The Gospel of Matthew', in Elizabeth Schüssler Fiorenza (ed.), *Searching the Scriptures: A Feminist Commentary*, II (New York: Crossroad, 1994), pp. 635-77, esp. pp. 642-44.

sented in Jewish legend as a user/composer of motherly wisdom to correct her son Solomon.

Wise Women: Counselors, Healers and Mourners

Many of the roles we have already seen women filling within the relatively private world of the home take them across that threshold and into the 'public domain' of the community at large. Women managing their household's economic stores might venture into buying and selling (Prov. 31.10-31; see discussion above); wives and mothers known for their common-sense teachings and ability to resolve conflicts might be drafted into the service of their neighborhoods, towns or cities. Such women are found in 2 Samuel as 'wise women', and their sisters are well attested in the Indo- European culture of the Hittites, a people who occupied Anatolia from the end of the Middle Bronze Age until the beginning of the Iron Age (see below).

Counselors

One of the most critical features of Israel's wise women was, once again, their excellent and timely use of language in the resolution of conflicts (2 Sam. 14, 20).[99] Like any male sage, they take up their public role without hesitation and with an expectation of being heard and valued, although 'mother' imagery is used to 'authorize' their interventions, at least in part. Proverbs and proverbial phrases, the tools of the sage, fall from their lips as needed and are as efficacious as the counsels of their brothers in the craft (2 Sam. 14.14; 20.18). We will explore the dynamics of these 'performances' of wisdom in the chapter to follow. What began as women's wisdom in the world of the home has clearly gone public, to the good of all.

Excursus: A Wise Woman's Composition in Old Norse

Though we have argued above that Israel's wise women were more known for their use of proverbial wisdom in roles associated with the counselor, we ought not to rule out the possibility of female authorship in at least some places in Proverbs, as we have seen above. If we conceptualize the voices of authority as female voices, we have seen that many proverbs and

---

99. Claudia Camp, 'The Wise Women of 2 Samuel: A Role Model for Women in Early Israel', *CBQ* 43 (1981), pp. 14-29, and also her 'Female Sage', pp. 187-90.

a few instructions might conceivably have had their origins in female culture and concerns. To this meager evidence we will add a foray across the time line to a corpus of literature reflecting the ninth-twelfth century of the Common Era from old Norse-Icelandic sources—*The Elder Edda*.[100]

Predating the Christian conversion of Scandinavia, the heroic, mythological and family sagas of this collection provide something of a window into old 'pagan' practices and beliefs of the Norse peoples. With respect to the roles and status of women, we find many of the same features echoing what has already been observed in the southern Levant. As one critic who has studied the corpus extensively has noted,

> Profoundly patriarchal in nature, Old Norse mythology does not simply subordinate female divinities to the more powerful male gods but requires associations among femaleness, evil, and wisdom, which suggests reactions of a predominant male society to an old belief in strong female deities.[101]

It is hypothesized that the power attributed to women derives from a world in which the maternal principle was at the heart of life-giving religious practices—as has been posited by some to be a feature of 'Old Europe' with its powerful mother-goddess figure.[102] Whether or not the poems collected in the *Elder Edda* do indeed reflect the Germanic tribes' reverence for strong mother figures, something already reported by the Roman historian Tacitus in classical times (*Germania* 8), the poems collected there present us with not only the usual proceedings of misogyny in the characterization of female figures, but also serve up a primal Wise Woman, the *vǫlva*, whose counsel is sought out by no less than the father of the gods, Odin, in the poem.

Given the overall patriarchal character of the collection, the presence of a Wise Woman/Seeress performing a positive action is itself remarkable.

---

100. *Poems of the Elder Edda* (trans. Patricia Terry; intro. Charles W. Dunn; Philadelphia: University of Pennsylvania Press, 1990); *The Poetic Edda*, a new translation by Carolyne Larrington (Oxford: Oxford University Press, 1996).

101. Jenny Jochens, 'Old Norse Sources on Women', in Joel Rosenthal (ed.), *Medieval Women and the Sources of Medieval History* (Athens: University of Georgia, 1990), pp. 155-87 (163).

102. Marija Gimbutas, *The Goddesses and Gods of Old Europe, 6500–3500 B.C.: Myth and Cult Images* (Berkeley: University of California Press, 1982). It should be noted that Gimbutas' work is on cultures that left no epigraphic records, so her reconstructions proceed from a method she has dubbed 'archeo-mythology'. Whether that method can read stable readings of symbols used over broad geographic and chronological ranges still requires investigation.

In general, the *Edda* marches to the same drummer as the cultures of the classical Mediterranean. Women are blamed for all the evils that afflict the world of the gods; it is the arrival of magic-working women from Giant-land who are responsible for disorder. When not viewed as simple sex objects related by and for male perception (such as the goddess Freyja), women, whether mythological or human, are seen as a source of strife for men.[103] In *The Sayings of the Wise One*, Odin, the father god and lord of wisdom, speaks a series of brief instructional stanzas, covering the usual topics of patriarchal wisdom (honor, greed, the fool, the wise, rewards and daily life), summing up the Viking creed in an alliterative refrain:

> Cattle die, kinsmen die,
> the self must also die;
> but glory never dies,
> for the man who is able to achieve it.[104]

About women, the Father of the Slain is less optimistic:

> At evening the day should be praised, the woman when she is cremated,
> the blade when it is tested, the girl when she is married,
> the ice when it is crossed, the ale when it is drunk…
>
> The words of a girl no one should trust,
> nor what a woman says;
> for on a whirling wheel their hearts were made,
> deceit lodged in their breasts…
>
> Such is the love of women, of those with false minds;
> it's like driving a horse without spiked shoes over slippery ice,
> a frisky two year old, badly broken in,
> or like steering, in a stiff wind, a rudderless boat,
> or trying to catch when you're lame a reindeer on a thawing hillside.[105]

Though students of ancient Near Eastern wisdom are not used to the cold metaphors of ice and reindeer, the sentiments conveyed by Odin's wisdom are all too familiar (Ben Sira would be in strong agreement). The god goes on to explain the primary insult that the existence of women offers to male dominance, glory and honor: even a wise man can be 'trapped' by a pretty face, and rendered foolish before other men! At least Odin is able to see that some blame might be attached to men in the ongoing struggle between the

---

103. Jenny Jochens, '*Vǫluspá*: Matrix of Norse Womanhood', *Journal of English and Germanic Philology* 88 (1989), pp. 344-62.
104. Larrington, *Edda*, p. 24.
105. Larrington, *Edda*, pp. 25-26.

sexes: 'the hearts of men are fickle towards women; when we speak most fairly, then we think most falsely, that entraps the wise mind'.[106]

One of the most potent images of the strong Viking woman and her role in the heroic doings of her men is that of 'inciting' menfolk to engage in brutal acts, often as a piece of revenge she herself cannot take on her own initiative. The lay, *The Whetting of Gudrun*, begins with just such a domestic scene, as she incites her sons to avenge the death of their sister Svanhild:

> 'Why do you sit, why do you sleep away your life? Why aren't you unhappy when you speak of cheerful things?...you would have tried to avenge her, if you had the temperaments of my brothers or the fierce spirits of the kings of the Huns...'[107]

Such women, like the 'nags' of Proverbs, provoke and goad their men into familial and social violence, egging on the poor, innocent warriors into carrying out their own nefarious, female designs. Such behavior even pushes a misogynist proverb into birth as a suitable refrain by the men: 'Cold are the counsels of women!' (*Kǫld eru kvenna ráô*).[108] While supplying a little too 'pat' an answer to the riddle of male violence, the portraits painted do suggest the presence of situations in which women take what leadership—or behind the scenes manipulation—that is available to them. A survey of the lays that bring such glory to men through their battles tells another tale when spoken in a woman's voice: loss of kin and suffering are the legacies of battle, not glory. No wonder the women had only cold counsels with which to warm themselves! With their men frequently away on raiding missions or, later, engaged in trade or exploration, women found extended opportunities for leadership; even men who were requested by absent husbands to 'help out' around the homestead were ultimately subject to the female head of household's approval.[109] It is more probable that this skewing of the 'natural' and appropriate patriarchal roles as viewed by men was more formative in creating the negative attitudes toward women shown in Icelandic literature than any primal flaw in womanhood itself.

How remarkable then is the situation in which a dominant god must seek his answers from a female! Elsewhere, in *Balder's Dreams*, Odin has

---

106. Larrington, *Edda*, p. 26.
107. Larrington, *Edda*, pp. 234-35.
108. Jochens, 'Old Norse Sources', pp. 162, 164-67, 173.
109. Jochens, 'Old Norse Sources', p. 175.

had to seek out the grave of a dead wise woman with 'corpse-reviving spells' in order to question her: 'Don't be silent, prophetess! I want to question you, until I know everything, I still want to know more...,' though her knowledge did him no good in trying to prevent Balder's death.[110] Jochens writes:

> ...the Nordic pantheon may be seen as the creation of a society dominated by males who made room for important female figures only when males— facing an unknown future—had to admit helplessness or when they voiced fear of women, a fear induced, perhaps, by the occasional success of women to predict the future.[111]

Our mythological Wise Woman was paralleled on a human level by women practicing the same profession as *vǫlur*, just as the wise women of Israel had their counterpart in Woman Wisdom. These women predicted the future and assisted their farming communities by practice of magic when needed. Essential and yet feared—the *vǫlur* shared in the dubious lot of 'professional' women in worlds where men are preeminent.

Our *vǫlva* begins by making clear that although she is responding to a request by the Father of the Slain, everyone ought to listen to what she has to say:

> Attention I ask from all the sacred people,
> greater and lesser, the offspring of Heimdall;
> Father of the Slain, you wished that I should declare
> the ancient histories of men and gods, those which I remember from the
>   first.
>
> I, born of giants, remember very early
> those who nurtured me then;
> I remember nine worlds...[112]

No ordinary human *vǫlva* then, our cosmic Wise Woman speaks with a triple authorization. She has been commissioned to speak her visions, as it were, by Odin, thus laying to rest the notion that a female ought not to be speaking so grandly. Further, she is very old and able to remember creation before it was peopled by humans; she speaks by the authority of her special memories because, like Woman Wisdom in Proverbs 8, she was there. Finally, she is 'born' of giants, a group that figures heavily and menacingly in Norse mythology. While perhaps only raised by giants, and not

110. Larrington, *Edda*, pp. 243-45.
111. Larrington, *Edda*, p. 162.
112. Larrington, *Edda*, p. 4.

one of their number,[113] nevertheless her association with them evokes power and disaster: it was the coming of three women of Giantland that ended the Golden Age of the gods, after all.

After enumerating the generations and doings of the Aesir and Vanir-gods and, following them, the dwarves, she tells of the Cosmic Tree and the coming of the three female Fates who guard its well/lake. Like all good Wise Women, cosmic or otherwise,[114] she is well informed on the role of the Tree as metaphor, and the role of female Norns in the lives of males:

> I know that an ash-tree stands called Yggdrasill,
> a high tree, soaked with shining loam;
> from there come the dews which fall in the valley,
> ever green, it stands over the well of fate.
>
> From there come three girls, knowing a great deal,
> from the lake which stands under the tree;
> Fated one is called, Becoming another—
> they carved on wooden slips—Must-be the third;
> they set down laws, they chose lives,
> for the sons of men the fates of men.[115]

These entities are followed closely by the appearance of a Strange Woman-type figure—seductive, knowledgeable in magics and up to cosmic trouble that make her beloved by wicked human females. Three times she is burned to death, but each time she returns to cause more difficulties. Scholars have identified her as a 'hypostasis' of the goddess Freyja (whom some scholars have seen as an Inanna/Anat variant),[116] as elsewhere Freyja is said to be cognizant of the kind of incantations[117] mentioned here:

---

113. Jochens, *Vǫluspá*, pp. 347-49.

114. Othmar Keel, *Goddesses and Trees, New Moon and Yahweh: Ancient Near Eastern Art and the Hebrew Bible* (JSOTSup, 261; Sheffield: Sheffield Academic Press, 1998), pp. 56-57.

115. Larrington, *Edda*, p. 6.

116. This so-called 'oriental hypothesis' (cf. Lotte Motz, 'Freyja, Anat, Ishtar and Inanna: Some Cross-Cultural Comparisons', *Mankind Quarterly* 23 (1982), pp. 195-212; Britt-Mari Näsström, *Freyja—the Great Goddess of the North* (Lund Studies in History of Religions, 5; Lund: Novapress, 1995), pp. 23-32). Note also the similarities in the Irish goddess Morrigna and the Valkyries in their manifestations as battle goddesses who also appear as birds.

117. While we do not know what such practices involved for the women who participated in them, scholars state that male transvestism was involved (even as the same feature is found in the cult of Inanna and elsewhere in the ancient Near East, thus

> Bright One they called her, wherever she came to houses,
> the seer with pleasing prophecies, she charmed them with spells;
> she made magic wherever she could, with magic she played with minds,
> she was always the favorite of wicked women...[118]

The wise woman then turns her attention to the coming Doom of the Gods, setting out the unavoidable fate that will plunge the world into Ragnarok, an icy and fiery end for all life. Just before she emerges from her trance, she glimpses a new creation, with earth rising out of the sea and some of the Aesir returning to inhabit it. In the last verse of the poem, however, the figure of a dreadful dark dragon (Nidhogg) appears, leaving the audience uncertain: is the coming of Ragnarok being evoked again, or does Nidhogg suggest that even in the new world, trouble lies brooding in the corpses beneath the dragon's wing?[119]

Midwives and Healers

We must add another category to the list of sage functions that mothers and public wise women perform: that of folk healer. Those dealing with the cuneiform traditions call our attention to the application of wisdom terminology to physicians in a number of places.[120] Training for the profession of physician (LU.AZU) doubtless required some sort of scribal education, even if an abbreviated one, because of the rituals and incantations necessary to the proper conduct of the role. For this reason, women must be excluded from the 'professional' or 'scientific' class of doctors, but this does not mean we should exclude them from the traditional roles of folk healers, nurses and midwives, all of which require some sort of training as well as innate common sense. In fact, the traditional roles of wife and mother include the job description of 'healer' and 'nurse', for the care of sick family members routinely falls to the women of the household.[121] In ancient times, as in modern ones, the first phase of health care was 'home care'.

---

forming part of the biblical polemic against cross-dressing that sees it as a participation in idolatry). See Carolyne Larrington, 'Scandinavia', *The Feminist Companion to Mythology* (London: Pandora; Harper Collins, 1992), p. 137.

118. Larrington, *Mythology*, p. 7.

119. Larrington, *Mythology*, pp. 12-13.

120. Harris, 'Female Sage', pp. 11-12, 15-16.

121. Sharon Sharp, 'Folk Medicine Practices. Women as Keepers and Carriers of Knowledge', *Women's Studies International Forum* 9 (1986), pp. 243-49; on the truth of this insight for the cultures of the ancient Near East, see Hector Avalos,

As might be assumed, the special care of women healers was most appropriate in situations that dealt with women and children: all those diseases and conditions having to do with fertility and infant health were especially important areas where a woman's expertise was considered indispensable. In the Old Babylonian version of the 'Flood Story', we find the 'birth-goddesses' assembled to welcome the first birth to the first human couple, and the goddess Nintu ('Lady') takes a joyous role in the labor and delivery:

> Wife and husband were [bliss]ful.
> The birth goddesses were assembled,
> And Nintu [sat rec]koning the months.
> [At the] destined [time] they summoned the tenth month.
> The tenth month arrived;
> …opened the womb.
> Her face beaming and joyful,
> She covered her head
> And performed the midwifery.
> She girded [the mother's] middle
> As she pronounced a blessing.
> She drew (a circle?) with meal and placed the brick,
>
> 'I am the one who created, my hands have made it!
> Let the midwife rejoice in the sacrosanct woman's house.
> Where the pregnant woman gives birth,
> And the mother of the baby is delivered,
> Let the brick[122] be in place for nine days,
> Let Nintu, the birth goddess, be honored…' (2.39.276-95).[123]

With a divine model instituting the role and functions of midwives, no wonder their word and deeds were held in high esteem—and perhaps some deferential male fear as well!—in their social worlds.

Study of Hittite texts provides us with some interesting parallels to interpreting the generally under-reported phenomenon of folk healing by women in Israel. These texts also point to an important connection

Illness and Health Care in the Ancient Near East: The Role of the Temple in Greece, Mesopotamia, and Israel (Harvard Semitic Museum, 54; Atlanta: Scholars Press, 1995); Hector Avalos, *Health Care and the Rise of Christianity* (Peabody, MA: Hendrickson, 1999).

122. We do not know of the custom of the placement of the 'brick' from any other text, nor do we know exactly what its role in midwifery was (A. Kilmer, 'The Brick of Birth', *JNES* 46 [1987], pp. 211-13).

123. Foster, *Before the Muses*, I, pp. 169-70.

between the wisdom traditions of cuneiform societies, where wisdom is more tied to incantational and magical rites, and less so to the literary and practical 'clan' wisdom traditions as they were known in ancient Israel.[124] In the rituals of the Hittite wise women, we find the missing link wherein 'proverbial' phrases and images, the tokens of the sages' art in Israel, are wed to the magical rituals of Mesopotamia and Anatolia to restore health and harmony.

Hittite wise women or 'Old Women' (literally, MI.ŠU.GI; Hittite: *ḫaššawa*) are first attested in the reign of Ḫattušili I, and appear to be associated with the old village power bases among the Hattians, the indigenous people of old central Anatolia. Hittite kings tended to become nervous if their palace women had too much contact with these tradents of the older order. The MI.ŠU.GI performed far more healing rituals than any of the other class of Hittite ritual personnel, and were in constant contact with ritual impurities among those they treated. (One wonders how this might have affected their status.) In modern terms, their work encompassed pediatrics, sex therapy, psychology, grief therapy and applied linguistics. Whether it was the proper ritual treatment of royal bones or a common household quarrel, these women were on duty, practicing their craft, burying angry words and turning sorcerous[125] assaults back onto their senders. One of the healing agents in their metaphorical 'black bag' was the proverbial phrase that linked set ritual action to the context in question.[126] The basic formula was 'Just as *x* in the natural world happens, so also may *x* happen in this life.' An example

---

124. These texts are not always as accessible as one would wish, but as a starting place, see Gary Beckman's 'Proverbs and Proverbial Allusions in Hittite', *JNES* 45 (1986), pp. 19-30; Ahmet Ünal, 'The Role of Magic in Ancient Anatolian Religions According to the Cuneiform Texts from Bogazkoy-Hattusha', in Prince Takahito Mikasa (ed.), *Essays on Anatolian Studies in the Second Millennium B.C.* (Leipzig: Otto Harrassowitz, 1988), pp. 52-85; Oliver Gurney, *Some Aspects of Hittite Religion* (Oxford: Oxford University Press, 1977); Fontaine, 'Queenly Proverb Performance', pp. 95-126, and 'Heifer'. *Biblical Archaeologist* 52.2, 3 (1989) is devoted entirely to the Hittite empire and makes a good entry point for those interested in this culture.

125. 'Sorcery' is the term usually given by anthropologists to magic practiced for illicit purposes. In fact, sorceresses and wise women appear to have used many of the same ritual methods, but for different ends, according to their societies' assessments.

126. Ünal lists 106 proverbial phrases embedded within ritual texts using analogical magic; not all are from rituals recorded from the wise women, but many are. In particular, one wonders if our wily women of 2 Sam. had a copy of KUB 13.3, because the proverbial phrases using water are a wonderful match.

from tablet 4, lines 7-14 of 'The Hittite Ritual of Tunnawi', which is
directed toward the cure of infertility, among other evils, reads as
follows:

> Then she seizes the horn of the fertile cow, and she says: 'Sun-god, my
> lord, as this cow is fertile, and she is in a fertile pen and she is filling the
> pen with bulls and cows, just so let this sacrificer be fertile; let her just so
> fill her house with sons and daughters, grandchildren and great grandchil-
> dren, descendants in successive generations!' Then they drive the fertile
> cow back to the pen.[127]

Keen observation of natural phenomena undergirded their practice of
medical magic; this is one place where we may observe nature wisdom—
the zeal for cataloguing—married to ritual practices. Even sharper esti-
mates of the appropriate use of such observations in context allowed these
wise women to make a metaphorical 'match' between the action in their
proverbial phrase, now enacted in ritual form before the sufferers and the
hoped-for goal in the sufferers' lives. In other words, in this paradigm of
proverbial action, 'proverb performance'[128] moves from the citation of
traditional wisdom to characterize or resolve social ambiguities to a ritualized, formal act whose goal is the same—the restoration of harmony. If a
parable might be considered a proverb with a plot-line, then the rituals of
the Hittite wise women are proverbs with props and stage direction. The
Hebrew word for 'proverb', '*māšāl*', carries two meanings, both reflected
in the work of these wise women. First, *māšāl* means 'to be similar to',
and, secondly, it carries the meaning of 'to rule over'. Every proverb encompasses these two ideas, encapsulating events to which the proverb is
'similar', and thus allowing its users to 'rule over' any situation in which
they find a similar set of circumstances in action. In these Hittite healing
rituals, the *māšāl* observed becomes the *māšāl* enacted, restructuring
reality along the lines indicated in the proverb's similitude, and thus
'ruling over' it.

Though there is little explicit mention of wise women healers in the
Hebrew Bible, some intriguing clues are present to suggest this ongoing
role for women in the world of folk wisdom. Midwives appear in Gen.
35.17 and 38.28, and are key characters in outwitting Pharaoh in Exodus

---

127. Albrecht Goetze, with E.H. Sturtevant, *The Hittite Ritual of Tunnawi* (New
Haven, CT: American Oriental Society, 1938), pp. 21-23.

128. 'Proverb performance' is the timely citation of a piece of proverbial wisdom in
a social interaction in order to evaluate events or influence outcomes. See the present
writer's *Traditional Sayings*, and Chapter 3, below, for discussion.

1. Within these stories, midwives execute the (semi?-)legal functions of pronouncing the child alive and announcing its sex; where twins are involved, the midwife certifies which child is the elder.[129] The parable of Ezekiel 16 reveals the typical functions performed for the newborn, no doubt also duties of the midwife:

> Thus says the Lord GOD to Jerusalem: Your origin and your birth were in the land of the Canaanites; your father was an Amorite, and your mother a Hittite.[130] As for your birth, on the day you were born your navel cord was not cut, nor were you washed with water to cleanse you, nor rubbed with salt, nor wrapped in cloths. No eye pitied you, to do any of these things for you out of compassion for you; but you were thrown out in the open field, for you were abhorred on the day you were born (Ezek. 16.3-5, NRSV).

The Wise Woman General Practitioner in Israel

Locating the 'wise woman' general practitioner whose expertise went beyond fertility matters in 'ancient Israel' is a more difficult matter, for a variety of reasons. Patriarchal agendas that relentlessly portray women's destiny as mothers have left us with explicit stories of barren wives, women in childbirth assisted by midwives, or stories where midwives play other important roles (see above). Few such stories exist covering more generalized medical problems that would have been dealt with by women in the home, or by specially trained (through family guilds, in all probability) wise women available to the whole community. However, the story of the captive Israelite slave woman in 2 Kings 5 is telling in this respect: it is in conversation between mistress and maid over the medical problem of the master that the important information about where a 'cure' may be sought outside the home. The foreign slave woman's knowledge of and concern for her master's illness is a hallmark of women's engagement in matters of family health; her 'referral' clearly indicates a recognition that the illness in question cannot be handled 'on site' in the home and demands an escalation of healing modalities.

---

129. For a more full description of the duties of the midwife, see Victor H. Matthews and Don C. Benjamin, *Social World of Ancient Israel, 1250–587 BCE* (Peabody, MA: Hendrickson, 1993), pp. 67-81.

130. Given the rather remarkable social status of Hittite women, in practice if not always in law, this pejorative statement by Ezekiel is fascinating. It is repeated in 16.45, following Ezekiel's citation of the proverb 'Like mother, like daughter' to characterize the evils of Jerusalem. One wonders if the phrase 'Your mother was Hittite' is also a *māšāl*, here used to express the author's discomfort with Jerusalem escaping from the control of its husband-god.

Female work in processing the subsistence materials of their household relating to food and textiles gave women a working knowledge of the effects of plant and animal products, minerals and other substances that typically form the bulk of the folk medicine pharmacopeia. These are precisely the sorts of materials traditionally neglected by earlier forms of 'biblical' archaeology oriented to the material culture of an urban elite, with its large edifices and lavish luxury items. Further, even when archaeology took a turn toward the subsistence economies of the central highlands of the late Bronze and early Iron Age Israel, such items are exactly the sort of fragile organic materials that would leave scant record in the evidence recovered from excavations. Add to this the difficulty of identifying a botanical listed in a medical or biblical text with the limited remains of material culture, and correctly correlating this with the medical name and properties of the actual botanical used,[131] and one can see why those who study this area of folk culture must cover greater geographical and chronological areas in order to piece together a general view of the cultural practices obtaining in the homes of women tradents of wisdom.

If we begin by thinking of the work and needs of the central unit of Israelite society, the 'family household' or *bêt 'āḇ*, we discover both the opportunity and necessity for training such resident female medical 'experts'. Living quarters consisted of three- and four-room compounds around central court that was used for group work projects (preserving foodstuffs, processing wool, flax, oils, etc.).[132] Families typically displayed multi-generational patterns, with membership in a constant state of flux: perhaps seven or eight persons on average in a domestic unit. Three or four of these units might share common walls and courtyards,

---

131. Based on a general search of the text, the standard biblical medicine chest seems to have included the following organic substances: Star of Bethlehem, rock rose, garlic, myrtle, mint (Mt. 23.23), rue, hyssop, coriander, saffron, cinnamon, frankincense, flax, lemon balm, figs, honey, olives, acacia, cedar, wine, mandrakes, vinegar, pistachio nuts, almonds, gums and myrrh. If the plant in Song 2.12 is to be identified with *Tulipa Montana* (arnica), then a powerful analgesic was also available to the Israelite healer.

132. This is the so-called 'pillared' house of the Iron I period, whose architecture used to be considered evidence of a distinctive 'new', ethnically different settlement population understanding itself to be tribal 'Israel'. For newer assessments of the archaeological record, see Paula McNutt, *Reconstructing the Society of Ancient Israel* (LAI; Louisville, KY: Westminster/John Knox Press, 1999), pp. 45-103, esp. pp. 49-51.

thus creating the broader living unit, sometimes identified with the biblical 'clan' or *mišpāḥāh*.[133]

Groups living together in such circumstances placed an understandable emphasis on group solidarity and self-sufficiency of the unit so necessary for their collective survival. Everyone was needed as a worker: children, females, males and elders, servants or clients, with most adult members putting in about ten hours of work a day. Everyone in the household then was at risk for work-related illness or injury, especially children and elders. In such a context, 'women's work' dealt with some limited agricultural tasks and the majority of technological 'processing' chores. In such domestic organization, our Western view of illness or injury in very personal, individual terms (as loss of ability for self-actualization, choice, resources or presence) and the need for health care does not reflect the harsh realities of life in a subsistence culture. Where each and every person in the household counts for the overall group's survival, illness is a threat to the successful exploitation of the environmental niche inhabited by the family. In order to return a group member to active productivity, it was essential to cultivate a working understanding of the causes of an illness and employ real and effective means of a procuring a cure. Women were the ones ideally suited to take on this critical task on behalf of the family.

Why women? a modern reader might ask. The women of the Israelite domestic unit had a unique combination of qualifications that made them the logical choice as care givers and healers.[134] These were drawn from the social construction of their biology as women, acculturation, availability for this kind of service, and special knowledge derived from their other economic behaviors. In the realm of biology, women's association with blood meant that they were habitually thinking about issues of purity,

---

133. These can be extremely fluid categories with considerable overlap, as we find them used in the biblical text (McNutt, *Reconstructing*, pp. 87-94; see also Meyers, 'Family', pp. 1-47).

134. In a text dealing with the cure of snake bites from Ugarit, we note the special healing role of the mother—even non-human ones—in seeking out care for children who have been bitten. It is the Mother-of-Horses who calls out to the Sun-goddess Shapshu, whom the text refers to as 'her mother', to summon the deities who will expel the venom from the suffering children (Baruch Levine and Jean-Michel de Tarragon, '"Shapshu Cries out in Heaven": Dealing with Snake-Bites at Ugarit [KTU 1.100, 1.107]', *RB* (1988), pp. 481-518). Note also the role of mothers' names in other magical healing practices (J. Naveh and S. Shaked, *Amulets and Magic Bowls: Aramaic Incantations in Late Antiquity*, 3rd edn with additions and corrections (Jerusalem: Magnes Press, 1998).

cleanliness and contagion. Women's birth-giving, nursing and child-rearing activities gave them incentive and opportunity to understand the body, from soothing a feverish or teething child to dealing with fertility matters (infertility, birth control and abortion) or mourning over the dead. Their expertise in butchery, cooking, preparation and food preservation gave them knowledge of local flora (especially herbcraft), fauna and their uses. In other areas of domestic division of labor, women's production of textiles made them the producers of other materials needed in healing practice: bandages, wool materials, clay or wax figurines, and so on, all used for healing purposes. The standard biblical remedy of cleansing with oil, followed by bandaging (and massage, where appropriate), puts the production—and no doubt, the application—of these remedies plainly in the hands of the womenfolk. It may be that Ezekiel's amulet-making women (ch. 13) were making protective amulets for household members —as one would expect a good *'eshet hayil* to do when faced with a strange set of hostile and unknown forces that have already proved lethal to the people of her land. Further, judging by comparative data from Hittite materials, and collections of Serbian healing charms used exclusively by women and passed down to daughters as part of their heritage, such mundane healing duties as massage, anointing, bandaging and administering herbs were probably accompanied by the recitation of incantations or proverbs, thereby bringing the practice of healing fully into the venue of 'efficacious speech' so prized by the wisdom movement.[135] After all, in such circumstances, 'pleasant words are like a honeycomb, sweetness to the soul and health to the body' (Prov. 16.24).

Women's cleaning activities, whether ritual or everyday in nature, may have been seminal in teaching the control of contagion; when someone was isolated in quarantine, it would have been the young or old women of the household who tended him or her by bringing food, water, cleaning and disposing of body waste.[136] Women, then as now, were the maids of the world, cleaning up the body wastes of infants, children, other women in their reproductive cycles, their own reproductive blood, and dealing with the aftermath of death. Indeed, women's association with cleaning is so routinized that it became a folktale motif in some strands of European

135. See above for discussion of Hittite proverbial analogies in healing; for Serbian healing charms, see John Miles Foley, *The Singer of Tales in Performance* (Bloomington: University of Indiana, 1995), pp. 99-135.

136. Access to body waste may have forged a significant connection of women, especially healers and midwives, with sorcery; see below.

fairy tales—where would Snow White or Cinderella have been without their ability to clean so well and so thoroughly?! In Israel, it was natural that an ill family member should turn to the Ladies of the House.

It is highly likely that some women who were especially good at these tasks became a living 'medical reference' for the gathered community. Reputation and experience would reinforce that specialty, causing it to be identified and passed along to suitable younger women. Such girls and young women probably trained as apprentices alongside their older female relatives, and this specialized knowledge, on analogy with other cultures, no doubt served as 'intellectual property' that was counted as part of their dowries. Thus, one might expect to see valued wise women and midwives coming from a particular household or *mišpāḥāh* to serve the broader village.

It is no accident, then, that many of the biblical passages that mention health or healing activities feature women and the family context are notable components of the enterprise. In several discussions of healing herbs (hyssop and balm), we find women also:

> Is there no balm in Gilead? is there no physician there? Why then has the health of the daughter of my people not been restored? (Jer. 8.22).

> Go up to Gilead and take balm, O virgin daughter of Egypt! In vain you have used many medicines; there is no healing for you (Jer. 46.11).

> Suddenly Babylon has fallen and been broken, wail for her! Take balm for her pain; perhaps she may be healed (Jer. 51.8).

Other biblical texts show an implicit if not explicit juxtaposition of women and healing elements or traditions. In Leviticus 14, purifications for leprosy include hyssop (a powerful purge when taken internally—who would have processed this herb for internal use?), cedar (a fumigant—who would have first used this wood smoke to preserve the household against pests?) and scarlet woolstuffs (surely processed and dyed by women). Further, some of these items are documented as part of the healing repertoire of wise women performing evocation magic elsewhere in the ancient Near East (p. 76 n 131, pp. 127, 184). Stories like Gen. 30.14, Leah's mandrakes and Rachel's use of them as a medicament for infertility locate women as interested in and knowledgeable about 'natural remedies'; note, too, that the boys and men have been trained to look for herbs and useful plants when out away from the living compound, and to bring them to the women of the household to be processed and used by them.

Postbiblical evidence continues to gesture toward the presence of women healers and midwives and their impact upon the community.

M. Šab. 18.3 tells us that midwives (or just the women, if there is no midwife) may decide what should be done medically for mother and her newborn child on the Sabbath, even where such directives may be at odds with
Sabbath regulations. In the Babylonian Talmud, we find that women healers' opinions on matters of health outrank male rituals, in that they, and
not the rabbi, can set the time for circumcision, based on a baby's health
circumstances (*Šab.* 134a). In *b. Sabbat* 134a, we discover R. Abaye's
mother/nurse cited as an authority on illness in infants and toddlers, and in
Niddah 20b, we meet Yalta, daughter of the Exilarch of Babylon (secular
leader of Jewish community in exile), who herself made determinations of
whether blood samples were clean or unclean. It is clear from the discussion there that women routinely examined themselves and other females as
well to determine ritual cleanness and/or the presence of gynecological
irregularities.[137] Extant amulets from the community in Ninevah were
constructed to protect against the child-strangling demoness Lilith: while it
is not clear if women made/wrote them, it is quite clear that they used
them.[138]

The Negative Side of the Wise Woman Healer: the Witch

Female sorcery—the negative use of the powers at the healer's command
—is alluded to and roundly condemned in Exod. 22.18, Lev. 20.27, Deut.
18.10, 1 Sam. 28 and 2 Chron. 33.6. The rabbis of the post-biblical period
give us the following enigmatic proverb from the Mishnaic Tractate *Pirke
Aboth* ('Sayings of the Fathers'): 'More women, more witchcraft' (2.8;
'*marbeh nāšîm, marbeh kešāpîm*').[139] Although the varieties of magical
practitioners excoriated in our texts do not include the healer, it is clear
from the various oblique references scattered throughout the Bible that
such roles for women did exist, and were recognized by the people as
specialized practices requiring training and skill. As always, the healer

---

137. Ilan, *Jewish Women*, p. 103.

138. Judith Z. Abrams, *The Women of the Talmud* (Northvale, NJ: Jason Aronson,
1995), pp. 123-51; Raphael Patai, *The Hebrew Goddess* (Detroit, MI: Wayne State
University Press, 3rd enlarged edn, 1978), pp. 236-44. One wonders if evidence of
such practices may have some bearing on the meaning of the use of so-called 'pillar'-
figures of females in Iron Age Israel.

139. R. Travers Herford, *Pirke Aboth, the Ethics of the Talmud: Sayings of the
Fathers* (New York: Schocken Books, 1962), p. 48; however, we do not know exactly
what the rabbis meant by 'witchcraft', but their association of it with the practices of
(especially foreign) women is indisputable.

who fails to heal becomes an easy target for charges of 'malpractice',[140] or
sorcery, and studies show that accusations of witchcraft are often the index
of social tensions at large.[141] It must be mentioned that it is not only in
Israel that the preoccupation with the malevolent use of such skills existed;
the Hittites, Egyptians and their Mesopotamian neighbors were obsessed
with averting the evils caused by wicked sorcerers.[142] The Apocryphal
book, the Ethiopian book of Enoch (*1 Enoch*), finds a particular way to
relate the healing work of women to the activities of witches. The problem
begins with the angels who see and desire the daughters of men:

> And they took wives for themselves, and everyone chose for himself one
> each. And they began to go in to them and were promiscuous with them.
> And they taught them charms and spells, and showed to them the cutting of
> roots and trees. And they became pregnant and bore large giants… (*1 En.*
> 7.1-3).[143]

The same special skills that women acquire in handling herbs and foodstuffs in order to sustain and heal their families become evidence against
them as practicing witches. Given these sorts of attitudes, we should not be
surprised to find the Palestinian Talmud going that extra mile: 'It was
taught: R. Shimeon b. Yohai says…even the most decent woman practices

---

140. Midwives, for example, were believed by Plato to be able to prolong or
increase the severity of labor pains by either medical or magical incantational means
(quoted in Julius Preuss, *Biblical and Talmudic Medicine* [trans. and ed. Fred Rossner;
Northvale, NJ: Jason Aronson, 1993], p. 37).

141. Stanley D. Walters, 'The Sorceress and Her Apprentice', *JCS* 23 (1970), pp.
27-38.

142. The literature on this subject is extensive. For a discussion of sorcery in Israel
with respect to women, see Athalya Brenner, *The Israelite Woman: Social Role and
Literary Type in Biblical Narrative* (Sheffield: JSOT Press, 1985), pp. 67-77. For
parallel cultures, see Walters, 'Sorceress'; Tsvi Abusch, *Babylonian Witchcraft
Literature: Case Studies* (BJS, 132; Atlanta: Scholars Press, 1987) and 'An Early Form
of the Witchcraft Ritual *Maqlû* and the Origin of a Babylonian Magical Ceremony', in
Tzvi Abusch, John Huehnergard and Piotr Steinkeller (eds.), *Lingering Over Words:
Studies in Ancient Near Eastern Literature in Honor of William L. Moran* (Atlanta:
Scholars Press, 1990), pp. 1-57; Sue Rollin, 'Women and Witchcraft in Ancient
Assyria (c. 900–600 BC)', in Averil Cameron and Amalie Kuhrt (eds.), *Images of
Women in Antiquity* (Detroit, MI: Wayne State University Press, 1983), pp. 34-45;
Maurice Vieyra, 'Le Sorcier Hittite', in Denise Bernot *et al.* (eds.), *Le Monde du
Sorcier* (Sources Orientales, 7; Paris: Seuil, 1966), pp. 101-25; and D.H. Englehard,
'Hittite Magical Practices: An Analysis' (PhD dissertation, Brandeis University, 1970).

143. '1 Enoch', trans. M.A. Knibb, in H.F.D. Sparks (ed.), *The Apocryphal Old
Testament* (Oxford: Clarendon Press, 1984), pp. 189-90.

witchcraft' (*y. Qid.* 4.11, 66c).[144] The Babylonian Talmud (*Sanhedrin* 100b) embellishes Ben Sira's litany of worries caused by a daughter (see our discussion above), adding 'if she grows old, lest she engage in witchcraft'.

Athalya Brenner's work on the peculiarly gendered form of the legal saying in Exod. 22.17, 'A sorceress—do not let her live!' raises another interesting possibility. Since many of the herbs and medicaments used by wise women for healing were also useful for birth control or to induce abortion[145]—either practice a primal violation of the patriarchal agenda of near-compulsory motherhood!—Brenner suggest that a sorceress is in fact a 'medicine woman' who is able to assist women in the control of their fertility. Brenner finds evidence that, throughout the Fertile Crescent, female birth control was

> known from the beginning of the second millennium BCE; acknowledged in medical records; considered efficient, at least to a certain degree (why bother with repeatedly administering or recording it otherwise?); is mostly drug-based; and is preserved in the on-going tradition.[146]

The deafening silence on this subject in the Hebrew Bible is for her another example both of the pro-mother agenda of its writers/compilers and the general lacuna on topics felt to fall within women's sphere of activity and interest.[147]

Professional Mourners

One more group of skilled or 'wise' women may be mentioned in the public domain of ancient Israel, and their existence points to how flexible the definition of 'wisdom' may be in actual practice. These are the professional mourning women, known to us from Jer. 9.17, 2 Chron. 35.25 and Ezek. 32.16. These women served an important function in their society, which may be related to those of the diplomatic wise women, midwives and healers, for their work in raising an outcry over the dead expressed their peoples' sense of orderly ritual at important times when the stability of the community had been threatened. Their 'art' or skill required training in the poetic conventions of ritual mourning, which some have related to

144. Quoted in Ilan, *Jewish Women*, p. 222.

145. Honey, dates, myrrh, acacia, onions, juniper and fir trees products, beans, beer and wine, celery, oil, birthwort, parsley, spikenard, coriander, cabbage, rue, dill, pepper, some ferns, cinnamon, and some kinds of mint (Athalya Brenner, *The Intercourse of Knowledge: On Gendering Desire and 'Sexuality' in the Hebrew Bible* [BIS, 26; Leiden: E.J. Brill, 1997], p. 78).

146. Brenner, *Intercourse*, p. 74.

147. Brenner, *Intercourse*, pp. 83-86.

Figure 6. Mourning Women (Fourteenth-century Castile. After Metzger and
Metzger, *Jewish Life*, p. 234, illus. 148.)

the high literary traditions of the epic poetry of their neighbors.[148] Women's
association with illness and grieving is attested in the earliest materials
available from the ancient Near East: when Dumuzi, the shepherd fertility
god of Sumerian Uruk, goes to the underworld, his wife, the goddess
Inanna, 'weeps bitterly for her young husband'; Sirtur, Dumuzi's mother,
weeps for him, saying, 'My heart plays the reed pipe of mourning,' and his
sister Geshtinanna wanders the city weeping for her lost brother.[149] Indeed,
the grief of Geshtinanna moves Inanna to accept her offer of taking
Dumuzi's place in death for half of every year, thus restoring fertility to
the land. The mourning of devoted sisters and daughters is attested in

148. Brenner, *Woman*, pp. 37-38.
149. Diane Wolkstein and Samuel Noah Kramer, *Inanna, Queen of Heaven and
Earth: Her Stories and Hymns from Sumer* (San Francisco: Harper & Row, 1983), pp.
85-89.

Ugaritic epics as well, and it is the mourning search of the Egyptian Isis for her dead mate Osiris that allows her to give birth to the redeemer-child god Horus.

Hence, the public work of mourning women is connected to both the language arts of the wise women of 2 Samuel and the ritual activity of the Hittite MI.ŠU.GI, one of whose activities was the funerary activities surrounding royalty. Indeed, the connection of these skilled practitioners to an even more distant past for women's public roles is intriguing. In the ancient Sumerian language, we discover that a special dialect, EME.SAL, existed and was spoken only by women, goddesses and eunuchs. This dialect is one associated with the high poetic arts, and in particular with the laments of the goddesses—and their female devotees—for the dead fertility god who was her yearly partner. When women first 'officially' find their language and raise their voice in public, it is in lament. The mourning women of Jer. 9.17 echo the Ugaritic lament for the fertility god slain by the god of Death, who climbs into the palace windows. Clearly, a long history of poetic composition and performance is buried beneath these brief references, and it is probably under this rubric that the work of women musicians, 'lay' or cultic, is probably to be understood (see Fig. 7). While musicians are not usually termed 'wise' per se, it seems that the notion of 'skilled performer' might very well qualify these women to be housed among the category of female sage.[150]

As we look at these three variations on the category of public wise woman—counselors, healers of various sorts and professional mourners—we may draw a number of conclusions. First of all, these women were all 'ritual experts' acting in complex, potentially volatile social situations. Next, deliberate, formalized language acts often constituted part of their duties, whether those language acts were the apt citation of proverbs (the wise women of 2 Samuel), healing incantations and pronouncements (midwives and healers), or formalized funeral dirges (professional mourners). Public wise women reoralized the powerful language traditions they had inherited and served as a reservoir of specialized knowledge that they shared in performance. In each 'occupation', training of some sort was

---

150. For work in this area, see Carol L. Meyers, 'Of Drums and Damsels: Women's Performance in Ancient Israel', *BA* 54 (1991), pp. 16-27; also her 'Guilds and Gatherings: Women's Groups in Ancient Israel', in Prescott H. Williams, Jr and Theodore Hiebert (eds.), *Realia Dei: Essays in Archaeology and Biblical Interpretation in Honor of Edward F. Campbell, Jr. at his Retirement* (Atlanta: Scholars Press, 1999), pp. 154-84.

Figure 7. Women Musicians. (Fourteenth-century Spain. After Metzger and Metzger, *Jewish Life*, p. 112, illus. 160).

required, even if that training took place primarily within the family unit. Finally, all of the skills that allowed women to fill these valued public roles originate in the roles attributed to wives, mothers, sisters and daughters within the world of the home. Each of these roles had negative correlates when female action was perceived to be challenging the boundaries of male control.

The Public Economic Manager/Business Woman: The Alewife

We have spoken earlier of the roles of management of the household economy which fell to wives and mothers, and whose commands were carried out by the lesser-status 'maidens' of the house (daughters and slaves). These roles too found their way into the public arena when enterprising women took the lessons they had learned in the home out into the town or village. In particular, women who ran 'alehouses' are mentioned in the law codes of Mesopotamia. While the alehouse was a site for the consumption of beer, it might also function as a guest-house or even a 'house of ill-repute' (the story of Rahab the business-woman or harlot, of Joshua 2 is a memory of such establishments). Women owning these businesses might 'run a tab' for regular customers, make various 'deals' as they traded for supplies, and were a ready source of loans to farmers and others who could afford to borrow. Clearly, their 'head for business' was translated from the household into a world where men usually held sway; this, of course, made them both valuable for the services they rendered, but also a target for male malcontentment whenever a dispute arose. One wonders how the city-states would have fared if the cloistered *naditu* women and alewives of the region had not taken on the role of 'banker' for the local community.[151]

Because of their presence at the 'center' of things in the town square, the alewife was also a source of information on the comings and goings of those in the community. It is for exactly this reason that Joshua's spies seek out Rahab in Joshua 2. Not only does this alewife seem to know the political scene better than the rulers of her city, she is also shown deftly managing the escape of the spies, the 'cover-up' of their getaway, and even manages to bargain shrewdly for the preservation of her own family when Israel's mighty force descends upon the city with destruction in mind. But politics and maintaining a safe establishment are not the only things the alewife has learned; the epic tradition of the ancient Near East suggests that she also has insight into the human heart that has a kind of wisdom all its own.

Returning to the Gilgamesh Epic, in Tablet X we meet a cosmic alewife, Siduri, whose name means 'she is my wall/protection'.[152] This alewife is a smart female; she sees Gilgamesh coming in her direction, draws conclusions and acts:

> The ale-wife Siduri, [who dwells by the deep sea]
> and sits [...]...
> The ale-wife gazes afar off;
> Speaking in her own heart [she says] (these) words,
> As she [takes counsel] with herself:
> 'Surely, this one is a killer]!
> Whither is he heading [...]?'
> As the ale-wife saw him, she locked [the door],
> She barred her gate, securing [the bolt].[153]

Clearly, this alewife knows 'trouble' when she sees it heading in her direction! Gilgamesh is not so easily turned off, however. He tells Siduri

---

151. Snell, *Life*, pp. 53, 81-82.

152. Gwendolyn Leick, *A Dictionary of Ancient Near Eastern Mythology* (New York: Routledge, 1991), p. 152.

153. Assyrian version, *ANET*, p. 90.

of his quest to understand the meaning of the death of Enkidu, his beloved 'double': 'Dwelling on the [sea-shore, O ale-wife, Thou dost see its depths, all [...]. Show (me) the way...'[154] Soundly oddly like Qoheleth (though considerably more upbeat in her assessment of family life!), Siduri replies to the hero with the message of a sage: seize the day; it's the only one you get!

> 'Gilgamesh, whither rovest thou?
> The life thou pursuest thou shalt not find.
> When the gods created mankind,
> Death for mankind they set aside,
> Life in their own hands retaining.
> Thou, Gilgamesh, let full be thy belly,
> Make thou merry by day and by night.
> Of each day make thou a feast of rejoicing,
> Day and night dance thou and play!
> Let thy garments be sparkling fresh,
> Thy head be washed; bathe thou in water.
> Pay heed to the little one that holds on to thy hand,
> Let thy spouse delight in thy bosom!
> For this is the task of [mankind]!'[155]

Though her appearance in the epic makes clear she is no ordinary mortal female, here Siduri the Alewife voices the definitive perspective of ancient women's wisdom. The good things of life are not discovered to be 'good' through their acquisition, but in their use within relationship.[156] To misunderstand this is to short change one's humanity, which begins and ends in the home, not the wilderness of epic adventures. Enjoyment of what life has to offer, attention to the needs of the next generation, and the joy found in the sexual 'other' with whom one makes a home—these are ultimately more satisfying (and available!) than any magic potion conferring eternal youth or life. Do we have here the origin of the motif of the 'bar-tender' as counselor, offering a listening ear and dispensing advice along with a stiff drink? Was it compassionate wisdom that caused the alewives of the ancient world to play such a role in the economic welfare of their customers and towns, or only shrewd self-interest? Either way, Siduri and her human sisters give us another portrait of women of the past, caught in the act of making wisdom manifest in daily life.

---

154. Supplement to the Old Babylonian Version, *ANET*, p. 507.
155. Old Babylonian version, Tablet X, col. iii (*ANET*, p. 90).
156. This is something with which Qoheleth can never quite come to terms.

Conclusions: Where Private and Public Overlap

We have seen in this survey that the wisdom tradition of ancient Israel allowed both private and public expressions of women's competence and contribution to the world of the wise. In many respects, these social roles of women are echoed on the literary level in the twin figures of Woman Wisdom and Woman Folly/Stranger. Together these two metaphorical figures embody the social roles, positive and negative, that women filled within society at large and the wisdom movement in particular. While the goddess traditions of surrounding cultures and within Israel itself may have had a significant impact in shaping the portrait and meaning of these two characters,[157] the actual lived experience of women contributed greatly as well. In particular, it is important to recognize that the roles played out in the private world of women in the household were a direct source of experience and authorization for much of their power when they moved out into the public arena (see Figure 8). In many cases, skills and training directly overlapped, and this fundamental identity was then reproduced and codified in the metaphors of 'womanhood' and women's roles explicated by the sages in figures of Woman Wisdom/Woman Stranger.

The Cosmic Domain: Where Is Wisdom to Be Found?

As we have examined the inventory of social roles filled by women and their representation in the book of Proverbs, so far we have omitted all but passing reference to the cosmic female figures of Proverbs 1–9, whose portraits are drawn with mythological brush strokes. The personification of Wisdom as a female has given and continues to give scholars and interpreters a nexus of problems concerning gender, role and function in their considerations of this figure.[158] I am no less beset by ambivalence, as witnessed in the very structure of this chapter. If Woman Wisdom is primarily a reservoir for all the positive roles that sages have perceived in real women, then surely she should have been treated under the various appropriate headings for the Private and Public Domains. But—and here

---

157. See Bernhard Lang, *Wisdom and the Book of Proverbs: An Israelite Goddess Redefined* (New York: Pilgrim Press, 1986), and Carole R. Fontaine, 'The Personification of Wisdom', in James L. Mays (ed.), *Harper's Bible Commentary* (San Francisco, CA: Harper & Row, 1988), pp. 501-503.

158. Woman Stranger/Woman Folly has caused considerably less trouble to the tradition—after all, that evil should appear in the guise of woman is no great surprise!

1. *Positive Roles*

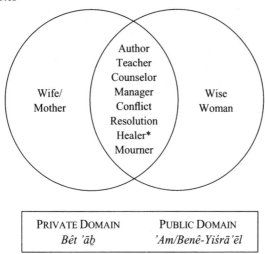

2. *Negative Roles*

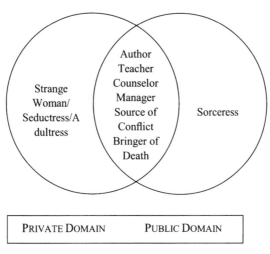

* Documented in parallel texts, but not in HB

Figure 8. Social Roles of Women in the Private and Public Domains.

we are faced with an enormous scholarly '*but*'—if she takes her derivation and function, at least in part, from the goddess mythologies of surrounding cultures, then perhaps she should be seen operating in her own domain, a cosmic one of creation, primal power, and the mythic realms of Life and Death. I am taking this latter option, if for no other reason than to present the notorious crux of a goddess-like figure, alive and well, in the ruthlessly patriarchal Hebrew Bible. Since modern interpretive programs still bear a trace of the need to be accountable to doctrinal formulations, it is always important to make a clear statement when textual markers directly contradict our desire to read the text in the patterns we have been taught.

Wisdom in the Cosmic Domain
She Who Was, Wasn't and Now Is: Goddesses in the Study of Hebrew Bible. Ḥokmâ has been through a lot:[159] She has been a 'Dame', a 'Lady', a 'Frau', a hypostasis, a figure ('Gestalt', Baumann), an 'exalted' female (Camp, the early years), a trickster (Camp, the later years), a cosmic scribe (Clifford),[160] a literary construct (Hadley), a convergence (McKinlay), a domesticated survival (Fontaine), and an inchoate personification (Fox).[161] She has been the voice of Creation, turned to men (*sic*) in self-revelation (von Rad), the voice of the Father's teaching (Newsom), or the rant of the scolding Mother (Brenner). The scholarly dithering over terminology is testimony to the sad fact that many, if not most, scholars are as captive to scholarly, religious and social constraints as any other group that seeks to make interpretations in a intellectual world where meanings are neither engraved on tablets nor sculpted in stone.[162] Despite early interpretations by Albright and Böstrom, and later Bauer-Kayatz, Lang and Fontaine,[163] that explored the goddess mythology used to shape the presentation of

159. Her plight is not unlike that of the African American woman pastor who told me, 'Well, first I was "colored", then I was a Negro, then a 'colored person', then suddenly I was black, then a "person of color", and now I'm African American. In fact, I'm a little tired...'
160. R.J. Clifford, *Proverbs*.
161. Fox, *Proverbs 1–9*, pp. 331-32.
162. Gentle Reader, I include myself among the fallible.
163. W.F. Albright, 'The Goddess of Life and Wisdom', *ASJL* 36 (1919–20), pp. 258-94, 'Some Canaanite-Phoenician Sources of Hebrew Wisdom', *VT* 3 (1955), pp. 1-15; G. Böström, *Proverbiastudien: Die Weisheit und das fremde Weib in Sprüche 1–9* (Lund: C.W.K. Gleerup, 1935); Lang, *Wisdom*; Christa (Bauer-)Kayatz, *Studien zu Proverbien 1–9* (WMANT; Neukirchen–Vluyn: Neukirchener Verlag, 1966); Fontaine, 'Personification', pp. 501-503.

Ḥokmâ, biblical scholars have often seemed reluctant to speak with conviction and freedom about their results in the study of the impact of goddess-worshiping cultures on the Bible. This is in marked contrast to classical scholars, Assyriologists, language specialists in the cultures surrounding ancient Israel and the like who have had less difficulty in taking up this question.[164]

The problem, of course, is that the text itself so roundly condemns worship of foreign deities that it is difficult to free oneself of that implicit characterization of the question as illegitimate or ancillary. Where monotheism in the later period of ancient Israel is likewise assumed as a 'textual given' and a doctrinal starting point for the reconstruction of the Bible's theology, again goddess worship must be labeled illegitimate or 'popular', and hence of less scholarly interest. But had such rigid monotheism been the norm for the postexilic period, surely the Bible would not have had to rail continuously against those who thought and acted otherwise.

Even though most biblical scholars might envision themselves as making socio-historical or literary inquiries into the *realia* of the kingdoms of Judah and Israel by investigating the texts or artifacts they left behind, the very fact that a great portion of the world (if not the academy) holds these texts as 'sacred' sometimes operates as a sort of unconscious 'gag order' on scholarly discourse, especially for those employed with traditional seminary settings. The finds coming out of the Judean desert and elsewhere for the last 30 years, detailed literary and iconographic studies, along with new studies into the nature of postexilic monotheism have changed the scholarly landscape enough for a more balanced approach to the contradictory traces of goddesses within our texts to emerge.[165] Scholarly opinion still ranges from minimal attention paid to the gender of Woman

---

164. This is not to suggest, of course, that it has been 'easy going' for feminist scholars in these areas of specialization, but rather that the simple fact of the presence of females among the pantheon could not be denied, even if analysis of the gender ideology in their portrayal was left largely untouched (Julia M. Asher-Greve, 'Stepping into the Maelstrom: Women, Gender and Ancient Near Eastern Scholarship', *NIN* 1 [2000], pp. 1-22).

165. See Judith Hadley's newest work, *The Cult of Asherah in Ancient Israel and Judah: Evidence for a Hebrew Goddess* (Cambridge: Cambridge University Press, 2000); see especially Sylvia Schroer, 'Die göttliche Weisheit und der nachexilische Monotheismus', in M.-T. Wacker and Erich Zenger (eds.), *Der Eine Gott und die Göttin: Gottesvorstellungen des biblischen Israel im Horizont feministicher Theologie* (Quaestiones Disputatae, 135; Freiburg: Herder, 1991), pp. 151-82, reprinted in Schroer, *Weisheit*, pp. 27-62.

Wisdom (the acknowledgment that abstract nouns [e.g. 'Torah', 'Under-standing', etc.] in Hebrew are feminine) to complex formulations that provide Woman Wisdom with a divine genealogy. Still, many scholars continue to proceed as though the reports in the Bible, so sketchy and so biased, are in fact accurate historical records of popular religious practice (the theological world to which goddess worship is usually relegated). One noted archaeologist, after reading a paper on the repression of Asherah worship, both in the Hebrew Bible itself and in the scholarly works devoted to it, to a polite but disinterested audience[166] was overheard muttering about 'denial' as he left the podium. We are reminded of the now-proverbial declaration by gay and lesbian persons, 'Denial ain't just a river in Egypt.'

Archaeology has made clear that Israel and Judah did *indeed* worship a consort goddess alongside Yahweh, and that for much of the history of the people, such worship was considered legitimate and routine.[167] It is not the intention here to lay out a blow-by-blow description of scholarly delusions, hiccoughs, and pooh-bahs for you patient and long-suffering readers. However, it *is* worth noting that the frequent disclaimers issuing from many experts that, while Woman Wisdom shares some traits with other scribal-, tree-, mother/lover- or redeemer-goddesses, that she can *in no way* be considered anything like a *real* goddess—this is ancient Israel and

---

166. Except for the more gutsy feminists, of course.

167. For an extensive bibliography, see Judith Hadley, 'From Goddess to Literary Construct: The Transformation of Asherah into Hokmah', in Athalya Brenner and Carole Fontaine (eds.), *A Feminist Companion to Reading the Bible: Approaches, Methods, Strategies* (FCB, 1, 2nd series; Sheffield: Sheffield Academic Press, 1997), pp. 360-99, as well as her new book (*The Cult of Asherah*); see also Judith McKinlay, *Gendering Wisdom the Host: Biblical Invitations to Eat and Drink* (JSOTSup, 216; GCT, 4; Sheffield: Sheffield Academic Press, 1996), pp. 17-37; Ze'ev Meshel, 'Did Yahweh Have a Consort?', *BARev* 5 (1979), pp. 24-35; Walter A. Maier, III, *'Asherah: Extrabiblical Evidence* (HSM, 37; Atlanta: Scholars Press, 1986); and Saul M. Olyan, *Asherah and the Cult of Yahweh in Israel* (SBLMS, 34; Atlanta, GA: Scholars Press, 1988). See also Steve Davies, 'The Canaanite-Hebrew Goddess, in Carl Olson (ed.), *The Book of the Goddess: Past and Present* (New York: Crossroad, 1985), pp. 68-79, and other articles in that volume. For a positive assessment of the Hebrew Bible's patriarchal monotheism in the context of goddesses in ancient Near Eastern culture, pressed into a defense, see Frymer-Kensky, *Goddesses*; for a different view, see Lang, *Wisdom*, and 'Lady Wisdom: A Polytheistic and Psychological Interpretation of a Biblical Goddess', in A. Brenner and C. Fontaine (eds.), *A Feminist Companion to Reading the Bible: Approaches, Methods, Strategies* (Sheffield: Sheffield Academic Press, 1997), pp. 400-25, as well as works by Keel and Schroer, mentioned above.

the thought-world of the Bible, whose putative purity must be protected at any costs!—are usually short on archaeology or literary analysis and long on apologetics, far more comfortable in choosing dates for Proverbs 1–9 that might be thought to exclude remnants of earlier goddess traditions. Fortunately, many beautifully trained, persuasive voices have been willing to call for the exploration of the No-Man's-Land of goddess worship out of whose mountains and clefts some traits of Woman Wisdom and Woman Stranger in Prov. 1–9 have been mined.

We might add that, given the work of Newsom, Camp, Keel, Lang, Yee, Maier and others,[168] the consideration of Woman Wisdom apart from her twin, Woman Stranger, is not a tenable working method. Both characters are bound up together, displacing and inverting the features of the other to suit the rhetorical strategy of the sages. In fact, it often seems to be the case that a 'great' goddess in all her ambiguous unity is 'divided' up when she comes to life in the pages of the Hebrew Bible: her good and noble features are projected upon Woman Wisdom; her negative characteristics are used to craft the figure of Woman Stranger. Neither is complete without the other: sun and shadow, they are twin sides of the same phenomenon—perceptions of genuine female power, and patriarchal society's acknowledgment of it in order to control it. This is not an uncommon development in cults and mythologies of a/the Great Goddess; Norse materials on the goddess Freyja show the same jumble of traits that are increasingly keyed into roles that emphasize her sexuality, as understood from the males' point of view.[169] Similarly, in the ancient Near East, we see over the course of time a consistent drive to attach other anomalous features to a 'great' goddess like Inanna-Ishtar or Isis, deriving from a conflation of local manifestations of the goddess from a variety of times

---

168. See nn. 40 and 42 above, as well as Christl Maier, *Die 'fremde Frau' in Proverbien 1-9: Eine exegetische und sozialgeschichtliche Studie* (OBO, 144; Göttingen: Universitätsverlag Freiburg Schweiz, Vandenhoeck & Ruprecht, 1995); Gale A. Yee, '"I Have Perfumed My Bed with Myrrh": The Foreign Woman ('iššâ zārâ) in Proverbs 1–9', in A. Brenner (ed.), *Feminist Companion to Wisdom Literature* (FCB, 9; Sheffield: Sheffield Academic Press, 1995), pp. 110-26; for Camp's most recent take on the Strange Woman, see her *Holy*, pp. 40-71.

169. Nässtrom, *Freyja*, p. 73. Nässtrom lists the following as qualities of a Great Goddess: she is autonomous, decides fate, is associated with earth but may appear as a sky-goddess; usually connected with the moon (seldom the sun), and has a character comprising both good and evil aspects that are often divided into two separate goddesses. Such goddesses have widespread cults that include both men and women worshipers.

and places. In fact, then, such replete entities are not examples of cosmic females with dangerous 'bi-polar' disorders, as some moderns would have it; rather, as we find them in their (often unrelated) texts, they have been the subjects of a long tradition of embellishment and amalgamation.[170] Even were this *not* so, literary theory suggests that fully developed characters routinely display inconsistencies, growth, change and unexpected features; this is the very mark of their fullness as characters. Woman Wisdom and Woman Stranger in Proverbs 1–9 might not, then, be simply a tricky splitting off of Madonna from Whore; rather, from the hands of our sages, we have characters whose motives and actions require us to view them as charmingly round and fruitfully substantive.

That Woman Wisdom and Woman Stranger are in some way *literary* all would agree; the meanings assigned to this personification vary widely, however. Attempts to understand this literary personification have proceeded in several directions: Woman Wisdom as a literary device that is an *abstract*, metonymic *concept* representing something else; or Woman Wisdom/Woman Stranger as a literary character best understood as *person*, real or divine. Within each group, scholars submit nuanced and differentiated positions for their readers' consideration. We need not rehearse here each and every variation on the scholarly themes, as others have already done so. Rather we will consider briefly the roles of Wisdom and Stranger as characters whose specialty is verbal performance.

Woman Wisdom as an Abstraction
Within this category, the figure of Woman Wisdom is understood as a hypostasis, the voice of creation or world-order reaching out to (male) humans, an abstraction of the sages' teachings, or simply a gendered personification.

Hypostasis. This position sees Woman Wisdom as an amplification of one of the qualities of the 'High God' Yahweh. The knowledge of God displays a separate, free-standing identity as Woman Wisdom.[171] The wisdom

---

170. See, for example, volume 1 of the new journal *NIN: Journal of Gender Studies in Antiquity*, which is entirely devoted to Inanna–Ishtar, and her polarities in character. Similarly, the 'early' Isis of the Middle and New Kingdoms in Egypt *is* a trickster and a magician, and not simply the splendid nurturing mother-goddess of the Hellenistic period.

171. From this perspective, one wonders what part of the divine character Woman Stranger represents!

of God, a phenomenon found mainly in late texts,[172] takes on a differentiated life of its own. God's wisdom essentially represents an aspect of
omniscience and the ability to act productively; and this becomes embodied as Woman Wisdom. Like the 'hand of God' in Ezekiel or the 'Word of
the Lord' in Jeremiah, this element of the divine serves as a surrogate
through which God's will is performed and fulfilled. The advantage of this
position is that it is able to downplay Wisdom's separation from God
(which might point to extra-biblical sources for the figure), which in turn
allows us to understand the figure as an authentically Israelite, Yahwistic
figure. Particularly important to this view is Woman Wisdom's origin
from and dependency on Yahweh (Prov. 8.22-31). If the period from
which these texts come is one of social disintegration and theological
anomie, then the *Ḥokmâ* hypostasy acts to fill the ever-widening gap
between God and humans—but in fact, this reading of the socio-political
background of Proverbs 1–9 is roundly disputed.[173]

This disadvantage of this position is that it takes a female character and
renders it male-by-implication (based on origin), without really accounting
for its presentation as female in the first place. While some may find this
advantageous for the attempt to craft more woman-friendly New Testament Christologies, it is less clear that this is a useful approach for
solving interpretive problems in Proverbs. Although the Hebrew Bible
makes full use of concepts of hypostasy, it is still true that we may better
account for the relationship between Yahweh and Woman Wisdom by
consideration of the various literary roles performed by these two figures
in wisdom texts, a strategy that allows us to retain the elements of Woman
Wisdom's character which hint at her pre-existence, or at least distinct
existence at Yahweh's side during creation.

What is of interest, from the point of view of the present work, is the
odd transformation at work in any such hypostatization: when the intellectual aspect of God takes on its new life as *Ḥokmâ*, 'it' becomes a 'she'!
Why? But, then again, why *not*? Some deeper message beyond that of
grammatical gender is being marked out by our texts when the authors
choose to clothe intellectual pursuit and rectitude in female dress.

Woman Wisdom as an Abstraction of Something Else. By ignoring the
human and divine prototypes of Woman Wisdom and Woman Stranger,

---

172. G. Baumann, *Die Weisheitsgestalt in Proverbien 1–9: Traditionsgeschichtliche
und theologische Studien* (FAT, 16; Tübingen: J.C.B. Mohr [Paul Siebeck], 1996).

173. Fox, *Proverbs 1–9*, pp. 342-45.

some commentators on the text have preferred to deal minimally with the significance of this female imagery. In such treatments, Woman Wisdom and Woman Stranger become bare literary maneuvers whose symbolic import *as female* becomes relatively inconsequential in the eyes of these readers, despite its atypical emergence in androcentric literature. Woman Wisdom is seen as the incarnation of the sages' teachings (but why as a female?) or the voice of the world-order addressing men (chosen because 'world', like 'woman', constitutes a philosophically 'contingent' category?), or as a sort of Teacher Temptress, prodding male students to greater erudition by use of sexually nuanced discourse (but wouldn't male students become distracted, thereby undercutting this strategy?). Some downplay the erotic character of Woman Wisdom's speeches, and note the way that poems about or speeches by Woman Wisdom often integrate prophetic techniques of rhetoric. As a result, the figure is then viewed as prophet, preacher and poet. However, it seems doubtful that any ancient male would have regarded a female figure raising her voice in the thoroughfares in such a favorable fashion. Brenner's image of the 'female scold' accounts for the same features of discourse, and has better social and literary parallels behind it.

For those who consider Woman Wisdom as a metonymic figure who represents something else that is bigger, more important or more abstract, the element of gender is evaluated in several ways. The metaphorization of the female body elsewhere in the Hebrew Bible seldom carries a positive interpretation: female sexuality becomes a metaphor for elite male political apostasy. Female barrenness (Hannah) or subjectivity in the moment of birth-giving (Yahweh in 2nd Isaiah) are likewise used to refer to negative features of experience attributed to the land or its god. So, the use of the female metaphor should not automatically suggest woman-friendly content. If creation reaches out as a woman, it is because in the patriarchal world Woman nurtures Man. Hence, the selection of female gender carries a negative message: caretaker rather than actor, this better expresses an anthropocentric theology of the earth as God's creation, inferior in status to both God and Man. Seldom does the female player in this drama function as an equal partner in a relationship of mutuality; she is no more than a bit player who empowers men's undertakings.

Carol Newsom argues that if the Sages' teachings are imagined as speaking in a woman's voice, then this voice is no friend to women. The teachings placed in Wisdom's mouth support an elite, hierarchical worldview that can hardly be characterized as attentive to issues of female worth and dignity. Wisdom, then, becomes the 'public' voice of the father-sage's 'private' teachings, male ideology incarnate. Again, the female gender is considered a negative feature of the text, construed as an example of the co-option and deformation of female experience such that it is made to witness against itself at the same time it suborns young men into the ideology that will make them masters rather than mistresses. Trapped within the patriarchal father's discourse, whose aim is to defeat the claims of all other competing voices, Wisdom's speech is powerful indeed. To turn a deaf ear to this voice is like ignoring one's own mother or father—a wonderful touch of guilt-tripping provided by the male sages to make their recommendations seem impossible to refute or refuse.[174]

Another trivialization of gender through abstraction comes with those who assert that the literary personification is a mere device, drawing its functional life from the simple fact that abstract nouns are feminine in Hebrew. But this view overlooks the feminist critique to be made of gender in language. Abstraction is understood as in some sense 'female' precisely because the *male* experience is the ontologically 'really Real' against which the language measures all else. Not without reason are the basic paradigms of verbs and nouns presented to first-year Hebrew students with the 'masculine singular' forms labeled as the 'base' or typical forms! All other endings that mark the feminine or the plural are created by *adding* particles to the third person masculine singular 'unmarked' or 'light' forms! This very concept of 'unmarked' forms tells us that the naked, base form—singular male!—is considered to be *the most commonplace and important* for understanding the language.[175]

With this critique in mind, we might ask why the gender of Woman Wisdom should go *un*remarked by scholars? The 'simple' literary device of an abstract feminine noun 'speaking' is itself a sign, marked at the most basic level of language, of the *a-typical*, the out-of-the-ordinary, that which is hard to know and even more difficult to express. If what is real and powerful is male, then what is female is unreal and ineffectual. Is this truly the most effective strategy for the presentation of teachings that the young should assimilate? In fact, in my reconstruction here the gender of the literary device signals a 'value' assessment by the authors of Proverbs

174. Newsom, 'Discourse', pp. 142-60.

175. An analogy for this might be made from the sporting world of American baseball. The 'balls' thrown by a pitcher (considered so because they fall outside of the zone for legal pitches) in baseball go unmarked by the referee since it is presumed that they are the norm. Only the 'strikes'—the balls that fly in the designated hitting zone—merit special notation by the referee, since they are *not* the norm.

1–9; it deserves *more* attention as an analytical category, not less, from scholars of a linguistic bent. The modern saying that 'Sticks and stones can break my bones, but words will never hurt me!' is often used by caregivers to offer comfort to those being teased or diminished by taunts and stereotypes, but closer analysis suggests another (an Other?) view. Academy or world of faith—we live by words, imposing meaning and creating worlds with them. Only when pressed into a corner by logical arguments do we resort to the fiction that words 'don't mean anything'. As in other areas, gender matters for interpretive work because it constitutes a category in those things being interpreted.

Woman Wisdom as Person
Woman Wisdom as an Israelite/Jewish Woman. The work of C. Camp, G. Baumann and S. Schroer, among others, has questioned the potentially misogynist argument for a divine precursor of Woman Wisdom that ignores the real, human role models that might have given rise to personified Wisdom in Israel. After examining the literary roles played by women in the Hebrew Bible and relating them to the social roles of real women, Camp was able to isolate a number of features present in Woman Wisdom and Woman Stranger that result from literary traditions about women and their roles in society. These include: wife and mother; lover; harlot and adulteress, the wise woman, the wily woman (uses indirect means to achieve her goals), and the female authenticator of written traditions (e.g. Huldah, Esther). Camp suggests that the social crises of the postexilic period provided the impetus for drawing on family-centered imagery to the wisdom tradition embodied in Proverbs. She further argues that Woman Wisdom replaces the king as mediator for those who seek to understand God's new ways of interacting with the human community.[176] Moreover, since the feminine is always viewed as ancillary and contingent within androcentric thought, it serves logically as a natural mediator between a male god and the male students who are the sages' implied audience.

In examining further the literary roles played by Israelite/Jewish women as these affect the interpretation of Woman Wisdom, we might note that many of these characterizations fall within the sphere of the 'sought-for person' (the 'princess-bride' awarded to successful heroes) so often found in folk literature. Although Woman Wisdom and Woman Stranger are literary—that is, written—constructs, they exist in and must be related to the world of oral literature with its tales, lullabies, love songs and

176. Camp, *Wisdom*, pp. 79-149.

proverbial teachings about gender. We should not be inordinately surprised then to find that Wisdom's 'story' is fleshed out along the lines of traditional storytelling, *and* told largely from the perspective of the male hero![177] In the world of oral conventions, we find the bride who is also an adviser and assistant to her prospective mate, the wife who brings a dowry of knowledge, blessings and experience to the hero through their marriage, and the (royal) father who awards the sought-for bride to the hero after his successful conclusion of a long search or set of arduous tasks. Later, when Bride becomes Mother, she is often the source for decoding the riddles of life, the meanings of dreams and the right path for her offspring. Most of these roles are preserved in the relationship between Yahweh, Woman Wisdom, and the scribal student (male) who is enjoined to seek her. Woman Wisdom is imaged as Yahweh's daughter in Prov. 8.23-25 (and the matter is open as to whether or not Yahweh should be considered 'father' or 'mother' to Woman Wisdom, as the Hebrew used in 8.25, usually translated as 'brought forth', refers primarily to the female role in birth-giving). Yahweh presents Wisdom, a better 'bride' than all those the king chose for himself, to Solomon in 1 Kings 3, thus legalizing the rule of an other-than-firstborn. Similarly, in Prov. 4.8, young men are told to 'embrace' Woman Wisdom as their mate and to 'grasp' her and her teachings (3.18; 4.13). Using this reconstruction, we can readily understand the figure of Woman Stranger as folk literature's 'false bride', whose claims sound so much like her legitimate rival's (cf. Prov. 9). The language of love and desire applied to the sought-for one, Woman Wisdom, continues into the Greco-Roman period (so Wisd. Sol. 6.12-16; 8.2, 16; Sir. 14; 15; 51), as does the ongoing demonization of Woman Stranger. From Qumran to the Zohar, Woman Stranger is made the epitome of demonic folly which leads men to death.

Scholars have become increasingly comfortable with assessing the role of goddesses who gave their gifts of character and action to the literary roles played by these two figures in wisdom texts, since it is quite possible to acknowledge such influences as models for Woman Wisdom and

177. My presumption is that if Woman Wisdom's story had been told by female storytellers, we would have been treated to many more domestic scenes involving marriage arrangements, household management and rearing of children in the home— that is, the marker's of 'women's culture' (J. Bekkenkamp and F. van Dijk, 'The Canon of the Old Testament and Women's Cultural Traditions', in Athalya Brenner (ed.), *A Feminist Companion to the Song of Songs* (FCB, 1; Sheffield: JSOT Press, 1993), pp. 67-85; A. Brenner, 'Women Poets and Authors', in *Song of Songs*, pp. 86-99; Meyers, 'Returning Home', pp. 85-115).

Woman Stranger without actually equating them with the figures presented in Proverbs.[178] As Baumann points out, although one is not *required* to understand Woman Wisdom as a personal scribal goddess, followers are urged to love her as if she *were* a personal goddess. The ambiguities of the description of the Wisdom Figure in Prov. 1–9 leave open a level of personal choice in how much one should allow this female source of Wisdom to function in a goddess-like capacity within a monotheistic, androcentric context.[179]

Woman Wisdom/Woman Stranger as Goddess Survivals. In acknowledging the international, especially Egyptian, influence on the first nine chapters of Proverbs, some scholars view Woman Wisdom as an Israelite/ Jewish adaptation of the legacy of goddess mythology in the ancient Near East, or as a survival of a legitimate[180] Canaanite/Israelite goddess who was once worshiped and known in the shape of a tree (Asherah).[181] McKinlay and Clifford have both convincingly dealt with the mythological 'banquet-type scene' that sets the stage for both cosmic females' offers in Proverbs 9.[182] It is not our purpose here to sift through each and every goddess known to us from the various cultures surrounding ancient Israel, since the major contenders for *Ḥokmâ*'s precursors have been so well studied in recent works. We will, however, survey both character traits and actions (functions) played in the plot patterns of the relevant goddess mythologies that have received less attention, and which form part of Hebrew *Ḥokmâ*'s genealogy. It should be emphasized here that such parallels are not meant to suggest Proverbs 1–9's *direct* dependence on foreign texts and models;[183] rather, these divine females existed in the oral world of storytellers, glyptic and monumental art, as well as the literary imagination of scribes. Our sages and scribes who composed and edited

178. Fox, *Proverbs 1–9*, pp. 334-38.
179. 'Eine gottähnliche Gestalt neben JHWH' (Baumann, *Weisheitsgestalt*, p. 313).
180. That is, known to and revered in the official cults of Israel and Judah.
181. McKinlay, *Gendering*, pp. 17-37.
182. McKinlay, *Gendering*, pp. 38-65; Clifford, *Proverbs 1–9*, pp. 27-28, 101-107; see also Carole Fontaine, 'The Deceptive Goddess in Ancient Near Eastern Myth: Inanna and Inaras', in J. Cheryl Exum and Johanna Bos (eds.), *Reasoning among the Foxes: Women in a World of Male Power* (Semeia, 42; Atlanta: Scholars Press, 1988), pp. 84-102, for discussion of the role of gender in the type-scene.
183. Of course, Prov. 22.17–24.22 *is* directly dependent on the Egyptian composition, *The Instruction of Amenemope*, so we must not dismiss the possibility of direct interaction between literary texts out of hand.

Proverbs 1–9 existed in that same world of orality and artifact, and even though they are the very circle whom we might consider *most* likely to have known and read the texts of other cultures, we can just as easily account for any parallels by reference to the larger fluid world of shared motifs and plots.

Egyptian Echoes in Proverbs
Maat. The goddess Maat stood for justice, rectitude, and social and cosmic order. She was literally the foundation of the throne of the Pharaoh (cf. Prov. 8.15-16) and provided the measure against which the hearts of the dead were judged in the underworld (see the biblical transformation of this motif in Prov. 16.2; 21.2; 24.12). Scholars who view her as a prototype or at least a close sister to the Hebrew Wisdom Figure offer the following traits in order to establish this link. Maat is the first creation of the creator god in one Egyptian myth, and in various texts she is conceived as both his daughter and the master plan by which he creates. Though never appearing as either a full-service 'personal goddess' or a particularly active character[184] in the mythological texts[185] that survive from ancient Egypt, she is nonetheless, an important figure/concept in Egyptian wisdom instructions. Protective amulets with her ostrich feather symbol were worn by sages as well as placed around the necks of the dead in hope of securing a good judgment. She is often depicted holding an ankh, the symbol of life in one hand and a scepter, a symbol of power, in the other. Such symbols remind one of the image of Woman Wisdom in 3.16, with long life in her right hand and honor and wealth in her left. In the *Book of the Dead*, the deceased was led into the Hall of Double Truth (Maat) for judgment; this 'doubling' of Maat may refer to both of the entrance pillars in the shape of this goddess in the judgment hall, or perhaps to the possibility of two *different judgments*, one positive, one negative, which might be made over the dead supplicant.[186] If the latter interpretation is the case, then we are

184. By active character, we mean one that is fully rounded, displaying ambiguities of behavior or ongoing growth over time, and one who engages in the activities of perceiving (usually 'seeing' or 'hearing' in the Hebrew Bible), speaking (which is also the way plans and feelings are conveyed in Hebrew narrative) and acting.

185. In the New Kingdom tale, *Truth and Falsehood*, Maat (Truth) is male rather than female, so this cannot be counted as a genuine occurrence of the goddess personified, and she plays no role in the *Contendings of Horus and Seth*, although Isis and Hathor both appear there as active characters.

186. J. Gwyn Griffiths, *The Conflict of Horus and Seth from Egyptian and Classical Sources* (Liverpool: Liverpool University Press, 1960), pp. 56-57.

put forcibly in mind of the cosmic female 'twins' of Proverbs 1–9, Woman Wisdom and Woman Stranger/Folly, association with whom signals markedly different fates—life or death!—to those who consort with them.

In fact, a close textual study made by Egyptologist M. Lichtheim shows that Maat is without question more a 'concept' than a 'person', despite her brief mythological notices mentioned above.[187] Scribes, state and city officials all speak of 'doing Maat', 'raising/lifting Maat up to the god X', or 'offering Maat', making it clear that this is public virtue rather than a private personal goddess, one expressing proper positive social values in one's conduct as a leader. The terminology linked with Maat in the context of public rectitude of leaders includes the following elements: benevolence, charity, justice, impartiality, conciliating litigants, shunning evil and evildoers, loyalty, obedience, self-knowledge, attention to the will of the gods.[188] The outcome of doing Maat is felt both during life and later in judgment during the afterlife—suggesting that there is a fair element of self-serving interest to be found in the personal piety of leaders. Maxims number 5 and 19 in the *Instruction of Ptahhotep* (5th Dynasty) sum up the didactic writers' approach to Maat:

> Great is Maat, lasting in effect,
> undisturbed since the time of Osiris.
> For one punishes the breaker of laws,
> though the greedy one…overlooks this.

> While baseness…may seize riches,
> crime…never lands its wares.
> In the end it is Maat that lasts,
> man says, 'it is my father's ground'.

> That man endures whose rule is Maat,
> who walks a straight line.
> He will make a will by it,
> one who is greedy has no tomb.[189]

At the end of the 18th Dynasty when the usurper Pharaoh Haremhab put an end to the monotheistic experiments of Akhenaton, we find in his tomb a brief, but more convincing occasion of a full-bodied personification of Maat. Haremhab's Memphis tomb contains a statue of that pharaoh in adoration of the gods Rē-Harakhti (the creator sun-god), Thoth (the scribal

---

187. *Maat in Egyptian Autobiographies and Related Studies* (OBO, 120; Freiburg: Universitätsverlag; Göttingen: Vandehoeck & Ruprecht, 1992).

188. Lichtheim, *Maat*, p. 151.

189. Lichtheim, *Maat*, p. 16.

god and secretary of the gods), and Maat, each addressed with a lyric prayer (BM Stele 551). Maat takes on full goddess-hood as the new Pharaoh invokes her to emphasize his public virtue in restoring the old faith:

> ...Praise to Maat, our Lady of the Northwind,
> who opens the nostrils of the living,
> and who gives air to the One in the midst his bark.
> Allow Prince Haremhab to breathe the breezes borne of heaven
> just as the Lady of Punt breathes her aromas from the Lake of Myrrh.[190]

From the same restoration period, we also have a 'Maat-litany' preserved in the Theban tomb of Neferhotep, chief scribe of Amun. Here again we see Maat more fully personified as the daughter of the sun-god Rē:

> O Rē who sets with Maat,
> Maat is joined to his brow.
> O Rē who rises with Maat,
> Maat embraces his beauty.
> O Rē, effective through Maat,
> Maat is secured to his bark.
> O Rē mighty through Maat,
> whereon he lives every day.
> O Rē who made Maat,
> and whom one offers Maat:
> You placed Maat in my heart
> that I may raise her up to your ka!
> I know you live by her
> and it is you who made her body.
> I am a straight one free of lies,
> who does not practice deception.
> Gods, lords of the two Maats,
> May you receive Amun's scribe Neferhotep, justified, in peace, in peace.[191]

Here, the portrait of Maat beautifully captures the gendered predicament of female figures in all of the ancient Near East's wisdom thinking: although strong and powerful, she is subordinated to the male god as a function of *his* nature. Her 'embrace' of the sun-god's beauty signifies her transition from active female character to a possession or trait manifested in the more important male. Like a human daughter, she is 'made' by her

---

190. J.L. Foster (trans.) and S.T. Hollis (ed.), *Hymns, Prayers, and Songs: An Anthology of Ancient Egyptian Lyric Poetry* (WAW, 8; Atlanta: Scholars Press, 1995), p. 113.

191. Lichtheim, *Maat*, p. 65.

father and belongs to him; she is 'placed' in the heart of another man, who offers her back to the giver! Both god and his follower almost seem to 'feed' off the female as she is passed back and forth between males, another analogue to the commodification of women throughout most of antiquity. What seems to be a celebration of a goddess is in reality praise of the god who possesses her—not so far from the thinking of Proverbs 8, as interpreted by most conventional scholars!

From the Persian period (Dynasty 27, c. 521–486 BCE), we find a hymn to Maat in the Temple of Amun at el-Hibis, with similar sentiments:

> Praise to you, Maat, daughter of Rē,
> > consort of god, whom Ptah loves,
> The one who adorns the breast of Thoth, who fashioned her own nature...
> Who pacified the two falcon gods through her good will...
> Skilled one who brought forth the gods from herself
> > and brought low the heads of the enemies;
> Who herself provides for the House of the All-Lord,
> > brings daily offerings for those who are on duty.
> Magnificent her throne before the judges—
> > and she consumes the enemies of Atum.
> She is just,
> > and there is no injustice in the Son of Rē, who lives forever...
>
> Rise splendidly, O Rē,
> > how beautiful you are because of Maat!
> As Maat shines splendid from the heart of Rē,
> > so are you splendid, O King, Son of Rē, who lives forever;
> You too are beautiful because of Maat...
>
> O Maat, build your throne in the head, in the mouth,
> > of the King, Son of Rē, who lives forever!
> May you make heaven and earth rejoice in Rē his father
> > from whom I, the King, have come forth.
> May you rise splendid from him on this beautiful day...
> And may your beautiful face give peace
> > to this good god, lord of the Two Lands, Darius,
> > > Son of the Sun and living forever.[192]

It is easy to see why Maat achieved her zenith of personification in the two periods from which these hymns come: in each case, there is some question about the status of right belief or a need to bolster the status of the pharaoh who lauds this goddess. Haremhab, though welcomed for his final subjugation of Akhenaton's experiment with Aton-worship, was

192. Foster, *Hymns*, pp. 122-23.

nevertheless *not* the legitimate ruler, and needed the extra cachet of Maat to sustain his claims to the throne. Darius, a Persian ruler, must somehow become the true son of Egypt by embracing the notion of divine parentage from the sun god Rē. In both contexts, the restoration of Maat by the king gestures toward the cosmic order of *right faith and practice*, so important to the ideology of rulership in Egypt. What better goddess than Maat to put the final seal of approval on the activities of these out-of-line monarchs!

Women and Maat. It is interesting to note that women are seldom accorded the virtues of Maat in their laudatory funeral inscriptions, nor are they a focus of 'doing Maat' except for the typical wisdom statements about protection of widows. This is precisely because the 'public' domain has been 'gendered' as male,[193] and so its ethical piety has very little to do with women, either as practitioners or recipients of Maat. One exception to this observation is the granddaughter of Osorkon II whose statue has been preserved among the those of the priests of Amun of Thebes during the 22nd and 23rd Dynasties in the so-called Karnak Cache. *Šb-n-spdt*'s statue was dedicated by her husband Hor, and on it she is accorded a Maat epithet:

> One virtuous like me, noble lady who knows her speech,
> king's daughter, good-natured, pure-handed withal...
>
> Skilled in speech whereof the fragrance of myrrh.
> While I dwelled on earth I spoke truth to all.[194]

Here then is another highborn female noted for her 'smooth words' of rectitude—her language skills are so heady that they are compared to the esteemed aromatic fragrance of myrrh. Like the Strong Woman of Proverbs 31 and Queen Tiye of the Amarna letters, knowledge and speech are the hallmarks of her ethical bearing. Though none of our texts actually portray Maat speaking, where human women and Maat *do* intersect, the disadvantaged (widows) find justice and the elite find a voice that can be valued within their culture. Given the talkative, energetic nature of *Ḥokmâ* and the skilled speech of her strange, foreign, foolish counterparts, the silent, static Maat does not present a very compelling paradigm from

---

193. Women in Egypt seldom held public office outside of temple service as musicians, chantresses and wab-priestesses.
194. Lichtheim, *Maat*, pp. 84-85.

which our sages might have borrowed the main features of the females of Proverbs' cosmic domain.

Hathor and Isis. Of the more 'active' Egyptian goddesses, Hathor, 'Lady of the Sycamore Tree', is well attested in glyptic and decorative arts in Canaan throughout the Bronze Age. This is accounted for not only by the proximity of Egypt to Canaan (and later Judah and Israel), but also the unceasing attempts of the Pharaohs to use the Levantine land-bridge as a buffer zone between themselves and first the Hittite Empire of Anatolia, then the Syrians, Assyrians, Babylonians and Persians. This political agenda insured that Egyptian art and preferences in depiction of the divine would find their way into the Bible's territory as surely as the colonists' defensive garrisons, which had been built to monitor border activities that might have imperiled their imperialist homeland. Literally, Hathor's name, *Ht.Hr*, means 'House of Horus', thus giving an example of an extra-biblical metaphorization of the goddess that links her to the 'appropriate' female role of enabler of the more important male. She was known in the southern Levant as 'Lady of the Turquoise' (Sinai peninsula) and in the north as 'Lady of Byblos', and her name occurs in the biblical place name 'Pihahiroth' (RSV), or 'House of Hathor' in Exod. 14.2, 9; Num. 33.7-8. Hathor is easily identified by the fact that she is shown frontally, rather than in profile, thus displaying her distinctive hairstyle (a sort of bouffant flip), her headgear (tell-tale cow ears, sometimes in conjunction with horns that flank a sun disk topped with the Uraeus), and her characteristic cultic, musical instruments, the *mnj.t.* and sistrum. As the Eye of the Sun, she was also especially associated with gold —its inexhaustible radiance and its preciousness. The iconography used to represent her as tree-goddess may also be behind some of the naked female figure pendants also popular in Bronze Age Canaan, since they sometimes show a blending of Egyptian traits with vegetal motifs.[195] Hathor was much more of a 'full-service' goddess than Maat; she was worshiped and revered by both sexes, although she was noted for her special connection to women. As the cosmic wild cow, she was a figure of power and fertility par excellence. As a tree-goddess, she offered hope of refreshment and immortality to the dead. Further, Hathor was featured in contexts of love and fertility, acrobatics and festivals, military might and revenge (imaged as a lioness),

195. Othmar Keel and Christoph Uehlinger, *Gods, Goddesses, and Images of God in Ancient Israel* (trans. T.H. Trapp; Philadelphia: Fortress Press, 1998), pp. 19-108; see esp. figures on pp. 21, 27, 55, 67.

and held the roles of mother of the sun and the wife of the sun-god in Helio-polis and Edfu. Clearly bearing aspects of sky-goddesses, she assimilated some traits of the Vulture protective mother-goddess Mut, the lion war-goddess Tefnut, and other tree-goddesses like Isis. Hathor was distinguished in at least 18 different versions in Egypt, and a special group of 'Seven Hathors' foretold the fate of particular children. From this brief summary, it is easy to see that she bears the same weight of contradictory images, origins and roles that may be observed parceled out among Yahweh and Woman Wisdom\Woman Stranger. However, the Hebrew Bible prefers to project the ambivalent aspects of the goddess onto Woman Stranger, thereby preserving the Wisdom Figure's positive, nurturing functions without much hint of her shadowy, aggressive side showing through.[196]

Hathor's role as the goddess of love, honored in acrobatic displays,[197] brings certain features of *Ḥokmâ* in Proverbs 1–9 forcibly to mind. *Ḥokmâ* is clearly imaged as a desirable lover for a man in 4.6-9 and 7.4-5 with vocabulary redolent of wholesome appetites described in the Song of Songs,[198] and this portrait would be familiar to those who adored Hathor. In the Egyptian love poetry corpus, Hathor plays a significant role in her aspect of the 'Golden Goddess'. In the Chester Beatty Love Songs, the restless girl bemoans her inability to be intimate with her lover, to whom Hathor has given her:

> My heart is troubled whenever he is thought of:
> his love possesses me.
> See, he is mindless,
> yet I am like him.

---

196. M. Heerma van Voss, 'Hathor', in K. Van der Toorn, B. Becking and P.W. van der Horst (eds.), *Dictionary of Deities and Demons in the Bible* (Leiden: E.J. Brill, 1995), pp. 732-33; C.J. Bleeker, *Hathor and Thoth: Two Key Figures of the Ancient Egyptian Religion* (SHR, 26; Leiden: E.J. Brill, 1973), excerpted in 'Isis and Hathor: Two Ancient Egyptian Goddess', in Carl Olson (ed.), *The Book of the Goddess: Past and Present* (New York: Crossroad, 1983), pp. 29-48.

197. Are these to be associated with erotic practices?

198. R.E. Murphy, 'Wisdom and Eros in Prov 1–9', *CBQ* 50 (1988), pp. 600-603, and *Proverbs*, pp. 27, 43; Clifford, *Proverbs*, pp. 61-62, 87; Fox, *Proverbs*, pp. 294-95. Interesting, however, is Fox's failure to cite 'lover' among his list in his discussion 'Models for Wisdom' (pp. 333-41). This may be because he sees the 'mother' role of Lady Wisdom excluding the possibility of a 'lover' role. Goddess mythology suggests otherwise: the Great Mother is often found in the role of consort to her Son (cf. discussion of Isis below).

> He does not know my lust to embrace him,
> or that he could write my mother.
> Lover, I am given over to you
> by the Golden Goddess of womankind.[199]

Later, the girl's lover, suffering from the same frustrated longing, turns directly to Hathor for help:

> I praise the Golden Goddess,
> I exalt Her Majesty.
> I raise high the Lady of Heaven,
> I make praise for Hathor,
> and chants for my Mistress.
>
> I tell Her all, that She may hear my plaints;
> so may my Lady give her to me...
>
> So I'll make a vow to my Goddess,
> and She'll give me the lady love as a present in return.[200]

Equally important is Hathor's connection to dancing and acrobatics, since this may be one of the many models for the notorious passage about *Ḥokmâ* in 8.30-31. *Ḥokmâ* says that at the time of creation, she was daily at Yahweh's side as an *'āmôn* (אמון), 'frolicking' (*meśaheqet*; cf. Ps. 104.26b for the same usage) before him. Although O. Keel made the argument based on Egyptian iconography that the forerunner of this scene must be Maat playing before the high gods, in fact (as Fox rightly points out), it is Hathor who is routinely imaged in such scenes.[201]

In an odd little tale from the New Kingdom in Egypt—a time period notable for the coarse humor and brusque images not usually found in the more 'sophisticated' literary traditions of Middle Kingdom Egypt—we meet both Hathor and Isis playing signal roles in 'The Contendings of Horus and Seth', a story about a dispute over power and succession among males.[202] The great gods are in dispute over whom shall receive the powers and rule of the dead god Osiris: should it be his (dastardly) brother

---

199. W.K. Simpson (ed.), *The Literature of Ancient Egypt: An Anthology of Stories, Instruction and Poetry* (New Haven: Yale University Press, new edn, 1973), p. 317.

200. Simpson, *Literature*, p. 319. The same sentiments appear in the Chester Beatty Cycle of Three Songs, voiced by the girl in third-person voice (p. 323).

201. O. Keel, 'Die Weisheit "spielt" vor Gott', *Freiburger Zeitschrift für Philosophie und Theologie* 21 (1974), pp. 1-66; Fox, *Proverbs 1–9*, p. 288.

202. Simpson, *Literature*, pp. 108-26; Lichtheim, *Literature*, II, pp. 214-23; see also Griffiths, *Conflict*.

Seth, who is roundly implicated in Osiris' death, or his son Horus, by the goddess Isis? At first, the god Shu rules that the son of Osiris should receive the offices of his father. While Horus's mother Isis shrieks delight-edly at this legal decision, Pre-Harakhti takes it badly (since he favored Seth's petition) and asks for another opinion. The gods requested to give the ruling suggest that the Universal Lord (the sun-god Re-Atum/Pre-Harakhti) to send to the Great Goddess Neith to judge between the uncle and the nephew. Letters are exchanged between Thoth and Neith, and Neith weighs in with her verdict: the office of Osiris should be given to the son Horus, but Seth's holdings should be doubled and his virility recog-nized with the gift of two Semitic goddesses (Anat and Astarte) to be his consorts. Should the gods do otherwise, the Great Mother Neith will cause the sky to crash to the ground in protest.

Again, Pre-Harakhti is filled with chagrin and insults Horus brutally: why, the young god's mouth still tastes bad—just like an infant's! The gathering of gods is no less pleased with Pre-Harakhti's verdict than that god was pleased with the decision of Neith, and more insults are ex-changed. 'Your shrine is empty!' cries the god Bebon to Pre-Harakhti, the Universal Lord, suggesting that a god who refuses to give justice in accordance with the general wishes of the gods is no god at all.[203] In response to the general divine outrage of the Ennead, Pre-Harakhti spends the day 'lying on his back in his pavilion very much saddened and alone by himself'.[204]

The situation is one that is not unfamiliar in the household of kings: when thwarted in their exercise of power, sulking is the order of the day and only an insult from a female is sufficient to prod the ruler from the solitary bed where he nurses his battered male ego. When Naboth the farmer refuses to sell Ahab of Israel his family garden, a similar vignette ensues:

> And Ahab went into his house vexed and sullen because of what Naboth the Jezreelite had said to him; for he had said, 'I will not give you the inheri-tance of my fathers'. And he lay down on his bed, and turned away his face, and would eat no food. But Jezebel his wife came to him, and said to him, 'Why is your spirit so vexed that you eat no food?' And he said to her,

---

203. Lichtheim (*Literature*, II, p. 223 n. 7) suggests this means something like 'Go home!' but given the nature of what follows, the insult seems greater than 'Get out of town!' Rather, we should understand here that the absence of the god's image occupy-ing its shrine is a symbol for the poverty of that god's power and presence.

204. Simpson, *Literature*, p. 112. This is twice repeated, indicating a major fit of pique on Pre-Harakhti's part.

> 'Because I spoke to Naboth the Jezreelite, and said to him,—"Give me your vineyard for money; or else, if it please you, I will give you another vineyard for it"; and he answered,—"I will not give you my vineyard"'. And Jezebel his wife said to him, 'Do you now govern Israel? Arise, and eat bread, and let your heart be cheerful; I will give you the vineyard of Naboth the Jezreelite' (1 Kgs 21.4-7, RSV).

In the Hebrew Bible, it is the jabbing comment of Queen Jezebel—meaning something like 'just *who* is king here, after all?'—which palliates Ahab's fit of the dismals. If he refuses to see himself as the real source of power, then his shrine will, in effect, be 'empty', too! However, Jezebel knows what she has to work with and sets about filling in for her husband's lack of decisive action. She manufactures a legal case that issues in a judgment that leaves Naboth dead and his land defaulted to the crown (Ahab!). Instead of the amusing scene of a Universal Lord sulking all alone in his pavilion after a 'walk-out' staged by the other gods, we are given a nasty editorial example of how female power begins in the bedroom but ends in the public spaces where innocent men die for their inability to control the wiles of women. (One could also choose to apportion a full range of blame to Ahab, but even with this hated king, the Bible prefers to shunt his failings onto the more 'evil' figure of his wife, as the gender code of the Deuteronomistic Historian requires.)

While Jezebel was able to exhort her supine spouse to a better mood, the god Pre-Harakhti, the Universal Lord, requires sterner measures to turn his mood sunny once more:

> After a considerable while Hathor, Lady of the Southern Sycamore, came and stood before her father, the Universal Lord, and she exposed her vagina before his very eyes. Thereupon the great god laughed at her. He got right up and sat down with the Great Ennead. He said to Horus and Seth, 'Speak concerning yourselves!'[205]

Hathor's curious action—one of those 'crude' elements of the late period—is certainly an effective strategy, far more so than the Great Goddess Neith's formal letter-message! We may wonder what it is about female genital display that causes the god's amusement, such that he can come to his senses and begin to hold court to settle the dispute between contenders for Osiris's power. Perhaps Pre-Harakhti, in the face of his own 'empty' shrine, is disempowered and potentially emasculated by Hathor's celebration and manifestation of the locus of female power and mother-right,

205. Simpson, *Literature*, p. 112.

especially since the latter is so prominently displayed in the goddesses' rulings on the dispute. Perhaps Hathor is completing the god's languid fantasy upon his couch in the vacant pavilion, allowing him to rise up, released from his troubles and with the ability to 'move on'.

But perhaps not: it is not so easy to recover the full intent of a mythological text that was probably meant to be taken as satiric even in its own time. We merely note here that, despite all Hathor's divine assistance in arranging matters of love between her human supplicants, she is also every bit as aggressive and dismissive of the male gender code as any wicked biblical queen or Strange Woman. Just as Woman Wisdom scoffs at the men who disregard her teachings, Hathor too is possessed of a self-hood that allows what is female to exist in positive, playful opposition to male 'emptyness'. When the parent-child imagery of Proverbs 8 used of Yahweh and Woman Wisdom at creation tells us that primal *Hokmâ* 'frolicks' before the Hebrew god, the subversive reader might also choose to remember Hathor at play before her father god.

The Older Isis. At this point in the tale, Isis, mother of the disputant Horus and enemy of Seth, moves into prominence as an active character. The features of the Ptolemaic Isis, grown into the role of universal, salvific mother-goddess of the ancient Mediterranean world through a long process of assimilation to other Egyptian goddesses,[206] has been much discussed with reference to its impact on the figuration of Woman Wisdom, and need not be repeated here.[207] Instead, we need to turn our

---

206. Most especially Hathor in the earlier period, and Neith in later times.

207. See, for example, L.V. Zabkar, *Hymns to Isis in her Temple at Philae* (Hanover: Brandeis University Press, 1988); J.S. Kloppenborg, 'Isis and Sophia in the Book of Wisdom', *HTR* 75 (1982), pp. 57-84; J.J. Collins, *Jewish Wisdom in the Hellenistic Age* (Louisville, KY: Westminster/John Knox Press, 1997); J.M. Robinson, 'Jesus as Sophos and Sophia: Wisdom Tradition and the Gospels', in Robert L. Wilken (ed.), *Aspects of Wisdom in Judaism and Early Christianity* (Notre Dame: University of Notre Dame Press, 1975), pp. 1-16; E. Schüssler Fiorenza, 'Wisdom Mythology and the Christological Hymns of the New Testament', in Wilken, *Aspects*, pp. 17-42; *idem*, *Jesus: Miriam's Child, Sophia's Prophet: Critical Issues in Feminist Christology* (New York: Continuum, 1994), pp. 131-62; Susan T. Hollis, 'Isis', in Serenity Young (ed.), *Encyclopedia of Women and World Religion*, I (New York: Macmillan Reference, 1999), pp. 487-88; J. Assmann, 'Isis', in K. van der Toorn, B. Becking and P.W. van der Horst (eds.), *Dictionary of Deities and Demons in the Bible* (Leiden: E.J. Brill, 1995), pp. 855-60; Fox, *Proverbs 1–9*, pp. 336-38; for a more general and 'spiritualized' study, see Caitlin Matthews, *Sophia, Goddess of Wisdom: The Divine Feminine from Black Goddess to World-Soul* (London: Grafton Books/HarperCollins, 1991).

attention to the 'early' Isis, whose roles as lady of magic and a trickster figure are of interest to us here, as a part of Woman Wisdom's and Woman Stranger's portrayal. While Isis is best known from her later cult in Ptolemaic Philae, her earlier appearances in Egyptian religion and mythology give her a rather different 'portfolio' of characterizations that go beyond her appearance as perfect wife-sister-mother of the Osiris–Horus funerary cycles. Outside of the cults of Osiris and Horus, she is associated in Koptos with the god Min, where she is understood as both his wife *and* his mother, thereby unifying the supposedly opposed roles of mother and wife to the male child who begets himself on her and then becomes her consort.

Isis's later perfection of the 'female redeemer' roles occurs, at least in part, through her assimilation of other goddesses. In the New Kingdom period, Isis is first being merged with Hathor (and Hathor-Tefnut), the fierce goddess of love and war, thus completing the Wise/Strange or Domestic/Wild continuum of female identity under patriarchal gender ideology: perfect sweetheart and perfect bitch come into creative tension in a single figure. She is identified with Sothis (Sirius), the star whose appearance heralds the beginning of the life-giving Inundation of the Nile. Writes J. Assmann of this first composite Isis:

> Isis-Hathor becomes an all-including deity: the mistress of heaven, the solar eye; the lady of the year and the inundations; the mistress of erotic love and of husbandry, motherhood and female fertility; the personification of pharaonic kingship who elects and initiates the legitimate heir; the chief magician who overcomes all dangers that menace the solar course, the life of the patient (especially the child), and even the fatal blows of death.[208]

In the Late Period, identification with Neith, another 'Cow of Heaven' in the Ramesside solar theology, gives Isis a trans-gendered aspect as a 'cosmic god'—both hidden and manifest, creator/creatrix who made the world and governs it. Further aspects of Neith[209] must be factored into the traditions of Isis and their impact on the goddess forerunners of our cosmic pair in Proverbs. Neith is a goddess of medicine, protective magic, weaving and other crafts, armaments and war, as well as the sciences. She is bisexual or beyond sex in her cosmogonic aspect; she is also associated with Maat and appears as the great serpent who protected pharaonic rulers. No wonder the Greeks so easily identified Neith with their Athena, male-

208. Assmann, 'Isis', pp. 856-57.
209. J. Assmann, 'Neith', in K. van der Toorn, B. Becking and P.W. van der Horst (eds.), *Dictionary of Deities and Demons in the Bible*, pp. 1159-63. Along with Isis, Nephthys and Serqet, Neith protects the corpse of Osiris in funerary texts.

identified goddess of wisdom! The Hellenistic transfer and then displacement of Isis mythology by Woman Wisdom as a sort of 'Jewish' substitute for the cult of the irresistible 'Cosmic Cow' of Egypt becomes a reasonable move on the part of those who sought a more 'indigenous' representation of the tradition of female embodiment of wisdom and intellectual pursuits.[210]

Returning to our tale of goddesses and their instrumental role in assuring proper succession goes to the 'correct' male,[211] the character of Isis emerges in its unusual combination of the Trickster-Mother.[212] When the Universal Lord ends his sulk and tells each rival for the office of Osiris to speak for himself, Seth leads off with a statement about his supreme virility among the Ennead, and goes on to cite his efficacy in slaying the nightly menace to the solar bark that carries the Sun through the underworld. Easily swayed by these notable conquests, the group of gods reverse their view and agree that Seth, and not Horus, should be king. But Isis becomes furious, takes an oath by Mother Neith, saying that these matters must be submitted to the gods Atum and Khepri, who actually *sit* in the Solar Bark nightly, and again the Ennead waffles its way to Isis's side. Now it is Seth's turn to be furious: he says he will kill one of the Ennead a day, and takes an oath, refusing to attend the tribunal deciding the issue should Isis the Great be part of it. Pre-Harakhti, on Seth's side all along, agrees: he tells Seth to go to a certain island and forbids the ferryman to carry across 'any woman resembling Isis'.[213]

The decrees of the male gods are no match for Isis the Trickster, however. She transforms herself into an old hag, hobbling along with a bowl full of flour. She asks for passage so she can give the young lad who is tending cattle this food, but the ferryman refuses, citing Pre-Harakhti's order. But, says the wily old woman, *that* was with respect to the woman Isis! Bribing the ferryman with a gold signet she wears, since he would not accept the cake she originally offered him, she successfully travels to the isle of the tribunal's proceedings. As she walks beneath the trees, she spots the Ennead eating with Seth and transforms herself into a gorgeous young woman, 'whose body was beautiful and whose like did not exist in the

---

210. So with Fox, *Proverbs 1–9*, p. 337.

211. Cf. the role of Wisdom as 'Power-Bride' or 'Princess-Bride' in the succession of Solomon (1 Kgs 3).

212. On tricksters generally, see Camp's *Holy*, pp. 72-143, and William J. Hynes and William G. Doty (eds.), *Mythical Trickster Figures: Contours, Contexts, and Criticisms* (Tuscaloosa: University of Alabama Press, 1993).

213. Simpson, *Literature*, p. 114.

entire land!'[214] Seth's great virility—his repeated 'selling point' to the
other gods—proves to be his undoing. As he accosts the beautiful young
maiden from behind a sycamore tree, we find ourselves in a familiar wisdom scenario: the male with power must be brought to judge himself, and
only the trickery of a woman using the ideology of motherhood can force
him to take responsibility for his actions. The disguised Isis replies to her
would-be seducer:

> Let me tell, my great lord: As for me, I was the wife of a herdsman and I
> bore him a son. My husband died, and the boy began to tend the cattle of
> his father. But then a stranger came. He sat down in my stable and spoke
> thus to my child: 'I shall beat you, I shall take your father's cattle, and I
> shall throw you out!' So he spoke to him. Now I wish to make you his
> defender.' Then Seth said to her: 'Shall one give the cattle to the stranger
> while the man's son is here?' Thereupon Isis changed herself into a kite,
> flew up, and sat on top of an acacia. She called to Seth and said to him:
> 'Weep for yourself! Your own mouth has said it. Your own cleverness has
> judged you!'[215]

Like the Wise Woman of Tekoa who uses the same strategy to get David
to condemn his own treatment of Absalom, or the prophet Nathan who
used a typical wisdom example story to bring David to knowledge of his
wrongdoing with the wife of Uriah the Hittite, Isis succeeds admirably in
the implementation of her cunning plan. Through her use of smooth speech,
deceptive transformation and the invocation of the hallowed state of a
mother concerned for her son, she accomplishes something the tribunal
could not in all the 80 (!) years of its deliberations.

Sadly for the exhausted tribunal (and reader), the 'contendings' of Seth,
Horus and Isis are *still* not over, and more transformations ensue. Seth,
still not satisfied with the Ennead's endorsement of his own verdict given
against himself, induces Horus to join him in transforming themselves into
hippopotamuses who will fight each other in the depths of the sea. As Isis
watches them sink beneath the waves, she mourns that Seth will kill her
Horus. No depressed layabout *mater dolorosa*, she immediately weaves
yarn into a rope and casts bronze into a harpoon that she tosses into the
ocean. It lands first in Horus, who cries out to her to remove it; next it
lands in Seth's flesh. Seth reminds Isis of their link as brother and sister
and she relents, recalling her harpoon from him as well. Infuriated at this
lack of partiality, Horus cuts off her head and carries it off to a mountain.

214. Simpson, *Literature*, p. 115.
215. Lichtheim, *Literature*, II, p. 217.

Headless but undaunted, Isis transforms herself into a headless statue. Upon seeing this outrage visited upon Isis the Great, the Ennead goes off to search out Horus and punish him for his act.

After Seth takes charge of the punishment of Horus and Hathor intervenes to cure the young god, Isis reappears for an important transformative role in yet another episode of contending. This time Seth attempts to rape Horus in the night, but he catches his uncle's semen in his hand and takes it to mother Isis. Horrified, she cuts off Horus's hand and flings it into the water, and thoughtfully makes him a new replacement. With a bit of ointment and a pot, she then induces an erection in her son and saves his semen in the pot. Later, she goes to Seth's garden and places Horus's semen in his favorite food, a lettuce, which he eats daily. When he eats the semen-dressed salad, he becomes pregnant with Horus's seed.[216] Seth and Horus go to the tribunal yet again. Seth insists he should triumph over Horus because, in his great virility, he has played 'the part of the man' over Horus, rendering the young god 'pseudo-female' through his act of homosexual rape. Now, however, the semen of both is called upon to give testimony: the semen of Seth answers from the marsh where Isis had thrown it (and her son's hand which held it), but Horus's semen answers from the body of Seth. Gendered judgment wins the day: again, the Ennead find in favor of Horus (since *he* is the one who did the deed of a man). Seth, even when rendered implicitly 'female', still refuses to take 'no' for an answer, and proposes boat races to settle the matter, which, of course, they do not.

In the end (thankfully, the myth *does* end), Osiris is polled by letter and he naturally decides in favor of his son rather than his murdering brother. Isis proudly hails her son as the proper lord to succeed his father and is even given the 'last word':

> 'Horus has risen as Ruler, life, prosperity, health!
> The Ennead is in feast, heaven in joy!
> They take garlands seeing Horus, son of Isis,
> Risen as great Ruler of Egypt.
> The hearts of the Ennead exult,
> The entire land rejoices
> As they see Horus, son of Isis
> Given the office of his father,
> Osiris, lord of Busiris.'[217]

216. The members of this divine household are in need of family therapy, and plenty of it! Can this be the implicit origin of the need to hold judgment scenes presided over by Osiris in the underworld?

217. Lichtheim, *Literature*, II, p. 223.

Kingship and its garlands are bestowed upon the young male by his salvific mother—who presumably has gotten her head back in order to proclaim such powerful words of installation over the son who decapitated her. Even among the gods, motherhood may not be all it's cracked up to be, and a mother who hopes to keep her head needs to keep her tricks at hand, as well. When reading the instructions for success to the elite young men found in Proverbs 1–9 against the mythological background of the Trickster-Mother, we become aware of the power struggles between males of the old and new generations, and the way mothers are drawn into those proceedings. The 'Mother's Torah', enlivened by Isis mythology, becomes a signal hallmark—a garland—of the road to success and appropriation of the father's power in the patriarchal world (Prov. 1.8b-9; 4.8-9). After all, even wise King Solomon had to be crowned with a garland of authority by his mother on his wedding day (Song 3.11)!

'The Contendings of Horus and Seth' is not the only place we see the trickery of Isis in full bloom, as it were. In the 19th Dynasty (c. 1350–1200 BCE) text 'The God and his Unknown Name of Power', Isis appears resplendent in her knowledge, trickery and effectiveness. Following a standard folktale plot pattern, we learn the story of how Isis tricked Re, a sun-god 'abounding in names',[218] into revealing his most secret name, hidden within his body at the beginning of time so that no sorcerer might gain power by improperly wielding the Name. Names, of course, function here as elsewhere in the ancient Near East as wondrous items of magical power: to know the proper name of an entity gives the knower full knowledge of that entity, and thus the power to compel by 'calling upon the Name'. For this reason, neither deities nor demons are especially eager to tell their true names of power.[219]

Isis is introduced to audience with full 'wisdom' credentials:

> Now Isis was a clever woman. Her heart was craftier than a million men;
> she was choicer than a million gods; she was more discerning than a million

---

218. John A. Wilson (trans.), 'The God and his Unknown Name of Power', *ANET*, 3rd edn, pp. 12-14.

219. Cf. Moses in Exod. 3 for a different version of this motif: Moses thinks that by asking for the Hebrew God's *real* name—which God will surely NOT tell him—he can exempt himself from going on the proposed mission of deliverance. This deity is full of surprises, however: 'he' does tell 'his' name (though oddly, in the first person form, 'I cause/I am', which is not gender marked as either male or female), thereby gifting Moses with genuine power to call and be answered, always a useful thing for a redeemer's hope of success.

of the noble dead. There was nothing which she did not know in heaven and earth, like Re, who made the content of the earth. The goddess purposed in her heart to learn the name of the august god...[220]

We may note here that Isis proposes no particular 'villainy'. Though practically 'all-knowing', she has a significant 'lack' in her knowledge: the god's name of power is unknown to her. Just as villainy sets a hero on the road to struggle and redemption, so the plot function of 'lack' requires the denouement of 'lack liquidated' brought about by the hero's searches, acquisitions and clever use of the wondrous people, objects and entities who come to aid him or her on the quest. Isis, then, is a seeker-hero who must liquidate her lack by means of the folktale plot function pair, 'Difficult Task'/'Solution'.

All will be well, however, for Isis has a cunning plan.[221] As the old god Re walks the fields as is his custom, his slackened features permit divine spittle to fall upon the earth. Finding this, Isis kneads it, together with the earth upon which it fell, into an 'august snake' that she leaves at the crossroads where Re is sure to come upon it. When he does, the magical snake bites him and inflicts him with a poison that sets his body on fire and shakes him to his core. He cries to his retinue, 'Let the children of the gods be brought to me, the beneficent of speech, who know their (magic) spells, whose wisdom reaches the heavens...' and '...Isis came with her skill, her speech having the breath of life, her utterances expelling pain, and her words reviving him whose throat was constricted.'[222]

Re tells Isis about the snake that bit him, and she requests that he tell her his secret name, for that is necessary for her magical cure to be effective. Re tells her many names, but the poison is not removed by Isis's actions. She tells him he must not have told her his *real* secret name (or he would have been cured), and asks him for it once more, and finally he tells her. In exultation, Isis begins her cure:

> Flow forth, scorpion poison! Come forth from Re, O Eye of Horus! Come forth from the burning god at my spell! It is I who acts; it is I who send (the message)! Come upon the ground, O mighty poison! Behold, the great god has divulged his name, and Re is living, the poison is dead. So-and-so, the [son] of So-and-so,[223] is living, and the poison is dead, through the speech

---

220. Wilson, 'God', p. 12.
221. Everyone seems to (Curtis and Elton, *Blackadder*, passim)!
222. Wilson, 'God', p. 13. The references to the throat probably refers to the constriction of the airway in anaphylactic shock as an allergic reaction to the poison.
223. The instructions clearly intend that the name of the current patient be inserted here.

of Isis the Great, the Mistress of the Gods, who knows Re (by) his own
name.'[224]

The true core of this myth comes into focus in the final phrases of Isis's
incantation against the poison: this is an aetiological myth about the origin
of the cure for scorpion sting, and it represents no idle tale. Rather, this
incantation was to be *performed* on behalf of injured members of the
community, as the instructions for its use given in its colophon make clear:

> WORDS TO BE SPOKEN OVER an image of Atum and of Horus-of-
> Praise, a figure of Isis, and an image of Horus, PAINTED (ON) THE
> HAND OF HIM WHO HAS THE STING AND LICKED OFF BY THE
> MAN—(OR) DONE SIMILARLY ON A STRIP OF FINE LINEN,
> PLACED AT THE THROAT OF HIM WHO HAS THE STING. IT IS
> *THE WAY OF CARING FOR* A SCORPION POISON. (OR) IT MAY BE
> WORKED UP WITH BEER OR WINE AND DRUNK BY THE MAN
> WHO HAS A SCORPION (BITE). IT IS WHAT KILLS THE POISON—
> REALLY SUCCESSFUL A MILLION TIMES.[225]

The Trickster Isis of this myth is not explicitly invoked as a mother,
though we may choose to see her in the mother's role of family nurse, and
she is certainly 'mother' of this incantation by both deed and word. Many
roles parcelled out among God, Woman Wisdom and Woman Stranger are
found here: the creator who uses the good earth to sculpt an active creature, the dangerous mistress of magic who can create a composite creature
to do her bidding, and the trickster who uses her wits to achieve her ends.
We might note, too, that ultimately Isis does not act solely on her own
behalf: she is like fire-bringer Prometheus who breaks solidarity with the
heavens to bring light to those of earth. Her trickery is on behalf of the
children of earth who suffer from poisonous stings, and her wisdom, skill
in planning and execution, and smooth use of words that contain 'the
breath of life' are all deployed in a redemptive way. Like the power attributed to the 'word in season' by the book of Proverbs (15.23), the no less
artful speech of the wise goddess 'revives the one whose throat is constricted', the one rendered voiceless by poisons of various sorts—really, it
works a million times!

Mesopotamian and Canaanite Echoes

The matriarchate of goddesses in Woman Wisdom's family tree is by no
means exhausted by reference to Egyptian parallels. Scholars also appeal

224. Wilson, 'God', pp. 13-14.
225. Wilson, 'God', p. 14. One of the texts of this spell contains a drawn vignette of
these four deities that could be copied and used in the charm as needed.

to connections between Woman Wisdom and Mesopotamian and Canaanite goddesses. Noting the striking similarities in the way Woman Wisdom
and Woman Stranger/Foreign Woman are described by the sages. Some
have considered the Babylonian Ishtar and her fertility cult to be the figure
behind Woman Wisdom's 'evil twin', Woman Stranger . Likewise, a
Canaanite vine-goddess, goddess of wisdom (still to be discovered) or
authentic tree-goddess (cf. Asherah below) have also been postulated as
figures from whom the sages adapted Israel's version of the divine
'totemic female' who confers the abundance of life's blessings on her
followers.

Mesopotamia. Using plot and character analysis as tools for reading Sumerian goddess texts, we must note the special relationship between the Sumerian goddess of love and war, Inanna (later fused with the Semitic Ishtar),[226]
and Enki, the god of wisdom and sweet (fertile) waters. As a result of her
crafty behavior, Inanna receives the *me*, divine ordinances by which human
society is organized, from the drunken Enki and successfully bears them
away to her city, thereby assuring its place among the competing city-states
of Sumer.[227] In other mythological texts, Inanna's dangerous journey to the
'Great Below', the underworld, seems to be a paradigm for the description
of Woman Stranger, whose house leads down to death (Prov. 2.18). Upon
Inanna's return, she consigns Dumuzi, her royal 'shepherd' mate, whose
rule is legitimated by his alliance with the goddess, to the demons of the
Great Below in her place. This punishment occurs because of his refusal to
mourn properly the loss of the divine wife. This motif reminds us of
Woman Wisdom in Proverbs 1, scoffing at those who ignored her and who
are now beset by calamity. Dumuzi's life is eventually restored for six
months of every year when his sister Geshtinanna, the vine-goddess (and
perhaps another fructifying aspect of Inanna), offers to take his place in the
underworld, thus presenting us with another divine female figure who, like
Woman Wisdom, brings life.

When Inanna is metamorphosed into the militant semitic Ishtar, great
goddess of ancient Israel's and Judah's enemies, we find yet another set of
plot and character associations that find their way into the portraits of the

---

226. For a comprehensive overview of this goddess and her cult in ancient Uruk, see
volume 1 (2000) of the journal *NIN: Journal of Gender Studies in Antiquity*, which is
entirely devoted to this topic.

227. Fontaine, 'Deceptive Goddess', pp. 88-93.

cosmic females of Proverbs 1–9.[228] In these materials, we discover a 'traditional-type scene' of goddesses who make invitations—to banquets, as in Proverbs 9, or to marriage—which may end in death for the hapless mortal who answers the goddess affirmatively.[229] Gilgamesh, when given a marriage proposal by Ishtar (Tablet VI), enumerates the other husband-lovers she has betrayed to death, and concludes, 'If thou shouldst love me, thou wouldst [treat me] like them.'[230] Here, the fractious king displays a pointed awareness of the potential dangers involved in consorting with goddesses, thereby displaying a great deal more sense than the young men of Proverbs 1–9. Of course, Ishtar also dislikes hearing 'no' from the human males she has favored, and Gilgamesh's churlish refusal only brings the tragedy of mortality home to him and his friend 'twin', Enkidu, in a crashing way when Ishtar demands Enkidu's death as punishment for slaying the Bull of Heaven.

Those Terrible Twins!: Ishtar and Saltu. From the Old Babylonian period we come upon an interesting text written in the Akkadian language, the Agushaya Hymn, which might suggest another line of interpretation for the marked resemblance found between the Wisdom Figure and her Strange/Foolish counterpart in the cosmic domain. This hymn tells what happened when the god of Wisdom, Ea (Sumerian Enki), constructs a 'double', the goddess Saltu, whose name means 'Discord', for the fierce, warlike Ishtar to distract her from troubling heaven and earth with her bloodlust.[231] Although the text is broken in many places, we find, as with Gilgamesh and Enkidu,[232] that paired, same-sex entities are no strangers to the storytelling world of the ancient Near East.

228. See n. 171, above.

229. Tzvi Abusch, 'Ishtar's Proposal and Gilgamesh's Refusal: An Interpretation of the Gilgamesh Epic, Tablet 6, Lines 1-79', *HR* 26 (1986), pp. 143-87.

230. *ANET*, p. 84.

231. For translations, see Foster, *Before the Muses*, I, pp. 78-88; B. Groneberg, 'Philologische Bearbeitung des Agušayahymnus', *RA* 75 (1981), pp. 107-34; Benjamin Foster, 'Ea and Saltu', in M. Ellis (ed.), *Essays on the Ancient Near East in Memory of Jacob Joel Finkelstein* (Memoirs of the Connecticut Academy of Arts and Sciences, 19; Hamden, CT: Archon Books, 1977), pp. 79-86; Frymer-Kensky, *Goddesses*, pp. 31, 67, 142.

232. For the symbolism of these 'twins', see Raymond Kuntzmann, *Le symbolisme des jumeaux au Proche-Orient ancient: Naissance, fonction et évolution d'un symbole* (Beauchesne Religions, 12; Parise: Beauchesne, 1983), pp. 51-78. While most of the previous research on this motif focused on the celestial symbolism of solar/lunar twins,

As the story has been reconstructed, both heaven and earth are suffering from Ishtar's incessant anger and battle-lust, just as the people of Uruk suffered under King Gilgamesh's unrestrained behavior toward his people. The god of wisdom, Ea, proposes a solution: let a twin be created! Ea describes his 'Bride of Frankenstein' to the council of the great gods:

> Let her be trusty [ ], let her have muscle,
> Let her raise riot, be always ready to fight.
> Let her be fierce!
> Let her hair [be ext]raordinary,
> More luxuriant than an orchard.
> Let her be strong of frame,
> Let her complain, she must be strong,
> Let her gasp for breath, she shall not tire,
> Let her not hold back her cry day nor night, let her rage![233]

From seven scrapings of the dirt beneath his nails, he creates a twin of the fierce goddess to draw off and exhaust Ishtar's outrageous energies for war. The goddess Discord, or Saltu, is then lectured by her 'father' Ea on the 'marks' by which she will recognize Ishtar. Ea makes her mission clear as he instructs Saltu in terms designed to make her envious of Ishtar and ready to vent her rage:

> I have created you to humiliate her:
> In my cleverness I gave your stature, valor, and might in abundance.
> Now be off, go off to her private quarters!...
> What advantage shall she have over you?
> You are the creature of my power!
> Speak out proudly what is on your tongue,
> As an equal before her.[234]

As Saltu approaches Ishtar's abode in a terrible rage, Ishtar sends out her servant Ninshubur,[235] to find out who or what is causing such a great disturbance. Ninshubur is frightened by this awful apparition, or caricature of his divine mistress, and relays this to Ishtar. Unfortunately, a large gap

---

Kuntzmann writes of this epical pair: 'While accepting violence as a basic "given" of the experience of being human and recognizing the undifferentiated state of being and matter as one of the sources for it, it clearly appears that the symbolism of twins narrates the ongoing drama of that confusion, and the necessity of ruptures needed to establish a differentiated vital world' (p. 78).

233. Foster, *Before the Muses*, I, p. 81.
234. Foster, *Before the Muses*, I, p. 83.
235. Though Ninshubur is male in our text, he often appears as a female in other Inanna-Ishtar texts.

in the text provides an equally large narrative gap as the hostile (?) encounter between the twins is lost.

We resume the story with Ishtar complaining to Ea about the creation of this worrisome doppelganger. She demands, 'Let her return to her lair!'[236] Ea tells Ishtar, 'As soon as you said it, I certainly did it!' and proceeds to tell the goddess a slightly altered version of Discord/Saltu's creation by him. *Now* the purpose of the twin's existence, he claims, was so that Ishtar's glorious might in battle, where she is known as the Whirling Dancer, might be remembered by later generations and commemorated by the yearly 'whirling dance' (*gūštu*) performed in the streets of the city.[237] This aetiology for the well-known celebrative dance seems to appear out of nowhere, given the parts of the text that have preceded, but allows the story to end happily ever after with an acceptable mythological origin for much-loved dance honoring Ishtar. Clearly, Ishtar has been 'sweet-talked' into accepting Ea's new version of events, and the story ends there.

We may make several observations here concerning the divine twins of the battle/love goddess of Mesopotamia and the cosmic ladies of Proverbs 1–9. Certainly, when we factor in the male variant of Gilgamesh and Enkidu, we see clearly enough that the wild, unacculturated 'twin' has no cause for existence outside of her or his relation to the 'original'. Though she is able to deal death to the young male adolescent who attends her banquet in an almost cosmic way, by leading him down to the Pit, Woman Stranger/Folly can in no way outshine or overcome Woman Wisdom.[238] She is only a shadowy double, and some scholars claim that it is *not* even Woman Wisdom whom she opposes, but rather the good wife in the Strong Woman passage found in Proverbs 31.[239] Whoever the 'twin' may be properly said to counter, we hear in Father Ea's words an echo of truth: the negative twin is indeed a creature of the author's power, given life to set up the original's credentials and behavior through a shifting dance of battles, both in public and in the inner chamber.

---

236. Or 'hole'.

237. Foster, *Before the Muses*, I, p. 87.

238. Fox sees Woman Stranger/Folly in Prov. 9 as a literary personification of the folly of human wisdom designed to serve as a foil to Woman Wisdom, but he feels she has 'no mythological roots' (*Proverbs 1–9*, p. 300). Obviously, the present writer disagrees: while it is true there is no direct dependence on any one myth from Mesopotamia or Egypt, significant motifs from dangerous goddesses have been transferred to the negative figure in Prov. 9.

239. Fox, *Proverbs 1–9*, p. 262.

Next, we might point out how much Saltu or Discord puts us in mind of the sages' description of the wicked females who step outside of their patriarchally inscribed roles of good-wife-and-mother. The loud, complaining shrew who speaks pridefully is a forerunner of the Scolding Wife, even though here she is set to devil her sister with a show of behavior too much like the original's to be tolerated. Her propensity to rage, her love of the riot, her hope of besting her 'sister'—all these are scarcely the traits of the docile female. While tolerated (within limits) in Ishtar, whose associations with law, right judgment and other socially redemptive activities are a given in the societies that worshiped her, in a twin, the very same features receive only censure. Like Woman Stranger whose house leads to Sheol, or Enkidu who must take his place in the underworld, in the end Saltu must return to her lair in the earth.

Figure 9. Twin or 'Girlfriend' Goddesses. (Perforated Sheet Gold; Alaca Huyuk, c. 2500–2000 BCE.)

One should not, of course, overdraw these lines of connection: after all, the sages of Proverbs are quick to craft their twins as light and dark, good and bad. Woman Stranger has not been constructed by our authors so that she can show Woman Wisdom a mirror of her own unrestrained behavior, or draw her into a cycle of girlfriend adventures as a 'Dynamic Duo' like Gilgamesh and Enkidu. This is no ancient 'chick-flick' of female bonding, but rather a sharply drawn rhetorical contrast that serves the ends of the patriarchal authors and their audiences. The figures in Proverbs 9 are *different*, and so men should pick one and *not* the other;

indeed, that's the whole point of the exercise. *But* these figures are also shockingly, intriguingly *alike* in the things they say and do. The Early Bronze Age town of Alaca Huyuk in Anatolia of the Hattic period presents us with a curious image of this female 'twinship', in the form of 'twin' idols made of perforated metal (see Fig. 9). The two females are joined by the hands in each version of this image, with similar headdresses and decorative perforated holes. Eyes and breasts on each female are clearly designated by larger and more noticeable perforations, but oddly, neither has a genital triangle marking, which is typical of female figurines of this period in Anatolia and Mesopotamia. If the females here are not twin goddesses, then they probably ought to be understood as 'girlfriends' or partners: they are missing the fertility marks of the genital triangle so typically used to suggest a female's biological role and identity. Whatever their interpretation ultimately turns out to be, it is clear that the iconographic traditions of the Near East know of female twins, or females choosing females with whom to partner. It may be that the mythological tradition of 'twinship' may provide a helpful reference for understanding the 'sameness' that exegetes have found so troubling and unexpected in Woman Wisdom and Woman Folly.

The She-Demon at the Crossroad: Lilith and Woman Stranger. Though many suggestions, all of them with some merit, have been put forward to understand the more cosmic dimensions of Woman Stranger/Woman Folly's presence and demeanor in the book of Proverbs (see above for discussion), she is not without precedent in the ancient world. Sumerian myth and Jewish storytelling have long spoken of an eternal would-be mother who wanders the margins, haunts the crossroads and is the target of all sorts of vicious lore. I submit here that Lilith, Adam's first wife made from earth like her mate, is the *original* wandering Jew(ess) whose story has been deferred in favor of the male protagonist, and that she functions as a prototype for Woman Stranger as well as the Queen of Sheba (see Chapter 3). Hence, we would do well to investigate her expulsion from the gardens of culture, and not only because she is much beloved by feminist scholars. As always, we must ask ourselves of patriarchal literature from any time or place: why does 'chaos' always seem to wear a female face (Figure 10)?

Figure 10. Hybrid Female Dragon. (Spain, c. 1300. After Metzger and Metzger, *Jewish Life*, p. 35, illus. 47.)

For feminists, the folk figure Lilith is in many ways our mother: it is no coincidence that such modern feminists as Judith Plaskow,[240] Ellen Frankel, Barbara Koltuv, and others have chosen Lilith as a key figure to represent the paradigm of the marginal, despised female who finds no rest in any community.[241] Here we take seriously the full afterlife of Woman Stranger/Folly in texts like those from Qumran and elsewhere, where she has become fully demonized and connected with the underworld in ways that evoke the epic traditions of the ancient Near East.[242] If she is really demonic, what might that mean for our interpretive task in Proverbs? First, a little history is in order.

240. 'The Coming of Lilith: Toward a Feminist Theology', in Carol P. Christ and Judith Plaskow (eds.), *Womanspirit Rising: A Feminist Reader in Religion* (San Francisco: Harper & Row, 1979), pp. 198-209.

241. Not only did Jewish feminists name their magazine after the demon, they gleefully explore her connection to the Queen of Sheba (Rachel Kranson, 'The Queen of Sheba's Fuzzy Legs', *Lilith* 26 (2001), pp. 10-12).

242. For an excellent discussion of this phenomenon, see Melissa Aubin, '"She Is the Beginning of All the Ways of Peversity": Femininity and Metaphor in 4Q184', *Women in Judaism* 2.2 (2001), on line at http://www.women-in-judaism.com.

Lilith of the Time Before. Unlike many scholars, I take demons seriously.[243] This is perhaps the result of growing up around Haitian communities in Miami, working as a feminist from time to time among conservative Christians, and dealing with Hollywood producers. Recognizing my minority position on this topic, I remind those who are less familiar with these elemental forces that the word 'demon' comes from the Greek 'daimon' for 'spirit', 'supernatural entity', and that we find the same concept much earlier in Mesopotamian materials (Akk; 'rabitsu'., Sumerian, 'Mashkim'). In all three languages, such a creature may be either evil *or* good. Iconography from incantation plaques and prayers from the Fertile Crescent suggest that the terms were applied to upright, two-footed human creatures, often of a hybrid nature. (Hence, demons are somewhat cherubim-like, but they are not the same as monsters, also hybrid creatures, but ones who do not walk upright.) [244]

Besides walking upright, demons have appetites, memories, desires and will. They have names; they can enter into contracts and form relationships. They have extended life spans, but they can die, mate and reproduce. They are, in many ways, *just like us*, only their animal natures and characteristics have been foregrounded, whereas homo sapiens usually prides himself on his distance from the world of creatures. So for feminist women, especially those reading the Bible in the line of professional duty, Lilith the demon is no alien flesh. She may have wings and bird feet, but we recognize those things in our own souls yearning to take flight from the restrictions of culture and its view of our so-called 'essential' natures. We recognize Lilith in our own cramped and aching feet, made hideous by the cultural foot-binding of high heels required in working women as a *de rigueur* part of 'power dressing'. Like demons, human women are often considered closer to the animal world of nature than men because of our biological differences from males of our species, our roles in reproduction and our primary care of little humans who are not very civilized at first. Our presence is often perceived as a source of 'dis-order' in the orderly logic of our men. (Why else are there so many books aimed at teaching women either how to behave like men so they can succeed in the public

243. I am not the only one, however: for a fascinating modern study, see Felicitas D. Goodman, *How about Demons? Possession and Exorcism in the Modern World* (Bloomington: Indiana University Press, 1988).

244. 'Demons and Monsters', in Jeremy Black and Anthony Green, *Gods, Demons and Symbols of Ancient Mesopotamia: An Illustrated Dictionary* (Austin, TX: University of Texas Press, in conjunction with the British Museum, 1992), p. 63.

world outside the home, or how to accept that our greatest fulfillment must naturally come from motherhood?) We know what Lilith is up against, and though it is not always peace between us, we *do* understand where she's coming from: a desert seldom inhabited by elite men.

Lilith, Attacker of the Sumerian 'Tree of Life'. Turning to Lilith's earliest textual life, before her commanding presence in mystical midrash on Genesis 1, the Court of Solomon and the Zohar, we find that she began literary life in ancient Sumer. Like any self-respecting demon, she is associated with the elemental powers of nature. Her name is derived from the Sumerogram for wind, 'LIL' and so, she was the entity whose presence was made known through the sudden storms that wrought havoc of the lower alluvial plain formed by the Tigris and the Euphrates.

Her first full-fledged literary appearance is in the third millennium in the 'Myth of Inanna, Gilgamesh and the Huluppu Tree'. The maiden goddess Inanna plants a seed she rescued from the river at the time of creation. This seed grows into a wondrous tree (a huluppu, probably the willow) that she tends, hoping to form from its trunk a 'shining bed and throne', the emblems of statecraft for our eager fertility goddess. But alas, before the tree is able to deliver these trappings of kingly culture, it is infested. The anzu-bird (a nasty lion-headed bird responsible for stirring up sand-storms) sits in the branches of the tree; in its trunk, the 'dark maid Lilith' makes herself right at home, and a 'snake who would not be charmed' gnaws away at the roots of the tree. In frustration, Inanna turns for help to the part human, part-god hero Gilgamesh. Perhaps not incidentally, his non-human father is said to be a lilu-demon (i.e. a male-lilith) in a king-list from about 2400 BCE. In our slightly later myth of the willow-tree, Gilgamesh with his mighty bronze axe sets upon the tree, causing the anzu-bird to fly away, Lilith to flee into the desert and the snake to set up shop elsewhere (Gen. 3, perhaps?).

As far as the poor Huluppu tree is concerned, the cure has clearly been worse than the disease, for with the lumber made from its violent exorcism-by-carpentry, Inanna finally gets her bed and throne. The implication is clearly that she shares both venues with the hero, who then becomes king of the Sumerian state. The ideological message is clear: nature is dangerous, fertility is ambiguous and in need of male control, and a male human champion is the only *possible* choice to hold these volatile forces in check. Score: patriarchal culture, 1; nature, 0, with the female element clearly linked with nature, while the male represents the saving graces of culture.

From the cultures that succeeded Sumer, we learn a little more. Lilith is a member of a family of lilu-demons, both male and female (Akkadian fem. sg. 'lilītu', masc. sg. 'lilû'; also '(w)ardat-lilî', 'maiden of the storm'; 'Irdu-lili', the male counterpart) who bear traits linked to the folkloric figures of vampires and succubae. In particular, our darling maid Lil, is now 'Lilitu' and has assimilated characteristics of the Babylonian goddess/demon, the succuba Lamashtu. Unlike most demons, who take orders from higher entities (the gods), Lamashtu has the sky-god for a father and acts on her own to do evil to the human community. Many demons were thought to cause disease; indeed, this was one of their primary activities. Lamashtu's medical 'speciality' in this area will be familiar to anyone who knows medieval European witchlore: she preyed upon pregnant women and newborn babies, seeking to cause miscarriage or crib death. She might be warded away by plaques and amulets, and other demons invoked in magical rituals could banish her to the underworld, there to travel a sunless sea in her divine boat.[245]

Lilitu takes over the characteristics of Lamashtu and becomes a sort of anti-maternal figure responsible for all mishaps surrounding pregnancy, childbirth and early infancy. The sexual characteristics of Lilith seem to be derived from the figure of the Ardat-Lili, an adolescent demoness whose name translates to something like 'the maiden of the storm'. Since she has no regular mate (one wonders here what makes the male demonic counterparts of Lilitu and Ardat-Lili so unsatisfying as mates), she seeks out unwitting young men at deserted crossroads or in the open country, hoping to conceive hybrid human-demon children through such encounters. In iconography, she is pictured as a beautiful nude, with wings, owl-feet, the occasional donkey-ear (Lamashtu's totem), a cap of horns, and stands flanked by lions and owls.[246]

By the time of the Hebrew Bible, the portrait of the she-demon seems to have reached full development, though later Jewish storytellers would add fabulous details and perfidious deeds. Her earlier names of LIL, Lilitu and Ardat-Lili and their stormy associations are forgotten, and now her name is associated with 'night' by a false etymology with the Hebrew term 'laylâ' (night). She is mentioned only once in the Hebrew Bible in Isa.

---

245. So, too, among the Hittites (T. Gaster, 'The child-stealing witch among the Hittites?', *Studi e materiali di storia delle religioni* 23 [1950/51], pp. 134-37).

246. M. Hutter, 'Lilith', in Karel van der Toorn, Bob Becking and Pieter W. van der Horst (eds.), *Dictionary of Deities and Demons in the Bible* (Leiden: E.J. Brill, 1995), pp. 973-76.

34.14 ('lîlît'; LXX, 'ὀνοκένταυρος; Vulgate, 'Lamia'). Here we find a prophetic oracle directed against Edom, which will be turned into a demon-haunted desert wilderness where even one such as Lilith might be comfortable. (Some translations demythologize the demoness and translate 'screech-owl', no doubt based on iconographic traditions, instead.)

However, Lilith emerges in postbiblical Jewish and Islamic folklore with a taste for a more convivial environment than barren desert. She appears as Adam's first wife in interpretations of the Priestly Creation story in Genesis 1. Later texts view her as a full-fledged succuba with her Mesopotamian traits of wings, long (red) hair and demon-feet (donkey, owl or vulture) fully intact. As such, she continues to be of special danger to pregnant women, newborns and men sleeping alone without a woman in their house, as is made clear from sixth-century CE Aramaic incantation bowls associated with the Jewish colony in Nippur. Although she receives only passing mention—all negative—in the Talmud (*'Erub.* 100b; *Nid.* 24b; *Šab.* 151b), by the time of the Zohar, the primary text of the thirteenth-century Spanish Kabbalists, she has a full, if somewhat contradictory, biography in place.[247]

Created on the same day and of the same material as Adam, God nevertheless chose to create the female earthling out of polluted matter rather than good earth. Fancying herself the equal of her mate due to these factors, she refuses Adam's male-dominant sexual advances, and eludes marital rape by uttering God's 'secret name' as an incantation that allows her to fly off safely into the desert (or Red Sea). Procreating with lecherous male demons of the wasteland, there she bears a demon-brood who are the source of humanity's diseases and misfortunes. Eventually, God dispatches three angels, Senoy, Sansenoy and Samangelof to bring her back to the Garden and Adam, but she refuses to comply. After some argument, she agrees to desist from her practice of strangling newborns and aborting pregnant women whenever she sees an amulet inscribed with the angels' names. Further, 100 of her demon children will be given up to death every day. The mother of many will also be the mother of many deaths.

Later, various postbiblical texts tell us that during Adam's penitential separation from Eve, Lilith returns to her former mate and bears demon children by him. She also produces more demons when she mates with Cain, the son of Eve by Satan/Sammael. Like the (w)ardat-lilî of Sumer and Akkad, her unnatural sexuality is blighted by her inability to find a

---

247. Patai, *The Hebrew Goddess*, pp. 221-54; Barbara Koltuv, *The Book of Lilith* (York Beach, ME: Nicolas–Hays, 1986).

permanent mate, so she haunts the crossroads, stalking lone men, flies in through their windows while they sleep alone, where her ministrations to her hapless prey are responsible for their nocturnal emissions. If she, or a male lilin, for that matter, managed to form an attachment to a human partner, the human spouse of Lilith's favorite was in grave danger: attacked, tormented, made infertile or driven mad. The succuba-wife or husband could only be driven out by the giving of a legitimate 'get' or 'writ of divorce'. We have the texts of such incantations, clearly used by the Jewish community of Nippur, about a hundred years after the formulation of the Babylonian Talmud.

Lilith's career continues as she is associated by later folklore with various females characters appearing in the Hebrew Bible and the Quran. She is the one who helps afflict Job in her association with the territory of Sheba, and later as Queen of Sheba and Zmargad, she engages in riddle contests with Solomon, king and demon-master (see Chapter 3). Likewise, with her cohort demoness, Naamah, she appears before Solomon to test his wisdom in 1 Kings 3, posing as one of the two harlots arguing over a surviving baby. Later she is considered to be the wife of Samael the demon (= Satan), and shares interesting iconographic traits related to the cherubim. When the Jerusalem Temple was destroyed, the Shekinah/Matronit descended from her place as God's consort in heaven to go into exile with her children, the Jews. Seeing a chance for advancement, Lilith ascends to the heights of heavens to become God's infernal consort in her stead.

The *Zohar* gives mixed testimony about Lilith's origins: she is either created after Adam from impure earth, or created simultaneously and attached to his side, later to be sawed apart by God. Another Kabbalistic variant has her emerging out of the Supernal Abyss, uncreated, and joined as an androgyne to Samael—again, not unlike the embracing cherubim of the Jerusalem temple. Thus she and her male counterpart form an infernal mirror image of the Adam–Eve androgyne. (There are other variants too: in all of them, Lilith's associations are generally negative, however exalted may be the description of her origins.) And so it goes: from Sumer to Spain, this untamed, aggressive, lustful being is somehow a major 'player' in humanity's gendered war with itself.

One other cherubim connection might be noted: after one of her mythical emergences, she is filled with desire for a mate. She flies about the earth and eventually breaches the zone of heaven, where she attaches herself to the 'little faces', the name given by the *Zohar* to those cherubim who surround the Throne of Glory (so named because their faces resemble those of small boys). Having succeeded in partnering herself, she refuses to leave the cherubim. After the creation of Adam, God wrests her from the cherubim and forces her descend to the earth. Coming upon the garden and Adam, she assumes this is to be her given partner—but Eve is attached to his side! Trying to regain her connection to the cherubim in heaven, she is thwarted yet again by the Watchers of the Gate Above, who cast her into the Red Sea. Her penchant for death continues in her watery abode, where it is even turned to serve divine purpose. Lilith and her demon brood drown the Egyptian armies of Pharaoh in the Red Sea as they harry the escaping Hebrew slaves during the Exodus. So even a demon like Lilith can pitch in and have her part in what Protestants call 'Salvation History'—she not only aids the proto-Israelite slaves, but she gets God off the theological hook by doing his dirty work for him.

Lilith of the Present. What is to be made of all this material derived from the popular culture and recorded by the learned elite, usually men, on the tablets from Mesopotamia and in the Bible and the literature created to interpret it? And how shall we relate the Women Strangers of Proverbs to this tradition of demonic female sexuality? When faced with supernatural phenomena, the modern/postmodern Western mind normally seeks other analytic categories than the 'indigenous' ones put forward from incantation text to Talmud. James Montgomery, an early twentieth-century translator of the Aramaic incantations, summed up what might be a standard conclusion of pre-feminist elite males: '[T]he Liliths were the most developed products of the morbid imagination—of the barren or neurotic woman, the mother in the time of maternity, the sleepless child.'[248] This account may very well hold for the unsuccessful *mother's* fear of Lamashtu side of Lilith's character, but what about that irresistible winged Venus at the crossroads, the muse of *men's* sexual dreams and forbidden associations?

Anthropologists of religion tell us that what we have here and in Proverbs' portrayal of the Woman at the Crossroads is an example of the 'demon-coping mechanism'.[249] In small, face-to-face communities, the assignment of interfamilial strife to a demonic source yields a variety of benefits. If Lilith is to blame for infertility, miscarriage, sudden infant death syndrome and every other manner of misfortune that befalls the

---

248. Quoted in Patai, *The Hebrew Goddess*, p. 225.
249. For an example of this social coping device in the New Testament, see Stevan L. Davies, *Jesus the Healer: Possession, Trance, and the Origins of Christianity* (New York: Continuum, 1995).

small child—well, then, all the human participants are exempted from blame and guilt. If it is the demonic spouse Lilith who steals a husband's seed during his erotic dreams, then it is hardly *his* fault that he has transgressed laws of purity, or cannot produce children with his human spouse. In Proverbs, the 'evil impulses' of unregulated, illegitimate sexual contact are assigned to Woman Stranger-as-Demon; the males bear no other role than that of unwitting victim who must be warned away. Discussion of male lust, adolescent vulnerability or the desperation of barren wives is conveniently foreclosed by this attribution of intentionality. Score: male humans, 2; Lilith, 0.

Further, anthropologists make clear that in such situations, it is usually a marginalized person within the family or community who is most at risk for demonic contact or possession. If the 'afflicted' person is an adolescent, pregnant, pre-menstrual or menopausal female, then the group is able to assign a known meaning to their behavioral oddities or flaunting of conventions of female submission, thus sparing the 'crazed' woman any punishment for her bizarre, unladylike conduct. There is a social gain here, too: such a person suddenly receives the attention and sympathy of the community, rather than its censure. Further, the community is able to affirm that young men or widowers must take mates *for their own good,* whether they want to or not: compulsory heterosexuality is offered as a remedy for demonic infection. For a woman, the offer of a ritual cure from Lilith's interference with the wife's achievement of motherhood encourages the barren, bereaved or betrayed wife to try again. A husband who strayed might not actually be 'guilty'; he is only a victim after all, and not responsible! Once more, community values of family and fertility are nicely balanced and given supernatural reinforcement. Everyone gains something by using the 'demon-coping mechanism'—but what about lonely, lovely, lustful, displaced Lilith?

Feminists are, of course, notorious for seeing things a bit differently, and we have some questions about the whole tradition on gendered matters. It seems to me that Lilith, rather than being the transgressor of the Garden, is the one who was cursed with the demonic lover! It is Adam and not Lilith—nor her meeker, curious sister Eve—who first introduces violence into gender relations into the Garden. Why *should* she submit to her partner? She knows the ineffable Name of God; it aids her in 'just saying "no!"' She is a worthy theological subject if she knows the Name! (No wonder she has wings to fly away!)

Next, let us examine the matter of her origin, entering into the mystical midrash on their own terms as story. Lilith is made of earth: who are the traditionalists who allege it was not *good* earth, but rather tainted? God, an exemplary potter, does not mind handling the substance from which she is made. Who is Adam to be so uppity? What taint can possibly exist at this stage of Creation? The only possibility is some sort of body waste produced by Adam himself, or that of the other creatures,[250] pure and innocent as God made them, fresh from their creator's hand. Those pieces of himself that the primal male cannot incorporate, tolerate or cling to, the interpreters of Adam project upon Lilith. Like Eve, she becomes the 'side' he does not want to acknowledge yet cannot help but cleave to: Adam's fascination with Lilith is his dance with his own Shadow side. No wonder he finds her at every crossroad of choice and blames her for every slip from the right path, and no wonder that this mythic path winds its way into the byways of the book of Proverbs. Woman Wisdom's Shadow clings to her skirts, displaced but still in existence. Whether as the Lamashtu-demon who murders children, or the Ardat-Lili who stalks her mate at twilight street corners, the lore of Lilith speaks the secret names of false gods, female and male: fulfillment through fertility; false consciousness of security through control of the 'Other' gender.

Does Lilith *want* to return to the same Garden she fled? Not on Adam's terms, she doesn't—as Judith Plaskow so playfully wrote in an early feminist midrash on the topic. She has already said 'No!' twice; she would rather endure a desert than be a slave. She prefers to strive for a place among the cherubim, or a seat next to God, rather than submit to gendered violence and trivialization by her own mate. The first female earthling is inspiring to her modern daughters, and *we* have ended her eternal wanderings by inviting her back into our waking consciousness. Ellen Frankel, in her splendid new work *The Five Books of Miriam: A Woman's Commentary on the Torah*, gives Lilith a place of honor as one of the women sages who speak to interpret the Way. She writes, in voice of 'Lilith the Rebel':

> 'I am the voice of protest. I challenge received wisdom, especially the truths taught by men who have not consulted their mothers, daughters, wives, and sisters. My goal is to upset the applecart, to bite the serpent back, to look back and see the fire without turning to salt, to give the Rabbis a piece of my mind. I seek the truth buried under the mountain of tradition. My spade is as sharp as my tongue and wit!'[251]

250. Otherwise valued when named 'compost'.
251. Ellen Frankel, *The Five Books of Miriam: A Woman's Commentary on the Torah* (New York: Putnam's Sons, 1996), p. xx.

The dark maid Lilith has finally come home to roost, and that may well be a sign of our times: the end is at hand. Perhaps we can all, all of us, Lilith included, return to a Paradise not yet experienced by our species. Perhaps the war is over, and we can all fly away together…or at very least, hear her wings fluttering in the darkness when we turn a dangerous corner.

A Tablet-Knowing Scribe: The Healing Wisdom of Gula. It is clear from a passage from the Atrahasis flood story of Mesopotamia, known through various versions in texts from the classical to the late Assyrian period, that the understanding of the role of the child-murdering she-demon Lilith or Lamashtu was conceived as part of an overall strategy for reducing the size of the noisy, unruly human population. First, the gods try to deal with their 'human question' with a flood of massive proportions. This is necessary, according to the thinking of the gods, because, although they need humans to perform the unpleasant labors they themselves do not wish to do, too many humans cause the riot of noise that disrupts their sleep. However, although the flood *did* have the effect of blotting out unneeded humans, it was also viewed as a bit of 'overkill', at least by the more compassionate deities. The birth-goddess Nintu (also called 'midwife of the gods, the wise Mami' in the same passage) weeps and wails, wondering how she could have consented to the irrational destruction of all the people. Her human children, without her help, have become like flies! In the future, she vows to wear forever a necklace of flies, in memory of her mistake and her commitment to the future of humankind. But what if the problem arises again?

The high god Enlil (sky/air) calls upon Enki (wisdom, sweet waters) to summon Nintu, the birth-goddess, so that she may institute death for all people. Like Eve, this mother to all living must also become the mother of all deaths—apparently there is a symbolic appropriateness to this equation in the mythological thinking of the peoples of the region. But even universal death might not be enough to control humanity; Enki tells Nintu to do more:

> Now then, let there be a third (woman) among the people,
> Among the people are the woman who has borne and the woman who has not borne.
> Let there be (also) among the people the (she)-demon,
> Let her snatch the baby from the lap of her who bore it,
> Establish high priestesses and priestesses,
> Let them be taboo, and so cut down childbirth.[252]

252. Tablet III, col. vii (Foster, *Before the Muses*, I, p. 183).

There is a certain sapience in this decree by the god of Wisdom: decreasing the number of potential mothers by allowing women into religious service, along with barrenness and infant mortality will produce an overall reduction in the group size at the 'front end' of the human life cycle. The text becomes fragmentary, then drifts into a large gap, leaving us to wonder what kind of response the grieved Nintu might make to wisdom's decree.

If the god of wisdom is involved with the onset of death, infant mortality, and the creation of women religious, where is the wisdom of the gods when the human community attempts to cope with these disasters (from the human point of view)? When the baby cries—perhaps heralding the onset of illness—or the body aches, the goddess Gula ('Great') comes in her wisdom to address the need at hand. In the 'Gula Hymn of Bullutsa-Rabi' (c. 1500–1000 BCE), a sufferer addresses the goddess and begs for her intercession on his behalf. Like Woman Wisdom, Gula traces her own biography and accomplishments in a long speech of self-praise, covering 'her astral character, her elevation to a position of authority, her interest in agriculture, her unalterable word, her healing abilities, her control of destinies, her sexual attractiveness, her upbringing and education, marriage and scholarship'.[253] The parallels with Proverbs 8 are clear enough from this description: here we have a 'full-service goddess' who evidences all of the categories of wise dealings and accomplishments we are used to seeing in Woman Wisdom, and some that we have only hypothesized, based on readings of Israelite women's roles in society, and relevant texts like this one from surrounding goddess mythology.

Before hearing Gula 'tell it like it is' in her own words, a summary of pertinent points that allow us to fill in some of the gaps of Woman Wisdom's duties in the cosmic domain. Gula is daughter of the god of highest heaven, An, and his wife, Antu, who taught her 'fair counsel'. Like Wisdom, then, she is associated with the heights and deeps of all creation, for she was taught and authorized by the god of wisdom: 'Ea in the depths gave me in full of his wisdom, / He gave me the tablet stylus from his own hand, / He entrusted to me the physician's craft, a secret of the gods…'[254] Interestingly, like the human incarnation of Woman Wisdom in Prov. 31.10-31, she is fully engaged in the management of the goods of the land, doing her accounts, and keeping track of what goes where, claiming, 'I am

---

253. Foster, *Before the Muses*, II, p. 491.
254. Foster, *Before the Muses*, II, p. 497.

daughter, I am bride, I am spouse, / I, indeed, manage the household.'[255]
No wonder Gula can say, 'Fair it is to hold me in mind, (it is) good health
and life. / People discourse of men (in) sickness (and in) health…'[256]
Concerning her wisdom in healing, she cites her qualifications at length:

> 'I am the physician, I can save life,
> I carry every herb, I banish illness.
> I gird on the sack with life-giving incantations,
> I carry the texts which make (one) well.
> I give health to mankind.
> (My) clean dressing salves the wound,
> (My) soft bandage relieves the pain.
> At my examination, the moribund revives,
> At a word from me, the feeble one arises.
> I am merciful, [I am] kindly [ ]…'[257]

Here at last we see a clear connection between the healing practices of the
female who manages the household and the scribal texts that form the
basis of 'official' medical training given to men in that occupation. We
should note here, too, that her healing wisdom goes well beyond the
'textual': she is wise in herbcraft, the making and application of medicines
—all activities that might be related to her general management of
agricultural and domestic crafts. Like Woman Wisdom, she hears when
people call:

> 'I am merciful, I hear (prayer) from afar off,
> I fetch up the dead from the netherworld,
> I am girded with the leather bag, I…the scalpel and knife.
> I examine the weary, I watch over the sick, I open(?) the sore,
> I am mistress of life.
> I am physician, I am diviner, I am exorcist,
> I, who am expert in calculations,
>   no one has explained (to me) a single wedge,
> I…every one of them. "There is life in my [ ],
> I am Ninlil[258], the merciful [goddess]".'[259]

She not only makes 'house calls' to the afflicted; when there, she engages
in nursing activities and renders a prognosis (via her astronomical calcula-

255. Foster, *Before the Muses*, II, p. 494.
256. Foster, *Before the Muses*, II, p. 492.
257. Foster, *Before the Muses*, II, p. 495.
258. 'Lady Wind', yet another name for Gula.
259. Foster, *Before the Muses*, II, pp. 498-99.

tions, perhaps). The combination of technical wisdom with motherly compassion for the sufferers in her 'human' household is especially note worthy: no ailing person turns Gula away because she is female! No wonder she can say, much like Lady Wisdom:

> I have mercy on the weak, I enrich the destitute,
> I bestow life on the one who reveres me.
> I make straight the path of the one who seeks after my ways...[260]

Like her Hebrew sister, Gula is no less skilled than a male deity in protecting her followers: whoever finds her, finds life!

The Levantine Connection: From Ugarit to Israel

It is a well-known truism in biblical archaeology that the culture of ancient Canaan was 'incubated' to the north in what are now Syria and Lebanon. As all the items of material culture display, forms that originate in the northern region move south in their patterns of dispersion and influence: we see this in pottery, grave goods, anthropomorphic representation of deities (in preference to zoomorphic forms preferred in Egypt or hybrid forms in Mesopotamia), and with the discovery of the Ugaritic texts of Ras Shamra, we have been able to add linguistic and epic traditions to the list of shared cultural artefacts that the ancient Hebrews adapted from their neighbors. Of course, the culture of the Levant did not emerge *ex nihilo*: trade ties, diplomacy and wars with Mesopotamia and Anatolia left their impact on that culture, as well as ongoing incursions from Egyptian imperialism. Situated at the crossroads of great empires, the Levant made its own unique mixture of borrowed elements, crafting a distinctive set of reinterpretations of their larger, more important neighbors. It should occasion no surprise, then, that this 'oral world' of shared storytelling traditions and motifs should form part of the tapestry of influences on the portraits of Woman Wisdom and Women Strangers in Proverbs.

Ugarit: Goddesses, Banquets and Untimely Ends. Such scholars as Albright, Boström, Lang and Clifford[261] have all seen a Canaanite goddess as a model for the depiction of Woman Wisdom and Women Strangers in the book of Proverbs. While Boström posited that Woman Stranger/Folly was a version of the Astarte-Aphrodite figure, such that Woman Wisdom was devised to constitute a counterpoint to this forbid-

---

260. Foster, *Before the Muses*, II, p. 496.
261. See nn. 158 and 161 above for references.

den goddess, Lang opted for a different explanation of the relation of the cosmic women of Proverbs 1–9 to Levantine traditions. In his earliest works on the personifications of chs. 1–9, Lang postulated that Woman Wisdom was a true Canaanite wisdom-goddess (the one Albright suggested but never found) who was the daughter of the mother-goddess Athirat (elsewhere known for crushing skulls and providing a model for Jael in Judg. 4–5)[262] and high god 'El, whose characterization undergirds much of Genesis's portrait of the God of the Ancestors. Like Athena, Greek goddess of wisdom, springing from the brow of father Zeus, or the birth of Thoth from the head of Seth, Lang sees a potential variant for his wisdom goddess's origin: she may be the product of a 'male birth' by 'El.[263] In this reconstruction, the orthodoxy (or deep forgetfulness, perhaps) of the later period forced the replacement of Athirat's and/or 'El's name in Proverbs 8 with that of Yahweh. Although Fox rightfully points out that this is a hypothetical reconstruction that depends largely on the 'absence' of evidence[264] to make its case, and hence must be considered suspect and unconvincing, this ignores the very real evidence, both literary and archaeological, of suppression of just such goddess traditions by the orthodox Yahwism of the Deuteronomists and their later descendants.[265] A larger problem of this reconstruction is that these goddesses, in action and personal character features, often bear little resemblance to the Woman Wisdom of Proverbs 1–9, though they have often contributed a banquet-type scene to the characterization of the Women Strangers. There is no way of recovering the fullness of the goddess tradition's 'lived theology' based on the limited survival of texts. Lang and others could very well be correct in interpreting Father 'El as the true creator god of Woman Wisdom in Proverbs 8, but it cannot be proved with anything like certainty. What *is* certain is that Fox consistently downplays the erotic aspects of the mother figure in the both biblical material and their parallels, choosing to see less when there is more.

While attempting to hear the final form of the text *and* its echoes of earlier models, I suggest a different, but more literal reading of the birth of

---

262. J. Glen Taylor, 'The Song of Deborah and Two Canaanite Goddesses', *JSOT* 23 (1981), pp. 99-108.

263. Lang, *Wisdom*, p. 64.

264. Fox, *Proverbs 1–9*, p. 335.

265. See Olyan, *Asherah*, for literary signs of this deliberate erasure of goddess traditions in Israel, and the works of Hadley for an archaeological analysis of the same process (n. 165 above).

Cosmic Wisdom in Prov. 8.22-31, a notorious passage over which much ink has been spilt and many trees cut down:

> Yahweh acquired me at the beginning of his work, the first of his acts of long ago.
> Ages ago I was womb-woven,[266] at the first, before the beginning of the earth.
> When there were no deeps I was birthed,[267] when there were no springs abounding with water.
> Before the mountains had been shaped, before the hills, I was birthed—
> when he had not yet made earth and fields, or the world's first clumps of soil.
> When he established the heavens, I was there, when he drew a circle on the face of the deep,
> when he made firm the skies above, when he established the fountains of the deep,
> when he assigned to the sea its limit, so that the waters might not transgress his command,[268] when he marked out the foundations of the earth,
> then I was beside him, like a skilled craftswoman;[269] and I was daily his delight, rejoicing before him always,
> rejoicing in his inhabited world and delighting in the children [lit. 'sons'] of earth!

This critical text reflects a primal birthing moment, both for the earth and for Woman Wisdom. Since it is not until the final verses of the poem that we meet any other characters, the identity of the birth-giver who is parent to Woman Wisdom can only be Yahweh, here described as taking a female role in the process of creating a darling child who is both adored offspring and masterly sage or artisan. Even though we may intuit an 'architectural' motif in the sections concerning earth's formation, when we compare this passage to Yahweh's speech in Job 38.4-11, we find the birthing imagery underscored once again in the context of world foundation:

266. Cf. Job 10.11; Ps. 139.13b.

267. This passive form of the verb clearly refers to the female's role in giving birth, rather than the male role of 'begetting'; so, too, Fox, *Proverbs 1–9*, p. 282

268. See Job 38.8-10, which is likewise replete with midwifery and birthing imagery.

269. Or 'darling child/'ward', 'nursling'; the translation of this word is much disputed (see R.B.Y. Scott, 'Wisdom in Creation: the 'Amon of Proverbs VIII 30', *VT* 10 [1960], pp. 213-23); for 'sage' based on Akkadian loan-word 'ummānu', see Clifford, *Proverbs*, pp. 24-26. For a measured philological discussion, see Fox, *Proverbs 1–9*, pp. 285-87.

'Where were you when I laid the foundation of the earth?
Tell me, if you have understanding.
Who determined its measurements—surely you know! Or who stretched the line upon it?
On what were its bases sunk, or who laid its cornerstone,
when the morning stars sang together, and all the sons of God shouted for joy?
'Or who shut in the sea with doors, when it burst forth from the womb;
when I made clouds its garment, and thick darkness its swaddling band,
and prescribed bounds for it, and set bars and doors,
and said, "Thus far shall you come, and no farther, and here shall your proud waves be stayed"?' (RSV)

Here, the Divine Architect, so familiar to moderns from the engravings of William Blake, is also caring, active midwife: 'he' catches the child as it emerges from the birth canal of creation, clothes it with appropriate garments, and takes pains to restrain the boisterous chaotic water-baby in its cradle, lest it come to harm. Here and in Prov. 8.22-32 we have the brilliance of the biblical writers in their appropriation, rejection and harmonization of goddess traditions: the relentlessly male god Yahweh has become both a birth-goddess and a mother-goddess[270] to creation and Woman Wisdom. While perhaps creating an unsolvable riddle for modern interpreters who expect linear 'plot development' and separation of spheres of divine action, the text creates a psychologically satisfying resolution in a way seen elsewhere in the mythopoeic theologies of the ancient Near East. The Hebrew god is a male who is *also* female with respect to roles played and character traits. It makes perfect sense: how else could both male and female humans be made in the image of this Divine Androgyne if the deity is *only* male? We do not have to revert to Canaanite theology of a male pregnancy by 'El; the text is perfectly lucid as it stands, once we put aside our own theories of the necessary gender of the Bible's god.

Goddesses and Sisters Who Bring Death: From Banquet to Bier. The goddesses of the Levant, with their Mesopotamian forerunners in the Inanna–Ishtar epic traditions, were not active solely in the 'positive' realm of birth and creation. They also brought death to young men and heroes who

---

270. 'Birth-goddesses' assist humans or goddesses in the birth-giving process; 'mother-goddesses' produce offspring. Many goddesses are mothers without being especially connected with the sphere of the process of birth.

refused their sexual advances or other offers. Gilgamesh rightly understands that Ishtar's offer of marriage is also an invitation to be king of the
dead (see discussion of Inanna–Ishtar above), a less than stellar fate for the
king who would be god. Anat, the maiden warrior with a taste for blood,
figures in a similar way in the 'Narrative of Aqhat'.[271]

The young hero Aqhat has been given a mighty, divinely constructed
bow, one designed to tempt the military tastes of any battle-goddess. Anat
is apparently banqueting[272] when she first catches sight of the boy and his
weapon. First, she offers silver and gold in exchange for his bow; after he
refuses, she claims she will give him immortality. Aqhat foolishly chooses
to be offensive in his reply: 'To a hero your guile is slime' (Tablet I, col.
vi, l. 35). To this insult—that she is unable to provide immortality, he adds
a gendered slight with a proverbial tang to it that becomes his undoing:
'Bows (are for) warriors, / Will womankind now be hunting?' (Tablet I,
col. vi, ll. 39-40).[273] Though Anat laughs in reply, Aqhat's goose is about
to be cooked, for 'in her heart[274] she devised [a plan]' to have the churlish
male murdered so she might take possession of his bow.

The parallels here with Woman Stranger/Folly are plain enough. In
Prov. 7.10 a woman 'dressed as a harlot' goes after her unsuspecting
young male prey with a 'guarded heart'. Earlier in the poem this *femme
fatale* has been connected with the 'loose woman' and 'adventuress' (7.5)
from whom 'Sister Wisdom' will protect her young male follower (7.4).
Female guile, hidden in the deepest inaccessible place—the heart—is on
full display in both Aqhat's tale of the covetous Anat and in the parent's
teaching about the dangerous sexual predator with her smooth words. But
the parallels do not end there, for after Aqhat's death at the hands of
Anat's henchman, it is his dutiful sister (and *not* his grieving father) Paghit
who dresses as a warrior beneath her woman's attire and sets out to kill

---

271. Simon B. Parker (ed.), *Ugaritic Narrative Poetry* (SBL Writings from the
Ancient World, 9; Atlanta: Scholars Press, 1997), pp. 49-80; Neal H. Walls, *The
Goddess Anat in Ugaritic Myth* (SBLDS, 135; Atlanta: Scholars Press, 1992).

272. 'She drinks the wine by flagons,/The vines' blood from goblets of gold'
(Parker, 'Aqhat', p. 60). Unfortunately, there is a large gap between these lines (Tablet
I, col. vi, ll. 5-6) and her covetous glance at Aqhat's bow (ll. 13-14), but since she
immediately spills her wine on the ground (ll. 15-16), we must assume that she had
been drinking. As usual in the ancient Near East, the flow of wine also heralds the flow
of power, and someone dies (Fontaine, 'Deceptive Goddess', pp. 97-98).

273. Parker, *Ugaritic*, pp. 60-62.

274. 'Wblb', Tablet I, col. vi, l. 42 (Walls, *Anat*, p. 189). Parker translates 'inwardly
she plotted' (*Ugaritic*, p. 62).

her brother's murderer. Called 'Paghit, bearer of water, /Collector of dew from the fleece, / Who knows the course of the stars' (Tablet III, col. ii, ll. 1-3, 5-7), she exhibits the same powerful connections with water and female domestic crafts that characterize the Israelite women who are the household incarnations of Sister Wisdom.

Clifford also points out in his commentary that in Anat's drunken offers to Aqhat we have a parallel of sorts to Woman Folly's invitation to come to *her* banquet, rather than Woman Wisdom's, in Prov. 9.13-18.[275] What underlies this episode is a 'type-scene' drawn from the mythological epic traditions: a series of fixed plot actions, character and item motifs, which commonly recur all together and usually in the same order. Such fixed storytelling conventions are a hallmark of oral composition, giving the performer a 'breathing space' through the employment of a 'set piece'. While reciting this conventional bundle of motifs at the appropriate point during the performance, she or he is then able internally to recall, compose, edit or rearrange the next episode to be performed. While Fox quibbles that neither Woman Folly's invitation to the unwary youth nor Anat's proposition to Aqhat constitute offers of marriage[276] (Gilgamesh and Ishtar), other variations on this banqueting motif in Hittite myth or the Hebrew Bible also omit the 'marriage' story-line but still clearly represent variations on the type-scene.[277] In fact, just as the Hittite goddess Inarash lures the Illuyankis-dragon to his death by setting out an alcoholic banquet, Ya'el lures Sisera and Esther entices Haman to their deaths at carefully staged 'banquets', Woman Folly's invitations take the type-scene in the same direction. In my reading of this set of conventions, Woman Folly's banquet *does* recall Anat's proposition to Aqhat: while Anat wants the desirable male 'weapon' that marks the boy as a warrior-hero, restless Folly wants a more personal, biological male weapon, which is also the subject of much heroic fantasy:[278] the phallus that will bring her satisfaction, related again in terms of eating ('Stolen water is sweet, and bread

---

275. 'Woman Wisdom in the Book of Proverbs', in G. Baraulik, W. Gross and S. McEvenue (eds.), *Biblische Theologies und gesellschaftlicher Wandel* (FS N. Lohfink; Freiburg: Herder, 1993); see also his commentary, pp. 101-105.

276. For an iconographic representation of the 'erotic' component in banquet scenes, see C. Maier, *Fremde Frau*, pp. 234-46, esp. p. 242.

277. Fontaine, 'Deceptive Goddess', pp. 92-97.

278. The 'proverb poem' used to teach young recruits correct terminology is apt here: 'This is my weapon (said while touching the firearm) / This is my 'gun' (touching crotch); / This is for killing (touching firearm); / This is for 'fun' (touching crotch).'

eaten in secret is pleasant,' 9.17). The young hero, the mighty dragon, the fleeing general, the wily villain and the silly adolescent all descend to their deaths when their appetites for male honor, heady wine or sex are allowed free reign—or as the old English proverb would have it, 'Whoever sups with the Devil must bring a long spoon!' A goblet in the hands of any other female but Woman Wisdom is a cue for circumspect response (just as the sages are so fond of teaching the young bureaucrats), for trouble is at hand!

Asherah, the Tree Goddess of Canaan: From Divine Female to Tree to Sacred Pole to Ḥokmâ. From the beginning of modern scholarship on Woman Wisdom, we have seen a persistent desire to find a goddess indigenous to the Levant whose vegetal connections might have provided the model for Woman Wisdom as the Tree of Life. While this was not such an easy matter to resolve based only on the recovery of epic materials from this region, newer archaeological inquiries into the worship and iconographic traditions of Israel, Judah and their neighbors have furnished us with materials not available to the first scholars, Albright and Boström, who tried to relate Lady Wisdom to an unknown vine-goddess or Astarte. Though mentioned in texts, it is not always easy to separate the goddess Astarte from the mother/tree-goddess Asherah (= Hebrew form of Ugaritic name of the goddess Athirat, consort of 'El), or the warrior maiden-goddess, Anat (sister to Ba'al); at least at our present state of the inquiry, and this without even addressing the problem of these goddesses' relationship to goddesses Qudshu (or Qodesh), Tannit, Elat, Ashratu or Atargatis! The scholarly literature on this topic is so extensive and complicated that the reader will be pleased to know that it is beyond the scope of our present study to do more than gesture toward it.[279] Astarte seems to be the most diffuse figure of the 'Big Three' Levantine goddesses, while it is fairly easy to tell Asherah from Anat, because of their different relationships to motherhood and the gods with whom they are correlated as partners. However these three and the others may ultimately turn out to be connected or fused, it is certain that the orthodox editors of official monothe-

---

279. At present, the two most extensive and useful works are Judith Hadley's recently published *The Cult of Asherah in Ancient Israel and Judah* (see nn. 163 and 165 above for full citations), and S. Schroer, *In Israel gab es Bilder: Nachrichten von darstellender Kunst im Alten Testament* (OBO, 74; Göttingen: Presses Universitaires Fribourg, 1987); other useful studies dealing with tree iconography by Keel are cited above in nn. 114 and 193).

ism would have despised their cults and devotees, and worked hard to expunge any trace of the once legitimate place they may have held in the worship of the god Yahweh.

When we compare the iconographic traditions of Canaan and later Israel and Judah (and some of the New 'New Historians' would argue that they are entirely the same group!) to the literary ones, we find a discrepancy that troubles those who privilege text over artefact. The Asherah of the Ugaritic mythology is a fairly bland, motherly figure: compared to Woman Wisdom, she doesn't have nearly the well-rounded personality as 'mover and shaker' of her group's traditions. In the epic materials, she is mainly noted for being 'creatress of the gods' and 'nursemaid of the gods', and counselor/intercessor with her husband 'El. She has connections to both the sea, 'treading' it in one her epithets, and the fields (perhaps indicative of an Amorite origin as Ashratu, goddess of the steppes). In one scene she is spinning and engaged in other domestic crafts; in another, she makes her way to 'El's abode while riding on a donkey, perhaps a sign of her high status (because Anat and others walk while she rides). She mourns when Ba'al kills 77 of her sons; in a peculiar Hittite myth that is an earlier variant of the Potiphar's Wife episode of Genesis (also found in an earlier Egyptian variation in The Tale of the Two Brothers), we find her in a love triangle with the young storm-god (Ba'al-Hadad) and her traditional consort, 'El-kunirsha, suggesting that she may have had connections to both gods. Though Asherah/ Athirat gives 'counsel' in some of these texts, that may well be an extension of her roles as consort and mother and bear no specific relationship to a textual wisdom tradition. Further, in these literary materials, she is not especially tree-like, and of course, Woman Wisdom in Proverbs is not marked by a particularly strong figuration as mother, though she does act as something like a consort to her followers. It should be added, too, that some scholars question whether the portrayal of the Ugaritic Athirat in these various capacities has any broad relevance outside of that particular city-state, preferring to the Hebrew Asherah as an import of the Akkadian Ishtar, forced upon Judah by her imperial overlords.[280]

When we turn to the iconographic record, we find a different set of developments that help us trace the goddess's path from the gynomorphic mother of the gods to the abomination of the Hebrew Bible, the 'sacred pole' or asherah, which was found as part of Yahweh's sanctuaries in many places and periods. Hadley hypothesizes, based on inscriptions and

---

280. For a path through this mare's nest, see Hadley, *The Cult of Asherah*, pp. 1-83.

Figure 11. Goddess Tree. ('Asherah') with Caprids (Conoid Seal, Iron I,
Taanach. Linoleum block print by author, after Othmar Keel and
Christoph Uehlinger, *Gods, Goddesses, and Images of God in Ancient
Israel* [Philadelphia: Fortress Press, 1998], p. 127, illus. 154b.)

material finds, that the goddess was often represented as a stylized tree,
usually flanked by caprids who feed from its outstretched branches (see
Fig. 11). Eventually, this tree-symbol of the goddess, which emphasized
her provision of food for all life as well as more general fertility aspects,
evolved into a symbol of a symbol, the sacred pole, whose connection
with the goddess may or may not have been retained. In 'official'
theology, this asherah probably functioned as a representation or hypostasy of the fertility aspects of the goddess assumed by Yahweh in his
evolution toward sole high god: certainly, we hear from the Judean desert
that it was possible to offer a legitimate blessing in the form of 'May
Yahweh and his asherah bless you!' Women weavers in the Jerusalem
temple seem to have held a special place in the Asherah's cult during the
time it was still considered to be an ordinary part of official Yahweh
worship, and their weavings may have been intended to adorn a wooden

image of the goddess or perhaps the sacred pole. Despite the Deuteronomistic reformers' attempt to relate the goddess Asherah to worship of the storm god Ba'al, who was Yahweh's most dangerous competitor for the hearts and minds of the people during monarchic times, textual analysis of both the Hebrew Bible and the Ugaritic materials confirm that, outside of the peculiar Hittite variant mentioned above, Asherah was primarily associated with 'El, and not Ba'al.

Figure 12. Tree Woman. (Etching by author).

The connections between the Canaanite god 'El and the Hebrew god Yahweh are well- known and need not be reviewed here.[281] Through these various lines of inquiry, we may posit a legitimate and ancient connection between Yahweh/'El and Asherah, one which was embodied in the presence of the asherah in Yahweh's sanctuary, the pole itself being a stylized, streamlined version of the 'Giving Tree' that 'stands' for Asherah the goddess. With the expunging of the goddess and her worship from her official, legitimate place in Yahweh's cult, a psychological and iconographic need was created: in what way was one to compensate for the loss of the female fertility element in the old religion? And what was to be made of the con-

---

281. Mark Smith, *The Early History of God: Yahweh and the Other Deities in Ancient Israel* (San Francisco: Harper & Row, 1990).

tinuing deep resonance felt in the symbol of the sacred tree, always a sign of life in the arid climates of the Near East?[282] Hadley suggests, as have others, that these 'lacks' were filled by the deliberate creation of a 'literary construct' with epic connections and a hidden history in images to be found on ewers, incense stands, pithoi and figurines—our Woman Wisdom (Fig. 11). Although the recollection of her connections with Asherah were even less than a distant memory to our late period sages editing and composing Proverbs 1–9, Woman Wisdom nevertheless stepped into the gap left when the Tree Goddess and/or her sacred pole was uprooted and burned down. Standing beside Yahweh at the moment of creation just as Asherah's asherah stood beside the standing stones in Yahweh's monarchic sanctuaries, Woman Wisdom embodies a forgotten past of divine female power: life-giving, nurturing, counseling.[283]

Final Remarks on the Cosmic Domain

Just as we saw considerable overlap in the private and public roles that real human women played in their societies reflected in the book of Proverbs, we find a similar process at work in the literary constructs of Woman Wisdom and Woman Stranger(s), but to a lesser degree. This is because goddesses in the cosmic domain, by their very nature, are not subject to the limitations placed on the regular women in the borders patriarchy tries to forbid them to cross. Indeed, human males (or scribal theologians?) in these mythological texts who have the temerity to suggest that the goddesses should keep to the 'female' boundaries between public and private, male and female action or attributes wind up meeting a very nasty end! No regular male dares attempt to harness the Maiden Anat to domestic female roles, nor do men who refuse the audacious sexual advances of goddesses escape their wrath. The extensive parallels between dangerous goddesses and Woman Stranger may be the source of our sages' restraint in attempting to control her: they understand that this ambivalent female *cannot* be controlled, and so they concentrate their efforts on the young men who are supposedly their prey. Indeed, female submission does not come naturally

282. Studies on the iconography and interpretation tree of life, and trees generally abound and cannot be reviewed here, but see Keel, *Goddesses and Trees*, pp. 20-59; Carol L. Meyers, *The Tabernacle Menorah: A Synthetic Study of a Symbol from the Bible Cult* (ASOR Diss, 2; Missoula, MT: Scholars Press, 1976), for an entry into that bibliography.

283. Hadley, 'From Goddess to Literary Construct'.

1. *Positive Roles*

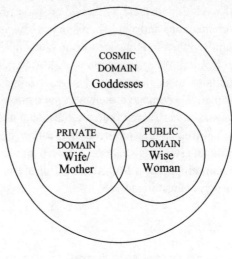

WOMAN WISDOM

2. *Negative Roles*

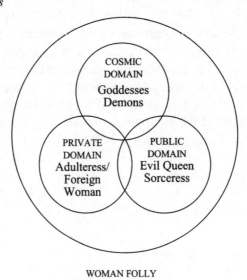

WOMAN FOLLY
WOMAN STRANGER

Figure 13. Sources of Characterization of Woman Wisdom and Woman Stranger.

or easily to these goddesses and demons; Lilith, Lamashtu, Gula, Mami, Nintu, Saltu, Ishtar, Isis, Anat, and even the motherly Asherah, all act with authority, and display wisdom fitting to their domains of power when they do. To be sure, they are shown in stereotyped female roles: mother, sister, consort, nursemaid, midwife, etc., on analogy with the human females whose lives and work helped shape the portraits of the goddesses. These texts, after all, are products of patriarchal thinking, but even so, the goddess mythologies give occasional voice to the chafing restrictions to which their human sisters are subject, and in doing so, raise an internal critique. Women's power did not, does not, and need not be seen as derived solely from their biology and gendered roles.

With this legacy of divine females lurking behind the composition of the cosmic figures in Proverbs 1–9, we are now able to see how these puzzling figures came to contain so many disparate elements. The characters of the cosmic pair in Proverbs are shaped not only by reference to the real social roles of women, but by goddess mythology as well, and this is why they stray so freely from private to public to cosmic venues and back again. Like the good girl/bad girl syndrome of the sages with respect to the women of the their culture—apparently there were *no* mediocre mothers or adulteresses!—the cosmic domain shows the same desire to bifurcate the goddesses into good, motherly ones, or wicked, sexual or warlike ones (Fig. 13). This is the very same redistribution of traits into good and bad 'bundles' of motifs that is the hallmark of the sages' presentation of Woman Wisdom and Woman Stranger. The goddesses do a better job of resisting this impulse in *their* texts; the cosmic twins of Proverbs are not quite so successful. It must remain the job of feminist readers to reunite these sisters, separated at their literary 'birth', in our valuation of what traits might be considered appropriate to 'females' and what texts ought to be read to daughters who would be whole.

Chapter 3

WOMEN USING WISDOM: PERFORMING THE TRADITION

Genre, Gender, and Performance

In folklore studies, the composition and social use of folk genres—proverbs, riddles, jokes, legends, etc.—have always been thought to provide a 'window' into a culture's true values and operating principles. Compared to expressive forms that demand detailed, long-term, specific education in their presentation and full-scale execution (such as Serbian folk epics or south Indian temple dancing), the 'little' everyday forms that anyone may use give critics an even larger cross-sampling for a group's broadly held 'folk ideas' and practices. Both the 'big' and the 'little' folk genres, then, offer us a gauge for assessing how units of folklore are used to impose, make and pass on meaning for the society that uses them.

One of those 'meanings' that a culture must continually reinscribe in its members is the whole concept of gender—that is, the 'import' assigned by that culture to the biological sex differences observed in male and females. A group's 'teachings' on this subject (as well as others) are both expressly and tacitly woven not only into the fabric of the genre items themselves, but also into the arrangements and uses made of those genres.[1] This means, among other things, that gender must be treated as an analytic category that must be traced in its overt occurrences in folklore (stories about waiting princesses told to girls; proverbs about women), and in its more subtle, sub-voce appearances in genres that may seem at first glance to have nothing to do with gender (stories about war-making told to boys; application of 'female' genres to men).

Folklorists initially took gender into account in their work primarily because many genres are sex-specific: lullabies and love lyrics among the

---

1. Marcia K. Lieberman, ' "Some Day my Prince Will Come": Female Acculturation through the Fairy Tale', in Jack Zipes (ed.), *Don't Bet on the Prince: Contemporary Feminist Fairy Tales in North America and England* (New York: Routledge, 1989), pp. 185-200.

ladies, war taunts and battle songs for the gentlemen, as it were. Even so, it took many more years of study before researchers working with living cultures became alert to the more subtle distinctions between the sexes' interactions with the lore of their society. Often, when a culture was studied and 'collected' by a male researcher, it was preeminently the experience of the *males* in the group that was recorded and considered normative for the whole culture. It took a feminist spirit of inquiry in anthropology to question this working method and legitimize the researcher's move from the men's tribal council into the menstrual hut. Once it was acknowledged that women might tell different stories from the men, or might tell the *same* stories as the men, *but with a different meaning,* the 'art' of studying oral verbal art had to be reframed.[2] In essence, this meant that more than the plain text of a folk item had to be collected. Along with the item itself, folklorists realized that their ethnographies must consider the context of group use of folk items, which is, more often than not, a *performance.* In performance, we encounter a nexus of interrelations that, taken as a whole, are used to calculate a 'meaning', however provisional or specific: the traditions of the past are engaged by means of an event taking place in the moment. The performance *event* enables the tradition; the tradition is the *referent* of the event.[3] It is at the point of this interaction that we will now take up the question of gender.

It cannot be emphasized enough here that someone who hopes to study the use of folk genres of the past is hampered by lack of evidence in a variety of ways.[4] The living society that developed and used the genre may have passed out of existence, leaving only an anthropologist's study to witness to their tradition and its use, or, as in the case of the ancient Near East, the only clue left may be the preservation of the folk item (and its use) within a literary text. Further, those texts that have been preserved are the victims of time and chance: some things that are probably *not* representative of the group as a whole may have been carefully maintained by a 'special-interest group' (scribes, bureaucrats, temple officials), while other articles in common use were not preserved, because they had no scribal

2.   Heda Jason, 'The Fairytale of the Active Heroine: An Outline for Discussion', in G. Galame-Griaule, V. Görög-Karady and M. Chiche (eds.), *Le conte, pourquoi, comment?* (Paris: Centre National de la Recherche scientifique, 1984), pp. 79-97.

3.   Foley, *Singer of Tales,* p. 27.

4.   For an excellent discussion of the parameters of using folkloristic methods to study the Bible, see Susan Niditch, *Folklore and the Hebrew Bible* (Minneapolis: Augsburg–Fortress, 1993), pp. 3-31.

advocates who cared about their collection. With a work like the Bible, which has been thoroughly edited, reformulated and rearranged to suit the later community's needs, there is no such thing as a pristine record of an actual oral interchange; a literary and ideological dimension always stands between the researcher and the oral performance or composition we are trying to understand. Finally, we must also note that in the patriarchal ideology of the ancient world, very little created by women, barred as they were from 'official' power or posts as authors, was considered worthy of transmission. This lack of a clear witness to the verbal expressiveness of women's wisdom necessitates a certain flexibility in method for the zealous researcher. We must take our evidence where we find it, and occasionally, even the gaps and silences will be counted as a proverbial 'word' spoken by women of the past. But the missing script of women's interactions with proverbial wisdom is an ever-felt poverty in the materials available for study, and must serve as a caution to the reader. I will give only one example here of how our theories about gender, genre and performance might be modified if only we had the kind of evidence that a living culture provides.

Of Babas *and Boys in a Serbian Village*

As is often the case, the unofficial, non-rational 'care' of sick family and village members in traditional societies usually falls to women, and in the Serbian villages studied by folklorists, the most efficacious and revered practitioners of such folk medicine are post-menopausal women, especially those who are mothers of mothers. Verbal charms and incantations (*bajanje*) are part of these women's heritage, passed on from generation to generation, and may even be reckoned as part of the dowry a bride brings when she marries into a new group. The performance of these charms is invariably undertaken by *women only*, and some gain more repute than others for their mastery of the 'dedicated register' of the charms and the successful outcomes of their practice. Optional ritual items may be used from time to time as well as other forms of intervention that 'modern' people would recognize more easily as 'paramedical'—massage, herbal remedies, etc.—but it is clear that it is the recitation and enactment of the charm in performance by a qualified *baba* that secures the desired outcome.[5]

For those of us raised on fairy tales or conversant with modern pagan feminist ritual reconstructions of (an imagined?) women's healing practice, we may be momentarily surprised that the *baba*, or granny, who

5.   Foley, *Singer*, pp. 99-104.

performs the cure is a perfectly ordinary and normal family woman. She does not arrive cloaked in darkness with snakes curling at her hands, nor does she, in her conversation or practice, revoke her 'official' religious allegiance to the Blessed Virgin as a beloved entity with special concern for women, children and families. Further, the village recognizes the importance of her work: she is normally paid in kind for her services.[6] Even more surprising, perhaps, is the fact that the delineated performance arena (the spatial, temporal and interpersonal location in which the performance is enacted) for her work is *not* characterized by any special time or place. Often, other family or village members are present and going on with their regular activities during the incantation of the *baba*. Once again, this tells us that the 'active' element in performance that secures the desired outcome is in the 'word power' of the charm, properly recited.

Assuming that one is a duly recognized *baba*, fluency in the 'register' of the charm is a necessary ingredient for the performance. Just as all forms of verbal art have a distinctive 'note' to sound, a linguistic and paralinguistic way of proceeding, so, too, charms are characterized by features particular to their specific register. The charm register is marked by the paralinguistic features of rapid speech, pauses and the whispered words that are delivered into the patient's ear, while the *bajalica* (a *baba* performing a *bajanje)* leans over him or her. Not all stanzas of the incantation must be pronounced, but some features are invariable and must always be present. Linguistically, the charm register also incorporates the frequent use of archaisms, and the typical form of 'women's prosody' familiar from other women's verbal traditions (symmetrical octosyllable). This type of verbal art foregrounds 'lyric, fleeting, intense moments' rather than the involved, sweeping, yet detailed narrative descriptions employed by men in epic recitations. Finally, the charm register makes extensive use of 'framing' as a device, using type-scene-like stanzas to introduce the different, essential portions of the charm recitation. In the Serbian charm of the 'Nine Winds', the frame consisted of a refrain ('Out of there comes...'), which calls up a 'therapeutic arrival' of healing entities who remove and dispel the wind-borne diseases afflicting the patient.[7]

During a performance by one Desanka at which folklorists were present, the granny began her recitation in a rapid, whispered voice[8], which was

---

6.   This form of payment is typical in the village for services performed by men *or* women.

7.   Foley, *Singer*, pp. 110-15.

8.   Originally, researchers thought this kinetic element was an atypical feature of a

followed by a pause caused, perhaps, by the unusual nature of her audience rather than the typical pause between frames. At this point, her seven-year-old grandson Marko broke in and prompted her with the beginning lines of the next required element. The performance then proceeded uninterrupted.[9]

We must stop here to observe the way in which our expectations about the role of gender in the performance arena, however well-informed, are directly contradicted by 'what actually happened'! A seven-year-old boy, according to the Serbian world-view, could not in any way be thought of as a viable performer of this women's folk genre, nor would we think of him as having the 'status' to interrupt his elder relative, especially in the presence of outsiders. Where critics might have thought that the charms used exclusively by women were jealously guarded by the women whose speciality they were, clearly the charms are so well known within the folk group that even a young boy can tell when the charm is being recited properly or improperly. The fact that the charms are employed in a context (performance arena) where many family members of various ages might be present has given this female folklore a broader currency. Had the researchers *not* been present for this interrupted performance, it is unlikely that they or we would have assumed that men and boys had any detailed knowledge of the charm register, the charm incantation itself, or its proper performance. This little episode (which is only of passing interest to the researchers themselves) underscores in the most serious way the necessarily partial and speculative nature of many of our reconstructions to follow, at least where they seek to designate the paralinguistic features of proverb performance. There is no substitute for evidence drawn directly from a living culture, and we readily concede that this is so. Still, there is much to be learned about the way a text and a culture manipulate the category of gender even in *literary* proverb performance, to which we now direct our attention.

Proverbs in Performance: Through a Woman's Eyes

From British television comes the chronicles of one Blackadder , a hapless Englishman whom we follow through various epochs and social locations, from princeling to servant. As an Elizabethan lord, he finds himself

performance before 'strangers'; as it happens, it turns out that these features are part of the standard charm register.

9.   Foley, *Singer*, p. 116.

mightily confused by his attraction to his new manservant 'Bob'—whom he does not know is in fact a young woman in disguise, bent on seeking her fortune as a lad. Concerned about his sexual identity, and having found no help from the leeches in his codpiece advised by the physician, he is told to consult the local wisewoman whom he has described as 'some deranged Druid who gives her professional address as 1 Dunghill Mansions, Putney'.[10] We join him there, where he greets a woman of middle years, sitting on a rock.

> *Blackadder:* Tell me, young crone, is this Putney?
> *Young Crone (broadly):* That it be, that it be!
> *Blackadder (pained):* 'Yes, it is', not 'That it be'. You don't have to talk in that stupid voice to me. I'm not a tourist.
> *Young Crone (slightly deflated):* Oh.
> *Blackadder:* I seek information about a wisewoman.
> *Young Crone:* Ah! The wisewoman! The wisewoman!
> *Blackadder:* Yes, the wisewoman.
> *Young Crone:* Two things must ye know of the the wisewoman!
> *Blackadder:* Yes?
> *Young Crone:* First! She is a woman! And second, she is…
> *Blackadder:* Wise?
> *Young Crone:* You do know her then?[11]

This comic interchange ushers us into a consideration of the power women seize from the common traditions of wisdom when they enter into the realm of *performance*. Lord Blackadder has tried the remedies of his enlightened times, but when 'push comes to shove', he is not unwilling to consult the 'final authority' in matters of health and conduct[12]—an old hag with no male protector in evidence, confined to the liminal margins of her village society, but absolutely indispensable for all of that. Throughout history, such women have sat off to the edge of official power, known and valued for their special crafts and display of counsel. Feared but functional, women have used their innate powers and special vision to carve out a place for themselves that is real, vigorous and prized by their communities, however much it may have been under-observed in historical and anthropological reconstructions of social history.

---

10. R. Curtis and B. Elton, 'Bells', in *Blackadder: The Whole Damn Dynasty, 1485–1917* (New York: Penguin Putnam, 2000), pp. 119-36 (127).

11. Curtis and Elton, 'Bells', p. 127.

12. For the record, her advice to the gender-addled lord is both wise and womanly: she says that whenever she fancies someone, she usually sleeps with them—though she has to drug them first, what with being so old and warty.

As we have seen in the last chapter, when speaking of women and the ancient wisdom traditions, we usually find ourselves speaking in a male tongue about what women *ought* to be, as encapsulated in the proverbs and teachings by men that refer to them. Only in limited places and with much speculation can we reconstruct a life for women as scribes, authors or patronesses of wisdom literature—the usual way in which earlier studies sought to locate women within the tradition as something other than the trope elite male authors make of them in order to educate young men into proper relation to patriarchal leadership. 'Beware the woman!' intone the sages, from Mesopotamia to Egypt, and all the places in between. Thanks to feminist studies, we are only too aware of the ideological deformation of the facts of daily life upon which this instruction relies. Were we to consider the actual axes of power and abuse in ancient societies of the biblical world, only the most biased observer would not conclude that the *real* proverbial truth to be learned there should be directed at young girls and women: *Beware the man!*

We will see shortly how proverbs about gender, genealogy and race are wielded in the mouth of the vituperative prophet Ezekiel, to the shame of men and the denigration and eventual erasure of the real females to whom they supposedly refer. Next to this, we will place those examples we have of women using women *differently*. To anticipate our conclusion, we must insist, once again, that *the gender* and the social location of the proverb user (as well as its original maker) affect the way in which supposedly 'neutral', traditional truths are deployed and exercised within society. Performance alone does not guarantee the female any great advantage; it depends on who uses the proverb, in what circumstances and to what end.

In folkloric terms, the meaningful citation of a proverb in a social situation in order to affect or evaluate speech or actions is named 'proverb performance'. It is a purposive, highly nuanced activity to be found all around the world, wherever traditional wisdom lives in a society as a construct of social knowledge and accepted truth. The *proverb image* (more specifically, the relation between the terms of the image)[13] is applied to a *context situation* by one member in an *interaction situation*. P. Seitel, early on in his studies of proverb use in African tribal societies, referred to this structured event as proverb performance, calling it a 'social use of

---

13. These relations may be ones of identification (A = B), contrast (A ≠ B), positive or negative causation (A → B; A →/ B respectively), with all their various structural permutations as these relationships are expressed linguistically.

metaphor', which it certainly is.[14] However, since not all proverbs are properly metaphorical in form (sayings being simply observational and not depending on metaphor as the base feature of their images), this remark has not always been properly understood or valued. In fact, it is the *application* of the proverb that makes use of metaphor, as the elements in the proverb are correlated with those of a context situation, in order to judge it or suggest an approved, traditional response to it.[15] It is in the rhetorical enactment or *performance* that the 'immanent referentiality' of the proverb as an item of folklore is given full scope. In order to achieve his or her desired effect, the proverb user depends on the audience's fluency in the tradition, and their ability to decode the pithy citation with all of the cultural knowledge to which that proverb pertains. It is in performance that the full nuances of the proverb are called into attention and strategically referenced to make the observation complete—what good is a proverb whom no one quotes? *Audience* is fully implied in any citation of a proverb as its most basic condition—though, to be sure, we may find at the end point of the tradition that a sage like Qoheleth will conduct a sort of irascible dialogue with former sages by citing current proverbs and then contrasting them with his own proverbially cast observations. Normally, however, we must be fully aware that proverb use is a *social* strategy and not simply a literary one, so that the full range of techniques used to study the dynamics of linguistic interactions are appropriate in any investigations of proverb use, and the role of gender there.

This metaphor-making behavior of calling up ancient wisdom coded in proverbs to speak to a present moment happens in the presence of a very specific sort of interaction between speaker and hearers/audience/readers, one that is governed by, among other things, features of status and gender. Since we do not always have a Young Crone before us, telling us that the Wise Woman is about to dispense wisdom, modern observers must ask what are the conditions and linguistic strategies that signal the movement

14. Peter Seitel, 'A Social Use of Metaphor', *Genre* 2 (1969), pp. 143-61, reprinted in Dan Ben-Amos (ed.), *Folklore Genres* (Austin: University of Texas Press, 1976), pp. 125-43.

15. G. Hasan-Rokem, *Proverbs in Israeli Folk Narratives: A Structural Semantic Analysis* (FFC, 232; Helsinki: Suomalainen Tiedeakatemia, Academia Scientiarum Fennica, 1982), p. 15; P. Grzybek, 'Foundations of Semiotic Proverb Study', *Proverbium* 4 (1987), pp. 39-85, reprinted in Wolfgang Mieder (ed.), *Wise Words: Essays on the Proverb* (Garland Folklore Casebooks, 6; New York: Garland, 1994), pp. 31-71, see discussion on pp. 49-51.

into the 'performance arena' of proverb use? How do we know that we are about to see and hear (or read) a proverb performed, rather than an epic poem, a charm or a lullaby?

The Performance Arena

Proverbs used in context seek to 'dis-ambiguate', that is, render meaning-*full* a situation that has arisen (or might arise) for which there are at least two distinct and largely contrasting interpretations. This interchange, in the language of folklore's 'ethnography of speaking', takes place in a 'performance arena'—a special location, spatial, temporal or interpersonal, where the oral performance occurs and a unit of folklore is invoked. It is the 'compressed' nature of the folklore item, its 'immanent referentiality', that accounts for its ability to call up a world of meanings, referencing a portion of a culture's thought world through employment of a compact linguistic idiom.[16] Since proverbs are an 'everyday' form that require no special training or membership within a specialized group in order to be able to use them, it is not surprising that the performance arena for their use differs substantially from that for covenant renewal ceremonies, love songs or prophetic oracles. Two key elements must exist in the arena (Seitel's *Interaction Situation)* of this humble, yet flexible form: a *conflict-ual situation* and *disparity in status,* at least a momentary one, between the proverb user and the audience who hears it.

Let us imagine a hypothetical interaction between two people, with observers looking on (Fig. 14). A *something* has happened or will happen. The participants in the interaction have sensed an inherent conflict: how should they 'read' the unfamiliar terrain? Which path should they take to evoke clarification, enforce unity or repress dissent? At this critical cross-road, someone cites/sites a proverb to suggest or impose a traditional construction of reality on the flux of unfamiliarity that threatens social coherence (or, at least, the threat is felt in the mind of the proverb user). This is sometimes referred to by the form-critical appellation, 'saying-appraisal'. A saying or proverb is put forward to offer an appraisal of the situation in socially accepted ways; in this critique by categorization, an implicit admonition to action is offered. If the participants recognize the proverb as 'true', agree that it 'fits' the situation to which it has been applied, then it follows that one ought to act in accordance with the weight of all that congruent wisdom. The audience/reader, then, is required to 'co-

16. Foley, *Singer*, p. 47.

create' cultural meaning, which, like God's word in 2nd Isaiah, goes out and does not return empty. In such ways, status quo is maintained, threats are defused and 'harmony' is restored. Sometimes. When we look at the relative status positions of the proverb user and the proverb hearers/ audience/readers, we see that a strategic and subversive use of tradition may also be at work in the performance arena. This strategic use of traditional wisdom is available to any group member who is fluent in the group's stock of proverbs, and has the impulse to employ it—not only women need apply!

**Proverb Performance:
Context Is Everything!**

Figure 14. The Performance Arena for Proverbs.

A Male-to-Male Example: Job 32–37
An example: when wisdom is so wholeheartedly associated with the 'aged' in traditional societies,[17] how is it possible for a young person to gain a

17. See Prov. 7.7; 16.31; 20.29; 22.6, 15; Job 12.12. Qoheleth, of course, makes a markedly divergent reading of this wisdom trope (4.13; 6.3, 6; 11.8-9; 12.1-7).

hearing for an alternative interpretation of the contextual reality that is in
dispute. We see this beautifully illustrated in Job 32–37, in the rhetorical
gyrations of Elihu the Buzite, the youngest of Job's interlocutors, as well
as in the textual commentaries made on this intrusive character. When his
elders attempted to argue Job into confessional conformity concerning the
meaning of his afflictions, Elihu had assumed the culturally assigned position of inferiority allocated to the young. How could an unseasoned group
member have the experience, the wisdom, or the wit to deploy it, which is
called for in the attempt to mend the momentous chasm in theology that
Job's laments have so detailed? Naturally, he should and must wait for his
elders to silence and confute Job's accusations against God's righteousness or moral intelligibility. When the three friends give up on their efforts
in reasoning with Job based on tradition, Elihu clearly defers to the accepted
wisdom that held him as a silent spectator[18] to the round of dialogues—or
does he? Like the young boy in the Serbian village who interrupted his
baba's recitation, Elihu also moves into the performance arena of Job and
the three friends:

> 'I am young in years, and you are aged; *therefore* I was timid and afraid to
> declare my opinion to you. *I said, "Let days speak, and many years teach
> wisdom."* But it is the spirit in a man, the breath of the Almighty, that
> makes him understand. It is not the old that are wise, nor the aged that
> understand what is right. *Therefore I say*, "Listen to me; let me also declare
> my opinion" ' (32.6b-10, RSV).

Elihu quotes a proverb about age and wisdom that links them in a basic
identity, *but* he then claims that the truth of that proverb has *not* held true
in the current situation. This refutation gives him a gap into which to insert
his own less typical perspective. God, and not age, bestows consciousness
—and hence, the capacity for wisdom—upon people, and the young as
well as the old may have access to *that* source of knowledge. His following speeches proceed to restate, sum up, and punctuate points that the
friends have actually raised previously, leading many commentators to
find him superfluous to the dialogue, an authorial afterthought of orthodoxy, or a bridge to the whirling theophany that *also* has no answer for Job
but silencing. Still, Elihu attempts to interpose a rhetorical space for his
speech, when faced with so much negative weight ranged against his
testimony:

---

18. Or so we the readers presume from his speeches, since no mention has been
made of him previously.

'Listen to my words, O Sages!
O Knowing Ones, hearken to me,
because *"ear-words-tries,
and-palate-tastes-food"*.
Justice let us choose for ourselves;
let us know between us what-is-good!' (34.2-4).

Just as at the beginning of his speeches, Elihu attempts to gain a hearing by entering the performance arena, signaled by his citation of an out-of-context proverb. We have not *really* been discussing the sense of taste, but Elihu invokes it here to make his point proverbially. Anyone can tell immediately when tasting if something is sweet or sour, good or bad. The sensation is just that intimate and unquestionable. Words, too, suggests Elihu, can be savored and explored by the organ that takes them in, the ear, just as the mouth does a foodstuff. Fitting words, so examined, may be relished and swallowed, if found pleasing and good! Words are the fare of the tongue, their sweet and wise product, and he invokes all the wisdom associations between wise speech, satisfaction and nourishment for his audience. Where his earlier attempt to suggest that God's breath of consciousness gave him the discernment to enter into the conversation served as a way to confute traditional thinking that silenced him, here he falls back upon the wisdom of the body, perhaps an even more basic assumption in his culture's lexicon of truth.[19]

Whether his attempt at gaining an ear is any more successful than before must be judged by the reader, but we find here, at least, a congruence with Job's own idiom. As his friends have spoken, basing their arguments in the rarefied and advanced logic of theological perception, Job has repeatedly answered with images of taste and touch, far more intimate and primitive sensations. Elihu's proverbial image has met Job 'where he lives'; Job, who cannot see or hear God in his current circumstances, aware of only the taste of bitterness of his own despair and pain, has been in a sense *heard* by the other culturally silenced participant in the dialogue. Whether this succeeds in carving out a hearing for the younger man is another matter entirely, but the proverb performance found here is a deft linguistic play on the previous words of Job, permeated as they are by the infantile senses rather than rational thought.

When we look at the two occasions where Elihu cites proverbs to smooth his entry into the debate of his elders, we see typical features that signal entrance into the performance arena. First, we have a *situation*—the

19. Food good, starvation bad; health good, pain bad; etc. throughout the whole of Job.

breakdown of the dialogues by which Job and friends hoped to convince the other of the correct interpretation of his suffering. This situation might be interpreted in a variety of ways, and hence constitutes an uncomfortable site of conflict. Who has won here, the silent, unrepentant Job or his now-speechless detractors? Are we to conclude that there *is* no answer that can make God good or Job guilty? Has conventional theological wisdom failed when brought face to face with concrete experience? Or have only the representatives of that wisdom failed? The conditions of contextual conflict over interpretation have been met.

Next, we find the *disparity in status* between Elihu and his audience, old and young, wise and foolish, that is a typical impetus to movement toward performance. Without 'outside' aid and the extra punch of authority lent by proverbial 'truth', Elihu can find no purchase for his words, as his citing of traditional wisdom about his status in 32.2-22, makes amply clear. In the performance arena, the strategic 'edge' goes to the deft user of an appropriate proverb, as Elihu shows himself to be in 34.2-4. At the same time the proverb user 'hides' behind group wisdom, he or she also sidles into the interactional role of 'counselor' or mentor to the audience—a method whereby a low-status participant temporarily aspires to and assumes the trappings of one of higher status—the educator versed in the wisdom of all. In other words, no matter where the proverb user began on the status continuum, the quotation of the proverb renders the performer 'one-up' on the audience.[20] What an advantageous verbal strategy for those who are routinely shut out of the circle of power! In verbal duels where each participant cites proverbs, of course, the field goes to the one whose citation seems to highlight the most congruence between the images in the proverb and the elements in the context to which it is applied. Each proverb user vies for the role of authoritative teacher, in an ever expanding game of one-up-manship. We have no evidence of this kind of interchange here in Elihu's speeches, however. The author allows the youngster to have the last word, so to speak, before the divine one comes.

Keying the Performance: The Proverb 'Register'

We see in the previous example how the basic conditions of performance arena (situation, status disparity) are met in Elihu's movement into the

---

20. N.R. Norrick, 'Proverbial Perlocutions: How to Do Things with Proverbs', *Grazer Linguistische Studien* 17–18 (1982), pp. 169-83; reprinted in Mieder, *Wise Words*, pp. 143-57, see especially discussion in section 3.2, pp. 149-50.

broken discourse of Job and his friends. We see also in our example some typical features that 'cue' the performer and audience to awareness that a proverb performance 'event' is about to take place. Those features that alert the participants to the special nature of the verbal event to follow are said to 'key the performance': they tell us that here we are to hear one kind of speech act and not some other, and which interpretive strategies we ought to employ to understand what follows. These attributes may include some or all of the following: appeal to tradition, disclaimers of performance, special codes or formulae, figurative language, paralinguistic features (volume, pause, gesture, etc.), parallelism, and so on.[21] Just as the reading of the Law may be keyed by the presence of Levites, scrolls from which those presiding might read, and a gathered, solemn audience, proverb performance is keyed when the user references the special features of the proverb 'register', that is, those features that set a proverbial statement off from normal spoken or written discourse.

Introductory Elements: Appeal to Tradition
Because proverbs represent a kind of educational code for a culture's hallowed beliefs and insights into the nature of the world, because they 'quote' the group's own former 'speech', users often key their performance by invoking the tradition itself. We may find, for example, some sort of formulae preceding (or sometimes, following) the citation, such as 'as the saying goes...', 'thus it is verily ever', 'a proverb of the men of Hatti says...',[22] or, in the case of the Hebrew Bible, 'as it is said...' (Gen. 22.14); 'therefore it is said...' (Gen. 10.9; 2 Sam. 5.8); 'as the proverb of the ancient says...' (1 Sam. 24.13); or 'therefore it became a proverb...' (1 Sam. 10.12). We also find the inversion of this appeal, when the Hebrew god seeks to find a clear way to *negate* tradition of the people by the denying the future applicability of certain proverbs (Ezek. 12.22-33; 18.2, 3). In fact, such vocative statements are *so* typical in keying proverb

21. R. Baumann, *Verbal Art as Performance* (Prospect Heights, IL: Waveland Press, 1977), pp. 8-22.
22. William W. Hallo, 'Proverbs Quoted in Epic', in T. Abusch, J. Huehnergard and P. Steinkeller (eds.), *Lingering over Words: Studies in Ancient Near Eastern Literature in Honor of William L. Moran* (Atlanta: Scholars Press, 1990), pp. 201-17 (213, 209). Along with others, Hallo lists his criteria for intertextual (= literary) proverb performance as (1) appeal to tradition, (2) out of context imagery, and (3) occurrence of the item in a proverb collection from the culture from which the relevant text comes.

performance that over-zealous translators often add them in as an introduction for proverb citations that seem to intrude, 'out of the blue', into
narratives or other genres. While Elihu does not use any of these typical
formulaic appeals in our example, his use of 'therefore' in v. 32.6bα[23] and
'I said...' (in the perfect rather than the more typical consecutive imper-
fect, in v. 32.7a), followed by a recognizable proverb, functions to
introduce his performance. We may safely conclude that the citation of a
whole proverb from the group's tradition, even without a formulaic introduction, operates as an invocation of the tradition and moves participants
into the arena of performance.

Out-of-Context Intrusion of Figurative Language
The next feature that keys our performance is also typical to use of proverbs in social or literary settings: the citation of a proverb is often jarring
in that it is '*out of context*'. That is, its *literal* referents in the proverb
image used to convey its meaning have no proximate referent in what has
just transpired. In our text in the Elihu speeches, the literary context begins
with Job's preceding speeches, starting in ch. 29, and runs through ch. 31.
'Days' (29.2, with 'months'; 29.4, 18; 30.27) have certainly been mentioned and the motif of silenced speakers has been explored (29.21-25).
However, Elihu's entry into the conversation, '*Let days speak, and many
years teach wisdom*', was immediately preceded by no mention of days,
years, teaching or wisdom, either by Job or his three 'official' counselors.
Similarly, Elihu's proverb about perception, '*ear-words-tries/and-palate-
tastes-food*' has no nearby antecedent in the conversation (his mention of
appetite in 33.20 refers to its loss, not its abilities) in the verses which
introduce it. While this episode is quite probably a *literary* construction
rather than a record of a genuine interaction, it still captures one of the
features that characterizes the performance arena for the social use of
proverbs—this surprising introduction of something that seems to be off
the mark, out of context, puzzling within its current context. In fact, when
a proverb user unleashes the proverb on the quizzical audience, the out-of-
context-*ness* alerts the audience to the performance and calls them in to
play their parts. The very *lack* of a literal congruence, or put another way,
the metaphorical mapping of the elements of the proverb image (ear,

---

23. This terminology also occurs routinely within prophetic oracles, after a summary of offences, in order to announce the judgment for those transgressions.
'Therefore' works as a pivot point within a performance, then, to introduce the next
phase.

word/palate, food) onto a situation, requires the hearers to search more deeply for connections and find a likely application for this unexpected citation.[24] Obviously, the speaker means to foreground *more* than the literal content of the proverb; the audience *must* be fluent in the group's proverbial stock to join in the bonding exercise of discovering the implied references to the situation at hand. The proverb user fades behind the community by calling its lore to mind, but simultaneously attains the one-up position of being the mentor who can impose appropriate standards, meanings and interpretations. Users and hearers, locked in conflict or ambiguity, come together in temporary unity as the exchange proceeds: both share a fluency in their culture's body of proverbs, and both are linked in the moment of the citation (and perhaps the context to which the proverb is applied as well). Group solidarity is maintained yet the speaker has voiced a (perhaps subversive) point of view, all the while from within a 'safety net' of shared assumptions.

The Proverb Register: Special Linguistic Features
Since our introductory formulae and the sudden intrusion of figurative language with no clear precedents in the verbal interaction have told us we are about to 'play' the score of proverb performance, we the audience are cued to attend closely to the special linguistic features of the proverb. Returning to our musical model, we need to know if the score is to be played as written for an oboe, or whether we should be playing a flute instead. In other words, we need to know the 'register' of biblical pro-verbial utterances.[25] This register includes some or all of the following features so typical in the construction of proverbs in general and biblical proverbs in particular: brevity, rhyme, alliteration, parataxis, parallelism and deviation from the normal syntax of discourse.

Proverbs are typically short statements, no more than two lines, usually exhibiting parallelism between the two half-lines. Rhyme may be present, either through the actual sounds or in the more abstract rhyming of word patterns.[26] Both of these generic features render the proverb easy to memorize, remember and repeat. This accounts for much of its didactic quality. Finally, proverbs in Hebrew are notorious for their abnormal syntax, which may be constructed through violation of the normal word order (verb-subject-object), and/or their penchant for parataxis—for

24. Norrick, 'Proverbial Perlocutions', pp. 147-48.
25. For a compact summary, see Niditch, *Folklore*, pp. 67-87.
26. That is, line 1: subject[1]-verb[1]-object[1]//line 2: subject[2]-verb[2]-object[2]).

example, the stark juxtaposition of nominal phrases without a connecting verb, or the failure to indicate *how* the elements of the image are related to each other (synonymous or antithetical connections). These features not only foreground the form as something *other* than normal conversation, but they summon the hearer to work through their potential ranges of meaning, deciding on what fits best in the current situation. All of these generic features of the proverb are present in Elihu's proverb performance.

Concluding Remarks: Enlarging the Playing Field

When the reader or audience finds itself witness to a performance event involving proverbs, several conclusions can be drawn. An interpretation of reality is at stake for participants, and at some level the parties share the same sets of cultural codes and world-view—otherwise, a proverb would not be summoned, nor would anyone understand its use even if it were. An African proverb puts this very well: 'When the truth is lost, we use a proverb to find it.' The compressed, brief utterance works like an 'entry heading' in a cultural encyclopedia, directing the hearers by this code to the full body of accepted group knowledge on that topic. The Hebrew Bible is well aware of the 'code' nature of the proverb (*mashal*), as it makes reference to situations that become a 'proverb' or 'byword' for future members of the group (Deut. 28.37; 1 Kgs 9.7; 2 Chron. 7.20).[27]

We may also conclude in such instances of performance that a gambit is being made by the one using the proverb to direct the players to read the situation according to the traditional 'score' as presented in the proverb. Whether of high or low status outside the performance arena, the proverb user attempts to take a favored position with respect to the hearers of the proverb. Further, this is accomplished in an economical, verbal way, whose bonding aspects intensify the performance's goal of defusing overt conflict. Finally, the user has also been offered a covert way of regaining, claiming or retaining social power: while hidden behind a saying to which everyone gives *some* level of assent, the user is able to put forward *alternate* 'traditional' versions of the truth, despite his or her ultimate status. Quoting the voice of tradition for *non*-traditional purposes, inferior group members—the young, the infirm, the usurper, the outsider, the female, the slave—find a way to reconstitute themselves as group members in good standing, of sufficiently high status to take up a mentoring stance vis-à-vis their audience. This 'indirection' is typical of those who do not have

27. Niditch, *Folklore*, p. 76.

assigned power, but rather must claim what power they can through use of their wits. The Hebrew Bible is aware of this nature of proverb performance, too:

> Like a lame man's legs, which hang useless,
> is a proverb in the mouth of fools (Prov. 26.7).

> Like a thorn that goes up into the hand of a drunkard
> is a proverb in the mouth of fools (Prov. 26.9).

Clearly, the Hebrew sages know that it is in *use* that proverb comes into its own as a didactic form. Fools, notorious for their inability to do anything properly, are equally inept when they try to use proverbs; Ben Sira sums it up: 'A proverb from a fool's lips will be rejected, for he does not tell it at its proper time' (20.20).[28]

We took as our original example a dispute between men of different ages and statuses. We saw, among other things, that patriarchy has a sliding scale of power and status that places some males at the direction of others, thus providing the circumstances where the performance arena might manifest itself in a verbal tussle over the right to speak. If this dynamic comes into play where all the participants are *male*, and the proverb images are male or neutral, then we must expect to see even greater differentials in prestige and position surface when a *female* element— either in the proverb image, or in the gender of the user—is introduced. If the use of the female in proverb images and content has been less than favorable (*sic*), then perhaps in contexts of *use*, we may find the text telling a different story in its gender ideology. Let us turn to the prophet Ezekiel to explore what happens when a female proverb image is invoked by a male to refer to *other males*.

Like mother, like daughter!: Gendering a Male Audience as Female
An angry prophet in exile by the banks of the river Kebar in Babylon directs a tirade against his co-exiles, the powerful men whose behavior led, in his opinion and that of his fellow prophets and later editors, to the current state of place-less-ness and cultural desolation. He uses a typical tactic to shame the men into hearing and internalizing his rant against their apostasy: he speaks to them as though they were women. This rhetorical strategy has been termed 'pornoprophetics' by feminist critics[29] and it has

---

28. For a more detailed discussion of these images and their construction of proverb use, see Fontaine, *Traditional Saying*, pp. 143-46.

29. See especially Athalya Brenner, 'Introduction', in Athalya Brenner (ed.), *A*

more to do with male psychology of manliness than with any innate female penchant for sexual perversity or wantonness. Ezekiel speaks—and presumes to speak out of God's authority and personality—as the savagely jealous and cuckolded husband of the 'female-men' of Jerusalem and Judah:

16.1 The word of the LORD came to me: 16.2 Mortal, make known to Jerusalem her abominations, 16.3 and say, Thus says the Lord GOD to Jerusalem: Your origin and your birth were in the land of the Canaanites; *your father was an Amorite, and your mother a Hittite.* 16.4 As for your birth, on the day you were born your navel cord was not cut, nor were you washed with water to cleanse you, nor rubbed with salt, nor wrapped in cloths. 16.5 No eye pitied you, to do any of these things for you out of compassion for you; but you were thrown out in the open field, for you were abhorred on the day you were born. 16.6 I passed by you, and saw you flailing about in your blood. As you lay in your blood, I said to you, 'Live! 16.7 and grow up like a plant of the field.' You grew up and became tall and arrived at full womanhood; your breasts were formed, and your hair had grown; yet you were naked and bare.

16.8 I passed by you again and looked on you; you were at the age for love. I spread the edge of my cloak over you, and covered your nakedness: I pledged myself to you and entered into a covenant with you, says the Lord God, and you became mine. 16.9 Then I bathed you with water and washed off the blood from you, and anointed you with oil. 16.10 I clothed you with embroidered cloth and with sandals of fine leather; I bound you in fine linen and covered you with rich fabric. 16.11 I adorned you with ornaments: I put bracelets on your arms, a chain on your neck, 16.12 a ring on your nose, earrings in your ears, and a beautiful crown upon your head. 16.13 You were adorned with gold and silver, while your clothing was of fine linen, rich fabric, and embroidered cloth. You had choice flour and honey and oil for food. You grew exceedingly beautiful, fit to be a queen. 16.14 Your fame spread among the nations on account of your beauty, for it was perfect because of my splendor that I had bestowed on you, says the Lord God.

16.15 But you trusted in your beauty, and played the whore because of your fame, and lavished your whorings on any passer-by. 16.16 You took some of your garments, and made for yourself colorful shrines, and on them played the whore; nothing like this has ever been or ever shall be. 16.17 You also took your beautiful jewels of my gold and my silver that I had given you, and made for yourself male images, and with them played the whore; 16.18 and you took your embroidered garments to cover them, and set my oil and my incense before them. 16.19 Also my bread that I gave

Feminist Companion to the Latter Prophets (FCB, 8; Sheffield: Sheffield Academic Press, 1995), pp. 21-37.

you—I fed you with choice flour and oil and honey—you set it before them as a pleasing odor; and so it was, says the Lord God. 16.20 You took your sons and your daughters, whom you had borne to me, and these you sacrificed to them to be devoured. As if your whorings were not enough! 16.21 You slaughtered my children and delivered them up as an offering to them. 16.22 And in all your abominations and your whorings you did not remember the days of your youth, when you were naked and bare, flailing about in your blood. 16.23 After all your wickedness (woe, woe to you! says the Lord God), 16.24 you built yourself a platform and made yourself a lofty place in every square; 16.25 at the head of every street you built your lofty place and prostituted your beauty, offering yourself to every passer-by, and multiplying your whoring. 16.26 You played the whore with the Egyptians, your lustful neighbors, multiplying your whoring, to provoke me to anger.

16.27 Therefore I stretched out my hand against you, reduced your rations, and gave you up to the will of your enemies, the daughters of the Philistines, who were ashamed of your lewd behavior. 16.28 You played the whore with the Assyrians, because you were insatiable; you played the whore with them, and still you were not satisfied. 16.29 You multiplied your whoring with Chaldea, the land of merchants; and even with this you were not satisfied. 16.30 How sick is your heart, says the Lord God, that you did all these things, the deeds of a brazen whore; 16.31 building your platform at the head of every street, and making your lofty place in every square! Yet you were not like a whore, because you scorned payment. 16.32 Adulterous wife, who receives strangers instead of her husband! 16.33 Gifts are given to all whores; but you gave your gifts to all your lovers, bribing them to come to you from all around for your whorings. 16.34 So you were different from other women in your whorings: no one solicited you to play the whore; and you gave payment, while no payment was given to you; you were different.

16.35 Therefore, O whore, hear the word of the LORD: 16.36 Thus says the Lord God, Because your lust was poured out and your nakedness uncovered in your whoring with your lovers, and because of all your abominable idols, and because of the blood of your children that you gave to them, 16.37 therefore, I will gather all your lovers, with whom you took pleasure, all those you loved and all those you hated; I will gather them against you from all around, and will uncover your nakedness to them, so that they may see all your nakedness. 16.38 I will judge you as women who commit adultery and shed blood are judged, and bring blood upon you in wrath and jealousy. 16.39 I will deliver you into their hands, and they shall throw down your platform and break down your lofty places; they shall strip you of your clothes and take your beautiful objects and leave you naked and bare. 16.40 They shall bring up a mob against you, and they shall stone you and cut you to pieces with their swords. 16.41 They shall burn your houses and execute judgments on you in the sight of many women; I will stop you from playing the whore, and you shall also make no more payments. 16.42 So I will satisfy my fury on you, and my jealousy shall turn away from you; I will be calm, and will be angry no longer. 16.43 Because you have not remembered the days of your youth, but have enraged me with all these things; therefore, I have returned your deeds upon your head, says the Lord God. Have you not committed lewdness beyond all your abominations? 16.44 *See, everyone who uses proverbs will use this proverb about you, 'Like mother, like daughter.'* (my italics) 16.45 You are the daughter of your mother, who loathed her husband and her children; and you are the sister of your sisters, who loathed their husbands and their children. *Your mother was a Hittite and your father an Amorite* (NRSV).

This passage is of interest to feminist theologians for any number of reasons, all of which go beyond the usual historical and literary critics' observations of formal elements, historical setting and textual antecedents. From world folklore, we are all too familiar with stories of abandoned children and the fates that befall them (Tale Type S300-S399 in the Motif Index).[30] Within the Hebrew Bible, this text stands out as an exilic example of trends already found in divorce/covenant lawsuit found in Hosea 2, the erotic language used to describe the relationship of God and Judah in Isaiah of Jerusalem's oracles of disaster, and the ravings of Jeremiah about the 'whoredom' of the people of the culture whose worship of other gods was perceived as an act of 'adultery' against the husband Yahweh.[31] Cities and their inhabitants are often likened to women, for they hold their people inside their walls as a fetus is held within the womb, so the images employed here are not unfamiliar ones.

Next, the passage is often quoted because it gives insight into the customary practices of the culture surrounding birth and marriage. The acts performed by the midwife at the time of birth included cutting the umbilical cord, cleansing the infant, rubbing it with salt and swaddling it,

30. For the rather different treatment received by abandoned males in ancient Near East, see Brian Lewis, *The Sargon Legend* (Cambridge, MA: ASOR, 1980).

31. Renita J. Weems, *Battered Love: Marriage, Sex, and Violence in the Hebrew Prophets* (OBT; Minneapolis: Augsburg–Fortress, 1995), pp. 35-67; Alice A. Keefe, 'The Female Body, the Body Politic and the Land: A Sociopolitical Reading of Hosea 1–2', in Brenner (ed.), *Latter Prophets*, pp. 70-100; and Pamela Gordon and Harold Washington, 'Rape as a Military Metaphor in the Hebrew Bible', in A. Brenner (ed.), *A Feminist Companion to the Latter Prophets* (FCB, 8; Sheffield: Sheffield Academic Press, 1995), pp. 308-25; Raymond C. Ortlund, Jr, *Whoredom: God's Unfaithful Wife in Biblical Theology* (Grand Rapids, MI: Eerdmans, 1996); Frymer-Kensky, *Goddesses*, pp. 144-52.

all actions that symbolize the father's acceptance of the child's legitimacy and membership in the family.[32] Beyond this, we also have a picture of the typical behavior of the betrothed husband toward his beloved future wife: the giving of gifts, whose function is both to delight and adorn the bride, but also to spell out the husband's social prominence and total possession of the young woman. In return for all this, the young bride is required to give total allegiance of body and soul to the male who has rightfully claimed and exclusively possessed her.

Elsewhere in the ancient Near East, we are familiar with the use of the 'great sin' of 'adultery' to metaphorize the breaking of covenant agreements between men or nations,[33] so our Hebrew prophets are merely rehearsing typical features of their androcentric culture that takes women's 'nature'—as construed by men and then internalized by 'good' women—and uses it as a metonym for something *far* more important to them than women—some aspect of themselves or their own concerns.[34] There is nothing special here in the use of the 'marriage metaphor',[35] as mainstream scholars so politely term this situation of forced possession and subjugation, though Ezekiel does develop it more thoroughly than previous prophets.[36] In theory, the 'woman/wife' Israel *ought* to have been thoroughly pleased and content to be drawn into such a patriarchal relationship to *her* discriminating god—he cares for *her* so *very* much; he is *just* like a husband!

This portrait of marital satisfaction and bliss is somewhat marred however, and this is so whether viewed through ancient male eyes or

32. Meir Malul, 'Adoption of Foundlings in the Bible and Mesopotamian Documents: A Study of Some Legal Metaphors in Ezekiel 16.1-7', *JSOT* 46 (1990), pp. 97-126.

33. F. Rachel Magdalene, 'Ancient Near Eastern Treaty-Curses and the Ultimate Texts of Terror: A Study of the Language of Divine Sexual Abuse in the Prophetic Corpus', in A. Brenner (ed.), *A Feminist Companion to the Latter Prophets* (FCB, 8; Sheffield: Sheffield Academic Press, 1995), pp. 326-53.

34. Fokkelien van Dijk-Hemmes, 'The Metaphorization of Woman in Prophetic Speech: An Analysis of Ezekiel 23', in A. Brenner (ed.), *A Feminist Companion to the Latter Prophets* (FCB, 8; Sheffield: Sheffield Academic Press, 1995), pp. 244-55.

35. Helmer Ringgren, 'The Marriage Motif in Israelite Religion', in Patrick D. Miller, Jr (ed.), *Ancient Israelite Religion* (Philadelphia: Fortress Press, 1987), pp. 421-28.

36. K.P. Darr, 'Ezekiel', in Carol Newsom and Sharon Ringe (eds.), *The Women's Bible Commentary* (Louisville, KY: Westminster/John Knox Press, 1992), pp. 183-90 (188).

modern feminist ones. The girl-child Judah/Jerusalem began her days as no legitimate child, fated to become the beloved bride of a betrothed chosen with care by her family. Rather, she was destined for female infanticide, left to die in the open field unreceived and untended. At the very starting point of this chapter, we learn that this girl-child is a 'designated victim', for something must have been very irregular indeed in her parentage or her birth to cause her to be so treated. We discover shortly thereafter, in the form of proverbial racism, that she was from her inception a 'mixed-breed': Hittite mother, Amorite father. Who could be expected to claim her and treat her well with such foreign, impure parentage as this for her heritage?[37] The whole of this introduction, of course, makes the actions of the midwife-like God all the more beneficent and shockingly tender: *he/she* takes pity on the child and her polluting blood, even when no one else does! Androcentric critics swoon with delight over their god's treatment of this female orphan—ah, we humans should *all* be as lucky as this![38] Born blighted by our 'original sin', tainted by the birth-blood of Eve, our snake-whoring mother, we are nevertheless made worthy to become the thoroughly dominated and transformed 'bride' of our Savior. (How nice.) In many such conventional applications of this story, the typology of blood pollution, female lasciviousness and human unworthiness proceeds unchallenged[39] through the two Testaments and beyond in the interpretations of sexist theologians.

But those who see in this passage a 'typical' example of the patriarchal god's unmerited love when *he* acts like a midwife toward orphan-girl-

37. Walther Eichrodt writes, '...this origin from heathen blood...presupposes that there is already present in the nature of the chosen people an original inclination towards heathenism, which it has received as an inherited family failing, and which cannot be expected to produce anything but bad results' (*Ezekiel: A Commentary* [London: SCM Press, 1970], p. 205). This masterful, positivist summary not only allows Westerners to place the 'chosen people' above the 'heathen', but then allows that group to be superceded by the more moral inheritor of this chosenness, Christianity. Thus, interpretation that accepts the Bible's self-referential history at face value continues the round-robin of racial and theological slurs, without critical comment on the specious nature of the claims.

38. See, for example, Joseph E. Coleson, 'Israel's Life Cycle from Birth to Resurrection', in A. Gileadi (ed.), *Israel's Apostasy and Restoration* (Grand Rapids, MI: Baker Book House, 1988), pp. 237-50.

39. See, for example, the analysis by Moshe Greenberg, 'Ezekiel 16: A Panorama of Passions', in J.H. Marks and R.M. Good (eds.), *Love and Death in the Ancient Near East: Essays in Honor of Marvin H. Pope* (Guilford, CT: Four Quarters, 1987), pp. 143-50.

Jerusalem need to read on further in Ezekiel's biography of the all-grown-up whore Jerusalem.[40] Only when God behaves like a woman does this passage speak of anything a feminist would recognize as 'divine' love. As soon as the little girl reaches puberty—breasts full and pubic hair appearing to welcome male possession—the character of her 'rescuer' changes from female to male. Before the girl had developed sexual characteristics, God loved the infant with the concrete and selfless actions of a midwife, rescuing a neglected child; now that she is palpably female in her sexual maturity, the rescuer turns incestuous in his desire for the child. Seeing a 'pay-off' for all that previous disinterested divine love, the male pedophile quickly acts to mark the young girl as *his* and his alone, for all to see—including the girl herself.

We might pause to wonder, how does *her* vision alter when she sees the 'man' in whose house she has been sheltered turn from 'father' to 'lover'? Has she read Deuteronomy or Leviticus? Is she ashamed of her new breasts and curious hair that bespeaks her 'shame' rather than her 'crowning glory'? Does she blame herself and her own tender expressions of daughterly affection for the new passion that she senses in the male who comes courting her with presents? Are those presents of finery welcomed, or do they seem to her more sinister? *Whatever* must she be thinking? Half-breed that she is, did she ever expect such an exalted marriage partner as her caring father? Is she grateful? Is she terrified?

We can only judge her early reactions from her subsequent behavior.[41] Yes, the later wife who is so free with her sexual favors, who gives away all the gifts lavished on her by her father-bedmate, who turns away callously from the living fruit of her incestuous coupling, does not seem particularly *grateful* for the tremendous gift of sexual attention she has received from the man who rescued her. Even her outraged 'husband' must admit that her behavior is no typical example of whoring—*she* is the one giving presents rather than receiving them! Indeed, she seems to strip herself gleefully of her father-husband's ownership in a calculated way, just as the Sumerian Inanna stripped off the garments marking her status as she moved through the gates of the Underworld to a death and rebirth that had momentous consequences for her culture. Whore-Jerusalem is a

---

40. Matthews and Benjamin, *Social World*, refer to vv. 4-6 as 'The Parable of the Good Parent' (p. 80). In my view, this is only feasible if one stops reading at v. 6.

41. Coleson writes (in reference to her *shameful* parentage), 'Beginning even here, she owed what she became to YHWH' ('Life Cycle', p. 238). Feminists would agree, though with a radically different construction of meaning.

'married' woman on fire, but not with desire for other men or gods; she is rather consumed by rage for the father-god who betrayed her innocence, and she takes every public opportunity to show him so. His betrayal preceded hers—or as we would say in modern proverbs, 'What's sauce for the goose is good for the gander.'

The passage is studded with wisdom terminology and makes a direct reference to the use of proverbs in social contexts: here, a pseudo-woman's behavior has been judged *so* horrendous that it will be come a proverbial code word for the future, and will elicit the use of a gendered proverb by everyone who hears about it: 'Like mother, like daughter!' It is clear that this innocent little saying, to which we would all agree at some level (resemblance, memory, family ties, etc.), stands here *not* simply to highlight the similarities between mothers and their offspring in a causational proverb image. The mother envisioned here is foreign (Hittite), misguided in her out-group marriage (Amorite), and unconcerned with the female child that issues from it. Her careless disregard for her daughter's well-being is then fated to be repeated in the next generation: the daughter will show similar neglect of social conventions of feminine behavior in *her* dealings with her divine husband.

The prophet selects *this* particular proverb to use in his rantings for reasons that have everything to do with gender ideology and very little to do with the 'plain sense' content of the proverb image and message. In fact, observations about parent–offspring similarities (and dissimilarities) abound in cross-cultural proverbial literature. English speakers not only use this biblical proverb itself, but add a variety of colorful expressions on the same topic: a child who resembles the parent is 'the very spit and image' ('spitting image' is the popular mutation of this proverbial phrase) of the parent, or 'a chip off the old block', because 'The apple doesn't fall far from the tree.' African proverbs tell the same story, but with indigenous images: 'The pup of the leopard claws like its mother' (the Akikuyu); 'The little mouse does not forget its mother's ways' (the Tonga) and 'The juice of the *mpfilwa* tree comes from its stem' (the Tonga).[42] Yet, in most cultures the opposite insight is also preserved: a child may be a 'throwback', a 'black sheep', a 'runt of the litter', a 'prodigal' or a 'changeling'. Tribal societies also bear witness to the ambivalence of alleged family resemblance: 'A hero begets a coward'; 'A good-looking person will not give birth to handsome children'; 'Fire begets ashes'; or 'A child forces

---

42. Friedemann W. Golka, *The Leopard's Spots: Biblical and African Wisdom in Proverbs* (Edinburgh: T. & T. Clark, 1993), pp. 104-105.

you to eat out of a dirty pot' (all from the Tonga). Among the Kamba, we find 'The mother of the ram has no horns'; 'The guinea fowl bears a francolin'; and the Nandi say, 'The lion bears a hyena.'[43] Like so many things in life, family resemblances, whether by nature or nurture, are not a 'sure thing'.

Elsewhere, Ezekiel is *not* unaware that his mother-daughter proverb has much contradictory evidence against it. In another occasion of proverb performance in ch. 18, we read the following:

> The word of the LORD came to me again:
> 'What do you mean by repeating this proverb concerning the land of Israel, "The fathers have eaten sour grapes, and the children's teeth are set on edge"?
> As I live, says the Lord GOD, this proverb shall no more be used by you in Israel.
> Behold, all souls are mine; the soul of the father as well as the soul of the son is mine: the soul that sins shall die' (18.1-4, RSV).

At this point, Ezekiel is citing a proverb, using God's 'voice', and explaining that it *no longer* applies within the folk group that previously held it as 'true'. That this proverb concerns *fathers* and *their* offspring alerts us to an underlying gap between the prophet's (and his culture's?) understanding of the causative relationship between the male parent's behavior and that of the children, and the features of that same relationship when the subject is *mothers*. Somehow, males have escaped the destiny of repetition; females, however, are not so lucky in the prophet's way of thinking. The dissimilarities based on the gender of the parents continue as we read on concerning fathers, good and bad, and their sons:

> If he begets a son who is a robber, a shedder of blood,
> who does none of these duties, but eats upon the mountains, defiles his neighbor's wife, oppresses the poor and needy, commits robbery, does not restore the pledge, lifts up his eyes to the idols, commits abomination,
> lends at interest, and takes increase; shall he then live? He shall not live. He has done all these abominable things; he shall surely die; his blood shall be upon himself.
> But if this man begets a son who sees all the sins which his father has done, and fears, and does not do likewise,
> who does not eat upon the mountains or lift up his eyes to the idols of the house of Israel, does not defile his neighbor's wife,
> does not wrong any one, exacts no pledge, commits no robbery, but gives his bread to the hungry and covers the naked with a garment,

43. Golka, *Spots*, pp. 105, 107.

withholds his hand from iniquity, takes no interest or increase, observes my
ordinances, and walks in my statutes; he shall not die for his father's
iniquity; he shall surely live.
As for his father, because he practiced extortion, robbed his brother, and did
what is not good among his people, behold, he shall die for his iniquity.
Yet you say, 'Why should not the son suffer for the iniquity of the father?'
When the son has done what is lawful and right, and has been careful to
observe all my statutes, he shall surely live.
The soul that sins shall die. The son shall not suffer for the iniquity of the
father, nor the father suffer for the iniquity of the son; the righteousness of
the righteous shall be upon himself, and the wickedness of the wicked shall
be upon himself (18.10-20, RSV).

So, good fathers might raise wretched sons, and sons of wretched fathers
might choose a different, more wholesome direction for their lives. Clearly,
neither nature nor nurture hampers free choice to follow the Law. 'Like
father, like son' is a lesson the prophet is not eager to emphasize, given his
call to repentance issued to the elite male exiles. Perhaps the difference in
Ezekiel's deployment of the notion of parental causation in the formation of
the offsprings' character is accounted for by the fact that *sons* have choice,
and reason, or because between chs. 16 and 18 God has decided to restore
the fortunes of Israel. Sons will someday grow to supplant their fathers as
full 'citizens' before the Law. Restored sons will do better than their exiled
fathers. Daughters, on the other hand, are *never* thought to outgrow some
male's authority, even when they marry and become mothers themselves:
'Like mother, like daughter,' both are perpetually maintained as dependents.
Gender ideology is firmly at work in Ezekiel's understanding of parents and
children. The proverb in 16.44, apart from this context of use in Ezekiel,
need *not* be *negative* in content or use: for example, it *could* mean and be
used to allude to the way a good and virtuous mother parents her girls to
similar virtues. This, however, is not the meaning Ezekiel's context forces
on us.

If we go beyond the literal content of what was probably a common
proverb used in Ezekiel's performance, we also see that he is not alluding
to some deeper psychological meaning. We have no sense that he is trying
to account for the behavior of the elite Jerusalem males by suggesting that
those who have themselves been abused and neglected will in turn abuse
and neglect others. No, his purpose is not so philosophically neutral as that.
Using the common biblical idea of 'corporate personality', he suggests
that the 'foreign' (= unacceptable) characteristics of the ancient Hittite–
Amorite parents of Judah continue into the present generation. The proverb, at its first level of contextual application, underscores identity and

genealogy. But the interpretation goes further than this in the prophet's diatribe: Ezekiel is indicting the powerful males of Judah in a way that underscores their current powerlessness in exile: they have become, from beginning to end, *females*. Their humiliation is made complete here by their fellow countryman as Ezekiel points out to them that their final arrival into exile is a both a derivation and an analog to their alleged earlier descent into *female* lasciviousness.[44] Now they are captive, as the females in their culture always are—but how can they, as men, bear that it has happened to *them*? Their shame is complete, and, for the prophet, *must* be complete if they are ever to repent and be renewed. The female image, when applied to the male, has become thoroughly negative in meaning. This is an ironic counterpoint to the earlier portrait of God who was caring and decent when a female midwife, but incestuous and brutal when he became a 'marrying man'.

A rebellious reader might come away from Ezekiel 16 with a different set of questions than those raised by mainstream critics: Why is having a Hittite mother such a bad thing (elsewhere, Uriah the Hittite seemed like a nice enough fellow)? What is distinctive about an Amorite father?[45] How would the foundling Jerusalem understand the prophet's citation of the mother-daughter proverb? Do women, high *or* low status, use proverbs so venomously, or in any way at all, for that matter? Are any of *their* performances recoverable, so that we might wash the bitter taste of Ezekiel's proverb from our mouths? At least *one* of Ezekiel's events of proverb performance holds true in our reading: this father did indeed fill his mouth with sour grapes, but it is the daughters' mouths who are blistered by the acid.

The Women Respond: Reversing Abuse through Use

Since we just left the low-status orphan who should have been grateful for any positive consideration whatsoever given to her by her 'rescuer', we will begin our—all too brief, given the lack of evidence—examination of women using proverbs with another female who is also among the lowest

---

44. Weems, *Battered Love*, p. 62.

45. For a possible peculiar occurrence of 'Amorite' as a pejorative in an ancient Near Eastern proverb, note the following proverb about gender-confusion, 'A [blockhead (or Amorite?) says [to] his wife, "[Yo}u be the young man, [I] will be the girl. [When} I turn to being the young man, [let...be] feminine, [let...] be masculine' (Foster, *Before the Muses*, I, p. 337).

of the low. We turn now to the Westcar Papyrus (P. Berlin 3033) from the 12th Dynasty of the Egyptian Middle Kingdom (1991–1786 BCE).[46]

The Tales of Wonder: *A Slave Woman's Proverb within a Tale within a Tale*

The Tales of Wonder is written in classical Middle Egyptian hieratic, but it is set within the Old Kingdom, during the reign of Khufu (Cheops). Assembled at the court of their father Khufu, the royal princes take turns telling wonder tales for the amusement of those gathered. Five tales in all were originally included, but only the third, fourth and fifth are complete in the manuscript. Our interest is in the third tale, told by Prince Baufre, about his grandfather, King Snefru.

As the tale goes, King Snefru had wandered about his palace, looking for a pleasant diversion to relax himself, but found nothing suitable. Discouraged, he called to his 'scribe-of-books', the lector-priest Djadja-em-ankh, who proposed the following solution:

> 'May your Majesty proceed to the lake of the palace. Fill a boat with all the beautiful girls of your palace. Your majesty's heart will be refreshed by seeing them row, a rowing up and down.'

Snefru agrees that this is an excellent remedy for his ennui, and proposes his own refinements to the plan of his scribe:

> 'Indeed, I shall go boating! Let there be brought to me twenty oars of ebony plated with gold, their handles of sandalwood plated with electrum. Let there be brought to me twenty women with the shapeliest bodies, breasts, and braids, who have not yet given birth. Also let there be brought to me twenty nets and give these nets to these women in place of their clothes!'[47]

All proceeded at his majesty's word, and indeed, his heart *was* refreshed by the sight of 20 naked slaves, virgins every one, rowing him back and forth. Soon, however, a complication ensues: the lead woman who was beating the stroke for her side of the rowers suddenly stopped rowing, causing the slave girls on her side of the boat to stop as well. Throwing status considerations to the winds, the Pharoah Snefru himself questions the girls as to why they have suddenly stopped rowing him, and they reply that their leader has stopped. When he questions the leader, she tells him that her brand-new, fish-shaped charm of new turquoise had fallen out of

---

46. Lichtheim, *Literature*, I, pp. 216-22; for the text transcribed into hieroglyphics, see K. Sethe, *Ägyptische Lesestück* (Leipzig, 1924), pp. 26-36.

47. Lichtheim, *Literature*, I, p. 216.

her braids and into the water, causing her to stop in distress. Snefru promises to give her another just like it, if only she will continue rowing for his enjoyment. With great *hutspah*, she 'talks back' to the great king, telling him, 'I like my pot down to its end!'[48] Though modern readers may not 'get' this proverbial allusion, clearly the participants in the story *do*. After the typical tale feature of retelling the whole incident (complete with proverb) to the scribe/lector-priest, Djadja-em-ankh performs a miracle of biblical proportions; he folds back the waters on one side of the lake onto the other,[49] revealing the turquoise fish-charm on the lake bottom. Retrieving it for its concerned owner, the scribe then replaces the 12 cubits of water that he had piled up on the first 12, returning the lake to its normal depth. All is well, and Pharaoh completes his day of pleasure excursions by feasting with the entire palace and giving a generous reward of 'all good things' to Djadja-em-ankh.

We may note a number of things in this paradigmatic example of proverb performance. A situation of concern has arisen—how can Pharaoh get his naked slave woman to stop thinking about *her* jewelry and start paying attention to *his* wishes?!—and it is marked by emblematic status differentials, since 'from pharaoh on his throne to the slave at her grindstone' is a merismus used in both biblical and Egyptian literature to designate the high (male elite) and low (female slave) ends of the status continuum (and hence every status in between; cf. Exod. 11.5; implicitly in the *Maxims of Ptahhotep* 5.10). The slave woman who leads the others shows the qualities of a leader in her spirited defense of her own actions, and, although she does not invoke the proverb tradition with a formulaic appeal, her citation of the pot proverb allows her to cushion herself against any potential royal anger at her behavior. Further, his majesty seems to accept her reasoning and turns the matter over to his scribe, who also accedes to the traditional wisdom cited by the woman. All three participants in the interaction are satisfied with the successful outcome.

Even though our slave woman functions as a literary 'prop' to stage the conflict situation that the scribe will successfully resolve, her challenge to

48. Simpson (ed.), *Literature*, p. 21. This is the literal translation, of which Simpson writes, 'Evidently a proverb with the sense that she wants the full amount or the same thing' (p. 21 n. 7). Lichtheim translates more generally, 'I prefer my thing to one like it' (*Literature*, I, p. 217), missing the proverb register of the 'out-of-context' citation.

49. One imagines this to be something like the crossing of the Reed Sea, with 'stiffened' water standing up on one side as though it were transparent Jello.

male authority stands out as a great wonder in this tale. Apparently, wisdom was not only to be found with the elite ladies of the harem, but with their less fortunate sisters as well. Cloaked by the security of a traditional citation, she not only stops the boat because of her own personal concerns, but she refuses to accept the solutions first offered to her by the infinitely more powerful males. Naked except for her netted overdress of pearls, the removal of her clothing has not removed her wit: she fights for the treasured turquoise amulet that adorned her tresses—and wins! Wisdom, known and deployed in a verbal interaction, carries the day, showing that cultural 'truth' can occasionally trump assigned status, to the advantage of those at the 'bottom' of the patriarchal pyramid of social worth.

We hear the same message about status and truth made explicit in another time of conflict and status differentials in fourteenth-century Spain. *Proverbios morales*, a proverbial corpus penned by the rabbi Santob de Carrión (= Shem Tov Ibn Ardutiel ben Isaac) was explicitly addressed to the Christian king of Castile, Pedro the Cruel (1334–69). Its introduction begins with two prologues, the most famous of which is quoted here:

> Even if my discourse is not great, it should not be despised because spoken by a modest person: for many a sword / Of good and fine steel comes from a torn sheath, and it is from the worm that fine silk is made. / And a miserable catapult can be most accurate, and a torn skin can [still manage to] cover up white breasts; / And a convincing messenger can bring good news, and a lowly lawyer can introduce truthful arguments. / For being born on the thornbush, the rose is certainly not worth less, nor is good wine if taken from the lesser branches of the vine. / Nor is the hawk worth less, if born in a poor nest; nor are good proverbs [of less value] if spoken by a Jew (lines 169-89).[50]

From the shelter of group solidarity implied by shared proverbs, a Jewish sage can instruct a Christian monarch and a female slave can gainsay a pharaoh. Once again, we see that 'You can't judge a book by its cover,' because even 'A cat may look at a king.'

A Warning to the King of Mari: Proverb Performance by a Prophetess
From the Old Babylonian town of Mari, located on the Euphrates, comes an archive of letters whose content has been a boon to the study of

---

50. T.A. Perry, *The Moral Proverbs of Santob de Carrión: Jewish Wisdom in Christian Spain* (Princeton: Princeton University Press, 1987), pp. 19-20; cf. discussion of the relationship of Shem Tov's images to Christian polemics, pp. 65-73. I am greatly indebted to Professor Perry for bringing this wonderful proverb's text to my attention.

women's roles in society in the ancient world. The classic work on this material done by Bernard Batto[51] continues to be a valuable resource for students of Israel and the ancient Near East. We are concerned here with the prophetic traditions at Mari, where women served equally with men (though not making use of the same medium), both in lay and professional capacities.[52] Oracles delivered by women were considered just as authentic and reliable as those received by men, and readers approaching these texts must shake off their sense of mistrust of that statement. Long years of reflecting on the Bible have created a readership only too used to women's perceptions of the divine being dismissed as an 'idle tale' (Lk. 24.8-11).

In a letter from Mari, we discover somewhat convoluted situation: a *qabbātum* priestess[53] serving the god Dagan of Terqa has received an oracle for the king of Mari. For some reason not clear from the text, she is not able to deliver this oracle in person, so gives it to a noble lady of the court, one Inib-šina, who then relays the oracle to the king.

> The offers of reconciliation of the man (ruler) of Ešnunna are only treachery. *Under the straw, the water flows.* But I will collect him into a net with which I will surround (him). I will ruin his city, and his property, which from ancient times has not been destroyed, I will destroy (ARM X 80.11-15).

The proverb 'Under the straw the water flows' operates in this oracle to suggest that hidden beneath the surface of diplomatic overtures, more sinister plans are afoot—but, not to worry! Dagan is on it, and the king will be protected from his enemy's machinations. The saying is built from observations made by people who live by rivers: a valued material may be afloat on the top of the water, but the current still moves beneath. It appears in an out-of-context statement applied metaphorically to a context situation. For our purposes, we need to ask here, To which voice among the three potential speakers should we attribute this proverb?

The oracle is quoted directly as the communication of Dagan to his priestess, so at some level Dagan must be considered the speaker.[54]

---

51. *Studies on Women at Mari* (Baltimore: The Johns Hopkins University Press, 1974).

52. Batto, *Women*, pp. 119-27.

53. For disputes over the correct translation of this term, see A. Marzal, *Gleanings from the Wisdom of Mari* (Studia Pohl, 11; Rome: Biblical Institute Press, 1976), pp. 69-70 n. 36. She is either a 'speaker' or an ecstatic priestess; either way, she is a duly authorized functionary serving Dagan of Terqa.

54. So, W.L. Moran, 'New Evidence from Mari on the History of Prophecy', *Bib* 50 (1969), pp. 15-56 (54).

However, we must bear in mind that, despite the quaint appeal of deities pictured trading proverbs with humans (so, too, 1 Sam. 16.7), in fact, this is a human-made utterance and there is a human voice behind the god's speech—a woman's voice, to be exact. As if the authority of speaking the god's words on his behalf were not strong enough, a lowly little peasant proverb about the state of the river is placed in the divine mouth to convey *his* message. Now, in Mari, a prophetess may expect to be believed and valued as she goes about her business, so we do not need to infer that the woman uses the proverb for fear that she will go unheard unless she has the weight of group tradition behind her. Local traditions have already validated her claim to speech. *But* if our discussion of proverb performance and its relationship to social struggle, ambiguity or claiming the power to speak holds true for this particular context, we may rightly wonder why the *qabbātum* cast her oracle in proverbial dress. The answer here may lie not in a status disparity between the *qabbātum* and the king, the *qabbātum* and the god, or the *qabbātum* and her noble go-between,[55] but in the context situation of the two kingdoms of Mari and Ešnunna. We know from other correspondence at Mari directed to Queen Shibtu that provincial governors from districts near Ešnunna frequently reported to Mari on the state of military readiness in their territories,[56] always with an anxious eye on their bigger, bellicose neighbor. Perhaps the conflict that inspires the need for a homely little proverb to bring it back 'down to earth' was the prospect of a cessation of the continuous struggles between Mari and Ešnunna. So powerful and mighty that it had never fallen to a conqueror (our letter claims), Ešnunna with hands outstretched in friendship might have been a mirage of peace too tempting to make the king willing to listen to the fearful whisperings of his counselors who thought otherwise. In this case, the prophetess offers up a truth straight from god's mouth to the king's ear, that even a peasant knows: appearances can be deceiving.

We do not have enough evidence to make further bold statements here about what role the *gender* of the prophetess might have played in this event of oracular-epistolary proverb performance. In fact, since women were so roundly accepted in leadership roles in Mari, we must suspect that

---

55. There are, in fact, several high-ranking women named Inib-šina at Mari: a priestess of some sort, and a governor's wife who served the king in official administrative capacities, either one of which may also have been a daughter of the king. At any rate, all of them enjoyed high rank (Batto, *Women*, pp. 59-61).

56. Batto, *Women*, p. 14.

gender is not a salient feature of this interaction.[57] We must simply content ourselves with the following observations: proverbs were not considered out of place in oracular contexts, they might be directed by gods to humans with metaphorical interpretive intent, and they carried weight when heard. Like the wise women of 2 Samuel and the 'old women' of Anatolia, the prophetess was simply going about her business of relaying the divine word, and she naturally included proverbs in those words when it was appropriate to do so. The fact that it is a woman's voice intoning the proverb that instructs the king on matters military and imperial should not go unnoticed. Here we see that the 'professional' women of the ancient Near East carried wisdom and deployed it as effectively as anyone else. How divine!

Hittite Women Talk Back: the Anatolian Différence

We have already discussed the role of Middle Bronze 'Wise Women/Old Women' of the Hittite Empire in Anatolia in Chapter 2, when we dealt with women as healers carrying on that particular wisdom tradition. These women, no doubt post-menopausal and trained by the women of their families, just as we saw among Serbian villages, also operated in the realms of divination. As noted before, the 'wisdom' traditions of Mesopotamia and Anatolia have often been characterized by their close relationship to the mantic arts. Hence, these traditions have been viewed as unlikely areas for general female participation, since women would not have had the scribal education needed to use mantic texts required in that line of work. And yet—the lay women of Mari were perfectly able to deliver and interpret oracles that were believed, so we should not be surprised that in Anatolia, too, women's words were considered valid vehicles for the interpretation of the divine will.

Morbidly fascinated with the world of impurity, from which the evil that caused disease and social conflict was thought to originate, the Hittites

57. While Mari was by no means an 'egalitarian' society to whose ideology we might attribute the somewhat stronger participation of women in public life, a variety of social features came together there to make it possible for some gifted women to excel in the public arena, even to the point of being awarded land holdings for their service to the city-state. However, given the plight of some princesses used as political pawns in strategic marriages, the fate of women captives placed into factory work, and the use of 'female humility formulae' in the correspondence, we have every reason to think that most women there met just as much gendered restriction of their life-choices as any where else (Fontaine, 'Heifer', pp. 167-70).

made constant use of the Wise Women (among others) to intuit the will of the gods, as well as administer the cure for such evils via 'analogic magic'.[58] Like the so-called 'nature wisdom' in the book of Proverbs (6.6-9; 30.24-31) and the wisdom of Solomon, which derived at least in part from his knowledge of natural phenomena (1 Kgs 4.33-34), the Hittite Wise Women interpreted the omens of birds (along with the 'Bird Observer'), and was instrumental in conducting the Snake Oracle. In this procedure, a water snake was released into a basin whose surface had been divided into various sections ('life', 'sin', 'temple', 'house', 'prison', 'bloody deed and oath', 'ghosts'), and the Wise Woman observed which subdivisions the snake traveled through on its escape from the basin, allowing her to return an answer of 'favorable' or 'unfavorable' to the one taking the omen.[59] This brings a different interpretive edge to the background of one of Proverbs' numerical sayings:

> Three things are too wonderful for me; four I do not understand:
> the way of an eagle in the sky,
> the way of a serpent on a rock,
> the way of a ship on the high seas,
> and the way of a man with a maiden (RSV 30.18-19).

We might note here that the wisdom of the Hittite Wise Woman exceeds that of our puzzled Israelite sage, for the quadrants of life indicated in our saying ('sky', 'rock', 'seas', 'love') are all within the ordinary provenance of her work. Some rituals required her to make a little toy boat, upon which she placed sins or prayers or images of hostile forces, to be sent to the sea by a small channel she had dug; she could give an answer to the meaning of the eagle's beak when it turned straight ahead; the way of the serpent was no mystery to her; and her normal duties included a highly specific understanding of the ways of fertility, desire and dysfunction.

It was, of course, in the practice of her healing analogic magic/medicine (and the 'counseling' that accompanied it!) that we see her most clearly in the role of a sage who manipulates words to change reality. In a ritual for the royal couple, she crushes a soap-root to work up suds, applies this to the limbs of the king and queen, while saying:

> As this soap plant cleanses soiled garments and these (thereby) become white, (thus/therefore) may it likewise purify the limbs of the king, the queen, the princes, and also the palace.[60]

58. Frantz-Szabó, 'Hittite', pp. 2007-20.
59. Frantz-Szabó, 'Witchcraft', p. 2017.
60. Frantz-Szabó, 'Witchcraft', p. 2012.

Examples of such performances of 'word-power' by these Wise Women abound in the archives they left.[61] We suggest here that Ezekiel's castigation of Judah for its 'shame' of having a Hittite female in its genealogy has, perhaps, some ancient memory of female wisdom and power in it, after all. Did the men of Judah think, perhaps, that they might manipulate God's treatment of them as their Hittite 'mother' might have used words to turn nature to the advantage of her people? Only speculation can be offered, not proof—but beneath the xenophobia that borders on racism may be a serious conflict of world-view that goes beyond the simple characterization of monotheists versus pagans.

Excursus: From Hittite Wise Woman to Desert Mother

The wise women of the Hittites may provide us with one of our first archival resources on women using words with mantic force as they bring about behavioral change, but they are certainly not the last. From the period of early Christianity, we have a set of 'Desert Mothers', nuns or anchoresses, whose reliance on the immanent referentiality of 'word-power' continues the practices of their much more ancient sisters. 'Amma' (mother) Theodora uses the familiar metaphor of the tree that 'stands' for human progress to teach a lesson:

> Let us strive to enter by the narrow gate. Just as the trees, if they have not stood before the winter's storms cannot bear fruit, so it is with us; this present age is a storm and it is only through many trials and temptations that we can obtain an inheritance in the kingdom of heaven.[62]

Theodora's use of the mantic mashal to teach a Christian lesson transports us back to the performance of the 'saying-appraisal': here, she starts with a paraphrase of a biblical quotation, but appends to it a *mashal* whose meaning she wisely explains to the untutored. Amma Syncletica likewise makes use of this method to teach the values of spiritual life: who would know more about making something clean, whether a soiled cloth or a

---

61. For echoes of these practices in southern Levant, see Jean-Michel de Tarragon, 'Witchcraft, Magic and Divination in Canaan in Ancient Israel', *CANE*, III, pp. 2071-81.

62. Benedicta Ward (trans.), *The Sayings of the Desert Fathers: The Alphabetical Collection* (Kalamazoo, MI: Cistercian Publications, 1975), p. 83; cf. A. Ünal, 'The Role of Magic in Ancient Anatolian Religions According to Text from Bagazkoy-Hattusha', in Prince T. Mikasa (ed.), *Essays on Ancient Anatolian Texts in the Second Millennium BC* (Wiesbaden: Otto Harrassowitz, 1988), pp. 52-85 (76-81).

soul, than a woman? Asked about the role of poverty in the perfection of Christian virtue, she replies that it certainly 'works' for those who can manage it:

> Those who can sustain it receive suffering in the body but rest in the soul, for just as one washes coarse clothes by trampling them underfoot and turning them about in all directions, even so the strong soul becomes much more stable thanks to voluntary poverty.[63]

Her other analogical teachings are even more reminiscent of the cornucopia of natural media which the ancient wise women used in their ritual-cum-saying practices:

> Just as the most bitter medicine drives out poisonous creatures, so prayer joined to fasting drives evil thoughts away.

> Just as the bird who abandons the eggs she was sitting on prevents them from hatching, so the monk or nun grows cold and their faith dies, when they go from one place to another.[64]

> She also said, 'Just as treasure that is exposed loses its value, so a virtue which is known vanishes; just as wax melts when it is near the fire, so the soul is destroyed by praise and loses all the results of its labour.[65]

The Hebrew Bible knows this pattern of teaching with a mantic flair as well; the construction usually makes use of the particle כ, 'just as, like', paired with באשר/כן, 'so, thus, accordingly' (see Jer. 18.6; 31.28; 32.42; 33.22; 42.18; Deut. 12.22; 28.63; Isa. 29.8; Zech. 8.13; 2 Chron. 32.17). Prov. 27.19 uses the construction to make a more observational saying, but its mantic possibilities should not be overlooked:

> Just as in water face answers to face, so accordingly the 'heart' (mind) of a person reflects the person.

Given the role of 'bitter waters' in revealing the inner truth of a woman's fidelity in the *Sotah* ritual in Numbers 5 and the river's role in determining guilt of the accused in Mesopotamia, this harmless little saying might be more than just a saying!

Just as striking as the Hittite Wise Woman's manipulation of language to empower her ritual actions is the pious prayer of a Late Bronze Age Hittite Queen who uses proverbs to wheedle the gods and goddesses into granting her prayerful request. Pudukhepa, the child-bride of Khattushili III, was the

---

63. Ward, *Sayings*, p. 231.
64. Ward, *Sayings*, p. 231.
65. Ward, *Sayings*, p. 234.

daughter of a priest of Kizzuwatna, a southern province most especially associated with the rituals of the Wise Women, as well as horse-breeding. In her move to the Hittite capital far away from her home, she coped with her new life 'theologically' by identifying the goddess of her homeland with the Sun-Goddess of Arinna, who was the protectress of the Empire (Fig. 15). It was to this goddess that she addressed her prayers that her aging husband be healed of his horrific case of 'fire-in-feet'.[66] After enumerating all the wonderful things her husband has done for the goddess (with the efficient help of an extremely able and zealous wife, of course), she prays:

> This is what I, Pudu-hepas,[67] thy handmaid, laid in prayer before the Sun-goddess of Arinna, my lady, the lady of the Hatti lands, the queen of heaven and earth. Sun-goddess of Arinna, my lady, yield to me, hearken to me! Among men[68] there is a saying: 'To a woman in travail the god yields her wish.' (Since) I, Pudu-hepas, am a woman in travail (and since) I have devoted myself to thy son,[69] yield to me, Sun-goddess of Arinna, my lady! Grant to me what (I ask)! Grant life to (Hattusilis, thy serv)ant! Through the Good-Women (and) Mother-goddesses[70] (long [and] enduring) years (and) days shall be (gi)ven him (KUB, xxi, 27.10-19).[71]

We may note here that all the features of the performance arena of proverb performance appear in Pudukhepa's prayer. There is disparity of status between the 'Lady' and her 'Handmaid', and the maid is in distress, which she interprets as one 'mother' to another. She invokes her audience, and cites her upcoming argument as based in the tradition of group wisdom concerning birth. Her saying is sufficiently 'out-of-context' that it may be recognized as a citation, even without the introductory formula the queen used to introduce it. She then thoughtfully supplies the correct contextual interpretation to her citation of a proverb: her mate, who has worn himself out in service to the goddess' son, is ill, and the queen

66. Medical friends tell me this most probably ought to be identified as 'athlete's foot'.

67. There has been considerable fluctuation in the conventions for the transcription of Hittite; I am quoting the forms used by the original translators.

68. Read 'people'. Hittite is a gender-neutral language, the 'feminist' implications of which were not readily apparent to early translators.

69. The son of the goddess and the Weather-god of Hatti, whose temples Khattu-shili had restored in a region reconquered by his family.

70. Both of these titles seem to be variants of the 'Old Women/Wise Women' functionaries whom we have been discussing.

71. Translated by Albrecht Goetze, 'Prayer of Pudu-hepas to the Sun-Goddess of Arinna and her Circle', *ANET*, pp. 393-94 (393).

experiences this as an analog of birth pangs. Since birth-giving is a time of great power and portent, when evil spirits must be averted and good ones drawn to succor the life of mother and child, we perceive by this metaphorical mapping onto the current situation that Pudukhepa's distress is of a high order, and of a type a divine mother will readily understand. Note also that in this portion of Pudukhepa's prayer, the 'life' (cure) that will be granted to the king is entirely in the hands of females: the wife pleads, the goddess grants and the Wise Women perform, causing the prayer to be realized.

Figure 15. Hittite Mother-Goddess (Sun-Goddess of Arinna). (1 in. × 2 ins. gold charm, Late Bronze Age Anatolia. Metropolitan Museum of Art, New York City, NY).

Lest readers suppose that this is an 'over-reading' of the element of gender in Pudukhepa's choice and citation of a proverb about women to the mother-goddess, later in her prayer she also addresses the son of the mother with the *same* proverb, but now with a different twist:

The Storm-god, thy father, (and) the Sun-goddess of Arinna, thy mother will (not re)ject thy word, they will hearken to thee. This (word) which I, Pudu-hepas, thy handmaid, have sp(oken) in prayer, announce and relay thou (to thy parents), Storm-god of Zippalanda, my lord! O god, my lord, yield to this word of mine! Because as a woman in travail I have in my own person made reparation to the god, my lord, intercede for me, god, my lord, with the Storm-god, thy father, and the Sun-goddess of Arinna, thy mother! (lines 30-39).

In this occurrence of the saying, it has been converted to a motive clause and requires no further citation of its traditional origin. The clear thrust of this section of the queen's prayer is that a beloved child cannot be denied by loving parents, so this god whom the king has served so well is invited to play the role of intercessor. But here is no sidelong bonding of mother to mother, a gentlewoman's agreement, as it were; rather we hear talk of a woman having made reparation through the birthing act of her own body. *Why* and *what kind of* reparation she has made, she does not say—this may refer either to the general notion that a mother serves the world by engaging in this dangerous yet critical occupation, or it may be a specific contextual reference to Pudukhepa's own efforts on behalf of the Storm-god in restoring his newly retaken temple and lands to their former glory. The text gives us no further hint as to how to unravel the queen's pointed reference, but the effect of it is clear enough: she is leaving no stone unturned in her efforts to intercede for the old king's health.[72] Between the proverb quoted first to a mother and then differently to her son by a mother who is a mate, we see a shift in focus and affect—from 'girl-talk' to a mother's subtle and not-so-subtle instruction to a divine 'son'. Since all other variables have remained the same, this difference may be attributed to the changes in gender and familial status of the proverb receivers. A mother's status *as mother* may allow her to outrank a son, and even the gods give in to a mother's request made under extreme duress. Although we cannot map out the precise correlations between text and context in the second citation, this intimate glimpse into the prayer life of a wily queen tells us that gender was a factor that ancients could recognize and manipulate. Whether Ezekiel might agree or not, there is clearly some merit to being able to claim a Hittite mother as a branch on Wisdom's family tree.

---

72. It is worth noting that her status is somewhat independent of his, so that she was in no particular personal fear for her own fate, should he die.

Back to the Bible: Women Using Wisdom

Our survey of women's proverb performance in ancient texts from the Bible's neighbors has been necessarily limited by the materials available to us, but they have given us some important insights as we return to biblical and postbiblical texts. From slaves to queens, women are portrayed using proverbs as part of their regular discourse, bearing out Ptahhotep's observation that, although wisdom is continuously pursued by male experts with varying results, it may still be found—almost shockingly!—among (low-status) women going about their regular 'female' activities. While we imagine none of our 'informants' had an actual scribal 'wisdom' education they nevertheless seem to know their group's proverb stock, and certainly understand the proper use of proverbs in interactions for strategic effect. Women are treated just as negatively as a trope when they appear in the collections of wisdom sayings in Egypt and Mesopotamia, yet in the *real world* of oral use of wisdom, they are equal players with native wit and full group membership.

While we may question the historical validity of the incident related in the tale of the slave woman in the Westcar Papyrus, some of our other sources bring us a far more credible view of genuine oral performance. Oracular texts, letters, and prayers—these kind of materials clearly have a closer 'factual' relationship to the events of which they speak, allowing us to speak with more confidence about a true 'performance' of the type that folklorists study. This allows us to speculate with greater accuracy about the dynamics found in examples of 'literary' proverb performance, where saying and story are more likely to have been crafted to 'fit' together. (Indeed, one of the marks of literary proverb performance is the fact that sayings and proverbs quoted within them are seldom so 'out-of-context' as noted in the texts which, show more social verisimilitude.) Even though such texts are layered with the rhetorical and ideological agendas of authors, editors and communities of readers, which must be taken into account, some characteristics of the performance arena and the proverb form itself still hold true. In both, gender has its role to play as part of the complex power equation between proverb user and proverb hearer(s).

Perhaps most intriguing of all is the recognition of the surprises to be found in our quest for women as bearers of the wisdom tradition in everyday life. In some ways, the archives we have searched have given us *more*, not less, than we expected, given the modern (mostly negative) conception of the roles allowed to women in the ancient world. Slaves who talk back, queens who wheedle, prophetesses who boldly 'tell it like it is' while instructing the king—is this what we would have expected to find if the women of the ancient world were as powerless and circumscribed as modern theological enforcers of patriarchal values would have us believe? As always, we are left wondering what the picture might look like if time and chance had not played its critical role in the materials from the ancient world that have been preserved in textual form. If we *had* the text of the letter Jezebel wrote in Ahab's name, what would we find there? We are all too apt to think that, when evidence is missing or partial, the total picture must inevitably be a negative one. The archives of Mari, Nuzi, Amarna and Khattuša serve as a telling reminder that 'it ain't necessarily so': if we are awed by the economic power and machinations of the *naditu* women, the diplomatic facility of the politically active queens, the *chutzpah* of the naked slave, should we expect any less of ancient Israel or the early Church, where slaves and debtors might expect to have some 'rights'[73] under law codes modified by a sense of divine compassion, or saved by a Spirit who listeth where she will? The position taken here is that we will not automatically assume that the biblical societies were *worse* than their neighbors with respect to women, just as we shall not make the knee-jerk assumption that those same groups to whom we like to trace our religious heritage were morally superior to the cultures surrounding them.

Biblical 'Professional Women': The Wise Women of 2 Samuel
The work of Claudia Camp takes center stage here, as in our discussions of the Strange Woman as trickster-twin of Woman Wisdom. Beginning with her study in 1981, Camp's work has sought to establish the literary antecedents of Woman Wisdom within the biblical corpus, as well as discover the locus of power in the informal roles by which women achieve distinction in tribal societies and those forms of social organization that succeed them.[74] Pointing out, quite reasonably, that we would not have matter-of-fact stories of 'wise women' from northern and southern villages in our historical books if that role were one unknown to the implied audience, Camp has increasingly focused on the literary or *verbal* behavior of women, wise or strange, as both that which authorizes their designation of 'wise' and as an example of that very wisdom. She finds that these women's roles are undergirded by the appropriation of 'mother' imagery to describe them. They function in situations where we might normally expect an 'elder', and give us some of our best models of 'clan' or

73. This is a very modern concept that I use with much reservation, but you get the idea.
74. 'Wise Women', pp. 14-29.

'family' wisdom. Finally, they are mediators of the covenantal values of land, inheritance and a Yahwism in which wisdom is a fully integrated value.[75] Other scholars have built on Camp's first studies, to enlarge and highlight various other aspects of these practitioners of female wisdom.[76]

The Wise Woman of Tekoa (2 Samuel 14). For our purposes here, we will be focusing on the Wise Woman of Abel, based on her use of a saying in the performance arena. We do not consider the Wise Woman of Tekoa any less 'wise' than her sister, even though Joab 'puts words in her mouth' (2 Sam. 14.3). Clearly, this woman was known for her wisdom, and it is the good report of her efficacy in difficult diplomatic situations that causes Joab to fetch her to instigate his plan for returning Absalom to the king's favor. That she listens to Joab as he puts words in her mouth is a sign of her wisdom, not some foolishness—the tradition is clear that a wise person listens to a variety of viewpoints, accounts and opinions before making a decision and putting it into action verbally. Further, the 'story within the story' calls up another aspect of women's wisdom, for Joab has her present herself as a female mourner and bereaved mother who tells what turns out to be an example-story to gain the king's self-conviction of wrong doing in the matter of his sons. In the decisive interview between the wise woman and the king, it is the wise woman who triumphs—with no puppet-master Joab standing behind a curtain giving her moment-by-moment advice. Whatever words David's general may have instructed her to say, it was her own experience, wisdom and ingenuity that allowed her to carry off her role. As a costumed mourner, she has invoked a different perform-ance arena than the one associated with proverb performance, and so we leave her to her recitation of woes.

The Wise Woman of Abel (2 Samuel 20). Here we have yet another story of General Joab and a Wise Woman. The broader meaning of this double set of stories deserves more attention, as does the whole concept of 'military wisdom' and ethos. However, we will content ourselves here simply by noting the important role of wise women in Hittite military rituals of drawing out enemy gods from their cities before a siege, as well as the role

75. 'Female Sage', pp. 187-88.
76. See Fontaine, 'Sage', pp. 155-64; Brenner, *Israelite Woman*, esp. pp. 33-45; Schroer, 'Wise', and Silvia Schroer, ' "And When the Next War Began...": The Wise Woman of Meth-maacah (2 Samuel 20.14-22)', in *Wisdom Has Built Her House: Studies on the Figure of Sophia in the Bible* (trans. L.M. Maloney and W. McDonough; Collegeville, MN: Liturgical Press, 2000), pp. 52-77.

of Mesopotamia goddesses and the *maš'artu*-priestess of Emar in authorizing military actions.[77] Clearly, there are some points of connection between the tasks of wise women and the skills of war-making. When we meet Joab in this context a second time, the wise woman is in her own venue, city of Abel, where a Benjaminite rebel, Sheba, has taken refuge.

> And Sheba passed through all the tribes of Israel to Abel of Bethmaacah; and all the Bichrites assembled, and followed him in. And all the men who were with Joab came and besieged him in Abel of Bethmaacah; they cast up a mound against the city, and it stood against the rampart; and they were battering the wall, to throw it down. Then a wise woman called from the city, 'Hear! Hear! Tell Joab, "Come here, that I may speak to you." ' And he came near her; and the woman said, 'Are you Joab?' He answered, 'I am.' Then she said to him, 'Listen to the words of your maidservant.' And he answered, 'I am listening.' Then she said, 'They were wont to say in old time, "Let them but ask counsel at Abel"; and so they settled a matter. I am one of those who are peaceable and faithful in Israel; you seek to destroy a city which is a mother in Israel; why will you swallow up the heritage of the LORD?' Joab answered, 'Far be it from me, far be it, that I should swallow up or destroy! That is not true. But a man of the hill country of Ephraim, called Sheba the son of Bichri, has lifted up his hand against King David; give up him alone, and I will withdraw from the city.' And the woman said to Joab, 'Behold, his head shall be thrown to you over the wall.' Then the woman went to all the people in her wisdom. And they cut off the head of Sheba the son of Bichri, and threw it out to Joab. So he blew the trumpet, and they dispersed from the city, every man to his home. And Joab returned to Jerusalem to the king (RSV, vv. 14-22).

We are immediately impressed by the ultimacy of the status variables in this telling little narrative: rebels versus military, north versus south, male versus female, indigenous versus transient. The scene of the fortified city walls, about which swarm the armies set to destroy, calls forth not some prophet, nor military hero of great stature and prodigious deeds, nor even an especially pretty shepherd with a way with stones and slings. What appears on the wall in defense of the city is a woman armed only with the wisdom of her words. By now, we should not be surprised to see her going about her business of adjudicating disputes and implementing solutions: we would expect nothing less than an old crone citing proverbs, referencing mother imagery and making quick decisions that she only later conveys to her townspeople 'in her wisdom'.

77. See Fontaine, 'Heifer', p. 173; Daniel E. Fleming, *The Installation of Baal's High Priestess at Emar* (HSM, 42; Atlanta: Scholars Press, 1992), pp. 209-11.

The wise woman makes no initial use of humility formula as she summons the general from among his men. No one has sent for her or put words in her mouth; she simply appears because a crisis is at hand, and it is her job and privilege to deal with it on behalf of her townspeople. She knows her own rank and power, and has no trouble displaying it before men who are of lesser rank when she calls the general to her. She wisely confirms that the general is who he says he is, subtly emphasizing her own status by assuming the role of interlocutor. Only when Joab has confirmed his identity does she become a 'handmaiden' to a man superior to her in status. Even so, her appropriately humble adoption of the 'subject position' of a serving woman approaching her more powerful master is coupled with an imperious command that the so-called master *heed her words*. It is her verbal activity that is *her* weapon, in this case the citation of a proverb coupled with the potent symbol of a mother violated—there is no worse illustration of the folly of political struggle for the people. Like a mother instructing a wayward son indulging in a violent tantrum that will only end in the destruction of all his favorite toys, our wise woman makes full use her vantage point on the city wall—could there be a better way to indicate the 'one-up' position of the Proverb User over the Proverb Hearer? Like Woman Wisdom who will take her place on the city walls centuries later, the woman here is a teacher and counselor who does not fear to show herself—though the mighty male rebel *does!*

She moves into the performance arena when she negotiates the identity of the men to whom she is speaking, commanding them to listen and do her bidding. Calling up tradition in the most potent way, she signals that what the general is about to hear is something more than the words of a mere woman: 'at the first' they used to quote the saying that follows, 'Let them ask for counsel at Abel!' 'At the first' or 'of old' (ראשנה) refers here not just to time, but to preeminence of rank and place, and the wise woman calls up this legacy of words and counsel to defend a town that is Yahweh's 'heritage'—a heritage of motherhood displayed through wise words.

But Joab has *not* asked for counsel at Abel before making his plans for a siege, and he stands convicted of his disrespect toward a 'mother'. His response is deferential and definitive: he uses a 'far be it!' oath to distance himself from his former foolishness. It is Sheba the rebel who is his enemy, not the mother-city with a distinguished history for settling disputes. Whether the wise woman agrees with this assessment or not, she knows that giving the head (ראש!) of one man is a better bargain than giving her city over to destruction. Without consultation of any male authorities in the town, she concludes the arrangement with the general. Only later does she tell the people the content of her bargain,[78] to which they assent. The 'head', the foremost part of the rebel, is substituted for the body of the foremost city of counsel. Thanks to the wise woman, Joab's army leaves the town in peace, its tradition of counsel now having one more story in its repertoire to repeat to the generations that follow.

Lions and Brides and Bears: Cross-gendering the Audience with Proverbial Allusions. Generals and other military 'professionals' use gender ideology in their 'pep talks' to the armies and those who lead them, shaming the troops by connecting to or disconnecting them from female imagery. In 1 Samuel 4, the Philistines rouse themselves from their pre-battle fears by use of this device : 'Take courage, and *be men*, O Philistines, in order not to become slaves to the Hebrews as they have been to you; *be men and fight!*' (v. 9, NRSV). A Hittite king berates his timid troops during the extended siege of Uršu:

> ...Why have you not given battle? You stand on chariots of water, you are almost turned into water yourself... You had only to kneel before him and you would have killed him or at least frightened him! But as it is *you have behaved like a woman!*[79]

Similar stratagems still obtain: among English speakers in the United States, young males in the process of coming to terms with their own gendered identity can easily be manipulated by the imputed slur that they 'throw like a girl', are 'wussies'[80] or 'Nancy-boys'.

A variation on this strategic use of gender ideology might choose to render the targeted enemies less threatening by cross-gendering them as female. Consider the conflicting counsels given to the rebellious Absalom by Ahithophel the Sage and Hushai the Archite traitor in 2 Samuel 17:

> Moreover Ahithophel said to Absalom, 'Let me choose twelve thousand men, and I will set out and pursue David tonight. I will come upon him while he is weary and discouraged, and throw him into a panic; and all the people who are with him will flee. I will strike down the king only, and I will bring all the people back to you *as a bride comes home to her husband.* You seek the life of only one man, and all the people will be at peace.' And the advice pleased Absalom and all the elders of Israel.

---

78. It is likely that the people are listening, out of harm's way, as in other city wall scenes (2 Kgs 18.26).

79. O.R. Gurney, *The Hittites* (London: Penguin Books, rev. edn, 1981), pp. 180-81.

80. This is a more polite term for 'pussy' (standard slang for female genital triangle), and has gained currency through usage in television and elsewhere.

Then Absalom said, 'Call Hushai the Archite also, and let us hear what he has to say.' And when Hushai came to Absalom, Absalom said to him, 'Thus has Ahithophel spoken; shall we do as he advises? If not, you speak.' Then Hushai said to Absalom, 'This time the counsel which Ahithophel has given is not good.' Hushai said moreover, 'You know that your father and his men are mighty men, and that they are enraged, *like a bear robbed of her cubs in the field*. Besides, your father is expert in war; he will not spend the night with the people. Behold, even now he has hidden himself in one of the pits, or in some other place. And when some of the people fall at the first attack, whoever hears it will say, "There has been a slaughter among the people who follow Absalom." Then even the valiant man, whose heart is *like the heart of a lion,* will utterly melt with fear; for all Israel knows that your father is a mighty man, and that those who are with him are valiant men. But my counsel is that all Israel be gathered to you, from Dan to Beer-sheba, *as the sand by the sea for multitude*, and that you go to battle in person. So we shall come upon him in some place where he is to be found, and we shall light upon him *as the dew falls on the ground*; and of him and all the men with him not one will be left. If he withdraws into a city, then all Israel will bring ropes to that city, and we shall drag it into the valley, *until not even a pebble is to be found there*' (RSV, vv. 1-13).

Here we have two 'counsel' speeches that are studded with the conventional language of proverbial phrases. In oral performance these traditional similes have the rhetorical purpose of stimulating the hearers into 'cocreation' of meaning by the powerful trigger of these 'integers' of oral tradition.[81] The older and higher status counselor, Ahithophel, characterizes the situation as being much like the one that confronts us on the walls of Abel: why slaughter a whole people when only one person need die? To render that 'people' as innocuous and desirable as possible, Ahithophel genders them as a 'bride' who will come joyfully to her master, thus allowing him to extend his power into the next generation. No hint here is given of a fractious, dangerous group that might easily overcome the rebel troops.

Hushai's counsel, meant to deceive Absalom into making poor choices that will ultimately restore David to the throne, takes a different direction, but the rhetorical strategy is the same. Now the 'people' whom Ahithophel imaged as a youthful bride in procession with her attendants is composed

---

81. Foley, *Singer*, pp. 56-59. This signifying 'word-power' in oral literature is in direct opposition to the occurrence of such stereotypic features in a text, where they may take on the aspect of the hackneyed 'cliche'—a sign of the author's inability to be 'creative' by generating new comparisons, rather than an audience-friendly tactic that invites the hearers to 'fill in the gaps' in oral performace.

of dangerous, seasoned 'mighty men' and champions. Hushai deploys
female imagery to make his point, too, only he extends the female language into a further stage of the 'reproductive' process. No bride, but
rather a mother bear whose cubs have been taken, will meet Absalom's
troops—a rather different proposition! The image of wild, maternal feroc-
ity renders the fleeing king and his followers 'female', both less-than and
more-than human, and calls up proverbial references:

> Let a man meet a she-bear robbed of her cubs,
> rather than a fool in his folly (17.12).

> Like a roaring lion or a charging bear
> is a wicked ruler over a poor people (28.15).

Weaving in the force of the traditional wisdom 'word-pair' of lions/
bears, Hushai conjures up the scene of the lion's den (pit) and the valiant
bravery of toughened troops. By this verbal maneuver, animal imagery
further distances the hearers from Ahithophel's marital rather than martial
reading of the enemy. It is this kind of dehumanization that undergirds
Hushai's suggestion of plundering a whole city. Other traditional phrases
describe positive and negative abundance (sand of the sea; not a pebble)
and ease (as dew falls), further moving the discussion into the natural
world in order to minimize the very real prospects of death and disorder
that Hushai's policy of 'over-kill' would create—*just* the kind of disaster
that Ahithophel and the Wise Woman of Abel are at pains to avoid.
Tellingly, the mother bear trumps the beaming bride, and the fool goes
unwittingly onto his folly. Such is the power of proverbial references
exploited by a skilled speaker.

On the walls of Abel, we again have another episode where a reader
may reasonably doubt the oral character of the interchange reported, at
least from the perspective of the requirements of the proverb register in
oral performance. The saying about Abel is applied to Abel directly and
literally. It also happens to coincide with what the wise woman hopes will
be the outcome of its citation: reasoned discussion about possible solutions
rather than wholesale violence applied indiscriminately. In this sense, the
saying is neither 'out-of-context' nor metaphorical—a textually effective,
if somewhat lackluster performance. In the light of the Hittite wise
woman's role of enticing the rebel gods out of a city so her armies can
conquer it successfully, we see a nice inversion here in 2 Samuel: our
Israelite wise woman entices her folk to fling the offending rebel's head
out of the city so that the town *won't* be conquered by armies. Whether
outside the walls attending to the ritual-symbolic needs of her army or

inside the walls tending the crisis about to breach the integrity of the
mother city and its people, matters military cannot be conducted without
some female presence—an interesting confluence of traditions we might
have considered exclusively 'male' and 'female' without our attention to
wisdom folk and wisdom forms.

What, we wonder, would our wise woman have done if there had been
no convenient folk tradition about Abel which had found its way into
saying form? No doubt the common stock of proverbs would have been
consulted, for the concerns of the Wise Woman of Abel do not go unre-
marked there:

> He who robs his father or his mother and says, 'That is no transgression,' is
> the companion of a man who destroys (RSV, Prov. 28.24).

> Scoffers set a city aflame,
> but wise men turn away wrath (RSV, 29.8).

All things considered, we must insist here on the NRSV's translation,
'Scoffers set a city aflame, but the wise turn away wrath,' rather than that
of other translations. Both forms are masculine plural, so why should we
accept the logic by which only the negative term is rendered inclusive?
When we ask about this dispute at Abel, her wise woman settles the matter, now as then.

Bath-Sheba Gives Counsel: the Afterlife of a Biblical Instruction

Long before the Hogwarts School of Witchcraft and Wizardry delighted its
students with a sky enchanted to look just like the real one outdoors, storytellers reading the book of Proverbs had provided a similar heaven for the
bedchamber of Solomon. Brought to him by Pharaoh's daughter Bithiah, the
wedded couple spent their first night beneath this unnatural ceiling, causing
Solomon to oversleep on the very day the Temple was to be dedicated
(gasp!). We meet him beneath this fraudulent firmament, with his mother
Bath-sheba giving instruction about the duties of kings:

> Over his bed she (Bithiah) spread a kind of canopy, in which she set all
> kinds of precious stones and pearls that shimmered like stars and planets, so
> that whenever Solomon was about to get up, he saw those stars and planets,
> and kept going back to sleep until the fourth hour in the day.
>
> R. Levi said, '…Israel grieved, for although it was the day of the Tem-
> ple's dedication, they could not bring the offering on time because Solomon
> was asleep with the keys of the Temple under his head, and, in their awe of
> royalty, they hesitated to wake him. So they went and told Bathsheba, his
> mother, who came in, woke him up, and chastised him. With regard to this,

it is said, "The utterance of his mother, followed by her chastising him" (Prov. 31.1). She took off her slipper and slapped him on one cheek, then on the other, as she said, "What, my son? And what, O son of my womb?" (Prov. 31.2)...

R. Yohanan said in the name of R. Simeon ben Yohai: '...In saying, "What, my son," she meant: All know that your father feared God, [but now it will be said: His mother made him what he is, and you will be spoken of not as your father's son, but as my son]. In saying, "And what, O son of my vows" she meant: Each woman in your father's household prayed, "May I have a son fit for the throne," while I made vows as I prayed, "May I have a son eager and keen to study the Torah, and fit for prophecy." Continuing her reprimand of Solomon, Bathsheba said, "Not with kings [who say], 'Lemuel'" (Prov. 31.4). Why do you imitate kings who say, "*Lamah lanu el*," "What need have we of God" "Not with kings who drink wine" (Prov. 31.4)—why do you act like those kings who imbibe wine, get drunk, then indulge in all kinds of lewdness?..." '

How do we know, said R. Isaac, that Solomon repented and admitted to his mother that she was right? From the verse 'Surely I am more brutish than that man, and have not the understanding of Adam' (Prov. 30.2).[82]

The materials made present in this midrashic contextualization of an extended proverb performance of an 'instruction' are gleaned from a variety of sources (Talmudic and medieval),[83] but the text presented here is from Bialik and Ravnitsky's *The Book of Legends (Sefer haAggadah)*, which I am going to treat as something of a modern 'version'. That is, although the authors gave wonderfully nuanced and thoughtful readings of much of the material they collected, they also conflated, added, deleted, and massaged the stories they collated, such that sometimes the text they produced must be viewed as an entirely new product. When one adds to this their somewhat casual and piecemeal approach to providing references to the original works they cite, we find that as a 'scholarly source', their *Book of Legends* must give way to L. Ginzberg's monumental *The Legends of the Jews*. There one may find a more thorough discussion of sources, even if Ginzberg's work gives less of a flavor of the originals and has its own problems in the handling of primary sources. Nevertheless, *The Book of Legends* is a 'popular' resource that makes an astonishing amount of legendary materials available in a single English volume for

82. H.N Bialik, and Y.H Ravnitzky (eds.), *The Book of Legends (Sefer HaAggadah): Legends from the Talmud and Midrash* (trans. W.G. Braude; intro. D. Stern; New York: Schocken Books, 1992), p. 126.

83. See p. 281 n. 13, in L. Ginzberg, *The Legends of the Jews*, VI (Philadelphia: Jewish Publication Society of America, 1936).

general readers. The desire to take the mother's instruction in Proverbs 30 and give it a *Sitz im Leben* within the broader tradition of Israelite wisdom began in Talmudic times (if not before); the little text cited above only continues the impulse with a kind of evangelical glee that heaps reading upon reading to create something we have not seen in quite this way previously.

If we turn to the Queen Mother's instruction as we find it in Proverbs 31, we see that it makes its point though interspersing intensely personal experience ('womb', 'son of my vows') with wisdom teachings on wine and women[84] that have already surfaced elsewhere in the book:

> The words of King Lemuel. An oracle that his mother taught him: No, my son! No, son of my womb! No, son of my vows! Do not give your strength to women, your ways to those who destroy kings. It is not for kings, O Lemuel, it is not for kings to drink wine, or for rulers to desire strong drink; or else they will drink and forget what has been decreed, and will pervert the rights of all the afflicted. Give strong drink to one who is perishing, and wine to those in bitter distress; let them drink and forget their poverty, and remember their misery no more. Speak out for those who cannot speak, for the rights of all the destitute (vv. 1-8, NRSV).

Given that this is our *only* extended example of a mother's instruction (unless one counts Naomi's program for seduction in Ruth 3.1-5), it is sad but useful to note how little the biblical text seems to care about its context. Despite the best efforts of scholars, this queen cannot be identified, nor can her son Lemuel (the LXX is even reluctant to consider this a personal name) be traced. The word translated 'oracle' may give a geographical reference: there is an area in Northern Arabia called Massa, from which this piece of 'foreign' (?) mothering may have originated, but the point is far from settled.[85] Foreign or not, the advice of this queen was easily understood as being in harmony with the instruction genre of the Hebrew Bible and the duties of queens.

Our legendary contextualization clearly belongs to the tradition that attempts to celebrate the accomplishments of David and Solomon in creating the monarchy's 'Golden Age', while also seeking to understand the negative dimensions of that time. While modern readers might raise issues

---

84. What, no 'song'?! See discussion below.

85. See James Crenshaw's treatment of this instruction in the context of ancient Near Eastern examples of the genre ('A Mother's Instruction to Her Son [Proverbs 31:1-9]', in *Urgent Advice and Probing Questions: Collected Writings on Old Testament Wisdom* [Macon, GA: Mercer University Press, 1995], pp. 383-95).

like treatment of women and children, even royal ones, in David's court to the forced labor that undergirded Solomon's magnificence, these kinds of political questions are less of an issue for later interpreters. While the Hebrew Bible gives copious 'hints' that all was not well among the people even when a fabulous Jerusalem was ruled by its very best kings, ancient and modern readings of the role of gender in the debacle of the 'United Monarchy' differ markedly. Feminist readers see the first kings' treatment of women and children as emblematic of a disruption of any social 'safety net' tribalized society might have held out to these pawns in male power games. For the Bible and its subsequent interpreters, however, exactly the reverse is true: it is the *women* (and the need to get sons through them) who are the *source* of the problem. It is the sight of a woman bathing that leads David to commit the 'sin of Uriah the Hittite'—not his malfeasance in lolling around Jerusalem while the army is at war, and *certainly* not any sin committed against Bathsheba herself as the silent pawn in David's adultery and cover-up, that causes the sword of God's judgment to fall on David's house, never to depart. Similarly, it is Solomon's political marriages to outsider princesses—the classic Strange Woman of high status—that incite him to the idolatries that cause God to judge him by rending the kingdom in two at his death. The deeds done to living women in this intense political mix of intrigue, shifting social ideologies and theology are again metaphorized to refer to something *more* important to the male writers: the fate of the Body Politic obliterates the fate of the Body Female.

Hence, our Queen Mother of Massa is easily given the identity of Bathsheba, the central link between David and Solomon, and in her instruction she is a staunch speaker on behalf of patriarchal gender ideology, both in the original text in Prov. 31.1-9 and our aggadic treatment of the text. Like Woman Wisdom's speeches that give a female voice to the denigration of female subjectivity, neither addressing women nor giving them much space to disagree with this exalted voice of parental Tradition, the queen's instruction gives the same reasons for kingly misconduct as does the rest of the Bible: women and their plots make men weak and sinful. The queen is certainly referring to 'harem politics', which were real and lethal in effect ('those who destroy kings'), since wives of various genealogies successfully married off and up into the royal harem served as the focus of their male relatives' power bids. The ancient Near East abounds with stories of the intrigues, coups and wars that stem from such maneuvering, and 2 Samuel is especially taken with this plot line as it describes how kingship is transferred from Ephraim to Judah.

Next, the queen speaks of the role that intoxicants play in very different situations, and here she shows a sensitive appreciation of the fact that context can make all the difference in the world. Those responsible for others, at ease and favored in their social locations, ought not to be seeking the release that one permits and encourages for those in despair. Again, the queen is on solid ground in her warnings: banquets in the world of Israel and its neighbors were occasions where power might be radically redistributed, and not always to the benefit of the 'afflicted'.[86] That the mother's instruction ends with an appeal to 'stick up for' the lowest of the social order is a nice piece of rhetoric—from her beginning rhetorical questions, we might have thought her concern was more for how her son's behavior reflected upon *her*, rather than a more general regard for the oppressed and their treatment under her son's rule.

The later treatment of this text as spoken by Bathsheba to Solomon, however, moves us from the ancient world of genuine court intrigue and royal ethics to the haunts of the Strange Woman *par excellence*, in the form of Pharaoh's daughter. Other legends about her effect on Solomon cling to this marriage like a magnet: Solomon had been sober for years upon years, as befitting a sage king, but during this wedding celebration he drank and hence overslept.[87] The rejoicing heard in heaven over the dedication of the Temple was less impressive than the rejoicing over the royal marriage, so enraging God that he set about engineering the end of Jerusalem at the hands of a future Rome at that very moment. Further, that night Bithiah danced 80 kinds of (erotic?) dances for her new husband, accompanied by one thousand kinds of different musical instruments, each with an explicit connection to a different idol.[88]

Here we have been given a compendium of the significant damage a Strange Woman can do to the wisest of men, *even* in the confines of consummation of a legal marriage. Drunkenness, lasciviousness, forbidden entertainments of both erotic and theological content—no wonder Solomon sleeps in! Even without the fabulous star-studded canopy Bithiah used to trick the king into thinking he slept beneath his usual sky, the man had been transported to new, exotic—and unacceptable—realms by his foreign wife. If the spur to the creation of midrash is 'the need to deal with

---

86. See Fontaine, 'Deceptive Goddess', pp. 84-102.

87. Ginzberg, *Legends*, VI, p. 281 n. 13. This is a much more reasonable, though not so magical, explanation for Solomon's tardiness in tending to matters in the Temple.

88. Bialik and Ravnitzky (eds.), *Legends*, pp. 125-26.

the presence of cultural or religious tension and discontinuity',[89] then we can only wonder at the stresses and fracture marks that must have strained the Jewish communities of antiquity and the Middle Ages, such that so much venom was directed at Out-Group wives, or the potential for forming such relationships. Whether this tendency is just another projection of disproportionate and hysterical male fear onto a distanced and demonic target found appealing for some psychological reason, or whether it reflects real social conditions of the periods when these legends were composed and retold must be left in the competent hands of students of those periods. What we *can* say in this connection is that the gender ideologies of the Hebrew Bible provided ample scope for elaborating on such tensions whenever they surfaced historically, and this ideology was propagated through wisdom teachings along with other forms for transmission of cultural values.

Our queenly proverb performance of a biblical instruction tells us a number of things. First of all, the Hebrew Bible's scanty superscription and introduction of this instruction left later readers as puzzled as modern ones, and so the impulse to put these words into a 'real' (= known) queen's mouth was born. Next, we are immediately aware of the distance between those puzzled earlier readers and ourselves: *they* need to fill in the gap concerning the nature of vows made by women longing to become successful mothers; we need to probe the superabundance of legendary material that largely exempts Solomon from any moral agency in the rule he instigates. *They* require an acceptable reason for Solomon's wickedness; *we* seek a more believable reading of Solomon's goodness. Cherchez la femme is no more credible than 'The Devil made me do it,' though both are staples of popular theological wisdom.

Though our 'performance' here is without doubt performance constructed by later readers, it follows all the patterns of saying-based proverb performance. The status differences in the Interaction Situation are not just between queens (own and foreign), but between generations (parent and child), classes (royal and non-royal), and female roles (mother and wife). The young woman has already given her 'performance' in the erotic, sensual domain; now the older woman challenges the bride's hegemony of influence over the besotted male—who will win, Wisdom or Folly? The charming premise that the only one capable of rebuking a king (smacking him with her slipper, no less—a Freudian tip-off if ever there was one!) is

---

89. B.W. Holtz, 'Midrash', in *Back to the Sources: Reading the Classic Jewish Texts* (New York: Simon & Schuster, 1984), pp. 177-212 (179).

his mother pays tribute to established folk ideas about the role of child-rearing as a source of authority and wisdom. The reluctance of underlings to challenge their royal lord is telling as well about the real conflicts underlying the narrative program of the legendary context.

The 'performance arena' is clearly demarcated by the introduction of the biblical verses with the formula 'as it is said', the typical way of beginning a biblical citation. Again, we know we are in the realm of literary, constructed performance because the instruction 'quoted' is not out-of-context at all. In fact, the opposite obtains: a context has been specifically and carefully constructed so these words of instruction will have some relevance to their current audiences, while the biblical 'hook' gives the aggadic material a template around which to weave a new scene in the life of ancient Israel's monarchy. Further, the exegetical elaboration that tells us what Bathsheba's instruction 'really' referred to succeeds nicely in shifting blame for David's sin back onto the woman where it belongs: if Solomon fails, it must be his mother's (and not his father's) fault. Solomon's 'own' proverbs confirm it: 'A wise son makes a glad father, but a foolish son is a sorrow to his mother' (10.1). That this directly contradicts the Hebrew Bible's testament that it was *David's* sin that caused the disruptions in his royal house (whatever the Bible or the reader may believe that sin to have been) is yet another triumph of gender ideology that simultaneously denies female moral agency *and* imputes to it great power.

But *there is a problem in the text*, maintains the feminist version of a medieval rabbi writing a *responsa*: where is Bithiah during this undignified tussle between mother and son? We presume that Pharaoh's daughter shared Solomon's bed and chamber during her Night of Eighty Dances to a Thousand Instruments. She is the origin of the offending false ceiling that mirrored the night sky, designed to keep Solomon at her side during the night and into the morning hours. She has been in every way a potent, patent presence, yet when the mother queen begins her chastisement, suddenly she disappears, voiceless. Why?

If our legends give Bithiah no voice but that of idolatrous instruments, we shall choose to hear her differently. We may compare Bithiah's performance for her new husband with that of another Strange Woman who seeks out a young fool rather than an old one:

> 'I had to offer sacrifices, and today I have paid my vows; so now I have come out to meet you, to seek you eagerly, and I have found you. I have decked my couch with coverings, colored spreads of Egyptian linen; I have

perfumed my bed with myrrh, aloes, and cinnamon. Come, let us take our
fill of love till morning; let us delight ourselves with love.' (NRSV Prov.
7.14-18)

Sacrifices and vows, couches and coverings, Egyptian spreads and exotic
scents—all these trappings of the seductress at her most outrageous are
echoed intertextually in the presentation of the Out-Group Bithiah and her
outrageous wiles. We hardly know whether we have strayed into the Song
of Songs or the Book of Esther—that Out-Group queen in a political marriage also brought 'whatever she desired to take with her from the harem to
the king's palace', though we are told she confined her choices for the
king's couch to those things advised by her eunuch 'coach' (2.13; cf. v. 15).
Esther, of course, may be Out-Group to her Persian husband, but she is In-
Group to the tellers of her story, so her behavior is approved while Bithiah's
is not. Bithiah's absence from our textual performance reminds us that it is
not just gender that can render strange and whose lines of belonging must
continually be redrawn; it is the foreignness of race that creates the Ultimate
Stranger. Only motherhood can convert a woman's standing from 'Other' to
'Own', when she holds the 'mixed' child of her 'foreign' womb and her
husband's 'own' seed in her arms. Bithiah is silenced because she has not
made this transition, so no words can be accorded her.

We have given Bithiah the voice of the Strange Woman who is *never*
imaged as a mother in the book of Proverbs, and we imagine her looking
on at Bathsheba's performance, still in bed beneath luxurious coverings,
perhaps with a knowing smile on her face. If *anyone* had detailed experience of the complexities of female power struggles in the harem for
control over the king's heart, it would be a daughter of Pharaoh! If the
sight of Solomon's cheek aflame with the imprint of his mother's slipper
leads Bithiah to consider him 'whipped', if he has been shamed before his
new bride for stealing a few hours for love out of the Temple's timetable,
we cannot say what this means for the future of their marriage. Though
our legends had no interest in such 'girl-talk', we will leave our Strange
Woman in conversation with the king's mother, a biblical quote on her lips
to go with the carefully constructed context of the legends:

> I adjure you, O daughter(s) of Jerusalem,
> by the gazelles or the wild does:
> do not stir up or awaken love until it is ready! (Song 2.7).

Of course, Solomon's exploits with Strange Woman have only just begun.
We have been working our way, Sheba by Bath-sheba, towards the greatest and strangest of all his loves: the Queen of Sheba.

The Queen of Sheba in the Hebrew Bible

Sheba's story, recorded in 1 Kgs 10.1-10, 13 (2 Chron. 9.1-9, 12; Josephus, *Ant.* 8.6.5-6), is nestled in among accounts of Solomon's international ventures and achievements:

> Now when the queen of Sheba heard of the fame of Solomon concerning the name of the LORD, she came to test him with hard questions. She came to Jerusalem with a very great retinue, with camels bearing spices, and very much gold, and precious stones; and when she came to Solomon, she told him all that was on her mind. And Solomon answered all her questions; there was nothing hidden from the king which he could not explain to her. And when the queen of Sheba had seen all the wisdom of Solomon, the house that he had built, the food of his table, the seating of his officials, and the attendance of his servants, their clothing, his cupbearers, and his burnt offerings which he offered at the house of the LORD, there was no more spirit in her. And she said to the king, 'The report was true which I heard in my own land of your affairs and of your wisdom, but I did not believe the reports until I came and my own eyes had seen it; and, behold, the half was not told me; your wisdom and prosperity surpass the report which I heard. Happy are your wives! Happy are these your servants, who continually stand before you and hear your wisdom! Blessed be the LORD your God, who has delighted in you and set you on the throne of Israel! Because the LORD loved Israel for ever, he has made you king, that you may execute justice and righteousness.' Then she gave the king a hundred and twenty talents of gold, and a very great quantity of spices, and precious stones; never again came such an abundance of spices as these which the queen of Sheba gave to King Solomon. Moreover the fleet of Hiram, which brought gold from Ophir, brought from Ophir a very great amount of almug wood and precious stones. And the king made of the almug wood supports for the house of the LORD, and for the king's house, lyres also and harps for the singers; no such almug wood has come or been seen, to this day. And King Solomon gave to the queen of Sheba all that she desired, whatever she asked besides what was given her by the bounty of King Solomon. So she turned and went back to her own land, with her servants (RSV, 1 Kgs 10.1-13).

Most critics agree that this is a legend clearly marked with wisdom forms (a praise speech including a blessing formula [v. 9a], and in v. 8, a beatitude or 'ashrê-saying') and characters (wise king, wise queen, diplomacy, riddle contest; eulogy (vv. 6-7, 9b).[90] This legendary character of

90. Burke O. Long, *1 Kings, with an Introduction to Historical Literature* (FOTL, 9; Grand Rapids, MI: Eerdmans, 1984), pp. 115-20; James A. Montgomery, *A Critical*

our riddle tale, and the narrative silences within it (why no texts of the riddles?) gives the story a vigorous 'afterlife'. Storytellers from different times and places, ethnic and religious traditions, have enhanced its details, guided by the preferences and needs of their own communities.

A historical report or notice of Hiram's fleet has been interpolated in vv. 11-12. We may note here that already, simply by consulting the standard 'objective' historical critical or literary research, we have entered into the realm where gender may be read as a forceful subtext influencing the reader: Hiram's fleet is 'historical'; Sheba's wealth, and even her very existence are relegated to the fairy-tale land of folk legend—lest we be inclined to take this very foreign, very astute queen as a real model for women in public leadership roles, or to see in her presence a gendered gap within the patriarchal hegemony over power politics.

Within the biblical text, two features spawned the intense speculation about Sheba's relation to Solomon. The verb בוא 'to come', a verb with connotations of sexual intercourse, is used in v. 2. The phrase 'And King Solomon gave to the Queen of Sheba all that she desired, whatever she asked...' in v. 13, seemed to underscore the sexual interpretation of v. 2 for some. This raises the evocative mystery of Sheba's origin and identity which is so evident in all the interpretative embellishments and historical research on her story which follow. In the New Testament, she is identified simply as the Queen of the South' (Mt. 12.42; Lk. 11.31).[91] Of the early sources, Josephus gives the most detailed and positive account of Sheba, who bears the personal name 'Nicaulis' and has now become equated with Egypt and Africa:

> There lived in those days a woman who was queen of Egypt and Ethiopia, a great student of philosophy, and on other accounts also one to be admired. When this queen heard of the virtue and wisdom of Solomon, she had a great mind to see him, and the reports that went every day abroad induced her to go to him. For being desirous to be satisfied by her own experience

and Exegetical Commentary on the Book of Kings (ed. H.S. Gehman; New York: Charles Scribner's Sons, 1951), pp. 212-19, and so with other commentators. It is probable that the insertion of Hiram's fleet here occurs because it is yoked to folk traditions of Hiram and Solomon holding riddle contests (see the account by Josephus), for which the loser had to pay a monetary fine.

91. For a discussion of Sheba in the New Testament, see Carole Fontaine, 'The Strange Face of Wisdom in the New Testament: On the Reuse of Wisdom Characters from the Hebrew Bible', in Athalya Brenner and Jan Willem van Henten (eds.), *Recycling Biblical Figures: Papers Read at a NOSTER Colloquium in Amsterdam, 12–13 May 1997* (STAR, 1; Leiden: Deo, 1999), pp. 205-29.

and not by bare hearsay (for reports thus heard are likely enough to be false, as they wholly depend on the credit of the relators), she resolved to visit him, especially in order to test his wisdom by propounding questions of very great difficulty, and entreating that he would solve their hidden meaning. So she came to Jerusalem... Now the king in his kind reception of her showed a great desire to please her, and easily comprehending in his mind the meaning of the curious questions she propounded to him, he resolved them sooner than anybody could have expected (*Ant.* 8.5.5).[92]

In the context of a discussion on Job 1.15, the Talmud declares, in the name of second-century CE sage R. Jonathan of Palestine, that Sheba refers to a kingdom or *region*, and not to a woman ruler at all, perhaps hoping to discount oral tales circulating about Solomon's erotic interest in Sheba that were then being used to discredit the ancestry of R. Judah the Patriarch.[93] In the *Targum of Job*, reference to Sheba is clearly intended to link her to the Sabeans who cause Job's misfortune, and is rendered '...and suddenly Lilith, the Queen of Smaragd, fell upon...', giving us one of our first demonizing tendencies in the quest for Sheba.[94] Following some of the same lines of thought found in Josephus, the later Ethiopian tradition

92. A.R. Shilleto (ed.), *The Works of Flavius Josephus: Whiston's Translation*, II (London: George Bell & Sons, 1889), p. 101. The name 'Nicaulis' is given by Josephus in *Ant.*, 8.6.2, where Josephus seems to be confusing her with Hatshepsut. The translator remarks, 'And indeed it must be confessed, that here, and in ERROR 5, we have more mistakes made by Josephus, relating to the kings of Egypt, and to the Queen of Egypt and Ethiopia whom he supposes to have come to see Solomon, than almost anywhere else in all the Antiquities' (p. 99).

93. *BT B. Bat.* 15, b. Lou H. Silberman, 'The Queen of Sheba in Judaic Tradition', in James Pritchard (ed.), *Solomon and Sheba* (London: Phaidon Press, 1974), pp. 67-68.

94. David M. Stec, *The Text of the Targum of Job: An Introduction and Critical Edition* (Leiden: E.J. Brill, 1994), p. 8*. The *11QTgJob*, a much earlier targum (first century CE) to Job, unfortunately does not contain this passage. The later *Targum of Job* represents a fascinating amalgam of multiple translations and midrashim, and has text groupings that reflect both Ashkenazic and Sephardic traditions. Unfortunately, it cannot be dated with any certainty and reflects a long and complex tradition history (E. Levine, *The Aramaic Version of the Bible* [BZAW, 174; Berlin: W. de Gruyter, 1988], p. 26; Stec, *Targum of Job*, pp. 86-94). Mangan posits a *terminus ad quem* for the eleventh century based on its extensive appearance in Saadya Gaon, and finds a very early core of material parallel to New Testament and pseudepigraphal writings (Célene Mangan, 'Some Observations on the Dating of Targum Job', in Kevin J. Cathcart and John F. Healey [eds.], *Back to the Sources: Biblical and Near Eastern Studies in Honour of Dermot Ryan* [Dublin: Glendale Press, 1989], pp. 67-78 [70, 75-76]).

conflates Sheba with 'Candace, Queen of the Ethiopians' (Acts 8.27), and under the name Makeda she becomes the founder of a royal dynasty (*Kebra Nagast* chs. 21, 33; written down around 1400 BCE).[95] This relation of Sheba to the horn of Africa, rather than the Arabian desert, will find its way into Christian Europe, where, by 1181, she is depicted as a black woman by Nicholas of Verdun in the altarpiece at Klosterneuburg, forming, along with various Old and New World 'Black Madonnas', one of the few positive associations between blackness and sacrality.[96] If early Christian Africans and their descendants found a powerfully beneficent way of understanding the 'otherness' of Sheba, inscribed in her blackness (which scarcely seemed 'other' to them), using it to ensure their rightful place in the fold of Christian nations, Sheba's 'strangeness' did not fare so well in her Judaic and Islamic retellings.

The story of Sheba's visit also appears in the *Quran* in Sura 27, 'The Ant'. In the *Quran*, we meet the still nameless Sheba, but we discover her first ruling in the midst of her people (vv. 15-45). Solomon is now Sulayman, a true Muslim and a prophet of the mighty one god Allah.[97] One of his fabulous bird-servants, the hoopoe, has seen Sheba ruling her people and worshiping the sun. Solomon sends the hoopoe back with a letter in Allah's name, commanding Sheba to come to submit to the king and his god. Deferential as befitting a woman in the *Quran*, especially a pagan one, she subserviently requests directions from her Council, saying, 'I am not used to decide an affair until you bear me witness' (v. 31). The Council replies that they have sufficient might to hold off any invader, but Sheba, a true diplomat, thinks otherwise. Even in the best of circumstances —winning—war causes disruptions to a kingdom that she is not willing to risk, even if her male advisors are. She wisely decides to try deflecting Solomon with a gift, hoping to abate his wrath and obviate the need for a tedious, uncertain journey that will end in her and her people's submis-

95. Edward Ullendorff, 'The Queen of Sheba', *Bulletin of the John Rylands Library* 45 (1963), pp. 496-98; *BT B. Bat.* 15, b. The *Kebra Nagast*, and the Christian versions based on it, follows a significantly different path in its explication of Sheba/Makeda's behavior and intent. There Sheba is a noble, wise, virginal ancestress who is tricked and seduced by Solomon and later bears him a son, Menelik. No mention of the hoopoe, demonic legs, body hair, a glass pavilion, bare legs or riddle texts is made.

96. Robert E. Hood, *Begrimed and Black: Christian Traditions on Blacks and Blackness* (Philadelphia: Fortress Press, 1994), p. 111.

97. All great heroes of the Hebrew Bible are treated as monotheistic 'true believers' by the Quran.

sion. Solomon rebuffs this overture, and demands her presence. He sends one of his enslaved jinns to fetch Sheba's throne while she is on her way to meet him—and tellingly, for the point of view of the narrator of this episode, Sheba's throne is described with the same terminology used for Allah's throne earlier in the Sura. For the *Quran*, Sheba is no illegitimate wielder of power, even though she is female, and she is portrayed sympathetically as more astute than the males who surround her. Like any good wisdom ruler, she takes 'counsel' with her wise ones, and includes them in her deliberations. When she reverses their advice, she does so in a way that highlights her as a caring ruler rather than a capricious female.

When Sheba appears at Solomon's court and a throne is set before her, we have a text which presents us with an 'iconic riddle', an action or event that itself is a riddle and requires a solution of some sort.[98] In a reverse of the biblical story where Sheba is the Riddler and Solomon the Riddlee, Solomon interrogates Sheba about the riddle of the throne: is it hers or not? Perhaps sensing a 'damned if you do, damned if you don't', Sheba waffles: she replies evasively that 'It seems the same,' and on account of her wisdom is bidden to enter Solomon's crystal pavilion, whose glass floor presents yet another iconic riddle. Thinking it to be water, she lifts her skirts, baring her ankles and feet in the process. Upon learning she has been tricked and has failed in her attempt to 'solve' the second riddle event, she immediately submits to Solomon and Allah, converting to Islam (vv. 40-45).[99] Following the logic of that Sura, the sense of this episode seems to be that, having seen her wisdom to be flawed in one arena, she recognizes that it may well be flawed in the theological realm as well. The one who brought her to this realization is clearly greater than her, so it is an act of greater wisdom to submit.

Gone is any attempt on *her* part to question Solomon, but in our interpretive journey, we discover at last a good reason for her tedious and time-consuming journey: rather than risk invasion by offending Allah's great king, she first tries diplomatic bribery but later, since he has quite literally stolen her throne from under her, she is forced into compliance. Only brief glimpses of Josephus's philosopher or the Bible's fabulously wealthy and astute ruler remains, since the Sura takes the point of view that no pagan, however eminent, can compare with one of the true faith

98. Galit Hasan-Rokem, *Web of Life: Folklore and Midrash in Rabbinic Literature* (trans. Batya Stein; Stanford: Stanford University Press, 2000), pp. 52-53.

99. A.J. Arberry (trans.), *The Koran Interpreted* (New York: Macmillan, 1955), pp. 76-85.

and sets out all its details to heighten that conclusion. (After all, a lone woman ruler's ability to recognize her own throne and return a crafty answer about it is not the stuff of which fabulous folktales are made, however much it may impress this Sura's author or implied audience.) While once again Sheba has no personal name and we are left with no actual riddle texts, only iconic riddle *events*, we find here for the first time the motif of Solomon's glass pavilion and Sheba's bared legs. No reasons for either are recorded overtly in the *Quran*, but clearly, we have a failed riddle test by Sheba, which is needed to bring about the dénouement of the queen's submission. Different elaborations on these motifs must have been circulating orally and would be fully fleshed out in by both Islamic and Jewish written versions to come.[100]

We find that a sexual encounter is presumed in the versions of this royal meeting from late antiquity and the medieval period, and Sheba bears a son to Solomon: in the *Alphabet of Ben Sira* (eleventh century CE, provenance in the Jewish Diaspora) the son is Nebuchadnezzar, as is also the case in the *Ma'aseh Malkath Sheba* of Saadiah ben-Yosef, a Yemenite version from Jewish and Islamic sources (text dated to 1702 CE, but with much earlier oral elements). In the eleventh-century CE Islamic version of al-Kasā'ī the son is Rehoboam and he is born after Sheba has converted to Islam. In the Ethiopian tradition of the *Kebra Nagast* (fourteenth century CE for its Ethiopic version), the most positive portrait of Sheba in all the medieval and later versions, Sheba also becomes a mother. After being tricked and seduced by Solomon, the noble queen gives birth to Menelik, who becomes the founder of the royal dynasty of that region. Later, after Menelik visits his father, he bears the Ark of the Covenant away to Africa where legend has it that it remains until this very day.[101] In one way or another, the union of Solomon and Sheba, from the Jewish point of view, was ill-fated because of their son's infliction of political suffering on the people of Israel.

---

100. For a discussion of the relationship between oral versions of Muslim and Jewish communities, and their interdependence, see the excellent study by Jacob Lassner, *Demonizing the Queen of Sheba: Boundaries of Gender and Culture in Post-biblical Judaism and Medieval Islam* (Chicago: University of Chicago Press, 1993).

101. Ullendorff, 'Queen', pp. 496-98; for translations of variant texts, see Lassner, *Demonizing*. See also W. Montgomery Watt, 'The Queen of Sheba in Islamic Tradition', in J. Prichard (ed.), *Solomon and Sheba* (London: Phaidon Press, 1974), pp. 85-103, and Silberman, 'Queen', pp. 65-84.

Table 1. Sheba Variants: Biblical and Early Post-biblical Period.

Text	1 Kings 10 2 Chronicles 9.1-12	New Testament: Matthew 12.42; Luke 11.31	New Testament: Acts 8.27	Josephus, *Ant.* 8.5.5	Babylonian Talmud	11QTgJob	Targum Job
Date and provenance	Tenth century BCE, Judah; presumed DH redaction in sixth century; Babylon	End first century CE (80–90 CE); Palestine/Antioch	80–90 CE	First century CE (c. 79 CE); Galilee; Rome	Sixth century CE (tradition from 2 CE Palestine); Babylon	First century CE; Palestine	First–eleventh century CE; Palestine to Babylon
Genre	Legend with embedded blessing/eulogy	Report (foreignness used to shame own group)	Report	Report	Response to slander of R. Judah the Patriarch	Aramaic Targum	Aramaic Targum with multiple translations
Sheba's PN	φ[102]	'Queen of the South'	Candace	Nicaulis	φ	φ	Lilith
Location	N or SW Arabia (Sabeans)	Ethiopia?	Meroe/Ethiopia	Horn of Africa/Egypt	Arabia	φ	Smargad/Arabia
Nature	Human	Human	Human	Human	A region, not a person	φ	Demon
Riddle contest	Yes	'To hear wisdom'	φ	Yes	φ	φ	φ
Riddle texts	φ	φ	φ	φ[103]	φ	φ	φ
Demonic hair	φ	φ	φ	φ	φ	φ	φ
Sexual encounter	Hinted	φ	φ	Hinted	Hinted	φ	φ (presumed)

102. φ = motif does not appear in this text.
103. Josephus also records Solomon had riddling contests with Hiram, but gives no riddle texts for either Hiram or Nicaulis.

Table 2. Sheba Variants: Midrashim.

Text	Targum Esther Sheni	Alphabet of Ben Sira	Midrash Mishle	Midrash HaHefez	Saadiah ben-Yosef (Ma'aseh Malkath Sheba)	Zohar: Parashat Balak 3.194b Hashmatot ha Zohar
Date and provenance	Fifth–tenth century CE Palestine	Eleventh century CE (after rise of Islam) Diaspora	Ninth century CE; eastern Diaspora	Fifteenth century CE (based on second century CE tradition); Yemenite	Written down in 1702 CE; Yemenite, with Jewish and Islamic sources	C. 1286 CE (Moses de Leon); Spain; Palestine
Genre	Aggadic midrash	Satire	Aggadic midrash	Aggadic midrash (oral sources)	Aggadic legends	Mystical aggadah
Sheba's PN	φ	φ	φ	φ	φ	Lilith
Location	Kitor, Arabia	Arabia	φ	φ	φ	φ
Nature	Human, but 'disfigured'	Human, but hairy (= foreign)	Human	Presumed human	Daughter of snake-princess/jinn	Demon
Riddle contest	Yes	No: 'to listen to Solomon's wisdom'[104]	Yes	Yes	Yes	Yes
Riddle texts	Yes[105]	No	Yes[106]	Yes[107]	Yes[108]	Yes[109]
Demonic hair	Yes	Yes (Solomon makes depilatory)	φ	φ	Yes depilatory made	Demon feet
Sexual encounter	Hinted	Yes; son Nebuchadnezzar	φ	φ	Yes; son Nebuchadnezzar	φ

104. Manuscript B: 'in order to *see* his wisdom'.
105. Riddle answers: eye make-up; naphtha; flax.
106. Riddle answers: menstrual cycle; daughters of Lot; determine gender; determine circumcised and uncircumcised.

Table 3. Sheba Variants: Islamic and Ethiopian Sources.

Text	Quran Sura XXVII 'The Ant'	At-Taʻlabî, 'Stories of the Prophets'	Al-Kasāʼī	Kebra Nagast 'The Glory of Kings'[110]
Date and provenance	Seventh-century CE Arabia	Eleventh-century CE Islamic	Eleventh century CE (seventh–thirteenth century Mss.)	Fourteenth-century CE (long oral history) Ethiopia
Genre	Poetry	Compiled legends	Compiled legends	Genealogical aetiology
Sheba's PN	φ	Bilqis	Bilqis	Makeda
Location	Arabia Felix	Arabia/Yemen	Arabia/Yemen	Africa
Nature	Human, but bare ankle episode is suggestive	Jinni's daughter (cuts off husband's head)	Jinni's daughter (cuts off husband's head)	Noble human ancestor
Riddle contest	φ	Yes	Yes	φ
Riddle texts	Solomon asks her questions	Yes: in letter form[111] Yes: in person[111]	Yes: in letter form[112] φ	φ
Demonic hair	Bare ankles	Hairy ankles: depilatory is made	Hairy ankles	φ
Sexual encounter	Converts to Islam	Yes Converts to Islam	Yes; converts to Islam, they marry; son: Rehoboam	Yes: Solomon tricks and seduces; son: Menelik

107. Riddle answers: same as note 3, with addition of God; primal earth; womb and its child; a boat; Tamar and her sons; Lot, daughters and their sons; Jonah; Abraham and three angels; Daniel and companions; Elijah and the Messiah; Golden Calf; a wick; Tamar with her husbands and sons; Samson and the Philistines.

108. Riddle answers: menstrual cycle, Lot and his daughters; distinguish gender; eye makeup box.

109. *Parashat*: use of enchanted snakes; *Hashmatot*: Solomon must make shoes for demon feet.

110. Christian Arabic, Coptic and Tigre variants follow the basic outlines of the *Kebra Nagast*.

111. Letter: determine gender; know contents of box; perforate pearl; string crooked shell; in person: sweat from horses.

112. Letter: determine gender; perforate pearl; string crooked onyx; sweat from horses.

Just who *is* Sheba, then, such that she has been transformed from foreign queen of fabulous wisdom and wealth in the Bible to bed-mate, lover and mother, wreaking havoc on Israel's later history? Storytellers elaborate in a variety of ways.[113] For some, the way to account for this evolution of the female character was to posit a more 'appropriate' genealogy for the woman: she is a full-scale demon in some Muslim and Jewish versions, with the *Zohar* even going so far as to name her (the better to control her?) —Lilith. This heritage of ultimate 'Other-hood' provides a fitting explanation for a woman ruling so well: she can't *possibly* be human, nor can her seizure of power be *really* legitimate! In some tellings, she is a jinni's daughter, and the jinn serving Solomon fear that a child of the pair would have both heritage and magic enough to enslave them all forever. In other versions, she seized power after killing her young husband, who had been defiling the laws of Allah. Either way, these demonic motifs work to deprive the woman ruler of the full-hearted support of either kin or court. Perhaps her nobles, who are so eager for war in the *Quran*, thought it might be an excellent way to rid themselves of an unwanted female leader; even the kin-jinn refuse her the familial assistance any ruler normally counts upon and deploys to manage the conflicts of leading groups with different interests. She is without the genuine support, then, that a king might have commanded. Fortunately, her abilities as a 'performer' of wisdom come to her aid to equalize the playing field of an arena in which men take and hold power as though it were indeed their divine right.

In the *Targum Sheni Esther* (dated to 500–1000 CE, Palestinian provenance) and the *Alphabet of Ben Sira* (eleventh century CE), along with the various medieval Arabic retellings, we finally come upon proverbs and riddles, plus some explanation for Solomon's need to see the foreign queen lift her skirts to reveal ankles—of course, the sources do not all agree upon the same riddles, nor do they give the same motifs or interpretation of Sheba's bared legs and Solomon's sight of them.[114] In the *Midrash Mishle* (c. ninth century; provenance uncertain) and the *Midrash HaHefez* (written in the fifteenth century CE, Yemenite provenance, but containing very early material), we again find riddles, although the racier

---

113. For a rousing, general introduction to the quest for Sheba's identity and recent archaeological findings of significance for this task, see Nicholas Clapp, *Sheba: Through the Desert in Search of the Legendary Queen* (New York: Houghton Mifflin, 2001).

114. Silberman, 'Queen', pp. 70ff; Lassner, *Demonizing*, pp. 161-214. For answers to the Sheba's riddles in the various sources, see notes to tables.

elements of Sheba and her visit are missing.[115] The *Zohar* gives us Sheba
as the composite demonic Lilith, as do related Kabbalistic texts of the
High Middle Ages and Early Modern period (see Tables). This fully
demonic portrait of Sheba in speculative mystical texts may be the reason
why Sheba's riddles play no significant part in Jewish riddling traditions
from the late medieval period onwards.[116]

To summarize the riddle of post-biblical traditions about the identity of
Sheba and her riddles, then, we must draw on both Jewish and Arabic
sources. The Queen Sheba, it is finally decided by the bulk of her commentators, is neither a region, be it the Horn of Africa or Arabia Felix,
nor a 'natural' human woman. Here we follow the 'social definition of
woman' proposed by Moss Blachman: a woman is 'a biological female
functioning as a wife and mother within the institution of the family'.[117]
In Arabic traditions, she is named Bilqis/Balkis (related to Hebrew
פילגש)[118] and is considered to be the daughter of either a jinni (aṭ-
Ṭaʿlabî's or al-Kasāʿî's version) or a snake-princess (the version of
Saadiah Ben Joseph, a Yemenite tale written down in 1702 CE, of Jewish
and Islamic provenance).[119] For medieval Jewish commentators and
mystics of the *Zohar*, she is the child-murdering, seed-stealing Lilith, a
she-demon of wind, storm and night, with a long and distinguished history beginning in Sumerian texts and continuing well into 'this very day'
in feminist revisioning of women's mythic heritage.[120] As an other-
worldly creature, she is thought to have either an extremely hairy body,
as is believed of demons (so with Ginzberg), or unnatural feet (footprints
of a rooster, an ass, a mule, a goat or clawed owl-feet).[121]

115. Lassner, *Demonizing*, pp. 13-14; Burton L. Visotzky, *The Midrash on Proverbs*
(New Haven, CT: Yale University Press, 1992), pp. 9-10; for riddles, see pp. 18-19.

116. Silberman, 'Queen', p. 76; for discussion of early modern and mystical Jewish
texts on Sheba, see also pp. 80-84. For late modern variants, see Lassner, *Demonizing*,
pp. 175-85.

117. Morris J. Blachman, *Eve in an Adamocracy: The Politics of Women in Brazil*
(Philadelphia: ISHI Press, 1979), quoted in Carolyn Matalene, 'Women as Witches', in
Brian P. Levack (ed.), *Witchcraft, Women and Society. Articles on Witchcraft, Magic
and Demonology: A Twelve Volume Anthology of Scholarly Articles*, X (New York:
Garland, 1992), pp. 51-65 (62).

118. Ullendorff, 'Queen', p. 494.

119. Lassner, *Demonizing*, p. 136.

120. Black and Green, *Gods*, p. 118; Patai, *The Hebrew Goddess*, pp. 221-54;
Barbara Hill Rigney, *Lilith's Daughters: Women and Religion in Contemporary
Fiction* (Madison, WI: University of Wisconsin, 1982).

121. Ginzberg, *Legends*, VI, p. 289. This motif is well attested in world folklore, see

Before dealing with the particulars of Sheba's demonic transfiguration and the riddle of how it happens that a powerful woman asking hard questions is so easily imagined to be a demon, we must pause for a feminist 'reality check'. Did our commentators plunge headlong into the realm of legend because the possibility of a woman ruler of a fabulously wealthy kingdom was simply historically unimaginable? Did ancient queens ever issue the kinds of challenges or engage in the display of political power that are ascribed to Sheba in the Hebrew Bible? Here modern historical critics, despite their tendency to relegate Sheba to the folkloric universe, call our attention to sources which may provide some light on the very possibility of a Sheba and her astonishing diplomatic, linguistically charged behavior. On the walls of the funerary temple of Queen Hatshepsut in Deir el- Bari, we learn that in year 9 (c. 1481 BCE) of her rule as Pharaoh, this famous queen mounted a fabulous trading expedition to Punt, land of incense (i.e. more or less the same region where Sheba is placed geographically).[122] The same tomb complex also shows reliefs that give Hatshepsut the required divine parentage by the god Amun, an ancestry needed for a woman to make her way in a powerful realm dominated by elite men.[123] Later in the New Kingdom, the Egyptian Queen 'Ankhesenamon, widow of Tutankhamon, wrote to the Hittite king Shuppiluliuma shortly after her husband's death, to request a Hittite prince be sent to Egypt to become her consort.[124] The Hittite monarch exclaimed in response, 'Since of old such a thing has never happened before me!' and sent envoys to determine the Queen's true intent. She replied in irritation:

> 'Why do you say, "They may try to deceive me"? If I had a son, would I write to a foreign country in a manner which is humiliating to myself and to my country? You do not trust me and tell me even such a thing. He who was my husband died and I have no sons. Shall I perhaps take one of my servants and make him my husband?...'[125]

As it happens, the Hittite king's suspicions were well founded, since the

Christopher R. Hallpike, 'Hair' in Mircea Eliade (ed.), *The Encyclopedia of Religion*, VI (New York: Macmillan, 1987), pp. 154-57 (155).

122. The areas where the diverging traditions place Sheba (Africa or Arabia) in fact show that the peoples on either side of the water had been trading, communicating and intermarrying since the earliest periods.

123. Sir Alan Gardiner, *Egypt of the Pharaohs: An Introduction* (Oxford: Oxford University Press, 1961), pp. 185-86.

124. Gardiner, *Egypt*, p. 241.

125. *ANET*, p. 319.

young prince sent to Egypt was murdered on the journey by an Egyptian faction. But we see in 'Ankhesenamon's correspondence a full appreciation of a lone queen's vulnerability and her need to form alliances with powerful foreign males. Her poignant question about marrying beneath her is echoed by Sheba in the Arabic version of at-Ṭa'labî's. After Solomon is done with Bilqis, he tells her to choose a man of her own people to which he might marry her off; she replies, 'O prophet of God, should the likes of me marry among (mere) men when I have already possessed such authority as I have in my domain and among my people?'[126] When Solomon tells her that Islam does indeed require such submission from her, she makes a reluctant choice, and is sent off to her own country properly under male control. Other ancient queens were equally engaged in the direction of matters matrimonial and political: for examples of Mesopotamian and Anatolian queenly involvement in international and regional politics during the Bronze Age, we may point to the vigorous correspondences carried on by Queen Shibtu of Mari and Puduḫepa of the LBA Hittite empire.[127]

Surveys of women in leadership roles in Pre-Islamic Arabia has also yielded 'some two dozen [examples], in a period of over sixteen centuries, and in territories that stretched from Ctesiphon to Rome and from the Black to the Arabian Sea'.[128] From Assyrian records, we meet several North Arabian queens, beginning in the ninth century BCE, which is, unfortunately, a bit late for any to be convincingly related to Sheba and Solomon. One Queen Zabibi is forced to pay tribute to Tiglath-pileser III (745–727 BCE), and her probable successor, the Sabaean Queen Shamshi, has an even worse experience of that leader. Although this text is poorly preserved, it alleges that Shamshi—the root (שמש) of whose name reminds us of the Arabic Sheba worshiping the sun in her own kingdom at the outset of her adventures with Solomon—broke an oath to Shamash (refusing to pay tribute to the Assyrian overlord?), causing Tiglath-pileser to drive her into the desert and force her to humble herself at his feet, along with paying heavy tribute.[129] Added to this list of Arabian queens, we must

---

126. Lassner, *Demonizing*, p. 201.

127. See above, and Fontaine, 'Heifer', pp. 167-72.

128. Abbot, 'Queens', *AJSL* 58 (1941), p. 22.

129. Abbot, 'Queens', p. 4; Daniel D. Luckenbill, *Ancient Records of Assyria and Babylonia*, I (Chicago: University of Chicago Press, 1929), p. 279; if we suppose an exilic editing of the book of Kings, done by exiles with access to the archives of their conquerors, we may choose to see in Shamshi a *real* (= historical) antecedent to Sheba, whose story has been transferred from the conqueror Tiglath-pileser to the conquered, Solomon.

also mention the later figures of Zenobia of Palmyra (third century CE)[130] and the queens of the House of Hind in the kingdom of Kindah in central Arabia (c. fifth century CE), all of whom provide adequate examples of genuine female leadership in this region of the world, if not the exact time, in which sources and scholars have placed Sheba.[131]

It was not necessary, then, for our versions to have transported Sheba either into the land of legend or the world of demons, at least not for want of any cultural memory of powerful women rulers. Clearly, some other impulse is at work, and we find it clearly stated in the *Targum Esther Sheni*'s interchange between Solomon and Sheba prior to her posing her riddles.

Solomon, Sheba and Performance

Though all the texts with riddles portray Sheba as the loser in her riddle contest with Solomon whose wisdom is the stuff of legend, in the *Targum Esther Sheni*, we see her make deft use of a proverb to handle both her retinue and the Israelites she has come to visit. Solomon, too, will take a turn at performance when, worried about her demonic origins, he tricks Sheba into showing her ankles so he may scan her nether parts for the tell-tale demon feet (either those of an ass or a bird). Our twice- and thrice-told tale bristles with wisdom rhetoric passing back and forth between the two rulers. First proverbs, then riddles—what should we make of this ordering of wisdom items in the interchange between the two royals? Proverbs attempt to 'dis-ambiguate' a conflict situation by categorizing it, just as riddles posit ambiguity through skewed categories in order to sort insiders from outsiders. We must be situated in the group's lore about order before we can venture safely into the world of riddling and disorder.

Sheba to Solomon: of Lions and Lairs

The first episode of proverb performance occurs before the presentation of iconic riddles to Sheba and riddle texts to Solomon. After sending a wealth of gifts to Jerusalem (some of which would figure as living iconic riddles in her later contest in other texts), she makes the journey from Kitor to Judah in record time (three years compared to the normal seven—all these are symbolic numbers, too, of course). The Targum continues:

---

130. In al-Kasā'ī's version, Solomon buries his wife Bilqis under the walls of Palmyra (Lassner, *Demonizing*, p. 212).
131. Abbot, 'Queens', pp. 13-17.

And so, after three years the Queen of Sheba came to King Solomon. When he heard of her arrival, he sent Benaiah son of Jehoiada to meet her. He was as handsome as the morning star shining nightly in the firmament and as elegant as the lily that graces the pond's edge. When she saw Benaiah son of Jehoiada, the queen dismounted and so he asked, 'Why do you dismount?' 'Are you not King Solomon?' she asked. 'I am not King Solomon,' he replied, 'only one of those who serve him.' *At once, she turned to her notables and offered the following based on a (well-known) proverb: 'If you do not see the lion, you see his lair.* (italics mine) So, if you do not see Solomon, then see the handsomeness of the man that stands before him.' Benaiah son of Jehoiada then escorted her to the king.[132]

Wisdom vocabulary and forms, wisdom characters (royals and advisors) and wisdom actions (diplomacy, proverb performance and exegesis) all occur together, marking this text as fully wisdom's own.[133] The occasion for the move into the performance arena is Sheba's very public and embarrassing mistake in taking the man for his master. She signals the performance immediately, knowing that she must retrieve what 'face' she can before her nobles: 'At once, she turned…and offered the following based on a (well-known) proverb…' The author, with the help of the zealous translator, must have at least some sympathy for Sheba, as it is he who supplies the invocation of tradition by characterizing what follows as part of the both groups' proverb stock. The Interaction Situation bristles with status differentials: own versus foreign, male versus female, master/mistress versus servant. No wonder our Sheba trots out a proverb at this juncture: in only one of these three categories does she take precedence over those who have seen her perspicacity fail her in greeting Benaiah in a manner befitting Solomon!

Here we see interesting twist on the familiar motif of cross-gendering an audience.[134] Normally, both the Bible and its subsequent 'post-texts' like to 'show up' the stupidity of out-group males by showing an in-group

---

132. Lassner, *Demonizing*, pp. 166-67. See also Bernard Grossfeld, *The Two Targums of Esther: Translated, with Apparatus and Notes* (The Aramaic Bible, 18; Collegeville, MN: Liturgical Press, 1986), p. 116. For a fuller discussion of this event, see Carole R. Fontaine, 'More Queenly Proverb Performance: The Queen of Sheba in Targum Esther Sheni', in M.L. Barré, S.S. (ed.), *Wisdom, You Are My Sister: Studies in Honor of Roland E. Murphy, O. Carm., on the Occasion of his Eightieth Birthday* (CBQMS, 29; Washington, DC: Catholic Biblical Association, 1997), pp. 216-33.

133. See discussion in Chapter 2.

134. For a spirited attempt at cross-gendering *an author*, see Camp's, *Holy*, pp. 144-90.

female outwitting them, either by her native wit or her in-group knowledge of divine plans or requirements (Jael versus Sisera; Judith versus Holofernes; the 'Virgin Israel' versus Sennacherib [2 Kgs 19.21b], etc.).[135]

Several variants are possible as a transformation of this action motif: an out-group female may be used to shame an in-group male,[136] a rhetorical strategy we saw employed by Ezekiel. Examples of this are found in the New Testament's use of Sheba in Mt. 12.42 (Lk. 11.31): the outsider 'Queen of the South' shames the insider males of Jesus' generation. Sheba only came to hear Solomon's wisdom after all, but the first-century men who reject Jesus have seen 'something greater even than Solomon'. Christians continue with this shaming of the (male) Jews in the medieval legends of the True Cross (*Legenda Aurea*, of Dominican Jacobus de Voragine, thirteenth century). When Sheba visits Solomon, she immediately notices that a 'bridge' made from a branch of the Tree of the Knowledge of Good and Evil is very strange indeed, and she refuses to cross it, preferring instead to sink down before it in homage. The very wood Solomon had tried to employ in building his Temple turns out to be the wood that will become the True Cross—but only wisdom's outsider, Queen Sheba, can perceive it.[137] Once again, an outsider, and a mere woman at that, has shamed the men on the inside of the holy city with her special sight—and the content of that sight leaves her where she should be: on her knees before male power.

In *Targum Esther Sheni,* this motif is inverted to doubly degrade the queen in our text by locating both negatives (female, out-group) in the same figure, Sheba. She comes to riddle Solomon, giving her a rhetorical edge as the Riddler, but before she can open her mouth, or lift her skirts to solve an iconic riddle, she is shown as a foreign bumpkin, shamed before

135. For women as keepers and teachers of Torah knowledge, see Anne Goldfeld, 'Women as Sources of Torah in the Rabbinic Tradition', in Elizabeth Koltun (ed.), *The Jewish Woman: New Perspectives* (New York: Schocken Books, 1976), pp. 257-71, and Abrams, *Women*. In fact, women's merit acquired in study of the Torah may protect them during the magical 'trial' of the Sotah (Num. 5); Judah Nadich, *The Legends of the Rabbis*, II (Northvale, NJ: Jason Aronson, 1994), p. 160 n. 113.

136. For the role of honor and shame in maintaining order in the definition of in-group/out-group boundaries, see Bruce J. Malina, 'Mediterranean Sacrifice: Dimensions of Domestic and Political Religion', *BTB* 26 (1996), pp. 26-37.

137. Paul F. Watson, 'The Queen of Sheba in Christian Tradition', in J. Pritchard (ed.), *Solomon and Sheba* (London: Phaidon Press, 1974), pp. 115-45 (121-23). Naturally, this event must precede her meeting with Solomon, since afterwards, the Hebrew Bible says, she had 'no spirit' left in her.

her own male advisors, and unable to discern the most basic status distinctions.

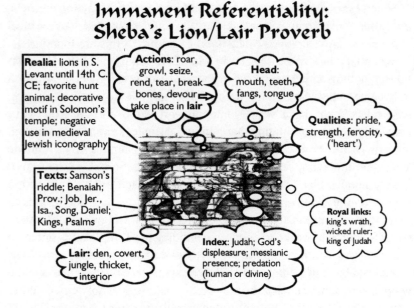

Figure 16. Immanent Referentiality: Sheba's Lion/Lair Proverb.

Sheba's proverb cited to her nobles meets the criterion of 'out-of-context' statement that is metaphorically mapped onto a contextual situation (her mistake), but it is 'out-of-context' only for those who are unfamiliar with the sublime intertextual connections the Targum's author has made to the Hebrew Bible. We have not been talking about lions or lairs—or have we (see Fig. 16)? In fact, the 'lion' and 'lair' are greatly reminiscent of Benaiah's previous career (2 Sam. 23.20-23):

> And Benaiah the son of Jehoiada was a valiant man of Kabzeel, a doer of great deeds; he smote two ariels[138] of Moab. He also went down and slew a lion in a pit on a day when snow had fallen. And he slew an Egyptian, a handsome man. The Egyptian had a spear in his hand; but Benaiah went down to him with a staff, and snatched the spear out of the Egyptian's hand, and slew him with his own spear. These things did Benaiah the son of Jehoiada, and won a name beside the three mighty men. He was renowned among the thirty, but he did not attain to the three. And David set him over his bodyguard (RSV).

138. Lions? Champions?

The intertextual connections invoked by the author tell us with certainty then, that Sheba's misidentification is actually not far off the mark, as she points out in her exegesis of her proverb citation: this servant is a Bad Man, around whom foreigners (however lovely) and wild animals (however fierce) would do well to tread lightly. The Targum conjures up other 'co-texts' in the minds of the audience, invoking images of the stock wisdom character, 'the lion (often likened to kings in the proverbial corpus), and prefiguring the erotic episode to come by use of language connected with the Song of Songs'.[139]

One might note, of course, the 'suspicious' nature of the citation of a proverb that so well captures previous textual comment on the referents to which the proverb image applies—this is a literary construction, after all, and not notes taken from a field worker's journal of observed performances. Just as Sheba's riddles will highlight her knowledge of Solomon's family history, her proverb shows her knowledge of his political history. We might note that there is a bit of a 'slip' in the rhetorical connections that she draws, however: a 'lion' is not related to his 'lair' in the same way a 'master' is related to his 'servant'. The failed metonymic correspondence that Sheba's exegesis discloses, however, must be related to the intertextual connections upon which the author drew to weave this episode into a narrative whose main points of action had already been set by the biblical text. We quote here from previous conclusions drawn about Sheba's proverb performance:

> ...to end our analysis with noting the somewhat skewed metaphorical 'fit' of Sheba's proverb to her context in this interaction is to underestimate the surplus of meaning woven into the episode. On the surface, the use of a figure of a proud, kingly, fierce, noble, powerful animal may seem to flatter both Solomon and his envoy, but, in fact, Sheba's proverb brings other possibilities to mind for the point she is trying to convey to her retinue. Above all, the citation of a proverbial lion at this point reminds us of the dangerous king, lurking in his covert/court, waiting to devour Sheba, personally and politically—Solomon is, after all, a Lion of Judah (Gen. 49.9), son of a shepherd who even as a boy could hunt and kill lions as well as any Assyrian king (1 Sam. 17.34-37). Further, Solomon is served by a courtier who will commit any violent act for his king, and who is associated with killing a lion in the close confines of its pit. Not without reason does Sheba think of lions and their dens at this moment, however much she may seem bedazzled by the handsome head of the king's servant who is to take her to his master's lair! She knows full well the heritage of Judah and its

king, the damage that proud, beastly head can do, and what is likely to befall her in the den to which she is being carried away. She cites a proverb which only loosely fits her context, but which nicely sums up her knowledge of the foreign king, his family traditions, his servants, the lore of his people, and her own intimations of her future encounter. This diplomatic maneuver is a skillful deployment of the language of wisdom. It may even be that Sheba sees more positive possibilities for herself: perhaps, like the Bride of the Song of Songs, she too may come forth from the den of lions as a lover with a devoted partner, rather than as a meal for a devouring predator. This alien woman proves her worthiness to craft her own fate through her astute knowledge and the quick wit which allows her to apply it in diplomatic interactions.[140]

Solomon to Sheba: Whose Hair, Where?

Deceived in her gaze by the illusion of the glass floor in the bath house where she greets Solomon, Sheba thinks the king must be sitting in water. She lifts her skirts and her bare, normal ankles are seen, but they are quite hairy. Unlike Sheba who *doesn't see*, Solomon plays the part of voyeur and sees clearly what he apparently set out to see. He comments in a form crafted with the typical verbless clauses that normally build the contrasts of a proverb or saying-appraisal (in this case, appearing as an appraisal followed by a saying), 'Thy beauty is the beauty of women, but thy hair is the hair of man; while *hair is an ornament to a man, but it is a disfigurement to a woman.*'[141] Though Sheba may not have demonic legs in this retelling, she is no normal woman; maleness deforms her body. Since the connection of feet and ankles with the male genitals is a well-established euphemism in texts from this part of the world, a further meaning may be gleaned from the fact that it is Sheba's *feet* that are hairy. Here we have a monster in the making, that woman who has so usurped male prerogatives of power that gendered male markings are visible upon her body. The implications are frightening: perhaps, as with the grotesque riddling Sphinx, failure to answer her questions will have dangerous consequences.[142] It may be that Sheba, like the Babylonian witch of the *Maqlû* incantations, has been transposed from the natural to the supra-natural

---

140. Fontaine, 'More Queenly', pp. 232-33.

141. Ullendorff, 'Queen', p. 496. שופרך שופרא דנשי וסערך סער דגברא וסער לגברא שפר ולאתתא גנאי. For slightly different translations, see Ginzberg, *Legends*, IV, p. 145; Lassner, *Demonizing*, p. 167; Angelo S. Rappoport, *Myth and Legend of Ancient Israel*, III (New York: Ktav, 1966), p. 125. Ullendorff's translation best preserves the parallelism of the non-verbal clauses.

142. Silberman, 'Queen', p. 79.

domain so that control of the danger she represents may be ritually instituted and maintained by male savants.[143] This is the same path of demonization followed by the European witch of the Early Modern period—
another dangerous female creature who must be shaved.

Solomon's proverb which is designed to put Sheba in her place, also,
highlights the text's gender ideology by placing its own concerns in the
mind of Solomon, the most wise of men—who *is* this woman who dares to
question *him?* The view of gender is clear: any male element, however
glorious, transferred to the female, is vainglorious and shameful. Although
we do not have the erotic motif in this targum, in a number of variants
Sheba's hairy feet and Solomon's need to shave them before he beds her
become the aetiology of Near Eastern depilatories using lime (*Alphabet of
Ben Sira*; *Ma'aseh Malkath Sheba*; *Stories of the Prophets*). Thus, she is
skinned of her hair and lightened in shade, not unlike the slaughtered lamb
whose hide is subjected to the same treatment in order to make parchment
for men's holy books. In the versions, Sheba's body becomes the palimp-
set upon which the authors who retold her story continually seek to
reinscribe appropriate female behavior.

The rumor of this hairy-footed peculiarity of Sheba/Bilqis/Lilith has two
origins within the texts studied here: sometimes, it is the ladies of Solomon's harem who spread the rumor of her abnormality in order to deflect
Solomon's interest away from her.[144] In other cases, it is the jinn themselves who tell Solomon of the demonic disfigurement of his potential
bed-mate, again hoping to derail a train of events they find disturbing to
their future. In Islamic versions, Bilqis is also acknowledged as queen by
the jinn, even though she has preferred the human world for her realm—no
doubt because the jinnis in the Land of the Jinn must occupy their time in
the weaving of magic carpets, an appropriate female occupation. The jinn,
already enslaved by the magician Solomon and his magic ring, fear that a
child of Solomon and Bilqis—part human, part jinn—will have ultimate
power over them, keeping them from obtaining their freedom upon Solomon's death.[145] In a choice between their own objectives and support of
their kinswoman and her continued right to rule in her own land without
interference, the jinn also find Bilqis 'out of place' and have no trouble in
trying to arrange her future to suit their own goals. Perhaps the relation-

143. Abusch, *Witchcraft*.
144. Rappoport, *Myth*, III, p. 201.
145. Lassner, *Demonizing*, pp. 199-201. Note Bilqis's refusal to submit to shaving in
at-Ta'labî's version.

ship between Bilqis and the jinn she rules is more adversarial and not so harmonious as one might suppose, given their kinship. One could easily imagine a different outcome to the episode, with Bilqis and her fellow jinn working together to secure both the Queen's independence and the freedom of the jinn. Bilqis's son by Solomon might just have easily been hailed as a savior for the jinn, had the text been of such a mind—there are such precedents in myth and legend (the LBA Hittite myth of Illuyanka, version 2, for example)[146]—perhaps the jinn are no more fond of half-breed children than are most human societies.

Several different 'folk ideas'[147] and cultural practices inform the intense scrutiny of Sheba's bare, but richly furry ankles. While in the Islamic variants Bilqis's ankles and body hair must be linked to her demonic parentage, the medieval Jewish midrashim containing this motif (*Targum Esther Sheni, Alphabet of Ben Sira*; Saadiah ben-Yosef's Yemenite version) are working from a different set of perceptions of 'otherness', one that encompasses demons but include dangerous (= out of place) human females as well. One set of traditions links membership in the house of Israel with Jacob, the 'smooth man' (Gen. 27.11), as compared to his brother, the hairy red Esau. Hence, Jacob, who stands for the In-Group, is 'a quiet man, dwelling in tents' (Gen. 25.27): he represents culture for the biblical storytellers, and so he is 'smooth'. Esau, the firstborn, who becomes outsider and foreigner, is 'a man of the field': he is the paradigm for 'nature' and so he must be hairy. (We may think here also of a similar nature/culture dichotomy operating in the characterization of Gilgamesh and Enkidu.) *The Alphabet of Ben Sira*, in introducing the origin of the depilatory, cites this tradition explicitly and adds 'that was a time when no Israelite woman had hair on those parts of her body ordinarily covered by garments'.[148] Following this idea back in time, we discover that the *BT Tractate Sanhedrin* 21a specifically states that 'the daughters of Israel had neither underarm nor pubic hair', though Rashi will later add that this was

---

146. Harry A. Hoffner, Jr (trans.), *Hittite Myths* (ed. G.M. Beckman; Atlanta: Scholars Press, 1990), pp. 12-14. Although showing clear signs of Hattic influence, extant texts are dated to the Hittite New Kingdom.

147. Folk ideas refer to the (largely unwritten) system of ideas that a folk group holds about itself, the nature of the human person, society and the world at large. See Alan Dundes, 'Folk Ideas as Units of Worldview', *JAF* 84 (1971), pp. 93-103; for discussion of the role of folk ideas in wisdom genres, see Fontaine, *Traditional Saying*, pp. 42-43.

148. Lassner, *Demonizing*, p. 167.

only the case before they sinned.[149] This unexpected anatomical feature is related in the context of Amnon's rape of Tamar. The rabbis record that because she was the daughter of a captive concubine, Tamar was marked by the fatal hairiness associated with foreign women. During the act of rape, Amnon's genitals are mutilated by one of her entangled hairs (*poor Amnon!*) and this is the origin of the rapist's subsequent hate for his victim.

We may also add other elements to the constellation of folk ideas and beliefs surrounding hair. Specific regulations about the shaving of captive foreign women appear in Deut. 21.10-14.[150] Hair, the crowning emblem of female beauty, might enhance the captor's desire for his foreign female booty, and so she must be shaved as she observes a mourning period for all she has lost. Ancient Near Eastern law codes provide regulations for the shaving and marking of female slaves, especially incorrigible run-aways.[151] Further, the shaving of female hair at puberty functions as a sign of a maiden's transition to sexually active status in certain marriage and fertility contexts,[152] though this should not always be interpreted solely as a sign of submission. The high priestess (NIN.DINGIR) of the Storm-God at the LBA city-state of Emar on the Euphrates observed a 'shaving day' in the ritual of separation that transferred her from the house of her father to the temple of her god-consort.[153]

Hair, then, as has been noted by anthropologists, serves as a marker for culture and gender in a variety of ways, because, among other things, it grows at the margins between the body and the world. These are precisely the boundary zones where gender must be continually reinscribed on the bodies of women and men. Mary Douglas, writing of bodily liminal zones, remarks:

---

149. *BT Tractate San.* 21a.114-15.

150. Susan Niditch, *War in the Hebrew Bible: A Study in the Ethics of Violence* (New York: Oxford University Press, 1993), pp. 85-86.

151. G.R. Driver and John C. Miles, *The Babylonian Laws*, I (Oxford: Clarendon Press, 1952), pp. 278-90; Orlando Patterson, *Slavery and Social Death: A Comparative Study* (Cambridge, MA: Harvard University Press, 1982), pp. 58-61.

152. Julian Morgenstern, *Rites of Birth, Marriage, Death and Kindred Occasions among the Semites* (Cincinnati: Hebrew Union College Press, 1966), pp. 93-116; for the role of hair in Jewish observance, see Leila Bronner, 'From Veil to Wig: Jewish Women's Hair Covering', *Judaism* 42 (1993), pp. 465-77.

153. Fleming, *Installation*, pp. 180-82.

...all margins are dangerous. If they are pulled this way or that, the shape of fundamental experience is altered. Any structure of ideas is vulnerable at its 'margins. We should expect the orifices of the body to symbolize its specially vulnerable points. Matter issuing from them is marginal stuff of the most obvious kind. Spittle, blood, milk, urine, faeces or tears by simply issuing forth have traversed the boundary of the body. So also have bodily parings, skin, nail, hair clippings and sweat. The mistake is to treat bodily margins in isolation from all other margins.[154]

We have traced, then, the full compass of our symbolic map of Sheba's strange, marginal body. While anthropologists of religion rightly point to texts that emphasize the transitional meaning of shaving (for which we have considerable evidence in the ancient Near East), Orlando Patterson properly calls our attention to the fact that the meaning of shaving must be correlated with the status of the one being shaved. Here in Solomon's court the shaving of Sheba's feet is symbolic of more than simple transition:

The shaving of the slave's head was clearly a highly significant symbolic act. Of all the parts of the body, hair has the most mystical associations. On the private or individual level, there is hardly a culture in which hair is not, for males, a symbol of power, manliness, freedom and even rebellion; and for women, the crowning expression of feminine beauty. The shorn head is, conversely, symbolic of castration—loss of manliness, power and 'freedom.' Even in modern societies we tend to shave the head of prisoners, although the deep symbolic meaning is usually camouflaged with overt hygienic explanations.[155]

We need not stop then, with the exegesis of Sheba's hair for its relationship to her hinted transition from her own throne to Solomon's bed, though certainly she is being made ready for her fastidious partner. The removal of Sheba's hair might not have been effective in making her fully human or even assuring her 'In-Group' membership, but it *does* fill the symbolic function of emasculating her. It is not her alleged demon-feet that present the problems in our Jewish and Islamic versions; it is her 'out of place'-ness as a female of power in a world ruled by men. She who was unnatural by nature of her birth, unnatural by her occupation, unnatural in her relationships, is now made 'natural' by the *un*natural act of having her hair removed. In Sheba's movement from the status of independent

154. Mary Douglas, *Purity and Danger: An Analysis of the Concepts of Pollution and Taboo* (London: Routledge & Kegan Paul, 1966), p. 121.
155. Patterson, *Slavery*, p. 60.

foreign queen to married woman and mother, we find, as in Samson's case, that the answer to the riddle of the outsider's independence is marked in shorn hair. Circling back around to the biblical text, we see our original Sheba there in a new light: humbled but human, spiritless but with her desires satisfied, without her revealing riddles but with her body chastely covered, her hair and her kingdom intact. As is sometimes the case, here the brevity and gaps of the Hebrew Bible are to be preferred—at least by feminists—for they mark the vulnerable margins of male power where women, demonic or otherwise, are invited to pose the hard questions and riddles of gender.

Sheba the Riddler

Riddles in Traditional Societies
Elsewhere in the Hebrew Bible (Judg. 14; 1 Esd. 3.1–5.6), Apocrypha, and Josephus, the eruption of a riddling contest signals competition, conflict, or social disruption of some sort, and often takes place in the public domain that may be categorized broadly as 'diplomatic'.[156] This is as it should be, for riddles are speech acts that test the boundaries of 'otherness'. Insiders sharing a common cultural context or experience will know the answer to the riddler's hard questions; outsiders are left literally without a clue, and their failure to answer the riddle reinforces the boundaries of belonging. Folklorist Galit Hasan-Rokem, in her study of riddling narratives in *Lamentations Rabbah*, writes of the appearance of riddle texts (the actual riddle) and riddling narratives (the story about the riddle and its solution in a context) in rabbinic literature:

> Narratives, and especially orally transmitted ones, are often the arena where the losers in military and political struggles have the upper hand. These tales convey the paradox of a narrative victory in the midst of an experience of physical and political destruction. The existential and experiential character of the riddle tale, however, manages to shatter the narrated victory of both riddlers and solvers...
>
> The riddle genre presents categories, meddles [*with?*] them, reconstitutes them, and constantly reenacts their inner collapse. Riddles thus truly express the chaotic and desperate wavering between stable, collective self-assurance, gained through the rabbis' perception of themselves as the

156. H.-P. Müller, 'Der Begriff "Rätsel" im Alten Testament', *VT* 20 (1970), pp. 465-89 (477-79), where he describes our passage as 'als Mittel des Wettkampfes unter Königen' (p. 477). For discussion of the relation of riddles to oracles and dreams, see pp. 471-77. It may be that YHWH is the original enigmatic, demonic Riddler.

bearers of true wisdom—contrary, for instance, to the Athenians—and the threat of individual and collective annihilation.[157]

At the linguistic level, riddles operate by suppressing the true referents of the Signifiers within the form, usually by the selection of Signifiers that misdirect the Riddlee's attention away from the true Signifieds.[158] Abstract Signifieds are personified and made concrete; concrete Signifieds are deformed into abstractions. Hence, riddles emphasize alternative visions and perceptions of reality; indeed, they depend for their effectiveness on a kind of 'double vision' that the Riddler exploits. Fittingly, then, given the genre, we shall see Sheba present a different view of herself from Solomon's through the elaborated riddle tale.

Folkloristic studies of riddling performance contexts outlines at least six broad categories, some of which are blended together in the biblical text, and others of which are explored in post-biblical accounts:

1. in rituals of initiation and death
2. courtship and marriage festivals
3. teacher/student interchanges
4. greeting exchanges upon meeting
5. embedded in other expressive genres (narrative and song)
6. leisure-time activities[159]

Clearly, the account in Kings fits into the wider context of exchanged greetings, and may even reflect the '*one-up-person-ship*' dynamic of teacher and student: Sheba, who takes the role of teacher, is taught that the student Solomon has wisdom even greater than the female sage who tests him. But the fact that the canonical text has suppressed the riddles posed by the Queen of Sheba should leave us with some hard questions of our own, questions so intriguing that subsequent retellings of the Sheba and Solomon story felt obliged to address. How could Sheba ever have believed that she would outwit the fabulous Solomon? Why would she even have engaged in such a contest in the first place? How could a woman challenge a man with any expectation of winning? What were her riddles about? Were they based on personal and idiosyncratic experi-

---

157. Hasan-Rokem, *Web*, pp. 51-52.

158. You will recall, Gentle Reader, from your structuralist days, that Signifiers are the linguistic signs (words) and Signifieds are the actual referents to which these signs refer.

159. Thomas A. Burns, 'Riddling: Occasion to Act', *JAF* 89 (1976), pp. 139-65 (143-45).

ence like Samson's honey-producing lion carcass (a so-called *neck riddle*, which must be solved by reference to information known only by the Riddler), or did her riddles appeal to common folk motifs like Zerubbabel's answer of 'women and truth' to the question posed, 'What one thing is strongest?' (1 Esd. 3.5a)? Are we to take the typical occurrence of riddles and riddle contests at marriage feasts[160] as a precursor of events to follow? Regardless of the types of riddle texts presented in the fleshed-out riddle narratives of the medieval period, one thing remains clear: Jews and Muslims must have shared a fund of oral traditions as this time, of which riddles texts were a part. The seesaw of political relations between the two groups forms part of the impulse to create riddle tales where Jew trumps Muslim, Muslim converts pagan and male returns female to her rightful role—one beneath him.

The brief biblical text clearly favors Sheba's capitulation (vv. 6-10) over her competition. Apparently, here the sex of the Riddler is so distracting that the riddles themselves, normally so crucial in the retelling of such events, are lost: the gendered, political identity of the Sheba is the *real* iconic riddle for the Hebrew Bible.[161] In such boundary confusion, faced with the liminal character of a foreign, female leader, we should not be overly surprised to find that the ambivalent presence of female body itself speaks louder than the words of challenge that issue from it.[162]

The Riddles: Texts and Icons
Sheba's riddles, when we finally come upon them in medieval and late Jewish texts (they are also found in one Islamic variant, At̲-T̲halabi's *Stories of the Prophets*), are remarkable for their *content*, and not simply for the fact that Solomon is portrayed as solving them so easily.[163] Not all

---

160. See Camp's *Holy*, for discussion of Samson's wedding riddle and its relation to the Strange Woman motif (pp. 94-143).

161. This explanation does not, of course, hold true for the suppression of the riddles of Hiram in Josephus.

162. Marina Warner, 'In and Out of the Fold: Wisdom, Danger, and Glamour in the Tale of the Queen of Sheba', in Christina Buchmann and Celina Spiegel (eds.), *Out of the Garden: Women Writers on the Bible* (New York: Fawcett Columbine, 1994), pp. 150-65; see the same author's *From the Beast to the Blonde: On Fairy Tales and their Tellers* (New York: Noonday Press, 1994), pp. 97-145.

163. For discussion of provenance of the riddles and this affect on the medieval audience, see Dina Stein, 'A King, a Queen, and the Riddle between: Riddles and Interpretation in a Late Midrashic Text', in Galit Hasan-Rokem and David Shulman (eds.), *Untying the Knot: On Riddles and Other Enigmatic Modes* (Oxford: Oxford

texts agree on the number and the content of her riddling, but in general it is safe to say that the ones presented all have to do with gender, genealogy, or nature (See Tables 1-3). In the *Second Targum to Esther*, three riddles are posed:

> Riddle one:
>> A cistern of wood: buckets of iron:
>> they draw up stones: they cause water to flow.
>
> Riddle two:
>> Like dust it comes forth from the earth:
>> it is nourished from the dust of earth:
>> it is poured out like water:
>> it illumines the house.
>
> Riddle three:
>> A storm-wind rushes through their tops:
>> it cries loudly and bitterly:
>> 'Its head is like a rush.'
>> It is praiseworthy for the free:
>> shameworthy for the poor:
>> honourable for the dead:
>> disgraceful for the poor:
>> joyous for the birds:
>> grievous for the fish.[164]

The answers to her riddles are, respectively, a tube of eye makeup, naphtha (a volatile mineral oil used for light) and flax. Sheba has riddled in such a way that the products of earth are characterized as living entities; she sees what is inanimate and imagines it as having life. Perhaps she is hoping that Solomon might take the hint: a woman, rendered publicly inanimate by gendered assumptions, might perhaps be viewed as a fitting ruler of her people, having life outside of the domestic unit. Critics have rightly pointed out that riddling tends to occur at the point of cultural and erotic tension, where categories are challenged.[165] Solomon easily 'gets' the answers to the riddles, but he still doesn't get it: his projected destiny for Sheba as erotic partner or submissive vassal does not change.

More riddles—texts and icons—are added in other texts, such as *Midrash Mishle*, the midrash on the book of Proverbs (ninth-century Palestine). We

University Press, 1996), pp. 125-50, where the author deals primarily with Midrash Mishle.

  164. Silberman, 'Queen', pp. 72-73.
  165. Stein, 'King', pp. 128-29.

must wonder here if Sheba is subtly poking fun or commenting on Solomon's legendary hoard of women, for she chooses riddles whose referent is the world of women, their biology or their role in genealogy. Perhaps she thinks he may not be so knowledgeable in this realm as in others—all those partners, yet so few sons![166] One example of these is

> Seven cease: nine begin:
> Two offer drink: one drinks.[167]

to which the answer is: menstruation, pregnancy, breasts, baby. Subsequent riddles concern themselves either with proper identification of members of Solomon's tribe of Judah or Israelite history generally (Lot and his daughters; other texts add riddles whose answers are Tamar and her sons, Abraham, Jonah, Elijah, Jonah, Samson; see Tables 1-3). Further riddles about gender are iconic in nature in *Midrash Mishle*: Solomon is required to discover the proper gender of boys and girls when it is deliberately concealed, or to tell the circumcised from the uncircumcised when that mark of belonging is hidden. His wisdom is equal to the task of correctly detecting both gender and ethnicity. Further riddle texts in other versions require the king to show correct understanding of the features of natural objects (how to perforate a pearl or string a crooked shell, etc.).

In all versions, Solomon answers the various types of riddles quickly and somewhat derisively, thinking them mere child's play. But perhaps Sheba has been riddling with a different purpose: if riddles are meant to keep outsiders *out* by referring to insider knowledge, then Sheba's ability to make riddles out of Solomon's heritage marks her for the boundary-crossing female that she is. Just as riddles introduce ambiguities into volatile situations, so Sheba's aggressive riddles have the effect of suggesting that her outsider status is at least an open question, since it is tempered by her knowledge of the world in general and Solomon's world in particular. Though Solomon can answer all of Sheba's riddles, Sheba has, through these contests, presented herself as a ruler equal in status and wisdom, one deserving of keeping her place in her own world.

A Final Riddle: The Kebra Nagast

What happens to our biblical Sheba when the story of her meeting with Solomon is told from *her* point of view, or that of her people? Where

---

166. Gentle Reader, I am making the literary assumption that the Sheba of these texts wants to win the riddle contest, and so chooses items that she believes will stump the king.

167. Visotzky (trans.), *Proverbs*, pp. 18-19; Silberman, 'Queen', p. 74.

'strangeness' and 'otherness' are features that Sheba shares with those who tell her story, we see that the solidarity of the group with their female leader creates a strikingly different portrait of the queen. Her anomalous role as a woman ruling on her own must be successfully negotiated by the text (by having her abdicate in favor of her son by Solomon, as well as declaring that henceforth females shall never rule alone). There is, however, no hint in the *Kebra Nagast* of the demonic resumé we have been investigating in Jewish and Islamic sources—but neither do we have anything so ambivalent or challenging as a woman putting a man to the test of riddles.[168] This national saga is written to claim a biblical heritage for the Ethiopian dynasty of Africa and so it is careful to silence any motifs of the Sheba story that cast the queen in a negative light.

In this last and somewhat more female-friendly version, Sheba's personal name is Makeda, and she is truly a daughter of wisdom. Solomon does not hear of her, but *she* hears of *him*—following the Bible rather than the *Quran*—and her desire to learn from him gives her the determination to listen to this sage in person. After being told of Solomon's doings by a trusted merchant named Tamrin, Makeda sets her kingdom in order for her journey, and addresses her people:

> 'Hearken, O ye who are my people, and give ye ear to my words. For I desire wisdom and my heart seeketh to find understanding. I am smitten with the love of wisdom, and I am constrained by the cords of understanding; for wisdom is far better than treasure of gold and silver, and wisdom is the best of everything that hath been created on the earth...[169]

After a continued eulogy extolling the benefits of wisdom, Makeda discerns a relationship between herself and wisdom whose female-to-female dimensions have not found in the biblical or subsequent retellings:

> Wisdom is an exalted thing and a rich thing: I will love her like a mother, and she shall embrace me like her child. I will follow the footprints of wisdom and she shall protect me for ever; I will seek after wisdom, and she shall be with me for ever; I will follow her footprints, and she shall not cast me away; I will lean upon her, and she shall be unto me a wall of adamant; I will seek asylum with her, and she shall be unto me power and strength; I will rejoice in her, and she shall be unto me abundant grace. For it is right

---

168. Carl Bezold (trans.), *Kebra Nagast: Die Herrlichkeit der Könige* (München: G. Franz Verlag, 1905); for English translations, see E.A. Wallis Budge (trans.), *Kebra Nagast (The Queen of Sheba and her Only Son Menyelek* (London: Oxford University Press, 2nd edn, 1932).

169. Budge, *Kebra*, p. 21.

for us to follow the footprints of wisdom, and for the soles of our feet to stand upon the threshold of the gates of wisdom. Let us seek her, and we shall find her; let us love her, and she will not withdraw herself from us; let us pursue her, and we shall overtake her; let us ask, and we shall receive; and let us turn our hearts to her so that we may never forget her...[170]

Unlike poor Bilqis in her struggles with councilors and jinn, or Sheba of medieval Judaism shown distanced from her entourage, Makeda gets a very different reception from those who serve her:

And her nobles, and her slaves, and her handmaidens, and her counselors answered and said unto her, 'O our Lady, as for wisdom, it is not lacking in thee, and it is because of thy wisdom that thou lovest wisdom. And as for us, if thou goest we will go with thee; and if thou sittest down we will sit down with thee; our death shall be with thy death, and our life with thy life.'[171]

The love language between Makeda and Wisdom, like that between Makeda and her people, reminds us of the affirmations of mutual possession made between the lovers of the Song of Songs or Ruth's devotion to Naomi. The slaves and serving women are addressed here as full persons, and because of this they reply as full partners in the enterprise, ones who choose as their queen has chosen, bound together in wisdom's journey of life and death. Because this is a Christian work determined to claim its Judaic roots, we hear echoes of a New Testament grace that easily associates wisdom with future messiah.

When Makeda and Solomon meet, we have only the threshold of the gates of wisdom—no glass floor, no bath house, no glorious throne masquerading. Tricks and riddles are nowhere in evidence, but wisdom is everywhere in the speech the two rulers exchange. Tests and diplomacy figure little in their conversations, which focus on the excellence of wisdom, and their pleasure in finding it in each other. Oddly, there is more lover-like language reported between Makeda and Wisdom, and Makeda's people, than between the famous 'lovers' themselves.[172] But Makeda finds the interchanges between the two to be a source of joy and new sight:

I am so happy when you question me, when you answer me! So great is my pleasure that my heart is touched, my very marrow glows, my soul is satisfied, my lips are like flowers and I walk without fear of stumbling. It is clear to me now: your intelligence knows no limit and there is no goodness

---

170. Budge, *Kebra*, p. 22.
171. Budge, *Kebra*, p. 23.
172. Poets—especially W.H. Auden— have, of course, felt free to fill in this gap.

lacking to your heart. In darkness I behold the light, I see the pomegranate
in the gardens, the pearl in the sea, the morning star in the midst of the
constellation of the stars, the moon beam at the hour of dawn...[173]

Solomon affirms that she is being led to wisdom by God, and then presents her with an iconic example of a wisdom insight—finally, *almost* a riddle. A workman heavy laden with burdens is passing by the royal couple, and Solomon commands him to stop without laying down the load he carries. He then asks Makeda how he, the wise king, is different from the worker: both were made by God, given their natures and status by God, and both will die. God *could* have given Solomon's glory and wisdom to the workman instead of the king—and at the moment the man is straining under his loads, sweat dripping down his legs into his shoes, God has given the worker more physical strength to bear his burdens than the king.[174]

The *Kebra Nagast* reads this interlude as yet another example of Solomon's wisdom, for he has the humility to know that all his accomplishments are to be attributed to God, and not to his own merit. Yet this is a telling extension of the 'class' background of the sages of Proverbs, now surfacing in a much later Christian text from Africa. While the wise king and queen discuss life's vagaries of status in the face of a death sentence that comes to all, they are quite able to take the sight of the workman encumbered with cargo as an intellectual conundrum for their speculation. This is because *they* are not the ones standing there, groaning beneath the weight of many burdens. Their thoughtful discussion of the man's lot in life, conducted with him paused before them, laden and straining like a beast of burden, ignores the subjectivity of the worker. He has no voice; he is not invited to answer Solomon's question to Makeda (Magda), 'Do you perceive any difference between this man and myself?' This riddle of class difference might evoke quite a different answer from this manual laborer —or a poor widow struggling to feed many children, or a chronically ill person for whom Solomon's vast array of life choices are only a fairy-tale dream of deliverance. Solomon and Sheba see no difference between themselves and the laborer because their sight, however expanded intellectually, has little of 'conscience' in it. Solomon does go on to speak of the need to perform 'good deeds', but he gives no content to this general phrase, and certainly, the record of his reign gives the reader little cause to

173. Mrs John van Vorst (trans.), *Magda, Queen of Sheba* (New York: Funk & Wagnalls, 1907), p. 41.

174. Van Vorst, *Magda*, pp. 42-44.

think that the welfare of common workers was a major focus of his king-ship. A fundamental option for the rights of the poor forms no part of the 'wisdom' these two members of the elite celebrate.[175]

Though we have been presented here only with the iconic riddle of the workman, there *are* more to follow. The tricks begin later when Solo-mon's lust for Makeda causes him to present a dastardly iconic water riddle for the queen's solution on the night before her departure from Jerusalem. Knowing that Makeda is virtuous, honest and heart-breakingly lovely, Solomon wonders if perhaps God might give him seed through her—is the same sort of sage prognostication that led Amnon the rapist to consult a wise counselor in order to discover how he might have his royal sister Tamar without going to the trouble of marrying her? The scene for 'forced' seduction[176] is set in Solomon's court, just as in his father's day: food, drink and an inner chamber let us know that Makeda's fate will be similar to Tamar's. Solomon resolves to have the queen, and orders a fare-well banquet prepared for her, one that is long on spicy dishes but short on drink. Makeda dines well and the king suggests she spend the night in the bedchamber in his palace. She thinks of reputation and her people's confidence in her virtue: a woman may only reign if she retains her virgin-ity. She begs Solomon to swear that he will lay no hand upon her to take her by force, and he agrees, if *she* will also swear to take nothing by force that belongs to him from his chamber. In a rush of indignation—why does the king speak like a fool? Does the Solomon believe her a thief, or a naïf to be awed by his treasures when she has so many of her own?—Makeda consents.

The rulers retire to separate couches in the different parts of the same chamber, and Solomon feigns sleep. Makeda wakens from her restless slumbers, tortured with thirst. Before retiring, she saw that Solomon had a vase filled with purest water, but when she seeks to drink from it, the king is suddenly at her side, awake and dangerous. Will she take water from him by force when she has sworn not to? Makeda, like Tamar, attempts reason in defense of her honor: 'Is the oath broken by my drinking water?'[177] To Makeda's dismay, he replies with a question that solves the iconic riddle: what, after all, is a greater treasure than water?

175. Legend remedies this, at least in Solomon's case, by making him into a beggar when the demon Ashmodai takes over his form and rules in Jerusalem in his place.

176. Many feminist readers might choose a different, four-letter word for these episodes.

177. Budge, *Kebra*, p. 35.

She has failed to understand the riddle that Solomon had constructed for her, though her own words suggested its double intent: when she asked why the king spoke like a fool, it was in direct contrast to all other reports of her evaluation of his speech as wise and illuminating. His supposed 'foolishness' in asking for her oath, then, was in reality the riddle that she failed to solve at the time. Makeda acknowledges her complicity in falling for his trick to bed her. She releases him from his oath, and, like so many of the men from his royal house, he takes her as though it is his divine right. She conceives and bears a son nine months later on her journey to return to Ethiopia.

After all the talk of Makeda's probity and wisdom, the narrative takes us by surprise with this sordid episode.[178] The Queen of Sheba's lovely form eclipsed her virtue and insight in the male gaze, and rendered her as any other woman at risk from a man of greater power, a fair prize for the taking. Her words of praise for Solomon certainly suggested that our heroine is a woman in love. Perhaps the text means us to think that she was really 'asking for it', and Solomon's riddle only provided her with the opportunity she secretly needed to overcome her virtuous misgivings. No doubt such an interpretation comes easily to patriarchal readers of our text, but we must raise other interpretations. Solomon's riddling strategem for bringing the Queen of Sheba to his bed for the noble purposes of procreation is introduced to us with God as a co-conspirator who might (emphasis on the *might*, as Solomon has posed this as a question) give the king a child through this woman. This need to show God's hand at work in the king's plot ought to raise readerly suspicions—this king doth protest too much! Divine direction on this path nicely relieves Solomon of the responsibility in the manufactured mating.

We wonder what Makeda thinks: is *this* another example of all that goodness and intelligence residing in the king's heart? How does she see that heart on the morning after the night before? Has Wisdom's child, who looked to her mother for protection, been deserted? Is the birth of a son, even one whom Solomon plans to acknowledge by means of a ring he has given to Makeda, true compensation for having her virtue cheated away in the night for a drink of water? Tellingly, after this incident, we hear no more reported speech between the two after Solomon presents her with the fateful ring in the morning (rather than the night before in a legitimate

---

178. The motif of drinking as the trigger to capture also appears in Solomon's capture of the demon Ashmodai (Ashmodeus), as well as in the Hittite myth of Illuyankas.

mating). The *Kebra Nagast* answers none of these questions for us, but its 'romance' of the royal couple does not end with Makeda's silence. After his tryst with Makeda is successfully consummated, Solomon has a dream in the night and now it is he who sees a light in the darkness:

> ...there appeared unto King Solomon a brilliant sun, and it came down from heaven and shed exceedingly great splendour over Israel. And when it had tarried there for a time it suddenly withdrew itself, and it flew away to the country of Ethiopia, and it shone there with exceedingly great brightness for ever, for it willed to dwell there. And [the King said], 'I waited [to see] if it would come back to Israel, but it did not return...'[179]

Solomon has seen the Shekinah, the feminine presence of God that dwells on earth with Israel hovering over the Ark of the Covenant like a glorious cloud, depart from him and his land. Within the *Kebra Nagast*, this dream prefigures the day when his son Menelik steals the Ark from Jerusalem while on a visit and bears it away to his mother's country, along with the bright young men who are his contemporaries. In the theological genealogy of Ethiopia's dynasty, necessity required that some reason be given why Africa had superceded Jerusalem as the home of the Ark of the Covenant, or become eminent among Christian nations.[180]

We give a different interpretation here of Solomon's dream and its outcome. A feminist reader might remember Tamar's cry to Amnon from a different royal inner chamber: '...such a thing is not done in Israel! do not do this wanton folly!' (2 Sam. 13.12b). Apparently, the Shekinah shares this female point of view, too: in a situation where the wisest of rulers can think of no better act of state than to force an honest, resisting woman into his bed, the female Divine Presence can hardly feel welcome. Like Makeda, she departs with the son and leaves the father to his own fate. One cannot sin against a wise woman, Wisdom's own, without consequences—though the outcome is not usually so cosmically satisfying to women's honor as this one.

The *Kebra Nagast* leaves us then with a final iconic riddle as we conclude our chart of the course of ancient women using wisdom, or used by wisdom. As exemplary as the character of Makeda is at the outset of her legendary journey to hear Solomon's wisdom, by patriarchy's measuring stick, she is still afflicted by a troubling 'lack' of fairy-tale proportions. She has no husband or son,[181] a condition that is unacceptable to patriar-

179. Budge, *Kebra*, p. 35.
180. For Christian folklore of Sheba, see Warner, *Blonde*, pp. 97-109.
181. Our story makes it quite clear that a daughter would not fill her 'lack', since the

chal ideology. This is *both* the reason why she is able to rule independently *and* the source of the only discomfort that the Ethiopian variant seems to feel with its noble ancestress. But the wise know how such a thing may be remedied: Makeda, through losing the iconic riddle test, receives the longed-for boon that motivates such loving quests for a fit helper. She becomes a mother. She has not needed to convert (though she did so), nor change her body into something more acceptable (though Solomon did so for her). At the same moment her intellectual wisdom failed her in the night, the gendered wisdom of the narrative triumphed. The noble queen is no longer an anomaly among women: wisdom's child will step down in favor of her son—as in the New Testament, Wisdom is vindicated by her children (Lk. 7.35). Makeda returns safely to her country as a fully functioning woman (a mother), yet she has been able to avoid the tedious political complication of marrying beneath her, or becoming an on-site subject to the ruler of some other country. Yet strangely, she continues to be a living riddle within the story told by her people: a pure woman of impeccable virtue who is both mother and unwed. This is a 'subject' position for which Christian history will have much inherent sympathy.

Perhaps Makeda, an eager seeker after light and water, had seen this satisfactory outcome for herself before she ever set out to visit the sage in Jerusalem: after all, riddles go with 'weddings' as clouds go with rain. We will leave her in her wisdom, gesturing verbally toward what is to come, as she explains her quest to her people:

> And I love him merely on hearing concerning him and without seeing him, and the whole story of him that hath been told me is to me as the desire of my heart, and like water to a thirsty man.[182]

But gender plays its role out to the last in her story: water for a thirsty man does not carry the same price exacted from this woman of wisdom:

> Seven cease: nine begin:
> Two offer drink: one drinks.

The price of Makeda's drinking is to be turned into a source of drink herself, as she is transformed from desiring subject to mother who satisfies the child's desires. As we conclude Sheba's story, we end in wonder and hope. Did she find in truth the heart's desire for which she traveled so far

point is to install sole male leadership for the upcoming dynasty. See Brenner's *Intercourse* for a pointed discussion on the 'gendering' of desire for a child.

182. Budge, *Kebra*, p. 23.

and gave so much? Answers will vary, depending on which version of the text one reads and how one chooses to interpret. We the readers have had better luck on *our* quest: we went looking for a wise woman who might speak to and for Wisdom in a woman's voice, and in this African queen, we have her—or at least as much of her as an androcentric text allows.

Chapter 4

THE WISDOM OF NEWTONS

Throughout our study of the ways in which women appear in ancient texts, both used by and using wisdom, we have noted the lacuna of the unedited, unvarnished female (F) voice in the tradition. What would it be like for us, we wondered, if we could hear Leah counseling Dinah? What if we could overhear more of what Naomi had to say to Ruth about life and men and God? Feminists everywhere have sought, as part of their task of recovery and reassessment of biblical traditions, to imagine those lost voices of the Mothers, if for no other reason than the desire to share those insights with the daughters who come after us. Since it is the position of the present work that Wisdom and her teachings are not exhausted by either time or the gendered preferences of ancient editors responsible for the book of Proverbs, I have asked my seminary students in wisdom courses to create those lost instructions, proverbs and poems in which female voice and experience are free to articulate themselves as true and valid expressions of the divine image. The result of those imaginings are presented here, following roughly the same organizational principles of Proverbs. Forms drawn from Hebrew poetry expanded to allow modern content; the trivialities of a specific little seminary, set on a hill in Newton, Massachusetts, mingle with the perpetual themes of child-rearing, spiritual quest and worldly experience. We decided that, in keeping with the book of Proverbs, we would leave our individual contributions to this modern wisdom 'book' anonymous, since what we have here is so clearly a *group* product.[1] We offer you up this body of wisdom, from a very particular time

1.　This does *not* mean, of course, that contributions should not be recognized: Sr. Nancy Citro collected, edited, arranged and provided unit titles for *The Wisdom of Newtons*; Rev. John Tamilio III made it digitally compatible with this manuscript. Other members of the class, many of whom are now ordained, who contributed are: Robert Bacon, Shawn Bracebridge, Ruth Bradshaw, H. Chan-Williams, Maureen Deneault, Inge Detweiler, Margaret Flad, Patty Gerry-Karajanes, Bob Hagopian, Jill

and place, as a present and a challenge: what wisdom are *you* hiding within yourself, Gentle Reader, and how will you make it known to the world?

The Gifts of Wisdom

Wisdom gives her children voice
　　to aid in self-disclosure.
Whoever gains her voice
　　grows in self-confidence.
Those who gain voice
　　rejoice in Wisdom.
It is Wisdom who is praised
　　for new found self-esteem.
Those who obey Wisdom
　　are never silenced again.
Blessed be Wisdom
　　who sets us free.

Wisdom calls me, arms outstretched,
　　a singing wind enveloping me.
Wisdom entreats me, come to the table,
　　singing a hymn, eating and drinking.
Wisdom's eyes are deep and knowing,
　　liquid stores of images.
Spilling pools of precious radiance
　　into my reflective gaze.
Wisdom takes my downcast eyesight,
　　lifts my eyes that I might see.
　　only to be seen with you.
Wisdom is my father all generous,
　　gifting me with eternal moments.
Wisdom is the holy breathing
　　causing my heart to beat with love.
Wisdom is the groom from heaven
　　joining himself in flesh to me.
Wisdom is my lover calling
　　with outstretched arms enveloping me.

Harvey, Zina Jacque, Robert Johansson, Pamela Langston-Daly, Carole Miller, Clarice Mitchell, Susan Murtha-Smith, David Nason, Susan Phoenix, Ted Pomfret, Katharine Preson, Michael Shrocki, Victoria Snow, Angelique Vernon, Kyoo Wan Yi and Meredith Manning Brown. To all of them, my deep thanks.

Wisdom Speaks of Creation

I, Wisdom, am the order that upholds the universe.
    Look around and you will see me.
Open your ears and you will hear my voice.
    Look to the planets, each in its orbit.
Look to the birds who know where to journey
    in spring and in autumn.
    See the fish who remember the stream of their spawning.

Listen to the rain
    when it comes in its season.
Listen to a mother as she sings to her children;
    Hear the voice of a father as he patiently teaches
    his sons and his daughters.

I, Wisdom, am a daughter of God,
    and I am the one who cares for her creation.
For lo, I was there when she brooded over
    the infant planet
    and when the clouds dispersed and the sun shone upon the waters.
I was there with the Holy One
    when the mountains were brought forth
    and when life appeared in the ancient oceans.

Listen to me, you children of earth.
    Listen and I will share with you the way of righteousness,
    and I will instruct you in the way that leads to life for all creatures.
Pay attention and honor the rhythms of creation.
    Love me and honor me and follow my precepts
    and my statutes:
Do not take more from the earth than you need.
    Treat all creatures with respect and honor.
Remember that your life is dependent upon other life.
    And order your families and communities with justice,
    that all might live in gratitude for the gifts of the Creator.

The Value of Wisdom

Happy the one who discovers Wisdom,
    life is refreshed by this beautiful find.
Ways to see clearly and walk the right path,
    enliven the soul and sharpen the mind.
If you read Wisdom with eyes fully open,
    hear all these words with a listening stance.

If you taste sweetness digesting the language
  feel the warm advice and cold admonitions,
Then you will know Wisdom in many ways;
  the Lord gave you senses to know it more fully.

Do not follow an alternate path,
  for there you'll get lost and perish from earth.
That path is dark, the sounds will be scary,
  the air will taste bitter and touch goes numb.
Walk down the path that follows Wisdom,
  and you will be nourished in every sense.
You'll use the gifts God gave you to know;
  you'll see creation in such greater fullness.
Those who ignore it will miss the beauty,
  God has revealed in life's places and moments.

Happy are those who find Wisdom,
  they know she will nurture them all of their days.
She is as the one who welcomes you home;
  she will embrace and feed you.
'I, Wisdom, am the path of ease
  through a jagged landscape,
  a way of safety through treacherous ways.
I am the star to steer your course towards,
  the star that shines in the darkest night.
I am the one who calms the seas
  of chaos, formless and terrible.
I am the way of the loving heart,
  the way of life and joy.'

The wise are happy;
  the fool is always anxious.
The fool is met by an empty doorway
  and silence.
The fool is like one starving who refuses to be fed by another;
  the fool grasps only emptiness.
Grow in Wisdom: she is not hiding,
  but invites you to join the community.

Happy is the daughter who finds Wisdom,
  and gains understanding of his ways.
He is as priceless as the most loving husband;
  more desired than the elusive house-husband.
In his bosom beats the heart of courage,
  and in his eyes flash the experience of joy.
Wisdom's hands produce the caresses of happiness,
  and all of his actions help sustain your life.

Admonition to Heed Wisdom

Wisdom cries out loud to her people
    calling them to heed her voice.
Into their lives she persistently calls
    through their video games and televisions.
'How long will you fill your ears with useless words,
    ignoring the power of my teachings?'
'Oh, listen, my people, to my words
    and follow my instructions for you.'
'For those who heed my teachings
    will find purpose, security, and peace.'

The True Security

Yahweh opens our hearts to receive love
    our hearts are open and we sing the praises of Yahweh.
We sing the praises with our hearts,
    but not our minds.
We close our minds to Yahweh
    so that we can stay in control.
Yahweh open our minds to you
    so that we can lose control.
For only when our hearts and minds sing the praises of Yahweh,
    are we one.

The True Path

Joys of life come from YHWH,
    the Creator and Sustainer of the world.
Every person listen, sing and rejoice!
Silly is the person who chooses to walk their own path,
    who seeks a way different from God's Way.
Unseen might be the image of God,
    but the Way of the Creator is known.
Surely the wise know
    their steps are already ordered in the Way.
Compassion is the Spirit of the way,
    in which the righteous work and play.
Honoring humanity as our friends,
    how better to honor YHWH!
Receiving from YHWH Yireh the gift of sacrifice,
    and learning how to serve another.

Instill in your children the true path,
    secure in them a foundation of faith.
Truly fear of YHWH is the Way to Wisdom;
    Wisdom is the ordered Way of Life.

The Care of Children

Hear my words, if the infant cries,
    do not procrastinate.
For one who acts decisively will generate smiles from all;
    but one who waits will deal with diaper rash for days.
Do not give her a bath before dinner,
    for those who bathe before they eat will bathe twice.
Always save junk food for last;
    junk food offered as a side order becomes the main dish.
Be a child and have children for life;
    be an adult and know not where your children have been.
Love your children and do not forget
    that they are your creation.
But remember that they are also
    their own creation.
All creations that are good are not copies of the original,
    but are new creations that build on the original creation.

Parental Advice to Daughters

Listen my daughter, to your mother's teachings,
    and learn from your father's example.
Your parents speak to you through love and experience,
    sharing the joy and pain of our lives with you.
Carry your parents' lessons with you always
    by writing them upon your heart.
My daughter, listen to my words
    and accept your mother's teaching.
Our culture does not value adolescents;
    it ignores our youth and places them in institutions called
    secondary schools.
Teens are full of energy;
    they are full of ideals.
Yet there is nothing for them to do in our culture;
    there is no real work or place for them.
We neglect them by having too few teachers in the schools;
    we neglect them by not being home to supervise.
We miss opportunities to awaken their souls;
    we give them tired, overworked teachers and boring curriculum.

And so, my child, strive to keep your spirit alive;
    never forget what kids need.

Hear the teaching of your mothers, oh daughter;
    follow the recipes of instruction from all those before you.
For their knowledge of the fire shall guide your production,
    and their technique shall be the tureen from which your broth
    serves nourishment.
Do not fall prey to the seduction of speed,
    or the ways of time-saving method.
For their yield is that of beauty without essence;
    like the colored, fizzy water with neither form nor sustenance.
Listen my daughter to these words of wisdom:
    your gifts are many and you have your whole life to discover
    them.
If you're not happy without a man
    you won't be happy with one either.
Never remain with anyone
    who fails to treat you with respect.

A Mother's Proverb Instruction

Our mothers taught us many things:
they had their proverbs, too,
but, Daughter, think of all the harm
were that the whole I gave to you.

'It's a Man's world,'
but 'it's a woman's prerogative
to change her mind.'
'A man may work from sun to sun,
but a woman's work is never done.'
('A woman's place is in the home.')
'The way to man's heart
is through his stomach'
(but is 'barefoot and pregnant'
the way to *yours*?).
'Why should a man keep a cow
when he can get milk for free?'
'Men don't make passes
at girls who wear glasses.'
'The hand that rocks the cradle
rules the world,'
But 'every baby, lose a tooth'.
'Behind every great man
there's a woman.'

'She lives for others;
you can tell by their hunted look'.

'Marry in haste, repent at leisure;'
'marry in black, wish yourself back!'
'You have to kiss a lot of frogs
before you find a prince;'
'it's as easy to love
a rich man as a poor one.'
'Better to be an old man's darling
than to be a young man's fool';
('there may be snow on the rooftop
but there's still a fire in the stove').
'Lie down with dogs
and get up with fleas';
'birds of a feather flock together,'
'you're known by the company you keep.'

Mothers' wisdom, mothers' woes—
did their proverbs speak of those?
Well, we are speaking *now:*
My girl, run from an angry man,
for a hot-tempered lover will do you no good.
Hit you once? Shame on him!
Hit you *twice*? Then shame on *you*!
If he hits you now, do you think it will change
because you have his ring and his name?
Don't go saying, 'Oh, *Mom!*' to me!
Do not think, 'It's because he *loves* me';
next you'll be saying, 'But it was *my* fault!'
A man who is jealous and violent, too,
will beat your children the way he beats you.
Leave him now before it's too late;
or wind up dead, should you try to wait!
Always keep money in your shoe,
and call a cab whenever you have to;
keep close your money and bank account,
or he'll give you something to cry about.
Better an ex-husband than an early grave.
Don't worry about him, don't try to save
your prison for some better day;
your only hope is to get away.
Better a little with fear of the Lord
than a fine house and violence!
Daughter, heed your mother's word!
Darling, will you show some sense?!

There are plenty of fish in the sea;
a man who can cry,
keep a job,
find his feet:
that one can teach you that love is sweet.
But flee from the bully, the addict, the drunk—
darling girl, shun him, or you'll be sunk,
and I'll be the one who raises your child
and remembers that once my daughter smiled.

Advice to Sons

Listen, my son, my streak of gray denotes Wisdom.
Our human form is wondrous in God's eye;
    our reflection on God, our blessing.
No less wondrous is the snake's skin;
    'his' reflection of the earth, 'his' blessing.
Snake and humankind are images of God;
    they are players in they system of creation.
Snake and humankind alone are but a breath;
    in relationship, they are Wisdom.
False pride destroys the fear of God;
    arrogance kills the snake underfoot.
Reverence and awe are the handmaids of Wisdom;
    respect follows the fleeing form.
Wisdom is not just in creation, but of it;
    She is the balm between humankind and the earth.
Her presence is the promise of this generation;
    and the hope for the seventh from now.

Listen, my son, to your father's words,
    and do not stray from your mother's care;
for our guidance will lead you to Wisdom,
    and our example to steadfast faith.
Follow the words of the Decalogue,
    and avoid those who think them folly.
Do not fall prey to drugs, alcohol, and loose living,
    for your strength will come in facing life with honor and dignity.
Come to us with your questions,
    for our hearts beat for you.
We are always available and at your service;
    we long to help you on your journey.
Even when we have returned to the breast of God,
    we will illumine your path with Wisdom's light.

Listen, my son, and do not turn away,
    for your mother loves you selflessly.

No one will ever love you as I do,
    for concern for you is all I have.
Follow all your dreams,
    but do not neglect your studies.
Enjoy the pleasures of life,
    but be aware of the future.
All the world lies before you,
    as on the day you were born.
All songs are your own,
    as when you first took breath.
Go, my son, and live,
    but remember your mother who loves you selflessly.
These are the lessons your mother and I
    teach you, my son,
    so that you may know how to survive in the 'hood',
by loving God as Creator, loving and respecting women as equals,
    and loving yourself, Spirit, Mind and Body.
They are to help you confront both the enemy within and the enemy
    within the world,
    and come out of battle the victor—all with the Creator's leadership,
    my princely prayer warrior.
Trust in God and follow the Divine Teacher's rules,
    so that you may be prosperous in all life's endeavors.
If a person lies in a gutter asking you for favors,
    give to them from the heart before you give from your hand,
For many times what they ask for
    is not what they truly need.
Love all women as colleagues
    and respect them as the mothers of the world's children.
A woman is no man's footstool
    nor is she his mantelpiece;
but she is his equal in life's journeys,
    either as partner or simply as friend.
Never follow a hoodrat or learn the ways of a player;
    for the Life Giver despises those who bring destruction to their
    communities,
    and abhors those who seek to defile their own sisters.
Truly, fear of YHWH is the Way to Wisdom;
    Wisdom is the ordered Way of life.

Listen, my son, my child of heart and soul;
    hear my words of counsel:
Befriend a woman with an inquiring mind;
    she knows the Wisdom in knowledge.
Befriend a woman with laughter in her heart;
    she knows the Wisdom in joy.

Befriend a woman with love for her body;
    she knows the Wisdom in health.
Befriend a woman who listens with care;
    she knows the wisdom in compassion.
Befriend a woman that pauses to listen to the call of flying geese,
    she hears Wisdom in many voices of God.

The Value of One's Unique Heritage

My child, listen well to your two mothers:
    you will be tempted to deny your parentage,
    and claim yourself alone in the world.
Beware, one who denies their family cannot
    seek warmth in the dead cold of winter;
none may share the warmth and light of the family home
    when denial lives there too.
Deny your home
    and you deny the only self you will ever know.
For Wisdom comes from insight,
    and insight comes from knowing your roots.
The tree cannot grow
    without its roots deep in the ground.
The gardener cannot hide
    that his fruits come from seeds.
So too, you cannot hide
    that you are grown from the love of two women.
Hold pride in the knowledge
    that love will bear fruits in time.
And that love can grow
    like a forest, thick and full of life.
Bring honesty to all relations,
    and the honest will stand by you.
Bring deceit, and you stand alone, in the cold.

A Father's Folly

My daughter, obey your father's rules,
    and forget who was your mother.
Listen to the one who raises you,
    who knows what is best for you.
Just do what you are told,
    never to ask questions.
If your feelings are hurt,
    just bite your lip;

for a slap will give you
    something to cry about.
A quiet daughter is the pride of her father,
    but a daughter who speaks is his disgrace.

A Daughter's Devotion and Strength

Spent my life waiting for mother;
    she's not coming, I'm on my own.
Give up the vigil, call off the search;
    the arms are not there, those days are gone.
Strength and wisdom are found within;
    they do not come from libations or rewards.
Let it go, stand tall, grow roots, bloom;
    I am my own tree now.
The faith comes from within,
    and from being a part of the whole.
The Spirit of Wisdom awaits within my heart;
    everything I'll ever be is already within me.
So rest in the knowledge that you were never alone;
    taste the fruit, enjoy the gift, join the dance.

Gay Wisdom

Listen, young fag, to this one who has been there,
    do not 'pooh, pooh' this experienced word.
My word is a key to a happier life,
    an escape from the locked world of deceitful games.
Do not enter bars where drinking and dancing,
    lead to drunk stupor and embarrassing moves.
The newspaper ad may tempt you with true love,
    but do not respond for those words are false.
Step out of the closet,
    it gives us all strength.
Prepare for rejections
    that make your heart sick.
Find your S.O. in your natural surroundings,
    same jobs and hobbies bring deeper respect.
These pointers I give you to help you along;
    endure, wait for true love to make your will strong.

General Maxims

One who is led by God,
    is as content as a nursing baby;
but those who lead themselves,
    are as frustrated as toddlers throwing temper tantrums.

Blessed is the one who holds tight to Wisdom,
  with hands and an open heart;
but the one who thinks Wisdom holds all answers,
  will have a closed heart.

Better are they who learn from their errors,
  than those who ignore and repeat their mistakes.
It is better to ask for forgiveness
  than it is to seek permission.
The pain on the inside shows on the outside,
  so treat the inside to cure the outside,
A wise mother sits with her child's grief;
  a foolish mother flees to games and toys.
He who uses his gifts wisely makes his mother glad;
  but a son who does not go to school wastes all his
  mother's life.
When the husband travels away from home,
  mechanical disasters will freely roam.
When you say to the Mechanic, 'It makes this sound,'
  silence will surely mock you.
A young family without a father
  is like a chair without four legs;
with him the mother has strength,
  without him she grows weak.
When a woman becomes disabled,
  the Lord blesses her with dustballs;
and the new courage to ask for help,
  yields cries of gratitude for a clean house.
When the mistress is ill, a household lacks salt;
  When the woman recovers, a village rejoices.
A woman without a man
  is like a fish without a bicycle.
It takes one heck of a man
  to be better than no man at all!
When crows are fussing,
  a hawk sits near.
If your friend loses lunch money, loan some;
  it may be your turn next.
If your friend loses lunch money daily,
  it is time to close the bank.

Woman Wisdom

Listen, my sisters, to one who precedes you,
  for the way is not wide for those of our kind.

My chances and choices may be helpful to you
    and your successes will cheer those whom you
    succeed and precede.
Build up your sisters and find common hope;
    stand together strengthened by difference, unafraid
    of its face!
For we are connected and what we do we will share;
    our job is to make wider the road as each passes.

Zina means strength, this is how I named my firstborn;
    A name not weak I offered to her.
Yearning for birth that was not to be lost;
    she was the one who found her way into life.
Xenos I served for nine months of not knowing;
    hoping to know her face and her spirit.
Wonderfully God introduced us in our birth;
    and now we stand two, made in one womb.
Victory came not in her forty years spent;
    but in the presence of God in our birth and our love.

A Wisdom Way of Learning

Attend, child, to the words of one who has gone through this,
    and has come out on the other side:
When teaching comes to you, be your own scribe,
    then learning comes to your heart through your own eye and hand.
Build your learning upon the gifts that God has given you,
    they are the strongest foundation.
When you are asked to give your knowledge to someone else, be generous;
    all teaching and learning is from God.
Arrange your library according to the subjects of the masters,
    thus the works are grouped together and easily found.
Learn the ways of the visitors,
    so that when you visit them you will not be a stranger.
Sleep and eat for the care of your body,
    so you may sing and praise God as you study.
Let music in your heart mingle with the quiet in your soul,
    then your voice will praise the Lord.
It is good to take pen in hand and write to your parents;
    they will know that you are well and you will prosper.

Seminary Wisdom

My friends, do not assume that you already know it all,
    but listen to what I have to tell you;

For I have been there three long years,
    and you may benefit from my experiences.
Be persistent when dealing with the Housing Coordinator,
    for she will forget you in an instant.
Get to know your advisor before your Mid-Program Review,
    for he ought to know your name before he walks in the door.
Talk to your professor about the problems you are having
    before the last day of classes;
so that neither of you will be in despair
    when you can't finish your work on time.
Pay attention to registration and drop-add deadlines,
    lest you pay extra fees that you really can't afford.
Read your Andover Newton catalog once in awhile,
    for it abounds with useful information.
Ignore my words if you enjoy struggle
    but heed them if you wish a smoother way on the Hill.

Hear, O young seminarians, the voice of one who graduates soon,
    and do not ignore the advice of those from before;
for they are like candles in the darkness,
    and beacons in the fog.
Do not believe what is written in the course catalog,
    speak, instead, directly to the professor;
for the class dates will change
    and pre-requisites will appear.
If your advisors say to you, 'Take Systematics, Church History, Christian
    Ethics, and Old Testament in your first semester,' do not consent;
for they delight in your suffering
    and enjoy tales of your confusion.
Wait not until the weekend or holiday break
    to make use of the library;
    go instead during class break, lunch, or chapel;
    for otherwise the hours are few and research time is limited.
Accept not the school's policy on anti-discrimination,
    support GLANTS in its efforts;
for same-sex relationships are still taboo
    and housing is not available to all.
Do not entrust any sacred document with the on-campus mailroom,
    hand deliver it instead;
for no one really knows what happens in there,
    and truly, it is an 'Ancient Mystery'.
If someone from your Field Ed site says to you, 'Come share our Sabbath
    meal,'
    do not refuse the invitation;
for while Sunday may be for spiritual nourishment
    your body will not be fed on campus.

If you are in need of administrative assistance,
> do not attempt to find help during office hours;
for the doors will be locked unto you
> and empty rooms answer your knock.

Listen, my child, and you will learn
> the ways of theological school.
The wise one buys books early,
> the fool waits until they are all gone.
If you need to concentrate
> do not sit near the one with the personal computer.
The personal computer can be a tool of the wise
> or the bane of the wise one's existence;
for the handicapped, a blessing;
> but for the able, just another burden to carry.
Happy is the student who registers early,
> for she shall have her first choice of classes,
> and be blessed with a reasonable course schedule.

A student rich with financial woes
> need only go to one office;
but a student poor in persistence,
> has a wealth of debt.

Read well a few pages—plunge deeply into the water;
> Skim a whole book—skate on the surface.
Wise are those who keep up with the readings;
> For the foolish will be scrambling at the end of term!
Honor the wisdom of women who have long served the church,
> and remember to uphold the importance of their work.
A busy coffee pot, the church's delight!
> A noisy parish hall, a joy!
Pursue knowledge with an open mind and heart;
> your compassion will increase along with your understanding.

Mistakes are the teachers of the wise,
> And thirst for knowledge their passion.
Remember that this church isn't seminary,
> And that the language you speak will sound foreign.
Learn all their names, and the names of their children,
> And the names of their pets: they will love you for this.
Smile and appreciate the joyful noise of your choir,
> No matter how off-key they sing.
Make changes slowly.
> Listen carefully when they say,
'We've always done it this way.'

Remember they have been there longer than you,
　　And will be there after you've gone.

Wisdom cries out on the quad,
　　from the grassy knoll she raises her voice:
Atop the holy hill she cries out,
　　at the entrance to halls of learning she speaks:
'How long, O Naive Ones, will you love being naive;
　　how long will innocence be blind to the truth,
　　and inexperience turn away from experience?
Listen closely to my warnings,
　　I will share my trials with you;
I will speak of the unspoken with you.

'Because I have spoken and you did not hear,
　　have warned at the Conference on Ministry days
and you laughed at my tales,
　　I, too, will smirk at your distress.
I will shake my head when panic strikes you,
　　when panic strikes at the use of the words ontological and hermaneu-
　　tical;
and your panic seizes you while preparing your first exegesis,
　　and realize lexicons are written in Aramaic, Hebrew, and Greek.
Then you will come to me with questions;
　　for advice, but I will not answer;
You will seek me at Union Street,
　　but will not see me behind Sam Adams.

Because you turned away from experienced knowledge
　　and did not choose the way of Wisdom;
would have none of my advice,
　　and followed not my example;
therefore, you shall become addicted to caffeine
　　and be afflicted with carpel-tunnel syndrome.
For the naivete` of new seminarians obscure the path,
　　and those who simply trust the institution will be lost.
But those who listen to me will have a chance,
　　and will, at least, know the E-mail address, fax number, and cell
　　phone,
　　to a good pastoral counselor.'

Blessed are they who are completing their take-home exams,
　　for the load lifted allows Wisdom to enter.
She fills their lightness
　　and lifts them on rivers of air like a great bird.
She flows into them
　　like cool water sliding over stones.

They drink in this water
    as the envelope takes in the pages.
Wisdom grows in their bodies
    like the strong tree of life,
who holds her weary students
    in her strong arms;
In her branches they rest
    before going to the post office.
Creation dances before them on the drive;
    snowflakes drift and then melt on the windshield.
The afternoon light is soft;
    the mail clerk is kind.
The clerk receives the envelope;
    the professor receives the work.
Wisdom grows,
    and connects.

Ministry Wisdom

The foolish one dies for office, work, and wealth;
    but the wise one lies with home, family, and love.

Wisdom cries out on the Hill,
    she raises her voice so that all may hear.
She calls out to the students as they rush to class,
    and weeps when they pass her by unheeded.

'You are indifferent to my counsel now,' she declares.
    'But you will wish you had listened when you are in your first
    church!'
For Wisdom knows that book learning is not enough
    for the one who would follow in the Shepherd's ways.
'Yes, there is much to do; there always is in the church;
    but your most important work is to take care of yourself.
For if you care not for yourself,
    why should the members of your congregation?
And if you cannot care for yourself,
    then how can you care for the sheep of your own flock?
They call business meetings on your day off and you go;
    have you no boundaries?
They expect you to do the work of your secretary when she quits
    two weeks before Christmas;
    so you take on her job in addition to your own.
They interrupt your dinner with routine concerns,
    and you leave your family to finish without you.

Do you not know the words, "Please come back another time";
    or do you only know how to say "Yes"?
Happy are the pastors who embrace my ways,
    for they shall enjoy many years of fruitful and healthy ministry.'

Wisdom sat in the back seat of my cart,
    I saw her out of the corner of my heart's eye.
'How did I do today?' I asked,
    thinking of tall children busy with colored ink and paper in my art
    room.
'How do I get my lesson message across
    to get their attention?
How do I get to their level of listening
    to reach their understanding?'
And she said in silent words,
    'God only knows!
I am just a messenger
    but God knows!
God also wonders how to touch the ears of people;
    God tries to reach the hearts of people.'
I answered, 'I am only a teacher
    and talk about color and painted lines on paper;
they create images which last for a day,
    like so much painted smoke; they do not care.'
'God cares,' said Wisdom, silent shadow of thought,
    and looked out the window.
'See God's creation! It lasts a day,
    like so much smoke! What will you do with it?
This is what you will do with it: Tell the Story again!
    Picture it again in art and music and song!
Tell it so all will hear! Sing it in color
    and portray it in melody!'
And I wondered how to write a sermon for Sunday,
    to tell the Story again;
so that we hear God's refreshing Story again,
    yet new for today.
Wisdom asked, 'How did you do?'
    And I answered, 'I learned that in reaching out I teach;
  I learned that whatever is in my heart and hand when I reach out,
    that is what I teach.'

Epilogue

    The path of the wise will never be barren,
        for it takes energy to learn.

There will never be a shortage of the needy,
    for need fills the hearts of us all.
The path of the wise leads to the heart,
    whereas the path of the ignorant takes the shortest route
    which is downtrodden from overuse.

Three things tickle the Holy One,
    Four make Shadday laugh out loud:
A convict who gets out,
    A cripple who gets well,
A woman who gets even,
    White trash with money!

Seek Wisdom in your soul,
    for it cannot be found in advertisements.
God will meet you there,
    and acquaint you with her.
Wisdom leads one through happiness,
    for happiness is but a by-product.
Pursuit of happiness is merely a misguided tour,
    in which the leader is intoxicated,
    directing his followers to streets with no names.
Pursue Wisdom for she has prepared your way;
    you will know happiness while she draws you to your soul
    and to the hearts of those around you.

A Good Man Is Hard to Find!

A man to be trusted—ah, who can find?!
        Perhaps only ten such come to each generation—
        (isn't that just what the rabbis say?).
They are more precious than stock options,
        but most who marry don't find them.
Few are those who share in the household,
        rising before dawn if a child should cry,
without expecting their heads to be patted,
        for doing what wives do every single day.
At work, a good man remembers his values;
        he does not check his ethics at the door of success.
He hires women workers, and promotes them;
        he does not regard breast size or grey hairs.
In board rooms, he is discretion and compromise;
        he knows when to be political
        for those with access denied there.
He does not sign reports he knows are untrue;
        design flaws and shortfalls he does not conceal

Even though he must think of his family,
　　　for a good man knows he can count on support
　　　from his mother, his spouse, sisters, daughters!
At home, he can mend and cook and clean;
　　　he knows his way through the supermarket aisles,
　　　and remembers his cats' special diets.
He knows about taxes, and credit and lawyers,
　　　and teaches his females the ways of his brothers.
Sisters, all ages, rise up and say,
　　　'Many men give lip service,
　　　but we see their acts!
We see their wives coming home tired,
　　　to do household tasks, while *they* relax
　　　content to be cushioned by her 'extra' paycheck.
But you are our equal, at home and at work:
　　　you are compassion, *you* are a man!'
Cherish him, sisters, should you find him,
　　　for he is very rare;
Praise him at feminist gatherings, saying,
　　　'Taste these! My mate himself made this brownie!'

Scribal colophon:
Here endeth our proverbs,
but not our journey.

Chapter 5

CONCLUDING SEMI-SCIENTIFIC POSTSCRIPT

Gentle Reader, our journey together through the proverb traditions of the ancient world has finally come to a close—at least for now! There is always one more proverb to add,[1] one more tradition to explore, one more reading to construct, especially for the engaged lover of word art. There are always more things to be said, more voices with which to enter into dialogue. Other views and discussions with modern critics could also be added, at length: to Fox's critique of Strange Woman, we might say, 'Pshaw!' even as we admire his addition of 'Energy' to Woman Wisdom's character profile; to Clifford's incorporation of Ugaritic epic traditions into our set of lenses for reading Israel's wisdom traditions, much applause could be raised; to Crenshaw's perceptive works on women in riddle performance as well as the motherly instruction,[2] published well before it was trendy to do so, we might turn an approving eye and wink for a critic who 'saw' women in wisdom as performers as well as tropes. The lyrical recovery of the oral ambiguities of proverbs so stunningly displayed in Murphy's translations for his Proverbs commentary even as it seeks a theological reading as its higher goal, deserves serious praise as well, as does van Leeuwen's perceptive insights on form and function.

Feminist critics have done their part to inform the 'lion's share' of this book's viewpoint and methodology. Susan Niditch's work on orality provides the framework needed properly to understand performance of

---

1.   'The bitch in going back and forth gave birth to blind puppies,' from the Mari letters (ARMT I 5.11-13), for example. The supposition is that this refers to the dog's characteristic of turning around in circles several times before lying down—but weakness in offspring is attributed to the mother's behavior.

2.   James L. Crenshaw, 'The Contest of Darius's Guards in 1 Esdras 3:1–5:3', in B.O. Long (ed.), *Images of Man and God: The Old Testament Short Story in Literary Focus* (Sheffield: Almond Press, 1981), pp. 74-88, 119-20; reprinted in the author's *Urgent Advice*, pp. 222-34.

proverbs. We read differently when we read with Camp, early or late;[3] we wisely are put on guard by the observations of Brenner and Newsom; we are heartened by the works of 'recovery' of a sacred past for our Tree of Life in the work of Hadley and McKinlay. Even where I must append a 'yes, *but...*' to the readings of white feminist critics and their sisters of every color and kind, there is a sharp awareness of the collective nature of our inquiries. We would be exactly nowhere without the 'head start' of those who have gone before, and all their work is gratefully acknowledged here.

During the long (*long!*) writing of this study, my dear conversation partner of the last decade and the 'Implied Reader' of my writing passed away after a long life filled to the brim with the fruits of scholarship and compassion. He had read many of the essays found here as they were in formation: to my complaints that women's voices were muted, distorted or absent in the book of Proverbs, he advised me, 'Then you must write them in!'; to the myriad analyses of all of the Sheba variants, he said, 'Very learned: imagine how pleased the Queen would be!' After our first argument over the necessity of feminist method and critique in the study of biblical traditions, he replied, 'But *this* changes *everything!*' At first discouraged ('But all my work needs to be redone, and I am old, old!'), he professed a sense of peace: 'I know the Torah is in good hands for the next century: women hold it now.' After all, no teacher has greater pride or sense of accomplishment than when those he has nurtured take his work further and add to it. Professor Claus Westermann's enormous support of women in the profession of biblical studies is one of the explicit legacies of the work presented here. Though he never got to write the Preface to this book as we had planned—nevertheless, I feel him here and on many, many pages that went before.

My work as a 'form critic' with a penchant for graphs, figures, tables and 'proof' was always a source of great amusement (and great trial?) to

---

3.   Though I do *not* think Solomon can properly be said to be female, as Camp whimsically suggests, I *can* propose an alternate reading of his dealings with Sheba: could it be that the Solomon who tricks and defiles our dark beauty is actually the king of the Demons, Ashmodai (Ashmodeus), who is said by Jewish storytellers to have tricked Solomon, seizing his physical form and then his throne to rule in his stead? And how appropriate it would be in this unconventional retelling to note that if Sheba is indeed Lilith by another name, then the mating of this demonic pair has implications for a reading of forced sex as liminally demonic, and hence, out of place—literally 'out of this world'— in the beds of human partners?

my Implied Reader, and it is thanks to him that I do not now pelt *you*, Gentle Reader, with a plethora of summarizing tables and insights. He taught me to 'keep it simple' by telling me this story in response to one of my first tortured drafts on Sheba:

> Once there was a very wise man, a scholar, who left off from his writing to walk in the market. While he was there, he found a most exquisite plum, so he bought it and took it home, preparing to enjoy it fully. But when he placed the plum on his kitchen table in preparation for eating it, he was struck again by its incredible magnificence. 'Surely', he said, 'this must be the most wondrous plum that has ever been grown!' And being a scholar, he set out to prove this was so. He returned to the market and bought a sample of every kind of plum that existed, always being careful to choose the very best version he could find of that variety of plum.
>
> After his shopping excursion, he returned to his house and set out each plum, by size and shape and color and variety, lining them up next to the first wondrous plum whose excellence he sought to prove. He ordered his plums carefully, cataloging each one, making minute observations and measurements of every part of the plum. Many days passed as he recorded his observations, for he was very thorough, but at last, he was finished, and was ready now to turn to his excellent plum for comparison. But that first plum, the wondrous plum that captured his intellect, was now wrinkled and moldy and entirely inedible! 'What a fool I am!' he exclaimed. 'It would have been better if I had eaten my plum, rather than studied it!'

While this *Beispielerzählung* may not be precisely what one hopes to hear in response to very earnest tabulations of data, the point was clear enough and certainly not lost on me. Study is good; finishing is better! As you wonder how such a little oral form as a saying or proverb could spawn so very many literary flourishes of response, at least pause to recall that there could have been more! In deference to my Reader, I eschew graphical wizardry and opt instead for a few brief observations on the matters covered elsewhere in this study.

Forms, Functions and Performance

Performance is the event where the latent potentialities of a unit of folk-lore are made present in all their radical possibilities. The occasion of performance of a tradition is redolent with contradictory impulses vying for ascendancy, impulses that contest the intersections of meaning at every multi-layered boundary in dispute. Through employment of a folk saying in the zone of one of these borders of meaning, a whole world of reference and cultural knowledge, familiar to and accepted by the members of that 'folk', is called up, perused, and negotiated.[4] Through performance, tradition takes root and bears fruit; without it, the saying is dead—on its way to obscurity in the catalogue of some scholar, but no longer a viable tool for living within the group that created it.

Hence, the humble sayings and honeyed proverbs of ancient Israel and Judah decline to specify a fixed meaning marked by syntax that marches the hearer down one path to one conclusion only, in a covert attempt at laying down the sure stepping-stones of ideology. No, not for the sages of the Bible's world were the overbearing law code or tendentious narration the preferred instrument of teaching for critical consciousness! These teachers and performers of the oral tradition opted for a different method: their proverbs are edgy and open-ended, with the potential for a range of meanings congruent with the relationships by which one chooses to understand the proverb's terms. Are the terms in opposition? Necessarily? Always? Is there perhaps another way of 'reading' and 'decoding' the situation at hand? Proverbs don't so much offer 'answers' as they seek to frame questions in terms of connection and disconnection. It is this core feature of the saying/proverb genre that causes our feeling of uneasy discontinuity and disorientation when we move from the patriarchal ideologies of ranting Wisdom and teaching Father in Proverbs 1–9 to the proverb collections themselves. It is *not* that their subject matter is disconnected, but rather that one chooses to force a position on the audience, while the other invites the audience to join in the process of meaning-making as a key element in the lesson to be taught.

The form embodies the function. The stark enjambments of images in the wisdom saying are like a literary fingerprint of the sages' and users' intentions and preferences. They want their students or audience to *hear*—then pause, assess, consider, and choose. They prefer not to over-designate meanings at any cursory level. Their proverbs are meant to tease and train the intellect, to the end of fostering the moral orientation approved by their society.

Further, the sages and performers choose to pose their word-puzzles in forms that call into the foreground the honed beauty of the clear insight, the stark surprise of the clever image. We often speak of a saying's poetic qualities as a mnemonic aid to memorization and recitation. But this ignores a more basic motive in the operation of the well-crafted proverb or

4.   For a wonderful introduction to performance studies, especially in the modern context, see Elizabeth C. Fine and Jean H. Speer (eds.), *Performance, Culture, and Identity* (Westport, CT: Praeger, 1992).

saying: the compulsive, reflexive need to respond to the world's ambiguity in poetic form betokens a powerful hunger for beauty on the sages' part. Oral poetry is by nature a fleeting thing, gone as soon as it is begun—but leaving the sounds of beauty echoing in the ear and in the heart. Where life can be brutal, chaotic and dangerous, the choice to know and respond to it through handsome phrases, intricately connected or oddly juxtaposed, says something about what it means to be human. We wonder, we grieve, we shout angrily—but in the end, we make art from the turns and twists of life. The sages have succeeded, at least in this lesson of basic beauty that they so eagerly sought to impart.

It is, then, a great sorrow that the beautiful forms in Proverbs have been the vehicle of so much that is perfectly *ugly* on the topic of women. Our survey of the ladies 'in the text' found, much as expected given the work of others that has gone before, that the sages made less space for the possibilities that women might *not* be accurately represented in the traditional wisdom about them. The women of the text are seen through the male lens, with only hints of counter-voices and female authorship to suggest that this cultural 'wisdom' might be mistaken, or at least incomplete. Women are understood by means of the roles, good or bad, that they play in men's lives. Our attempt to excavate the social reality behind those roles gave us a bit more to work with: images of caring and competence, public visibility, social responsibility, cultic participation, and cosmic females whose features 'underwrote' the portraits of Woman Wisdom and Woman Stranger/Folly. In this respect, our attention to iconography and parallel texts provided a valuable 'control' group for the literary images in Proverbs. Even where we used medieval images from Jewish texts to fill in our gaps on women's practice, images that might reasonably be said to carry little weight in interpreting our texts, since they postdate the Bible, we would argue that they represent a visual 'afterlife' of work of women inscribed in the text of Proverbs, and hence are relevant indeed.

The study of women's verbal performance of the ancient proverbial tradition was necessarily limited in several ways, by the nature of the material available to us. First, we do *not* have access to direct field notes of some anthropologist on hand to record actual verbal interactions, and so many nuances are lost to us, however versed we may be in the proverb corpus, their images and referents and their customary meanings. Next, most of the texts we *do* have come to us mediated by the literate 'elite'— the folk (the poor, the young, the foreign, the female) remain largely hidden from us, for this reason. If we seem to have found ourselves caught up

in the royal struggles of queens and their menfolk, this bias of elite survivals accounts for this fact as much as any notion that royalty are the sole
possessors of wisdom, taught or endowed with it by the gods. Another
limitation stems directly from the ancient gender codes that condition the
texts that come to us: due to the patriarchal nature of the ancient world, not
many texts by women have been preserved (and even if they were, it is
highly unlikely that ancient views of 'authorship' correspond to ours).
Hence, we are working more often than not with male-authored texts in
which the voice of woman (Brenner's so-called 'F voice') is allowed to
speak—but with what degree of censorship or projected conformance to
male views of female abilities and behavior, we cannot always say. Have
we really been able to progress from the unsatisfactory situation of
studying men's proverbs *about* women into something more closely tied to
women's reality? When the rabbinic storytellers contextualize Prov. 31.1-
9 as the words of Bath-sheba to Solomon in his bedroom, we are still in
the world of male fantasy, which attributes male attitudes to the female
characters it permits to appear. This is the reason why this study privileges
real, historical women's correspondence, which incorporates proverb performance over all the other genres upon which we been required to rely.

Still, it is possible to make *some* observations about women's use of the
wisdom tradition in performance. Clearly, from our various sources, we
see that in many situations involving women there is a routine 'expectation' that they can, should, and do perform this traditional genre during
conflictual situations, framing it in such a way that it is clearly marked *as*
performance. None of our audiences, the hearers/readers of the women's
citation of a proverb, fall over in astonishment that a woman might speak,
and speak decisively, from tradition. Women appear to be 'authorized
performers' of the cultural tradition: they are expected to be competent
in their group's lore, and they display this competence when required.
Whether it is a king listening to the warning of a prophetess, a general
heeding a wise woman's advice, or a slave woman 'speaking up' for her
own point of view, those who hear, listen, and those who speak have an
expectation of being heard. Unlike the portrait of women *in* the book of
Proverbs that often sees women as a threat or some sort of adjunct to male
dreams of achievement, the women of these societies were 'out there'
doing wisdom, rather than writing it—just as feminist theologians 'do' theologies, rather than 'write a theology' as their male colleagues do.

Women's presence as performers of proverbial traditions is all the more
striking because of the general misogyny to be found in proverb collections not only from our time periods and geographical locations, but around

the world as well. African theologians like Mercy Oduyoye and Edda Gachukia, for example, note that quotation of traditional sayings and proverbs are one of the primary tools for perpetuating female oppression in Africa, and that new proverbs must be written to challenge and realign gender relations and female stereotypes toward the ideals of justice.[5] Like little 'proof texts' whose basic assumptions go unquestioned, proverbs and sayings are indeed powerful instruments for stifling change, silencing questions and closing discussions—*depending* on how they are used. While I grant that such tools in the hands of those defending the gender status quo do not automatically seem to disclose a rhetoric of resistance to male oppression, our study suggests that even a proverb with negative content about women can be strategically deployed to teach its opposite. I think here of the marvelous framing devices employed by Jesus of Nazareth to suggest a different path for finding one's relationship to tradition. Though he is usually responding to a citation of the law codes, these legal sayings function as group wisdom, which the Teacher then reframes:

> You have heard that it was said, 'You shall love your neighbor and hate your enemy.' But I say to you, Love your enemies and pray for those who persecute you, so that you may be children of your Father in heaven; for he makes his sun rise on the evil and on the good, and sends rain on the righteous and on the unrighteous (Mt. 5.43-45).

Jesus' appraisal of the legal saying opens with the traditional proverb performance frame that invokes tradition...*but* then moves on to seize proverbial authority on behalf of the speaker and hearers. Where proverbs are used to restrict and bind, their citation can be undermined in a variety of ways in the arena of performance, opening the group to new directions in action and thought. So, while granting the full range of disquieting and unfair 'teachings' about gender that are to be found in the wisdom tradition, our study indicates ways in which even gendered proverbs can serve the program of liberation of gender attitudes.

One striking feature of the proverbs cited by women (or placed in their mouth in stories by men) is the prominent position of 'motherhood', real or symbolic, in both proverb content ('The gods grant the prayer of a woman in labor') and 'midrash' on its meaning in context (Bath-sheba's view that any lapse in Solomon's behavior will be attributed to his mother

---

5.   Quoted in Joseph Healy, MM, and Donald Sybertz, MM, *Towards an African Narrative Theology* (Faith and Culture Series; Maryknoll, NY: Orbis Books, 1996), p. 36.

and *not* his father). Our study has shown that Camp's very early recognition of the connection between wise women traditions and symbolic motherhood is, in fact, right on the money. So, although women might have been considered authorized performers, their authorization is still linked in a primal way to their sex roles and the way those biological activities are 'gendered' or understood by their culture. Like Elizabeth I of England, ruling alone as a Protestant and so forced to become a symbolic 'Virgin Queen' in order to be 'mother' to her people, many of them still Catholic, our performers naturally assume the mother's cloak when they seek to influence events. Hittite queen or Hebrew wise woman, astute women sought the extra 'edge' of approval that archetypal patterns of motherhood could provide.

Women who found their status, high or low, *outside* of motherhood seem to feel more free—or, more appropriately, are *shown* as more freely using frames and proverbs that do not depend on the tropes of motherhood for their legitimacy. The prophetess of Dagan needs to make no flourish about her motherly advice to the king; she simply delivers the god's message in proverb form, explains its reference, and that is that. Likewise, the slave woman from the Westcar papyrus doesn't bother invoking Isis, her own motherhood, or any feature of her relationship to a man who might give her status. She is a slave; she *has* no power base and no 'social existence' apart from her slavery, so she speaks her own truth simply in a proverb with nothing to do with motherhood, though one might relate the term 'pot' to women's domestic duties. Hittite wise women do not invoke mother goddesses in any marked way, even when dealing with fertility issues—they just go about their ritual business. Sheba in the *Targum Esther Sheni* speaks of lions and lairs, not her nurturing role as a mother to her people (even though the analysis of that text sees her with an ulterior motive that is very much related to nurturing the lives of her subjects). We should not be surprised then that the archetypal Strange Women of Proverbs 1–9 are never shown as mothers, nor do they speak as mothers when they ply their smooth words on male 'victims': their status is negatively derived from their *lack* of motherhood. They are faithless to their legitimate partners, foreign, ritually suspect, 'off limits', and the passage to *their* womb is in fact a tunnel leading to the Underworld. With no child to relieve their 'foreignness' by converting them into mothers of a new group member, these women, painted in harsh tones from a palette of negative female archetypes, are doomed like Lilith to wander the boundaries of 'wholesome' culture—childless, embittered, envious, demonic.

But we must not end with the overdrawn caricatures of men whose obsession with their own honor and wisdom made them less than accurate observers of Woman and women, Wisdom and wisdom. Though we have had much to do with queens in this study, the original hope was to recover the ordinary, non-elite woman's connection, if any, to the wisdom tradition. There has been some success, but only when we were willing to leave the 'official' scribal domain of wisdom text production and venture into the marketplace, the bedroom or the hearth side where living wisdom was performed.

Like mother, like daughter! Women, then as now, draw wisdom from the deep well of their daily experience in the world. The ancient women studied here were curious and able observers of events and things, accustomed to making minute yet critical decisions for the successful execution of women's domestic crafts. In this daily world of women's work, they could see when the yarn was about to break or the pot to boil, and they acted on that information. Perhaps we cannot say that they were producers of wisdom texts, but they were, of necessity, producers of *meanings* for those texts when used in an oral setting, times when the common threads of their groups were stretched to the breaking point, and conflict was on the verge of boiling over. Into these moments, they spoke their 'word in season', opening their mouths in wisdom (Prov. 31.26), and made a difference by 'performing' a 'torah of hesed'. This is a legacy of Wisdom to her human daughters that is worth remembering—and performing in the days to come.

BIBLIOGRAPHY

Abbott, N., 'Pre-Islamic Arab Queens', *AJSL* 8 (1941), pp. 1-22.

Abrams, J.Z., *The Women of the Talmud* (Northvale, NJ: Jason Aronson, 1995).

Abusch, T., 'An Early Form of the Witchcraft Ritual *Maqlu* and the Origin of a Babylonian Magical Ceremony', in T. Abusch, J. Huehnergard and P. Steinkeller (eds.), *Lingering over Words: Studies in Ancient Near Eastern Literature in Honor of William L. Moran* (Atlanta: Scholars Press, 1990), pp. 1-57.

—*Babylonian Witchcraft Literature: Case Studies* (BJS, 132; Atlanta: Scholars Press, 1987).

—'Ishtar's Proposal and Gilgamesh's Refusal: An Interpretation of the Gilgamesh Epic, Tablet 6, Lines 1-79', *HR* 26 (1986), pp. 143-87.

Abusch, T., J. Huehnergard and P. Steinkeller (eds.), *Lingering over Work: Studies in Ancient Near Eastern Literature in Honor of William L. Moran* (Atlanta: Scholars Press, 1990).

Akurgal, E., *The Art of the Hittites* (trans. C. McNab; New York: Harry Abrams, 1962).

Albright, W.F., 'The Goddess of Life and Wisdom', *ASJL* 36 (1919–20), pp. 258-94.

—'Some Canaanite-Phoenican Sources of Hebrew Wisdom', *VTS* 3 (1955), pp. 1-15.

Alexander, J.G., *Medieval Illuminators and their Methods of Work* (New Haven: Yale University Press, 1992).

Arberry, A.J. (trans.), *The Koran Interpreted* (New York: Macmillan, 1955).

Arnold, D., *The Royal Women of Amarna: Images of Beauty from Ancient Egypt* (New York: Metropolitan Museum of Art; Harry N. Abrams, 1996).

Asher-Greve, Julia M., 'Stepping into the Maelstrom: Women, Gender and Ancient Near Eastern Scholarship', *NIN* 1 (2000), pp. 1-22.

Assmann, J. 'Isis', in van der Toorn, Becking and van der Horst (eds.), *Deities and Demons*, pp. 855-60.

—'Neith', in van der Toorn, Becking and van der Horst (eds.), *Deities and Demons*, pp.1159-63.

Aubin, Melissa, ' "She Is the Beginning of All the Ways of Peversity": Femininity and Metaphor in 4Q184', *Women in Judaism* 2.2 (2001), on line at http://www.women-in-judaism.com.

Avalos, H., *Health Care and the Rise of Christianity* (Peabody, MA: Hendrickson, 1999).

—*Illness and Health Care in the Ancient Near East: The Role of the Temple in Greece, Mesopotamia, and Israel* (HSM, 54; Atlanta: Scholars Press, 1995).

Barber, Elizabeth Wayland, *Women's Work: The First 20,000 Years* (New York: W.W. Norton, 1994).

Batto, B., *Studies on Women at Mari* (Baltimore: The Johns Hopkins University Press, 1974).

(Bauer-)Kayatz, Christa, *Studien zu Proverbien 1–9* (WMANT; Neukirchen–Vluyn: Neukirchener Verlag, 1966).

Baumann, G., 'A Figure with Many Facets: The Literary and Theological Functions of Personified Wisdom in Proverbs 1–9', in Brenner and Fontaine (eds.), *Wisdom and Psalms*, pp. 44-91.

—*Die Weisheitsgestalt in Proverbien 1–9: Traditionsgeschichtliche und theologische Studien* (FAT, 16; Tübingen: J.C.B.Mohr [Paul Siebeck], 1996).

Baumann, R., *Verbal Art as Performance* (Prospect Heights, IL: Waveland Press, 1977).

Bechtel, L.M., 'Shame as a Sanction of Social Control in Biblical Israel: Judicial, Political, and Social Shaming', *JSOT* 49 (1991), pp. 47-76.

Beckman, G., 'Proverbs and Proverbial Allusions in Hittite', *JNES* 45 (1986), pp. 19-30.

Bekkenkamp, J., and F. van Dijk, 'The Canon of the Old Testament and Women's Cultural Traditions', in Brenner (ed.), *Song of Songs*, pp. 67-85.

Bergant, D., *Israel's Wisdom Literature: A Liberation-Critical Reading* (Philadelphia: Fortress Press, 1997).

Bezold, Carl (trans.), *Kebra Nagast: Die Herrlichkeit der Könige* (München: G. Franz Verlag, 1905).

Bialik, H.N., and Y.H. Ravnitzky (eds.), *The Book of Legends (Sefer HaAggadah): Legends from the Talmud and Midrash* (trans. W.G. Braude; intro. D. Stern; New York: Schocken Books, 1992).

Bin-Nun, S.R., *The Tawannana in the Hittite Kingdom* (THeth, 5; Heidelberg: Carl Winter, 1975).

Binger, T., *Asherah: Goddesses in Ugarit, Israel and the Old Testament* (JSOTSup, 232; CIS, 2; Sheffield: Sheffield Academic Press, 1997).

Blachman, M.J., *Eve in an Adamocracy: The Politics of Women in Brazil* (Philadelphia: ISHI Press, 1979).

Black, Jeremy, and Anthony Green, *Gods, Demons and Symbols of Ancient Mesopotamia: An Illustrated Dictionary* (Austin: University of Texas Press, 1992).

Bleeker, C.J., *Hathor and Thoth: Two Key Figures of the Ancient Egyptian Religion* (SHR, 26; Leiden: E.J. Brill, 1973).

—'Isis and Hathor: Two Ancient Egyptian Goddesses', in Olson (ed.), *Goddess*, pp. 29-48.

Blenkinsopp, J., 'The Social Context of the "Outsider Woman" in Proverbs 1–9', *Bib* 72 (1991), pp. 457-73.

Bloch, H.R., *Medieval Misogyny and the Invention of Western Romantic Love* (Chicago: University of Chicago Press, 1991).

Borghouts, J.F., 'Witchcraft, Magic, and Divination in Ancient Egypt', *CANE*, III, pp. 1775-85.

Boström, G., *Proverbiastudien: Die Weisheit und das fremde Weib in Sprüche 1–9* (Lund: C.W.K. Gleerup, 1935).

Boyarin, D., *Carnal Israel: Reading Sex in Talmudic Culture* (New Historicism: Studies in Cultural Poetics; Berkeley: University of California Press, 1993*)*.

—*Intertextuality and The Reading of Midrash* (Bloomington, IN: Indiana University Press, 1990).

Brenner, A.,

—'Introduction', in Brenner (ed.), *Latter Prophets* (FCB, 8; Sheffield: Sheffield Academic Press, 1995), pp. 21-37.

—'Introduction', in Brenner and Fontaine (eds.), *Wisdom and Psalms*, pp. 23-30.

—'Some Observations on the Figurations of Woman in Wisdom Literature', in Brenner (ed.), *Wisdom Literature*, pp. 50-66.

—*The Intercourse of Knowledge: On Gendering Desire and 'Sexuality' in the Hebrew Bible* (BIS, 26; Leiden, E.J. Brill, 1997).

—'Women Poets and Authors', in Brenner (ed.), *Song of Songs*, pp. 86-99.

Brenner, A. (ed.), *A Feminist Companion to Esther, Judith and Susanna* (FCB, 7; Sheffield: Sheffield Academic Press, 1995).

—*A Feminist Companion to Latter Prophets* (FCB, 8; Sheffield: Sheffield Academic Press, 1995).

—*A Feminist Companion to Ruth* (FCB, 3; Sheffield: Sheffield Academic Press, 1993).

—*A Feminist Companion to Song of Songs* (FCB, 1; Sheffield: Sheffield Academic Press, 1995).

—*A Feminist Companion to Wisdom Literature* (FCB, 9; Sheffield: Sheffield Academic Press, 1995).

—*The Israelite Woman: Social Role and Literary Type in Biblical Narrative* (Sheffield: JSOT Press, 1985).

Brenner, A., and F. van Dijk-Hemmes (eds.), *On Gendering Texts: Female and Male Voices in the Hebrew Bible* (BIS, 1; Leiden, E.J. Brill, 1993).

Brenner, A., and C. Fontaine (eds.), *A Feminist Companion to Reading the Bible: Approaches, Methods, Strategies* (Sheffield: Sheffield Academic Press, 1997).

—*A Feminist Companion to Wisdom and Psalms* (FCB, 2 [Second Series]; Sheffield: Sheffield Academic Press, 1998).

Bronner, L.L., 'From Veil to Wig: Jewish Women's Hair Covering', *Judaism* 42 (1993), pp. 465-77.

Brown, J., 'Note on the Division of Labor by Sex', in E.W. Barber (ed.), *Women's Work: The First 20,000 Years* (New York: W.W. Norton, 1994), pp. 29-30.

Budge, E.A. Wallis (trans.), *Kebra Nagast (The Queen of Sheba and her Only Son Menyelek)* (London: Oxford University Press, 2nd edn, 1932).

Burns, T.A., 'Riddling: Occasion to Act', *JAF* 89 (1976), pp. 139-65.

Camp, C., 'The Female Sage in Ancient Israel and in the Biblical Wisdom Literature', in Gammie and Perdue (eds.), *Sage*, pp. 185-204.

—'The Wise Women of 2 Samuel: A Role Model for Women in Early Israel', *CBQ* 43 (1981), pp. 14-29.

—'Understanding a Patriarchy: Women in Second Century Jerusalem Through the Eyes of Ben Sira', in A.-J. Levine (ed.), *'Women Like This: New Perspectives on Jewish Women in the Greco-Roman World* (Atlanta: Scholars Press, 1991), pp. 1-40.

—'What's So Strange about the Strange Woman?', in D. Jobling, P.L. Day and G.T. Sheppard (eds.), *The Bible and the Politics of Exegesis* (Cleveland, OH: Pilgrim Press, 1991), pp. 17-31.

—*Wisdom and the Feminine in the Book of Proverbs* (BL, 11; Sheffield: Almond Press, 1985).

—*Wise, Strange and Holy: The Strange Woman and the Making of the Hebrew Bible* (JSOTSup, 320; GCT, 9; Sheffield: Sheffield Academic Press, 2000).

—'Wise and Strange: An Interpretation of Female Imagery in Light of Trickster Mythology', in Brenner (ed.), *Wisdom Literature*, pp. 131-56.

—'Woman Wisdom as Root Metaphor: A Theological Consideration', in Hoglund *et al.* (eds.), *The Listening Heart*, pp. 45-76.

Camp, C.V., and C.R. Fontaine, 'The Words of the Wise and Their Riddles', in. S. Niditch (ed.), *Text and Tradition: The Hebrew Bible and Folklore* (Semeia Studies; Atlanta: Scholars Press, 1990), pp. 127-52.

Carroll, B.A. (ed.), *Liberating Women's History: Theoretical and Critical Essays* (Chicago: University of Illinois Press, 1976).

Ceresko, Anthony R., *Introduction to Old Testament Wisdom: A Spirituality for Liberation* (Quezon City, Philippines: Claretian Publications, 1999).

Clapp, Nicholas, *Sheba: Through the Desert in Search of the Legendary Queen* (New York: Houghton Mifflin, 2001).

Clifford, R.J., *Proverbs: A Commentary* (OTL; Louisville, KY: Westminster/John Knox Press, 1999).

—*The Wisdom Literature* (IBT; Nashville, TN: Abingdon Press, 1998).

—'Woman Wisdom in the Book of Proverbs', in G. Braulik, W. Gross and S. McEvenue (eds.), *Biblische Theologie und gesellschaflicher Wandel: Für Norbert Lohfink SJ* (Freiburg: Herder, 1993), pp. 61-72.

Coleson, Joseph E., 'Israel's Life Cycle from Birth to Resurrection', in A. Gileadi (ed.), *Israel's Apostasy and Restoration* (Grand Rapids, MI: Baker Book House, 1988), pp. 237-50.

Collins, J.J., *Jewish Wisdom in the Hellenistic Age* (Louisville, KY: Westminster/John Knox Press, 1997).

Coogan, M., 'Aqhat', in *Stories from Ancient Canaan* (trans. M. Coogan; Louisville, KY: Westminster Press, 1978), pp. 27-47.

Coudert, A.P., 'The Myth of the Improved Status of Protestant Women: The Case of the Witchcraze', in Levack (ed.), *Witchcraft, Women and Society*, pp. 85-113.

Crenshaw, J.L.,

—'A Mother's Instruction to Her Son (Proverbs 31:1-9)', in *Urgent Advice and Probing Questions: Collected Writings on Old Testament Wisdom* (Macon, GA: Mercer University Press, 1995), pp. 383-95.

—*Education in Ancient Israel: Across the Deadening Silence* (ABRL; New York: Doubleday, 1998).

—*Old Testament Wisdom* (Atlanta: John Knox Press; London: SCM Press, 1981).

—*Samson: A Secret Betrayed, a Vow Ignored* (Atlanta: John Knox Press, 1978).

—'The Contest of Darius's Guards in 1 Esdras 3:1–5:3', in B.O. Long (ed.), *Images of Man and God: The Old Testament Short Story in Literary Focus* (Sheffield: Almond Press, 1981), pp. 74-88, 119-20; reprinted in the author's *Urgent Advice*, pp. 222-34.

Curtis, R., and B. Elton, 'Bells', in *Blackadder: The Whole Damn Dynasty 1485–1917* (New York: Penguin Putnam, 2000), pp. 119-36.

Darr, K.P., 'Ezekiel', in Carol Newsom and Sharon Ringe (eds.), *The Women's Bible Commentary* (Louisville, KY: Westminster/John Knox Press, 1992), pp. 183-90.

Davies, Stevan, *Jesus the Healer: Possession, Trance, and the Origins of Christianity* (New York: Continuum, 1995).

—'The Canaanite-Hebrew Goddess', in Olson (ed.), *Goddess*, pp. 68-79.

—*The Revolt of the Widows: The Social World of the Apocryphal Acts* (Carbondale, IL: Southern Illinois University Press, 1980).

Douglas, M., *Purity and Danger: An Analysis of the Concepts of Pollution and Taboo* (London: Routledge & Kegan Paul, 1966).

Driver, G.R., and John C. Miles, *The Babylonian Laws* (2 vols.; Oxford: Clarendon Press, 1952).

Dundes, Alan, 'Folk Ideas as Units of Worldview', *JAF* 84 (1971), pp. 93-103.

Ecker, G. (ed.), *Feminist Aesthetics* (trans. H. Anderson; Boston: Beacon Press, 1986).

Ego, B., 'Targumization as Theologization: Aggadic Additions in the Targum Sheni of Esther', in D.R.G. Beattie and M.J. McNamara (eds.), *The Aramaic Bible: Targums in their Historical Context* (JSOTSup, 166; Sheffield: Sheffield Academic Press, 1994), pp. 354-61.

Eichler, B.L., 'Another Look at the Nuzi Sistership Contracts', in Ellis (ed.), *Essays*, 19, pp. 45-59.

Eichrodt, Walther, *Ezekiel: A Commentary* (London: SCM Press, 1970).

Ellis, M. (ed.), *Essays on the Ancient Near East in Memory of Jacob Joel Finkelstein* (Memoirs of the Connecticut Academy of Arts and Sciences, 19; Hamden, CT: Archon Books, 1977).

Englehard, D.H., 'Hittite Magical Practices: An Analysis' (PhD dissertation, Brandeis University, 1970).

Epstein, I. (ed.), *The Babylonian Talmud* (Hindhead: Soncino, 1948).

Eskenazi, T., 'Out from the Shadows: Biblical Women in the Post-Exilic Era', in Athalya Brenner (ed.), *A Feminist Companion to Samuel–Kings* (FCB, 5; Sheffield: Sheffield Academic Press, 1994), pp. 252-71.

Exum, J.C., *Fragmented Women: Feminist (Sub)versions of Biblical Narrative* (Valley Forge, PA: Trinity Press International, 1993).

Fine, Elizabeth C., and Jean H. Speer (eds.), *Performance, Culture, and Identity* (Westport, CT: Praeger, 1992).

Fleming, D.E., *The Installation of Baal's High Priestess at Emar: A Window on Ancient Syrian Religion* (Harvard Semitic Studies, 42; Atlanta: Scholars Press, 1992).

Foley, J.M., *Immanent Art: From Structure to Meaning in Traditional Oral Epic* (Bloomington: Indiana University Press, 1991).

—*The Singer of Tales in Performance* (Bloomington: Indiana University Press, 1995).

Fontaine, Carole R., 'A Modern Look at Ancient Wisdom: The Instruction of Ptahhotep, Revisited', *Biblical Archaeologist* 44 (1981), pp. 155-60.

—'Folktale Structure in the Book of Job: A Formalist Reading', in E. Follis (ed.), *Directions in Biblical Hebrew Poetry* (JSOTSup, 40; Sheffield: JSOT Press, 1987), pp. 215-16.

—' "A Heifer from Thy Stable": On Goddesses and the Status of Women in the Ancient Near East', in A. Bach (ed.), *Women in the Hebrew Bible: A Reader* (New York: Routledge, 1999), pp.159-78.

—'Journey through the Pit: A Pictorial Account of One Woman's Descent into Shadow and Beyond', *Anima* 15 (1988), pp. 53-66.

—'More Queenly Proverb Performance: The Queen of Sheba in Targum Esther Sheni', in M.L. Barré, S.S. (ed.), *Wisdom, You Are my Sister: Studies in Honor of Roland E. Murphy, O.Carm., on the Occasion of his Eightieth Birthday* (CBQMS, 29; Washington, DC: Catholic Biblical Association, 1997), pp. 216-33.

—'Proverbs', in James L. Mays (ed.), *Harper Collins Bible Commentary* (San Francisco: Harper, rev. edn, 2000), pp. 447-65.

—'Queenly Proverb Performance: The Prayer of Puduhepa (KUB XXI, 27)', in Hoglund *et al.* (eds.), *The Listening Heart*, pp. 95-126.

—'The Deceptive Goddess in Ancient Near Eastern Myth: Inanna and Inaras', in J.C. Exum and J. Bos (eds.), *Reasoning among the Foxes: Women in a World of Male Power* (Semeia, 42; Atlanta: Scholars Press, 1988), pp. 84-102.

—'The Personification of Wisdom', in J.L. Mays (ed.), *Harper's Bible Commentary* (San Francisco: Harper & Row, 1988), pp. 501-503.

—'The Sage in Family and Tribe', in Gammie and Perdue (eds.), *Sage*, pp. 155-64.

—'The Social Roles of Women in the World of Wisdom', in Brenner (ed.), *Wisdom Literature*, pp. 24-49.

—'The Strange Face of Wisdom in the New Testament: On the Reuse of Wisdom Characters from the Hebrew Bible', in Athalya Brenner and Jan Willem van Henten (eds.),

Recycling Biblical Figures: Papers Read at a NOSTER Colloquium in Amsterdam, 12–13 May 1997 (STAR, 1; Leiden: Deo, 1999), pp. 205-29.

—*Traditional Sayings in the Old Testament: A Contextual Study* (BL, 5; Sheffield: Almond Press, 1982).

Foster, Benjamin R., *Before the Muses: An Anthology of Akkadian Literature. Vol. I: Archaic, Classical, Mature* (Bethesda, MD: CDL Press, 1993).

—*Before the Muses: An Anthology of Akkadian Literature. II. Mature, Late* (Bethesda, MD: CDL Press, 1993).

—'Ea and Saltu', in Ellis (ed.), *Essays*, pp. 79-86.

Foster, J.L. (trans.) and S.T. Hollis (ed.), *Hymns, Prayers, and Songs: An Anthology of Ancient Egyptian Lyric Poetry* (WAB, 8; Atlanta: Scholars Press, 1995).

Fox, Michael V., *Proverbs 1–9* (AB, 18a; New York: Doubleday, 2000).

Frankel, Ellen, *The Five Books of Miriam: A Woman's Commentary on the Torah* (New York: Putnam's Sons, 1996).

Frantz-Szabó, Gabriella, 'Hittite Witchcraft, Magic and Divination', in Sasson (ed.), *Civilizations*, III, pp. 2007-20.

Frymer-Kensky, T.S., *In the Wake of the Goddesses: Women, Culture and the Biblical Transformation of Pagan Myth* (Glencoe: Free Press, 1992).

Fuchs, E., '"For I Have the Way of Women": Deception, Gender, and Ideology in Biblical Narrative', *Semeia* 42 (1988), pp. 68-83.

—'Who Is Hiding the Truth? Deceptive Women and Biblical Androcentrism', in A. Yarbro Collins (ed.), *Feminist Perspectives on Biblical Scholarship* (Chico, CA: Scholars Press, 1985), pp. 137-44.

Gammie, J.G., and L.G. Perdue (eds.), *The Sage in Israel and the Ancient Near East* (Winona Lake, IN: Eisenbrauns, 1990).

Gardiner, Sir Alan, *Egypt of the Pharaohs: An Introduction* (Oxford: Oxford University Press, 1961).

Gaster, T., 'The Child-Stealing Witch among the Hittites?', *Studi e materiali di storia delle religioni* 23 (1950/51), pp. 134-37.

Gilmore, D.D. (ed.), *Honor and Shame and the Unity of the Mediterranean* (Washington, DC: American Anthropological Association, 1987).

Gimbutas, M., *The Goddesses and Gods of Old Europe, 6500–3500 B.C.: Myth and Cult Images* (Berkeley: University of California Press, 1982).

Ginzberg, L., *The Legends of the Jews* (7 vols.; Philadelphia: Jewish Publication Society of America, 1936), pp. 65-84.

Goetze, Albrecht, 'Prayer of Pudu-hepas to the Sun-Goddess of Arinna and her Circle', *ANET*, pp. 393-94.

Goetze, A., and E.H. Sturtevant, *The Hittite Ritual of Tunnawi* (New Haven, CT: American Oriental Society, 1938).

Goldfeld, Anne, 'Women as Sources of Torah in the Rabbinic Tradition', in Elizabeth Koltun (ed.), *The Jewish Woman: New Perspectives* (New York: Schocken Books, 1976), pp. 257-71.

Golka, Friedemann W., *The Leopard's Spots: Biblical and African Wisdom in Proverbs* (Edinburgh: T. & T. Clark, 1993).

Goodman, Felicitas D., *How about Demons? Possession and Exorcism in the Modern World* (Bloomington: Indiana University Press, 1988).

Gordon, Pamela, and Harold Washington, 'Rape as a Military Metaphor in the Hebrew Bible', in Brenner (ed.), *Latter Prophets*, pp. 308-25.

Greenberg, Moshe, 'Ezekiel 16: A Panorama of Passions', in J.H. Marks and R.M. Good (eds.), *Love and Death in the Ancient Near East: Essays in Honor of Marvin H. Pope* (Guilford, CT: Four Quarters, 1987), pp. 143-50.

Griffiths, J. Gwyn, *The Conflict of Horus and Seth from Egyptian and Classical Sources* (Liverpool: Liverpool University Press, 1960).

Groneberg, B., 'Philologische Bearbeitung des Agušayahymnus', *RA* 75 (1981), pp. 107-34.

Grossfeld, Bernard, *The Two Targums of Esther: Translated, with Apparatus and Notes* (Aramaic Bible, 18; Collegeville, MN: Liturgical Press, 1986).

Grzybek, P., 'Foundations of Semiotic Proverb Study', *Proverbium* 4 (1987), pp. 39-85, reprinted in Mieder (ed.), *Wise Words*, pp. 31-71.

Gurney, O.R., *Some Aspects of Hittite Religion* (Oxford: Oxford University Press, 1977).

—*The Hittites* (London: Penguin Books, rev. edn, 1981).

Hadley, J.M., 'From Goddess to Literary Construct: the Transformation of Asherah into Hokma', in A. Brenner and C. Fontaine (eds.), *A Feminist Companion to Reading the Bible: Approaches, Methods, Strategies* (Sheffield: Sheffield Academic Press, 1997), pp. 360-99.

—*The Cult of Asherah in Ancient Israel and Judah: Evidence for a Hebrew Goddess* (Cambridge: Cambridge University Press, 2000).

—'Wisdom and the Goddess', in J. Day, R.P. Gordon and H.G.M. Williamson (eds.), *Wisdom in Ancient Israel: Essays in Honour of J.A. Emerton* (Cambridge: Cambridge University Press, 1995), pp. 234-43.

Hallo, W.W., 'Proverbs Quoted in Epic', in Abusch, Huehnergard and Steinkeller (eds.), *Lingering over Words*, pp. 201-17.

—'Sumerian Historiography', in H. Tadmor and M. Weinfield (eds.), *History, Historiography, and Interpretation: Studies in Biblical and Cuneiform Literatures* (Jerusalem: Magnes Press, 1983), pp. 9-20.

—'The Women of Sumer', in D. Schmandt-Besserat (ed.), *The Legacy of Sumer* (BM, 4; Malibu, CA: Undena Publications, 1976), pp. 23-34.

Hallpike, C.R., 'Hair', in M. Eliade (ed.), *The Encyclopedia of Religion*, VI (New York: Macmillan, 1987), pp. 154-57.

Harris, R., 'The Female "Sage" in Mesopotamian Literature (with an Appendix on Egypt)', in Gammie and Perdue (eds.), *Sage*, pp. 3-10.

Hasan-Rokem, G., *Proverbs in Israeli folk Narratives: A Structural Semantic Analysis* (FFC, 232; Helsinki: Suomalainen Tiedeakatemia, Academia Scientiarum Fennica, 1982).

—*Web of Life: Folklore and Midrash in Rabbinic Literature* (trans. Batya Stein; Stanford: Stanford University Press, 2000).

Healy, Joseph, MM, and Donald Sybertz MM, *Towards an African Narrative Theology* (Faith and Culture Series; Maryknoll, NY: Orbis Books, 1996).

Herford, T., *Pirke Aboth, the Ethics of the Talmud: Sayings of the Fathers* (New York: Schocken Books, 1962).

Hermisson, H.J., *Studien zur israelitischen Spruchweisheit* (WMANT, 28; Neukirchen–Vluyn: Neukirchener Verlag, 1968).

Hoffner, Jr, Harry A. (trans.), 'Birth and Name-Giving in Hittite Texts', *JNES* 27 (1968), pp. 198-203.

—*Hittite Myths* (ed. Gary M. Beckman; Atlanta: Scholars Press, 1990).

Hogland, K.G., E.F. Huwiler, J.T. Glass and R.W. Lee (eds.), *The Listening Heart: Essays in Wisdom and the Psalms in Honor of Roland E. Murphy* (JSOTSup, 58; Sheffield: JSOT Press, 1987).

Hollis, Susan T., 'Isis', in Serenity Young (ed.), *Encyclopedia of Women and World Religion*, I (New York: Macmillan, 1999), pp. 487-88.

Holtz, B.W., 'Midrash', in *Back to the Sources: Reading the Classic Jewish Texts* (New York: Simon & Schuster, 1984), pp. 177-212.

Hood, R.E., *Begrimed and Black: Christian Traditions on Blacks and Blackness* (Philadelphia: Fortress Press, 1994).

Hutter, M., 'Lilith', in van der Toorn, Becking and van der Horst (eds.), *Deities and Demons*, pp. 973-76.

Hynes, William J., and William G. Doty (eds.), *Mythical Trickster Figures: Contours, Contexts, and Criticisms* (Tuscaloosa: University of Alabama Press, 1993).

Ilan, T., *Jewish Women in Greco-Roman Palestine* (Peabody, MA: Hendrickson, 1995).

Jason, Heda, 'The Fairytale of the Active Heroine: An Outline for Discussion', in G. Galame-Griaule, V. Görög-Karady and M. Chiche (eds.), *Le conte, pourquoi, comment?* (Paris: Centre National de la Recherche scientifique, 1984), pp. 79-97.

Jochens, J., 'Old Norse Sources on Women', in J. Rosenthal (ed.), *Medieval Women and the Sources of Medieval History* (Athens: University of Georgia, 1990), pp. 155-87.

—'*Vǫlupsá*: Matrix of Norse Womanhood', *Journal of English and Germanic Philology* 88 (1989), pp. 344-62.

Kalugila, L., *The Wise King: Studies in Royal Wisdom as Divine Revelation in the Old Testament and its Environment* (Coniectanea Biblica, 15; Uppsala: C.W.K. Gleerup, 1980).

Kaplan, A.E., 'Is the Gaze Male?', in A. Snitow, C. Stansell and S. Thompson (eds.), *Powers of Desire: The Politics of Sexuality* (New York: Monthly Review Press, 1983), pp. 309-27.

Keefe, Alice A., 'The Female Body, the Body Politic and the Land: A Sociopolitical Reading of Hosea 1–2', in Brenner (ed.), *Latter Prophets*, pp. 70-100.

Keel, O., 'Die Weisheit "spielt" vor Gott', *Freiburger Zeitschrift für Philosophie und Theologie* 21 (1974), pp. 1-66.

—*Goddesses and Trees, New Moon and Yahweh: Ancient Near Eastern Art and the Hebrew Bible* (JSOTSup, 261; Sheffield: Sheffield Academic Press, 1998).

Keel, Othmar, and Christoph Uehlinger, *Gods, Goddesses, and Images of God in Ancient Israel* (trans. T.H. Trapp; Philadelphia: Fortress Press, 1998).

Kilmer, A., 'The Brick of Birth', *JNES* 46 (1987), pp. 211-13.

Klein, L.R., 'Honor and Shame in Esther', in A. Brenner (ed.), *A Feminist Companion to Esther, Judith, and Susanna* (FCB, 7; Sheffield: Sheffield Academic Press, 1998), pp.149-75.

Kloppenborg, J.S., 'Isis and Sophia in the Book of Wisdom', *HTR* 75 (1982), pp. 57-84.

Knibb, M.A. (trans.), '1 Enoch', in H.F.D. Sparks (ed.), *The Apocryphal Old Testament* (Oxford: Clarendon Press, 1984), pp. 169-319.

Koltuv, Barbara., *The Book of Lilith* (York Beach, ME: Nicolas–Hays), 1986.

Kranson, Rachel, 'The Queen of Sheba's Fuzzy Legs', *Lilith* 26 (2001), pp. 10-12.

Kuntzmann, Raymond, *Le symbolisme des jumeaux au Proche-Orient Ancien* (Beauchesne Religions, 12; Paris: Beauchesne, 1983).

Lambert, William, *Babylonian Wisdom Literature* (Oxford: Clarendon Press, 1960).

Lang, B., *Wisdom and the Book of Proverbs: An Israelite Goddess Redefined* (New York: Pilgrim Press, 1986).

—'Lady Wisdom: A Polytheistic and Psychological Interpretation of a Biblical Goddess', in Brenner and Fontaine (eds.), *Reading the Bible*, pp. 400-25.

Lassner, J., *Demonizing the Queen of Sheba: Boundaries of Gender and Culture in Postbiblical Judaism and Medieval Islam* (Chicago: University of Chicago Press, 1993).

Larrington, C., 'Scandinavia', in *The Feminist Companion to Mythology* (London: Pandora/ HarperCollins, 1992), pp. 137-61.

Larrington, C. (trans.), *The Poetic Edda* (Oxford: Oxford University Press, 1996).

Leick, Gwendolyn, *A Dictionary of Ancient Near Eastern Mythology* (New York: Routledge, 1991).

Lerner, G., *The Creation of Patriarchy* (Oxford: Oxford University Press, 1986).

Lesko, B.S., *The Remarkable Women of Ancient Egypt* (Providence, RI: B.C. Scribe Publications, 1987).

Levack, B.P. (ed.), *Witchcraft, Women and Society. Articles on Witchcraft, Magic and Demonology: A Twelve Volume Anthology of Scholarly Articles* (New York: Garland, 1992).

Levine, E., *The Aramaic Version of the Bible* (BZAW, 174; Berlin: W. de Gruyter, 1988).

Levine, Baruch, and Jean-Michel de Tarragon, ' "Shapshu Cries out in Heaven": Dealing with Snake-Bites at Ugarit (KTU 1.100, 1.107)', *RB* (1988), pp. 481-518.

Lewis, Brian, *The Sargon Legend* (Cambridge, MA: ASOR, 1980).

Lichtheim, M., *Ancient Egyptian Literature: A Book of Readings*. I. *The Old and Middle Kingdoms* (Berkeley: University of California, 1973).

—*Ancient Egyptian Literature: A Book of Readings*. II. *The New Kingdom* (Berkeley: University of California, 1976).

—*Ancient Egyptian Literature: A Book of Readings*. III. *The Late Period* (Berkeley: University of California, 1980).

—*Maat in Egyptian Autobiographies and Related Studies* (OBO, 120; Freiburg: Universitätsverlag; Göttingen: Vandenhoeck & Ruprecht, 1992).

Lieberman, Marcia K., ' "Some Day My Prince Will Come": Female Acculturation through the Fairy Tale', in Jack Zipes (ed.), *Don't Bet on the Prince: Contemporary Feminist Fairy Tales in North America and England* (New York: Routledge, 1989), pp. 185-200.

Lincoln, B., 'Treatment of the Hair and Fingernails among the Indo-Europeans', *HR* 16 (1977), pp. 351-62.

Lomperis, L., and S. Stanbury (eds.), *Feminist Approaches to the Body in Medieval Literature* (Philadelphia: University of Pennsylvania Press, 1993).

Long, B.O., *1 Kings, with an Introduction to Historical Literature* (FOTL, 9; Grand Rapids: Eerdmans, 1984).

Luckenbill, Daniel D., *Ancient Records of Assyria and Babylonia*, I (Chicago: University of Chicago Press, 1929).

McKinlay, J.E., *Gendering Wisdom the Host: Biblical Invitations to Eat and Drink* (JSOTSup, 216; GCT, 4; Sheffield: Sheffield Academic Press, 1996).

McNutt, P., *Reconstructing the Society of Ancient Israel* (LAI; Louisville, KY: Westminster/ John Knox Press, 1999).

Magdalene, F. Rachel, 'Ancient Near Eastern Treaty-Curses and the Ultimate Texts of Terror: A Study of the Language of Divine Sexual Abuse in the Prophetic Corpus', in Brenner (ed.), *Latter Prophets*, pp. 326-53.

Maier, Christl, *Die "fremde Frau" in Proverbien 1–9: Eine exegetische und sozialgeschichtliche Studie* (OBO, 144; Freiburg: Universitätsverlag; Göttingen: Vandenhoeck & Ruprecht, 1995).

Maier, III, Walter A., *'Asherah: Extrabiblical Evidence* (HSM, 37; Atlanta: Scholars Press, 1986).

Malina, Bruce J., 'Mediterranean Sacrifice: Dimensions of Domestic and Political Religion', *BTB* 26 (1996), pp. 26-37.

Malul, Meir, 'Adoption of Foundlings in the Bible and Mesopotamian Documents: A Study of Some Legal Metaphors in Ezekiel 16.1-7', *JSOT* 46 (1990), pp. 97-126.

Mangan, C., 'Some Observations on the Dating of Targum Job', in K.J. Cathcart and J.F. Healey (eds.), *Back to the Sources: Biblical and Near Eastern Studies In Honour of Dermot Ryan* (Dublin: Glendale Press, 1989), pp. 67-78.

Marzal, A., *Gleanings from the Wisdom of Mari* (Studia Pohl, 11; Rome: Biblical Institute Press, 1976).

Matalene, C., 'Women as Witches', in Levack (ed.), *Witchcraft, Women and Society*, X, pp. 51-65.

Matthews, Caitlin, *Sophia, Goddess of Wisdom: The Divine Feminine from Black Goddess to World-Soul* (London: Grafton Books; HarperCollins, 1991).

Matthews, V.H., and D.C. Benjamin, *Social World of Ancient Israel, 1250–587 BCE* (Peabody, MA: Hendrickson, 1993).

Meshel, Ze'ev, 'Did Yahweh Have a Consort?', *BAR* 5 (1979), pp. 24-35.

Metzger, T., and M. Metzger, *Jewish Life in the Middle Ages: Illuminated Hebrew Manuscripts of the Thirteenth to the Sixteenth Centuries* (New York: Alpine Fine Arts Collection, 1982).

Meyers, C.L., *Discovering Eve: Ancient Israelite Women in Context* (Oxford: Oxford University Press, 1988).

—'Guilds and Gatherings: Women's Groups in Ancient Israel', in Prescott H. Williams, Jr and Theodore Hiebert (eds.), *Realia Dei: Essays in Archaeology and Biblical Interpretation in Honor of Edward F. Campbell, Jr. at his Retirement* (Atlanta: Scholars Press, 1999), pp. 154-84.

—'Of Drums and Damsels: Women's Performance in Ancient Israel', *BA* 54 (1991), pp. 16-27.

—'Returning Home: Ruth 1.8 and the Gendering of the Book of Ruth', in A. Brenner (ed.), *A Feminist Companion to Ruth* (FCB, 3; Sheffield: Sheffield Academic Press, 1993), pp. 85-114.

—'The Family in Early Israel', in L.G. Perdue, J. Blenkinsopp, J.J. Collins and C.Meyers, *Families in Ancient Israel* (Louisville, KY: Westminster/John Knox Press, 1997), pp. 1-47.

—*The Tabernacle Menorah: A Synthetic Study of a Symbol from the Bible Cult* (ASOR Diss, 2; Missoula, MT: Scholars Press, 1976).

Meyers, C., T. Craven and R.S. Kraemer (eds.), *Women in Scripture: A Dictionary of Named and Unnamed Women in the Hebrew Bible, the Apocrypha/Deuterocanonical Books, and the New Testament* (Boston: Houghton Mifflin, 2000).

Mieder, Wolfgang (ed.), Wise Words: Essays on the Proverb (GFC, 6; New York: Garland, 1994).

Montgomery, J.A., *A Critical and Exegetical Commentary on the Book of Kings* (ed. H.S. Gehman; New York: Charles Scribner's Sons, 1951).

Moran, W.L., 'New Evidence from Mari on the History of Prophecy', *Bib* 50 (1969), pp. 15-56.

Moran, W.L. (trans. and ed.), *The Amarna Letters* (Baltimore: The Johns Hopkins University Press, 1992).

Morgenstern, J., *Rites of Birth, Marriage, Death and Kindred Occasions among the Semites* (Cincinnati, OH: Hebrew Union College Press, 1966).

Motz, Lotte, 'Freyja, Anat, Ishtar and Inanna: Some Cross-Cultural Comparisons', *Mankind Quarterly* 23 (1982), pp. 195-212.

Müller, H.-P., 'Der Begriff "Rätsel" im Alten Testament', *VT* 20 (1970), pp. 465-89.

Murphy, R.E., *Proverbs* (WBC; Dallas, TX: Word Books), 1998.

—*The Tree of Life: An Exploration of Biblical Wisdom Literature* (Grand Rapids, MI: Eerdmans, 2nd edn, 1996).

—'Wisdom and Eros in Prov 1–9', *CBQ* 50 (1988), pp. 600-603.

Murphy, Roland, and E. Huwiler, *New International Biblical Commentary: Proverbs, Ecclesiastes, Song of Songs* (Peabody, MA: Hendrickson, 1999).

Nadich, Judah, *The Legends of the Rabbis*, II (Northvale, NJ: Jason Aronson, 1994).

Näsström, Britt-Mari, *Freyja—the Great Goddess of the North* (Lund Studies in History of Religions, 5; Lund: Novapress, 1995).

Naveh J., and S. Shaked, *Amulets and Magic Bowls: Aramaic Incantations in Late Antiquity* (Jerusalem: Magnes Press, 3rd edn, 1988).

Newsom, C.A., 'Woman and Discourse of Patriarchal Wisdom: A Study of Proverbs 1–9', in P.L. Day (ed.), *Gender and Difference in Ancient Israel* (Philadelphia: Fortress Press, 1989), pp. 142-60.

Niditch, S., *Folklore and the Hebrew Bible* (Philadelphia: Fortress Press, 1993).

—*Oral World and Written Word: Ancient Israelite Literature* (LAI; Louisville, KY: Westminster/John Knox Press, 1996).

—*War in the Hebrew Bible: A Study in the Ethics of Violence* (New York: Oxford University Press, 1993).

NIN: Journal of Gender Studies in Antiquity 1 (2000).

Norrick, N.R., 'Proverbial Perlocutions: How to Do Things with Proverbs', *Grazer Linguistische Studien* 17–18 (1982), pp. 169-83, reprinted in Mieder (ed.), *Wise Words*, pp. 143-57.

Olson, Carl (ed.), *The Book of the Goddess: Past and Present* (New York: Crossroad, 1985).

Olyan, Saul M., *Asherah and the Cult of Yahweh in Israel* (SBLMS, 34; Atlanta, GA: Scholars Press, 1988).

Ortlund, Jr, Raymond C., *Whoredom: God's Unfaithful Wife in Biblical Theology* (Grand Rapids, MI: Eerdmans, 1996).

Parker, Rozsicka, *The Subversive Stitch: Embroidery and the Making of the Feminine* (London: Woman's Press, 1986).

Parker, Simon B. (ed.), *Ugaritic Narrative Poetry* (WAW, 9; Atlanta: Scholars Press, 1997).

Patai, R., *The Hebrew Goddess* (Detroit, MI: Wayne State University, 3rd edn, 1990).

Patterson, O., *Slavery and Social Death: A Comparative Study* (Cambridge, MA: Harvard University Press, 1982).

Perdue, L.G., J. Blenkinsopp, J. Collins and C. Meyers, *Families in Ancient Israel* (Louisville, KY: Westminster/John Knox Press, 1997).

Perry, T.A., 'Quadripartite Wisdom Sayings and the Structure of Proverbs', *Proverbium* 4 (1987), pp. 187-210.

—*The Moral Proverbs of Santob de Carrión: Jewish Wisdom in Christian Spain* (Princeton: Princeton University Press, 1987).

Peskowitz, Miriam B., *Spinning Fantasies: Rabbis, Gender, and History* (Berkeley: University of California Press, 1997).

Pilch, J.J., ' "Beat his Ribs While He Is Young" (Sirach 30:12): A Window on the Mediterranean World', *BTB* 23 (1993), pp. 101-13.

Plaskow, Judith, 'The Coming of Lilith: Toward a Feminist Theology', in Carol P. Christ and

Judith Plaskow (eds.), *Womanspirit Rising: A Feminist Reader in Religion* (San Francisco: Harper & Row, 1979), pp. 198-209.

Preuss, Julius, *Biblical and Talmudic Medicine* (trans. and ed. Fred Rossner; Northvale, NJ: Jason Aronson, 1993).

Pritchard, J.B. (ed.), *Ancient Near Eastern Texts Relating to the Old Testament* (Princeton: Princeton University Press, 3rd edn, 1969).

—*Solomon and Sheba* (London: Phaidon Press, 1974).

Rappoport, Angelo S., *Myth and Legend of Ancient Israel* (3 vols.; New York: Ktav, 1966).

Richler, B., *Hebrew Manuscripts: A Treasured Legacy* (Cleveland; Jerusalem: Ofeq Institute, 1990).

Rigney, Barbara Hill, *Lilith's Daughters: Women and Religion in Contemporary Fiction* (Madison, WI: University of Wisconsin Press, 1982).

Ringgren, Helmer, 'The Marriage Motif in Israelite Religion', in Patrick D. Miller, Jr (ed.), *Ancient Israelite Religion* (Philadelphia: Fortress Press, 1987), pp. 421-28.

Robbins, G., *Women in Ancient Egypt* (Cambridge, MA: Harvard University Press, 1993).

Robinson, J.M., 'Jesus as Sophos and Sophia: Wisdom Tradition and the Gospels', in Wilken (ed.), *Aspects of Wisdom*, pp. 1-16.

Rollin, S., 'Women and Witchcraft in Ancient Assyria (c. 900–600BC)', in A. Cameron and A. Kuhrt (eds.), *Images of Women in Antiquity* (Detroit, MI: Wayne State University Press, 1983), pp. 34-45.

Rosen, Tova, 'Circumcised Cinderella: The Fantasies of a 14th Century Jewish Author', *Prooftexts* 20 (2000), pp. 87-110.

Rutledge, D., *Reading Marginally: Feminism, Deconstruction and the Bible* (BIS, 21; Leiden: E.J. Brill, 1996).

Sasson, J.M. (ed.), *Civilizations of the Ancient Near East*, III (New York: Charles Scribner's Sons, 1995).

Satran, D., 'Fingernails and Hair: Anatomy and Exegesis in Tertullian', *JTS* 40 (1989), pp. 116-20.

Schroer, Silvia, ' "And When the Next War Began...": The Wise Woman of Meth-maacah (2 Samuel 20:14-22)', *Wisdom Has Built her House*, pp. 52-77.

—'Die göttliche Weisheit und der nachexilische Monotheismus', in M.-T. Wacker and Erich Zenger (eds.), *Der Eine Gott und die Göttin: Gottesvorstellungen des biblischen Israel im Horizont feministicher Theologie* (Quaestiones Disputatae, 135; Freiburg: Herder, 1991), pp. 151-82.

—*Die Weisheit hat ihr Haus gebaut: Studien zur Gestalt der Sophia in den biblischen Schriften* (Mainz: Matthias-Grünewald-Verlag, 1996).

—*In Israel gab es Bilder: Nachrichten von darstellender Kunst im Alten Testament* (OBO, 74; Fribourg and Göttingen Presses Universitaires Fribourg, 1987).

—*Wisdom Has Built her House: Studies on the Figure of Sophia in the Bible* (trans. L.M. Maloney and W. McDonough; Collegeville, MN: Liturgical Press, 2000).

—'Wise and Counselling Women in Ancient Israel: Literary and Historical Ideals of the Personified ḥokmâ', in Brenner (ed.), *Wisdom Literature*, pp. 67-84.

Schüssler Fiorenza, E., *In Memory of Her: A Feminist Theological Reconstruction of Christian Origins* (London: SCM Press, 1983).

—*Jesus: Miriam's Child, Sophia's Prophet: Critical Issues in Feminist Christology* (New York: Continuum, 1994).

—'Wisdom Mythology and the Christological Hymns of the New Testament', in Wilken (ed.), *Aspects of Wisdom*, pp. 17-42.

Scott, R.B.Y., 'Wisdom in Creation: the 'Amon of Proverbs VIII 30', *VT* 10 (1960), pp. 213-23.

Sed-Rajna, G., *The Hebrew Bible in Medieval Illuminated Manuscripts* (New York: Rizzoli, 1987).

Seibert, Ilse, *Women in the Ancient Near East* (New York: Abner Schram, 1974).

Seitel, Peter, 'A Social Use of Metaphor', *Genre* 2 (1969): pp. 143-61, reprinted in Dan Ben-Amos (ed.), *Folklore Genres* (Austin: University of Texas Press, 1976), pp. 125-43.

Sethe, K. *Ägyptische Lesestück* (Leipzig, 1924).

Sharp, S., 'Folk Medicine Practices. Women as Keepers and Carriers of Knowledge', *Women's Studies International Forum* 9 (1986), pp. 243-49.

Shilleto, A.R. (ed.), *The Works of Flavius Josephus*, II (London: George Bell & Sons, 1989).

Silberman, L.H., 'The Queen of Sheba in Judaic Tradition', in Pritchard (ed.), *Solomon*, pp. 65-84.

Simpson, W.K. (ed.), *The Literature of Ancient Egypt: An Anthology of Stories, Instructions and Poetry* (New Haven: Yale University Press, 1973).

Smith, M.S., *The Early History of God: Yahweh and the Other Deities in Ancient Israel* (San Francisco: Harper & Row, 1990).

Snell, Daniel C., *Life in the Ancient Near East, 3100–332 B.C.E.* (New Haven: Yale University Press, 1997).

Speiser, E.A. (trans.), 'The Epic of Gilgamesh', *ANET*, pp. 72-99.

Stec, D.M., *The Text of the Targum of Job: An Introduction and Critical Edition* (Leiden: E.J. Brill, 1994).

Stein, Dina, 'A King, a Queen, and the Riddle between: Riddles and Interpretation in a Late Midrashic Text', in Galit Hasan-Rokem and David Shulman (eds.), *Untying the Knot: On Riddles and Other Enigmatic Modes* (Oxford: Oxford University Press, 1996), pp. 125-50.

de Tarragon, Jean-Michel, 'Witchcraft, Magic and Divination in Canaan in Ancient Israel', in Sasson (ed.), *Civilizations*, III, pp. 2071-81.

Taylor, A., 'Armenian Illumination under Georgian, Turkish, and Mongol Rule in the Thirteenth, Fourteenth, and Fifteenth Centuries', in T.F. Matthews and R.S. Wieck (eds.), *Treasures in Heaven: Armenian Illuminated Manuscripts* (New York: Pierpont Morgan Library, 1994), pp. 84-103.

Taylor, J. Glen, 'The Song of Deborah and Two Canaanite Goddesses', *JSOT* 23 (1981), pp. 99-108.

Terry, P. (trans.), *Poems of the Elder Edda* (intro. Charles W. Dunn; Philadelphia: University of Pennsylvania Press, 1990).

Tonomura, H., 'Black Hair and Red Trousers: Gendering the Flesh in Medieval Japan', *American Historical Review* 99 (1994), pp. 129-54.

Tractenberg, J., *The Devil and the Jews* (Philadelphia: Jewish Publication Society of America, 2nd edn, 1983).

Trenchard, W.C., *Ben Sira's View of Women: A Literary Analysis* (BJS, 38; Chico, CA: Scholars Press, 1982).

Ullendorff, E., 'The Queen of Sheba', *Bulletin of the John Rylands Library* 45 (1963), pp. 486-504.

Ünal, A., 'The Role of Magic in Ancient Anatolian Religions According to the Cuneiform Texts from Bogazkoy-Hattusha', in Prince T. Mikasa (ed.), *Essays on Ancient Anatolia in the Second Millennium BC* (Wiesbaden: Otto Harrassowitz, 1988), pp. 52-85.

van der Toorn, K., B. Becking and P.W. van der Horst (eds.), *Dictionary of Deities and Demons in the Bible* (Leiden: E.J. Brill, 1995).

van Dijk-Hemmes, Fokkelien, 'The Metaphorization of Women in Prophetic Speech: An Analysis of Ezekiel 23', in Brenner (ed.), *Latter Prophets*, pp. 244-55.

van Leeuwen, R.C., 'Proverbs', in Carol Newsom *et al.* (eds.), *New Interpreters Bible*, V (Nashville: Abingdon Press, 1997).

van Vorst, Mrs John (trans.), *Magda, Queen of Sheba* (New York: Funk & Wagnalls, 1907).

van Voss, M. Heerma, 'Hathor', in van der Toorn, Becking and van der Horst (eds.), *Deities and Demons*, pp. 732-33.

Vieyra, Maurice, 'Le sorcier Hittite', in Denise Bernot *et al.* (eds.), *Le monde du sorcier* (Sources Orientales, 7; Paris: Seuil, 1966), pp. 101-25.

Visotzky, B.L., *The Midrash on Proverbs* (New Haven: Yale University Press, 1992).

von Rad, G., *Wisdom in Israel* (trans. J.D. Martin; London: SCM Press, 1972).

Wainwright, Elaine, 'The Gospel of Matthew', in Elizabeth Schüssler Fiorenza (ed.), *Searching the Scriptures: A Feminist Commentary*, II (New York: Crossroad, 1994), pp. 635-77.

Walls, Neal H., *The Goddess Anat in Ugaritic Myth* (SBLDS, 135; Atlanta: Scholars Press, 1992).

Walters, S., 'The Sorceress and Her Apprentice', *JCS* 23 (1970), pp. 27-38.

Ward, Benedicta (trans.), *The Sayings of the Desert Fathers: The Alphabetical Collection* (Kalamazoo, MI: Cistercian Publications, 1975).

Warner, M., *From the Beast to the Blonde: On Fairy Tales and their Tellers* (New York: Noonday Press, 1994).

—'In and out of the Fold: Wisdom, Danger, and Glamour in the Tale of the Queen of Sheba', in C. Buchmann and C. Spiegel (eds.), *Out of the Garden: Women Writers on the Bible* (New York: Fawcett Columbine, 1994), pp. 150-65.

Washington, H.C., 'The Strange Woman (נכריה/זרה אׁשה) of Prov 1-9 and Post-Exilic Judaean Society', in Brenner (ed.), *Wisdom Literature*, pp. 157-85.

Watson, Paul F., 'The Queen of Sheba in Christian Tradition', in Pritchard, *Solomon*, pp. 115-45.

Watt, W.M., 'The Queen of Sheba in Islamic Tradition', in Pritchard (ed.), *Solomon*, pp. 85-103.

Weeks, Kent R., 'Medicine, Surgery and Public Health in Ancient Egypt', *CANE*, III, pp. 1787-98.

Weems, Renita J., *Battered Love: Marriage, Sex, and Violence in the Hebrew Prophets* (OBT; (Minneapolis: Augsburg–Fortress, 1995).

Westermann, C., *Roots of Wisdom: The Oldest Proverbs of Israel and Other Peoples* (trans. J.D. Charles; Louisville, KY: Westminster/John Knox Press, 1995).

—*Wurzeln der Weisheit: Die ältesten Sprüche Israels und anderer Völker* (Göttingen: Vandenhoeck & Ruprecht, 1990).

Wilken, Robert L. (ed.), *Aspects of Wisdom in Judaism and Early Christianity* (Notre Dame: University of Notre Dame Press, 1975).

Wilson, John A. (trans.), 'The God and his Unknown Name of Power', *ANET*, pp. 12-14.

Wolkstein, D., and S.N. Kramer, *Inanna, Queen of Heaven and Earth: Her Stories and Hymns from Sumer* (San Francisco: Harper & Row, 1983).

Yee, G., 'The Socio-Literary Production of the "Foreign Woman" in Proverbs', in A.Brenner (ed.), *FemCompWisLit*, pp. 127-30.

—'"I Have Perfumed my Bed with Myrrh": The Foreign Woman (*'iššâ zārâ*) in Proverbs 1–9', in Brenner (ed.), *FemCompWisLit*, pp. 110-26.

Zabkar, L.V., *Hymns to Isis in her Temple at Philae* (Hanover: Brandeis University Press, 1988).

INDEXES

INDEX OF PROVERBS AND INSTRUCTIONS

French

Hittite

Jewish

Old Norse

Spanish

Ugarit

BIBLE

INDEX OF AUTHORS